BY LESLIE T. CHANG

Factory Girls: From Village to City in a Changing China

Egyptian Made: Women, Work, and the Promise of Liberation

EGYPTIAN
MADE

EGYPTIAN MADE

WOMEN, WORK, AND THE
PROMISE OF LIBERATION

LESLIE T. CHANG

RANDOM HOUSE
NEW YORK

Hardback ISBN 978-0-525-50921-9
Ebook ISBN 978-0-525-50922-6

Printed in the United States of America on acid-free paper

randomhousebooks.com

2   4   6   8   9   7   5   3   1

First Edition

Title-page art and chapter-opener art by
Oleksandr Babich © Adobe Stock Photos

Book design by Sara Bereta

Map by Angela Hessler

For Peter

CONTENTS

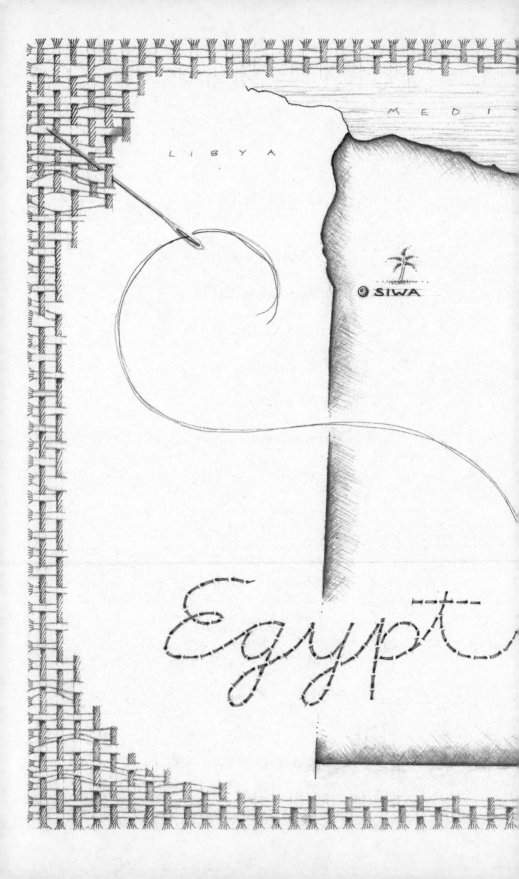

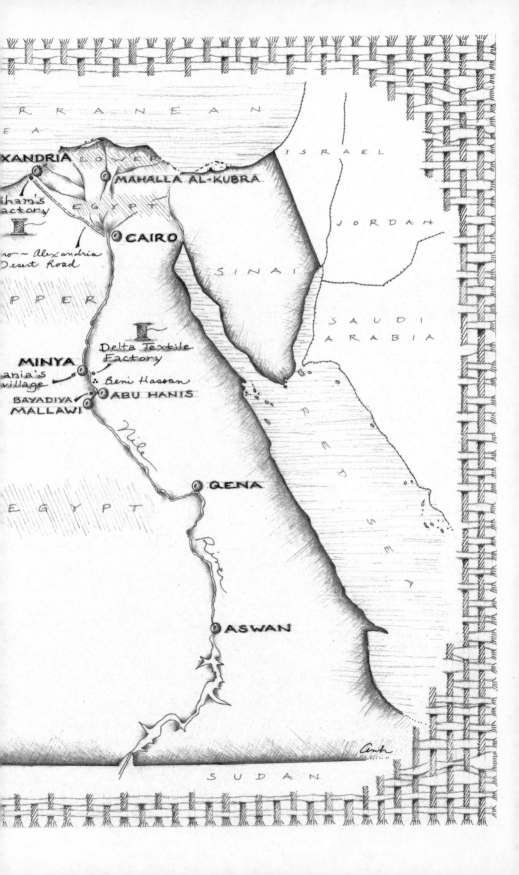

EGYPTIAN
MADE

1

THE BEST WORKERS ON EARTH

ALMOST NO ONE WORKED IN an Egyptian factory because she wanted to. Teenage girls might do it for a while to buy things for their *gihaz*—the china plates and serving bowls, the big and the small teapots, the bedsheets and nightgowns and ten or twelve or twenty sets of everything they needed in their trousseau before a man would agree to marry them. Some of the older women were divorced or widowed and had children to support. The married ones usually needed money badly enough that their husbands had agreed, reluctantly, to let them work outside the home.

Rania Saeed Mohamed didn't fit into any of these groups. She was twenty-two and married but living apart from her husband when she started working at a men's underwear factory outside the city of Minya. The plant was an hour's bus ride from her village, and normally a wife would have asked her husband's permission before taking such a step. But Rania didn't consult anyone. Unhappiness gave her freedom, although that wasn't a trade she would have made on her own. As with almost everything else in her life, she didn't have a choice.

On Rania's second day in the factory, a Romanian American manager named Elena asked a group of new recruits: "Who wants to work in quality control?"

Rania raised her hand. "I can do it." She wasn't sure what quality control was.

Elena was the first foreigner she had ever met. She trained Rania to spot every potential problem in a pair of men's underpants. If a leg was a few millimeters short, or the seams around the crotch didn't lie flat, a client could reject the order and cost the company thousands of dollars. Inside every garment factory, there's a never-ending battle between production and quality—hour after hour, workers must turn out hundreds of items to exacting standards. Rania developed a preternatural ability to keep the assembly line moving while catching mistakes almost as soon as they happened. *Rania isn't just a factory girl,* Elena began telling her colleagues. *She's a manager. She sees and knows everything.*

Elena taught Rania another important lesson: When someone criticizes your work, stand your ground and answer back. In Rania's early days, a trainer named Rabab El-Sayyid often shouted at her—shouting being an act as common as breathing inside an Egyptian factory. Rania learned to respond directly and calmly to the attacks from the older woman. One day she realized that she wasn't scared of Rabab anymore. Two years after she entered the factory, Rania was promoted to supervise her own line, just as Elena had promised.

There are no secrets in a clothing factory. Every hour, each production line's output is recorded on a whiteboard in black marker. The numbers are printed out daily, stapled together, and passed around from hand to hand like factory samizdat, and supervisors who missed their targets are called into the manager's office to explain themselves. Rania's capacity for work was legendary. She was *bi-mit ragil,* as the Egyptians say—"worth a hundred men" (even in a factory that employed over 90 percent women, men remained the gold standard). Every month, the factory gave awards to its most productive workers, and Rania's line placed first more times than she could count. The prize dinnerware sets and teakettles cluttered her kitchen cabinet at home, useless in their abundance.

Some people in the factory said that Rania manipulated production figures to make herself look better, and her tendency to play favorites didn't sit well with everyone. She had a way of attracting notice and charging into conversations, and executives or clients visiting the plant always asked who she was. "Whenever management comes, there's just a little more interaction with Rania than with other people. She's always in their face" is how one senior manager put it. "Arrogant, bullying, bossy," another executive rapped out between pursed lips. With her red supervisor's tunic, wide-legged black trousers, and silver bracelets jangling on her wrists, Rania stood out for her authority and sense of style. She was often the only woman in the factory who was wearing pants.

Rania didn't know it yet, but her bosses had big plans for her. Most of the executives in the factory came from outside Egypt, and they were eager to promote a woman into a leadership position as a way to show all their other female employees what was possible. Little by little, they would add to Rania's production and management responsibilities. But they needed to be careful. If she took on too much at once, she might fail spectacularly and turn into a warning about what happens to women with too much ambition.

For every Egyptian woman who works, four others stay home. The nation's percentage of women in the labor force is among the lowest in the world, and the number has remained flat for the past quarter of a century; among some groups, such as college graduates, it has actually fallen. These facts contradict the common belief that globalization will bring opportunity, create jobs for women, and overturn social norms. It did happen this way in Taiwan, South Korea, China, India, and in conservative Muslim nations such as Malaysia and Bangladesh.

Since the 1970s, Egypt has become deeply integrated into the international economy through its political alliances along with increased trade, tourism, and migration. But the prospects for Egyptian women are getting worse. They're less likely to enter the workforce than they were ten years ago. They're more focused on making a good marriage and becoming more financially dependent on men. In the experience of these women, globalization has closed more doors than it has opened.

In other social realms, the country has made some progress toward equalizing opportunity for women. Girls and boys now attend school in comparable numbers, and Egyptian universities enroll more female than male students. Women are living longer, marrying later, and having fewer children than they did several decades ago. But the MENA region—the Middle East and North Africa—is the only part of the world in which such gains have not propelled women into the workforce, a puzzle that economists call "the gender equality paradox." A World Bank study estimated that average household income would rise by as much as 25 percent if women in the Middle East worked at the same rates as their peers in other parts of the world. The bank also estimated that at the current rate of increase in female employment, it would take the region's women a hundred fifty years to catch up to the rest of the world.

Resistance to female employment is grounded in a specific idea about male dignity. When a woman works outside the home, her family and community often interpret this act as a failure on the part of her husband. Chapter 4, verse 34, of the Quran says: *Men are the protectors and maintainers of women, because God has given the one more than the other, and because they support them from their means.* Marriage is a complementary arrangement—the man supports his wife, and she obeys him in return—and wifely submission is written into the Egyptian legal code. A woman who leaves the house without her husband's permission is considered *nashiz*—rebellious—and forfeits her right to his financial support.

Even when women work, their range of social acceptability is narrow.

Most women are reluctant to travel far from home on public transportation, for fear of sexual harassment; they don't want to spend their days in small workplaces or shops, which may bring them into close contact with male co-workers or strangers; they would rather leave work in time to be home to cook dinner for their husbands. Unemployment in Egypt is four times higher for women than for men—20 percent, compared with 5 percent—in large part because women turn down jobs that might compromise their domestic responsibilities or their reputation.

"It's not about the wage. It's really about the working conditions," Ragui Assaad, an economist at the University of Minnesota who studies labor and development, told me. Many of the jobs available in the Egyptian economy, he continued, are with small or informal enterprises that may require women to travel great distances, work long hours, or be exposed to sexual harassment. "If the working conditions are met, women are ready to work in droves. But if they're not met, very few are willing to work."

Since the 1960s, when Gamal Abdel Nasser guaranteed jobs for all high school and college graduates, women have seen the government as the ideal employer. These positions offer gender-blind hiring and wages, good benefits, short workdays, and large workplaces with the stamp of respectability. But the public sector is shrinking—it employs 5.6 million people, down from almost six million two decades ago—and female labor participation has dropped in tandem. More than 40 percent of all working women are still concentrated there as administrators, clerks, nurses, and teachers. Even better than a sinking ship, though, may be no ship at all: Between 2006 and 2012, the number of women in the workforce fell by six hundred thousand, and it has continued to decrease since then.

Outside the public sector, work comes with a warning label. Serving as a maid or a nanny in a stranger's house ranks particularly low, since it leaves a woman vulnerable to mistreatment or scandal. Selling goods in a shop is risky because it might invite sexual harassment by the owner, one's co-workers, or customers. Any job that makes a woman arrive home late at night so that the neighbors talk: That's considered *haram*, forbidden. Peddling insurance door to door, collecting bill payments, or visiting the homes of strangers: *Haram, haram,* and *haram.* Only if a woman is very poor, or her parents have died and left her no inheritance, or she has younger brothers and sisters to care for or a crippled leg or some other condition that makes it unlikely that anyone will marry her, only then will the people in her village praise her for going out to work. Otherwise, no.

Factory work is roughly on par with being a cook or selling vegetables in the market, but even in manufacturing there are moral judgments that don't entirely make sense. One woman I knew was embarrassed to work in a pickle factory that was run out of her neighbor's house. "I'll go into the house of a married man in my village to make pickles? It doesn't sound good." Another factory in the area made crystal figurines—there was nothing *haram* about that, but the close work could harm one's eyes. Clothing factories rank high in women's estimation, because sewing is a useful female skill, and most of the workers in the industry are women. Making men's underwear is acceptable, although a woman might spend most of her waking hours fingering, aligning, smoothing, and stitching together pieces of fabric that will someday touch the intimate parts of a man she doesn't know. For obscure reasons, it's still better than making pickles.

The big factories are often far from the villages, which requires a woman to wake up before dawn and walk through streets where she has no business being at that hour. Construction workers might make comments. The minibuses are another humiliation—they're like sardine cans on wheels, packed to bursting with marinating human bodies, male and female, that might accidentally rub against each other in embarrassing ways. The only thing worse is when the bus doesn't come at all. Then a worker might have to pay precious pounds for a *tuk-tuk* or a taxi so she won't show up late.

At the end of the month she might be paid £E700, or the equivalent of $80. Even if that makes her the family's steadiest earner, her husband might still spend the money as he likes and tell people that he lets her work for fun. "Working for fun"—that's how men often describe female labor, as if getting up at five in the morning and bending over a sewing machine for eight or ten or twelve hours until a person's vision blurs and her back aches and her shoulder muscles scream for mercy is a form of entertainment. Wives also tend to downplay the value of what they earn: They often say that they're working for pocket money, or just to buy clothes or makeup for themselves. Statements like this seem to mix pride and self-preservation. If a woman says her income helps support her family, that implies her husband can't do it by himself. That might make him angry.

Women give different reasons for why they work:

I just want to learn.

I love working here. I love seeing my friends.

To be honest, we're just bored of being at home. That's the bottom line.

You just come here and you're in a different world. You forget about everything.

I get up in the morning and I have places to go and things to do, rather than just serving my husband.

I'm here to feel I have some role in the universe.

Young women often take jobs to save up for marriage—this is generally accepted, as long as the work is acknowledged to be short-term. In this society a woman, like a basket of eggs, has a sell-by date, and it's considered best for her to quit once she finds someone to marry.

The alternative is to spend every day being shouted at on the assembly line and then hurry home to chop vegetables, cook dinner, oversee the children's homework, put them to bed, wash the dishes, clean the house, and give her husband her full attention. More shouting: He might accuse her of no longer being the devoted housewife he married. The important thing is for her to prove that working hasn't changed her at all.

When a couple starts talking about marriage, the first request he usually makes of her is to stop working. It goes on from there: *Wear longer dresses and looser tops. Get home early. Pray more. Stop using makeup. Don't hang laundry on the balcony.* Young men are fickle, and young women feel pressure to agree to whatever is asked of them. It's not much of a negotiation, but it's a pretty good preview of what being married will be like.

Most women don't have ambitions to rise in the factory; almost no one dreams of being promoted to supervisor or production manager. The ideal is to stay home and be a *sitt bayt,* a housewife—or if one has to work, to quit as soon as she can, the way a person leaves a hospital waiting room quickly to avoid catching an illness. Women sometimes brag that their husbands don't let them work, because what appears from one angle to be repressive behavior looks, from another, like love. To spend one's days sitting at home is a blessing. It means that God is smiling on you, *al-hamdulillah.*

I MET RANIA one afternoon in June 2016—characteristically, she ambushed me on the factory floor while I was talking to someone else.

"Are you working here now?" she interrupted, speaking to me through my translator, Amira. "Because I'd like to be friends with you."

Of course, I already knew who she was. I had been visiting the Delta Textile Factory for two months to speak with the assembly line workers there. Many of the women I met impressed me as strong-willed—heroic, even—for working against the wishes of their families. But these rebellions didn't usually last very long. The single women planned to quit as soon as they got engaged. When I asked the married ones about their future, they would talk about their dreams for their husbands or their children, as if their own lives were already over. *I want my son to be a doctor. My priority is my husband's happiness; when he's happy, I'm happy.* The job where they spent most of their waking hours never figured into the conversation. I came to see the factory floor as a kind of waiting room. It was a place where a woman marked time until something really important—engagement, marriage, childbirth—happened and took her away from here.

Later that afternoon, I had the chance to speak with Rania in the company conference room. Up close, she appeared intent on occupying as little space as possible—which surprised me, given her reputation as the factory's star supervisor. She had acne-scarred cheeks, full lips, and a black wool *hijab* that wrapped her face in a tight oval and made her look younger than she was. She spoke in a subdued voice, and she didn't laugh or make jokes, the way I'd noticed most Egyptians did no matter how bad their circumstances.

I asked Rania how old she was and what she did at work.

"I'm twenty-eight—no, I turn twenty-nine tomorrow," she corrected herself. "I'm the best supervisor in the production area."

She told me how Elena had asked for volunteers on Rania's second day at work and she had raised her hand. Rania would later tell me this story again and again. It was an anointment of sorts, a promise that her future would be different from everyone else's.

I asked Rania how she had learned to manage people.

"The key is that the girls should feel comfortable dealing with you. If you give them instructions or even if you're strict, they'll follow you if they feel comfortable with you."

"What happens next for you?"

Rania sat up straighter in her chair. "I want to be a manager, *insha'allah*."

She had always loved working. When she was a girl, she'd dreamed of being a police officer or a doctor one day. Like most of the young women in her village, she got married while she was still in her teens—she was fifteen or sixteen, she can't remember exactly now. At an age when adolescents in other parts of the world are playing in volleyball tournaments or hanging out at the mall, Rania set up house with Yasser, a man she didn't love or even like very much. Her father had insisted on the match out of "just stubbornness," she told me.

Rania remembers taking her final exams in her second year of trade school—her specialty was sewing—and then rushing home to breast-feed her newborn son, Kareem. By the time their daughter, Dina, was born, three years later, she and Yasser were barely on speaking terms. Rania moved out to live in her father's house for some months but later returned home for the sake of her children. Now they were eleven and eight, and they stayed in the house alone after school until she came back from work.

"*Sab*," I said. "It's hard."

"*Mish sab*," she replied automatically. "It's not hard."

Rania told me a lot more that day, about her solitary childhood and her parents' divorce, her abusive uncles and her overbearing father and her husband whose main character trait was indifference. Every development was like another chapter in a fairy tale that was destined to end unhappily. Only the story of Elena—*Who wants to work in quality control?*—broke the template and sent Rania's life story off in a different direction.

From Rania I learned that the workplace could be not just a waiting room but a place of refuge. Inside the factory, the disappointments of personal life might fall away, so that a woman could become someone else and even forget her own birthday.

I had heard this story before, but still it surprised me.

BETWEEN 2004 AND 2006, I spent a week or two every month in Dong-guan, a city in South China that was the global epicenter of manufac-turing. My focus was the teenage girls who labored on the city's assembly lines six days a week, for eight or eleven or thirteen hours each day. I met them in the evenings, or on those rare weekend after-noons when the lines were idle, my working day beginning when theirs finally ended. Rural Chinese had been migrating to the cities for two decades, and most foreign newspapers—including *The Wall Street Journal,* where I worked—had published stories about the harsh con-ditions inside the factories. I wanted to write about something else: how coming to the city had changed these young women's lives, if in-deed it had.

Almost everything I learned in those early days was a surprise. The factory girls were younger than I expected, some of them still in their midteens; they were unschooled in the trades they needed, inexperi-enced, and fearless. I met girls who had spent their first nights in the city sleeping in a bus station or under a highway overpass, and others who had been cheated out of their meager savings soon after they ar-rived. Newcomers quickly learned how to survive, which included lying about their qualifications, talking their way into jobs they had no busi-ness doing, staging small protests, and standing up to their bosses to demand better treatment. Quitting a job was as easy as changing one's hairstyle (actually, getting your hair colored or straightened was the big-ger commitment, because it cost most of a month's pay).

The details of the workplace were often of no interest to them, and when I asked these young women who owned the factory where they worked or what the object they made was used for, they couldn't say. The factory mattered only insofar as it intersected with their own concerns—whether it allowed them to save money or learn skills or obtain the promotion they wanted. Over and over, I watched young women use factories, just as surely as the factories used them, to craft new lives for themselves.

The factories fascinated me. They were like giant, silent beasts crouched on the landscape, as alive in their own way as the young men and women who darted in and out and all around them. Over most of a year, I paid monthly visits to the Yue Yuen shoe factory, which employed seventy thousand people and manufactured athletic shoes for brands like Nike and Adidas. This single production facility was so large that it had its own power plant and fire department, its own hospital and kindergarten, even its own seasons that followed the buying habits of consumers fifteen time zones away. To live here was to know the sudden rush of orders in late spring, the brief summer lull, and the ramping up of machines starting in September in the long lead-up to Christmas. Yue Yuen had its rules and hierarchies, its quarrels, cliques, love triangles, suicides, gangs, and criminal enterprises. "We have seventy thousand people: It's a city," Luke Lee, an executive who oversaw worker health and safety at Yue Yuen, told me. "Whatever problems a city has, we have in the factory."

Occasionally I found myself in a workshop at the other end of the scale, where a dozen women sat bent over their chairs, sewing shoe uppers or pleather purses in a dim room not much bigger than a garage. Even a factory this small is connected to every other manufacturer in the world that produces the same thing—a change in price, or supply, or technology can come from anywhere and require a response—and this is what makes factories interesting. A store can exist, day after day and month after month, without anything of significance happening inside. A company can go dormant and become a void hiding behind a name on a business card. A factory has to make something and find someone willing to pay for it; failing that, it must either shut down or change into something else. That was like Newton's First Law in action: A factory in motion tends to stay in motion. For a journalist, that was a guarantee that something interesting would happen, if you just waited around for a while.

I moved to Cairo in October 2011 with my husband, Peter Hessler, and our one-and-a-half-year-old twin daughters. Initially I had no intention of writing about factories. China is the manufacturing center of the world, and what happens on its assembly lines matters to a lot of people, but Egypt has no such importance. I was curious about women, though—like Chinese factory workers, women in the Arab world are a fraught subject that people tend to have strong opinions about. Women had helped drive the region's political uprisings, including the Arab Spring demonstrations that had toppled the regime of Hosni Mubarak earlier that year. They had joined marches and hunger strikes, given speeches, and organized food deliveries and medical help for protesters; from Tunisia to Bahrain, there was hope that this newfound visibility would win them greater rights and respect. News coverage about women in the Middle East tended to focus on a few types—activists or political prisoners, or those who had been the victims of honor killings or kidnapped into ISIS. I wanted to meet ordinary women and understand what this moment meant to them.

To embed myself in an Egyptian village and write about the dynamics I found—that was my initial fantasy, but it was a terrible idea. Egypt is a military regime, and it feels like one: The heavy presence of soldiers, police, and security guards fosters a suspicion about anything that might upset the normal order of things. As a Chinese American female journalist—three troublesome qualities, all in one person—I would draw attention fast and probably last only a few hours before being found out and booted back to Cairo. It was easier to talk to women outside the home, and that's how I started to think about the female labor force, though in a context that was the opposite of the world I knew. In China, almost all the women I met were working, sometimes in several jobs at the same time. I had watched, day by day, the ways in which employment changed the fates of the women I knew in Dongguan. Economics trumped tradition: That was the lesson. Why couldn't the same transformation play out even in a country with a different culture and history on the other side of the world?

So I found my way onto the factory floor again—specifically focusing on the textile and garment industry that has been central to the Egyptian economy for more than a century. In small workshops and on massive production floors, and later in villages and homes, I talked to women who sewed clothes for a living in order to understand what the work brought them. Guided by their concerns, I learned about the country's divorce laws, its educational policies, and its changing interpretations of Islam, all of which continue to shape the daily lives of ordinary women. The government barely came up in our conversations, but that absence was significant: By failing to build a competitive manufacturing sector, as other countries have done, the Egyptian government has diminished opportunities for the women who risk so much to work at all.

No matter how much time I've spent in factories, I always feel a thrill when I enter one for the first time. Here, at once, are all its secrets revealed: the closely guarded products and designs, the clients' names and price tags, the daily production targets and efficiency rates that are written on whiteboards for anyone to see. It takes time and patience to understand the workings of such a place. The factory has its rules and hierarchies, its quarrels and crimes, its private knowledge of who are friends and who are enemies and what's really going on behind its walls.

Which is how I ended up writing about the Egyptian village after all.

ON A BALMY spring morning in 2016, a white minibus belonging to the Delta Textile Factory pulled into the village of Beni Mahdi, which is a half-hour drive south of Minya on the Aswan Western Agricultural Road. Out jumped Mohamed Hanafy Ali, the company's personnel manager. After him came Fatima Metwally, who ran a local organization that provided job training and other services for women. The two of them looked around—dirt roads, donkey-drawn carts, packs of children heading to or from school.

Minya and the surrounding villages make up one of the poorest parts of the country, and the region ranks near the bottom in national surveys of income, literacy, and life expectancy. Delta needed six hundred people to work at its new facility in the city's industrial zone, and it was prepared to pay them well. That seemed like a straightforward equation, except that in Egypt there's rarely such a thing as an easy math problem.

"In Upper Egypt, having women work is seen as a mistake," Mohamed had explained to me. "When a girl gets engaged, her fiancé tells her to stay home, because"—and here he squared his shoulders and puffed out his chest—"'I am a man!'"

Delta executives had posted flyers, placed ads in newspapers, visited local high schools, and contacted churches and organizations that were active around Minya, but recruiting women into a factory in these parts takes a lot more ingenuity than that. One company executive interrogated the waitstaff at Makanik, a fashionable café downtown, about whether they would like to work in the textile industry ("and they're looking at me like I'm mad"). The company was now venturing into "the backwaters"—farming communities that lay about an hour and a half by car from Minya in every direction—to meet rural women face-to-face and encourage them to give Delta a try.

I followed Mohamed and Fatima into the front room of a village house. Its four walls were lined with hard benches, where twenty-two women sat squeezed together, along with several toddlers and infants. Fatima, who had been hired by Delta to recruit workers, spoke first.

"Today I'm here to tell you about a new opportunity," she said. "I can see in your eyes that you really want to be independent, and work, and earn your own money." She was tall with blazing brown eyes, the kind of woman who is always in a hurry and brings energy into a room with her. Even the babies in the audience would quiet down and pay attention when she spoke.

Fatima continued, "When we go down to the villages to look for women to work, we're aiming to empower women. We want to create an independent life for them. As women, we never feel our independence unless we go out to work. We feel that we have worth and a social community. We have options in life."

She outlined the terms of employment. The women would work eight hours each day, with a half-hour break for lunch, six days a week. Their starting salary would be £E700 a month, the equivalent of $80. Delta would provide free transportation and medical insurance.

Mohamed, who was mild in temperament with pale blue eyes, turned on a laptop and a projector and began showing photographs on one wall of the room. Images of women sitting at modern assembly lines appeared, the figures looking pale and blurry against the rough stone surface.

"The factory is beautiful," Fatima narrated, as the women watched and murmured among themselves. "It's like the factories you see on television. There are chairs, and everything is automated. Everyone has a uniform, and they're all women, as you see.

"When you see this in reality," she continued, "it will be even more beautiful than in the pictures."

Mohamed shut off the projector.

"If a woman has children in the nursery, how can she leave at six-thirty in the morning?" a woman wearing a black *hijab* edged in gold demanded.

"Everyone should arrange their lives and manage their timing," Fatima answered, as several women started a debate about the opening hours of nurseries.

Do we get paid during the training period?

What about the treatment? Because some people just treat us badly.

If a woman doesn't even know how to thread a needle, will they shout at her?

What if I'm pregnant and in the sixth month?

The women asked blunt questions and challenged the company's policies and talked loudly over one another. The room began to feel hot and close. It was hard to believe that such outspoken women had stayed home their entire adult lives.

Afterward, I spoke with Nadia Mahmoud, a twenty-one-year-old housewife in a black full-face covering known as the *niqab*, who had mentioned her pregnancy. Nadia had a three-year-old at home and no work experience, yet she was determined to sign on at Delta. "I'll try to convince my husband tonight, *insha'allah*, and then I'll work until I give birth to my baby," she told me.

Not one man from the village attended the meeting, but their presences were felt like ghostly apparitions. Later that day, the women would go home, cook dinner, and make their case for factory employment; the men would fill their bellies, weigh the pros and cons, and decide. It was a good bet that there would be more shouting.

Fatima called over the din of conversations, "Who agrees to work and will now go home to ask your husbands?" Thirteen women raised their hands.

A woman wearing a long pink *abaya* stood up. "I'm leaving now," she announced. "I'm going to ask my husband and come right back."

"Some personal advice from me," Fatima said. "We don't just ask our families. We also try to convince them, because this is very important for our existence."

Later I asked her, "Do husbands ever get angry at you for stirring up trouble?"

"Yes," she said. "I meet men who are very severe: 'Why are you talking to my wife? Why are you making her more aware? We don't want our women to work. We want them to stay home.'" In such situations, Fatima chose her words carefully, she told me. "We don't talk to the women about their rights—we try to tackle their needs. We say, 'You need to earn money to help your husband, to support your family, and to take care of your house.'"

And yet I noticed that when she spoke to the women of Beni Mahdi, Fatima hadn't taken a pragmatic approach at all. The women faced economic difficulties—that was why they had come—but Fatima had appealed to their emotions. She talked about goals and dreams; she spoke of *worth* and *social community* and *an independent life*. She assumed that these women living in an Upper Egyptian village wanted to get out of the house, to meet new people, and to change their lives.

The next morning, a white minibus belonging to the Delta Textile Factory pulled into Beni Mahdi again. More than a dozen women got on. Altogether, Fatima Metwally's organization recruited three hundred women in the villages around Minya to join the workforce at Delta. The company impressed the women as respectable, and the pay was decent, but its main selling point appeared to be its fleet of minibuses—like hermetically sealed containers, these would deliver the women to and from the factory with minimal risk of contamination. Through this sleight of hand, the women could work in the outside world without coming into contact with it. If the conditions are right, as the economist Ragui Assaad told me, women will work in droves.

IN A COUNTRY where people often run late, sleep through breakfast, and eat lunch around dinnertime, the Delta Textile Factory had an optimistic timetable. It had just built a $2.5 million state-of-the-art manufacturing facility in an industrial zone outside Minya. The company wanted to have six hundred fully trained workers by the middle of 2016, and to have them reach global standards of efficiency within the following twelve months. Most of the recruits would be women from farming villages who had never worked outside the home; a quarter were illiterate. And the mid-2016 deadline fell smack in the middle of the month of Ramadan, when women are expected to stay home to cook, clean, and spend time with their families.

"I'm expecting that one-third of the workforce won't be here the first week," Kevin Meyer announced in early June, one day before the start of the holiday. He's a black South African man in his forties with close-cropped hair, sharp cheekbones, and an air of suppressed energy beneath his button-down shirt and khakis. The Delta factory had ten assembly lines when he arrived a few months earlier to oversee its expansion; now it had twenty-two. On a calendar taped to the wall, the date June 30 was circled, accompanied by a message written in bold block letters: 30 LINES TO BE COMPLETED.

"We've basically doubled the factory," Meyer said, "and now we need to do it again." He had never scaled up a facility so fast. "In all my years of helping factories build, it is completely abnormal."

Mohamed Hanafy Ali, the personnel manager, cracked open the office door and said something I didn't catch.

"What the fuck are they thinking?" Meyer exploded. "They've just set me back two weeks!" Four of the six instructors he'd hired from Cairo to instill professionalism in his new work staff had not shown up that day. Nor had they bothered to call in.

He thought about it, weighed his options ("I'm not going to treat them like children"), and decided to dock the missing days from the employees' pay. "In other factories, there would be punitive measures," he told me, calm and buttoned down again. "But our company policy is about giving chances."

Making boxers and briefs may not seem particularly high-minded, but Delta is here in part for idealistic reasons. The company, which manufactures clothing and underwear for brands such as Tommy Hilfiger and Calvin Klein, established its first plant in Egypt in 1996 in a Cairo industrial zone. That was a political act: Delta is owned by an Israeli American businessman and based in Tel Aviv, and the investment was a gesture of Arab-Israeli friendship. Through the years, the investment has grown into six factories in which knitting, dyeing, cutting, and sewing are coordinated in a vertically integrated operation. But building friendship is harder. Although Egypt signed a peace treaty with Israel in 1979, most ordinary citizens are opposed to the country's existence, and anti-Semitism is widespread. Delta's Egyptian branch plays down its Jewish parentage, and its employees don't know who owns it. Or so I've been told by the management, which allowed me to report in its factories, interview workers, trail supervisors, poke around storerooms, and sit in on training sessions where corporate secrets were divulged, on the condition that I never talk to its employees about who owned the company.

Delta's expansion is also based on cold hard calculation. Where other investors look at Egypt and see corruption and inefficiency, Delta focuses on a different metric: The country has one of the lowest-paid workforces in the world. Making a T-shirt in Minya, for example, costs one-third of what it would in China, and it's also less than in places like Indonesia and Sri Lanka. Thanks to Egypt's web of free trade agreements, plus the luck of geography, manufacturers enjoy quicker and cheaper access to markets in the United States and Europe than their Asian rivals. And Delta can draw on two decades' experience in the country, plus generous local government support, to help build its Minya operation. "We've got an advantage on tax, we've got an advantage on labor costs, and we have a bigger pool of people to pull from," Ian Ross, the CEO of Delta Textile Egypt, told me. "It's not as stupid as everybody thinks."

One day that spring, I sat in on an orientation for new hires. The women sat at long tables in the factory canteen divided by village of origin, like high school cliques at lunchtime. A bored-looking young man from Personnel rattled off the rules.

You need to be at the bus stop five minutes before the bus arrives. If you're at home eating a sandwich, the bus won't wait for you.

If someone is absent for two days, we'll cut a hundred pounds from her salary.

In the production area, training starts from the simplest things—the parts of a sewing machine, how to thread a needle. A supervisor named

Mahmoud demonstrated how to move the machine's needle up and down by pressing the foot pedal.

"You have to watch the needle, and put your hands like this," he told a young woman, as he placed his palms flat on either side of the needle plate. "Are you ready?"

"Just stay with me," she replied tensely. She sat down and pressed with her foot. The needle jumped up and down violently, like a tiny jackhammer.

"No, like this." He sat down at the machine again.

The next step would be to sew straight lines on a piece of cloth; a trainee might complete fifty rectangles before moving on. "We've been told to be patient and let them take as long as they need," Mahmoud told me. Eventually, the recruits would know where they stood. Those with the most basic sewing skills would be assigned to the Singer single-stitch machine, and from there the hierarchy ascended to the Overlock, the Juki, the triple-stitch, the Flat Lock, and finally the elastic, which was the most difficult machine on the floor.

Most of the new employees sat in chairs lined up against the walls, like basketball subs waiting on the bench. Delta was hiring workers so fast that it didn't have the capacity to train everyone at once.

I spoke with one of these women, whose name was Hind Hassan. She sat with her hands clasped in her lap and wore heavy layers of black, like a grandmother in an old Italian movie. I was surprised to learn she was only thirty.

"I want to work to buy things for my marriage," she told me. Her parents were in their seventies and she had six older siblings, all of them married. Hind rarely left home and had never gone to school—"I don't know how to write my name"—but what she did know, down to the last *ersh*, or Egyptian cent, was how much money she needed to get married. The bride's side had to contribute £E40,000, and the groom—whoever he might be, because he didn't exist yet—would pay another £E30,000 for an apartment, furniture, and gold jewelry.

I showed Hind photos of my twin daughters, who had just turned six. She glanced at them.

"You should have two more children—boys. Boys are better than girls."

I put the pictures away. "I like my girls fine, and I have to work, so I don't want to have more children."

"Boys are better. You should have two more," Hind repeated, as if I hadn't spoken.

A fly buzzed around us and occasionally settled on her cheek or the edge of her lip, but she didn't brush it away with her hand. Her obstinacy was starting to bother me. That and her passivity—*Please smack that fly!*—although a woman who went into a factory to earn £E40,000 for marriage could hardly be called passive.

"Have two more boys, okay?" she said one last time. "It's settled, then?"

Delta's biggest challenge is teaching women like Hind, who often have poor education and no work experience, how to function in a global workplace. Many of these new hires have little contact with women outside their families, let alone with men they don't know. They operate on village time: *The bus won't wait for you.* Following set schedules, obeying bosses, handling conflicts with strangers—these are new experiences for them. Kevin Meyer was struggling to find female supervisors, he told me, because the women were so accustomed to deferring to their husbands that they hesitated to make decisions on their own.

"If there's a problem in the family, it's easy to solve because the father has the last word," Fatima Metwally, the recruiter for Delta, told me. "But the factory and the world don't work that way. For the girls, the easiest solution is always to leave this environment and run away."

Women quit the factory for the flimsiest of reasons, and Delta executives were frustrated that they didn't see a future for themselves in the industry. In rural India, Meyer once built up a clothing factory from twenty-five hundred to six thousand employees in a year and a half. "We recruited from rice paddies, people doing vegetable farming, people who had never seen a white person before." The women became productive workers, and some of them later went into business for themselves. Two female industrial engineers he'd trained set up their own consulting firm; another young woman sat in on merchandising meetings in her spare time and landed a senior position at Adidas. Ordinary workers saved up money to buy sewing machines and sell saris in their villages. In China, Delta Egypt's Ian Ross told me, some of the most impressive entrepreneurs he knew were women who had come from humble beginnings. But in Egypt—nothing.

It wasn't because the women lacked talent or drive. "Female workers are better than men. Seriously," Ross said one day, with characteristic bluntness, when we talked in the factory's conference room. "The men here believe that they can just go for a smoke, get a drink of coffee, that they don't have to do anything—gosh, the women even have to bring them lunch. It's very, very Victorian."

He noticed me laughing and stopped. "Don't you think so?"

"Oh, yes."

Ross was a native of Manchester, and he had bright blue eyes and an air of canny shrewdness. He had grown up in the textile trade. He quit school at fifteen to operate a sewing machine, and he worked his way up to the corner office of an international corporation without ever losing the instincts of a factory foreman. He spent his days on his feet, moving from the production floor to the cutting room to the warehouse and back again and taking note of talent wherever he found it ("I'm a great believer that there's intelligence everywhere, it's just how you bring it out and use it").

He noticed that Egyptian women took the jobs that men considered beneath them. They worked harder and endured more. He admired their grit. "I like people who fight their way through the world, and I like strong characters."

On his rounds in the Minya factory, Ross made a point of praising women workers in front of their bosses. He planned to recruit them into the cutting room—it was one of the few departments inside Delta that was all-male, for no other reason than that it had always been that way. The factory's top positions were all occupied by men, and he wanted to change that, too. A couple of weeks before Ramadan, Ross and his executives met and decided they would promote a woman from within the company's ranks into management, and she would be a local resident— the first female production manager in Upper Egypt. Through this act, they hoped to encourage all the other women in the factory to stay and to set ambitious goals for themselves.

"We have to make money, but we'd also like to develop women so they become stronger within their communities," Ross told me. "I don't know whether that's achievable in Egypt, especially rural Egypt. But it would be a nice tick in the box, wouldn't it?"

Maybe it was because the factory felt like a microcosm of the world outside, but I had met many factory managers who thought the way Ross did. At first he was there to produce goods and make a profit. Then he made a simple and surprising observation: *Female workers are better than men.* And he set about trying to reform the society in which they lived.

Two days after I met Rania, I returned to the Delta plant. It was the second day of Ramadan; for the entire month, workers would be laboring without food or water for seven and a half hours straight. The women wore long sleeves and long dresses, undershirts and overshirts, headscarves that wrapped under their chins or draped down their torsos, on a production floor that felt like a Finnish steam bath. It was the first week of June, and the temperature outside was forecast to reach a hundred and nine degrees.

As a test of her management abilities—on top of the challenges of a Ramadan at the height of summer—Rania had been asked to oversee a second production line along with her own. At 7:30 A.M. sharp, she walked rapidly up and down her two lines clapping her hands, like a teacher calling students to attention. A large sign on the wall proclaimed:

Happy Girls ☺
Happy Garments

Rania hugged one worker, kissed another on the cheek, and playfully boxed the ears of a young woman who was staring into space. "Where is Aida? Let's go. *Yella!*" The soft whirr of sewing machines started against the deep thrum of the ventilation system and the drone of Quranic verses over a loudspeaker.

Rania was trying out a new worker—a young deaf woman, also named Rania, who had just finished two weeks' training on the elastic machine. This Rania had a slender face and long-lashed dark eyes that were perpetually downcast, like a bashful puppy's. She conveyed in pantomime that she wanted to trade her orange trainee's smock for the white one of a regular worker. Rania promised to get her one.

At 8:14 A.M., Rania reminded an employee that the seam on a pair of boxers must fall exactly in the middle of the waistband, so that the two legs matched. She sat down at the deaf worker's machine to demonstrate. The junior Rania screwed up her face, signaling that she didn't like the pressures of working on the regular line.

At 8:30 A.M., a woman named Zizi came up to Rania and asked to be switched over to her team. "She motivates girls and makes them produce a lot of work," Zizi told me. "It's good to see her face in the morning." Rania agreed to make the change.

At 8:52 A.M., the first casualty of the day: A worker fainted. The young woman leaned back in a chair on the side of the production floor, surrounded by a gaggle of excited co-workers. When Rania arrived, tears were trickling out of the woman's eyes. Rania wiped them away with the edge of her headscarf.

"Come on, you're scaring me," she whispered, as someone fanned the woman with a production calendar.

The worker was upset because she had recently been transferred off Rania's line to work under a different supervisor. Her fainting spell—possibly faked—was a dramatic bid to reverse the factory's decision.

At 9:11 A.M., Rania took her stopwatch out of her pocket and checked it. The deaf Rania had expressed that she was unhappy because she couldn't keep up with the worker next to her. She struck me as a demanding employee, but Rania took it in stride. She went over to the young woman's station, folded a pair of boxers in half to make sure that the two legs matched, and nodded her approval.

At 9:16 A.M., Zizi returned to her original line because her transfer had upset another worker, but she asked Rania to talk to her supervisor to make sure she was treated well. Rania promised that she would.

At 9:30 A.M., Rania went upstairs for the morning meeting and received her target for the day: six hundred pairs of boxer shorts. The supervisors spoke back and forth—about production targets, pieces, people—in such rapid-fire bursts that I couldn't keep track of who or what they were talking about.

Today I need you to produce five hundred. Can you do that?

Yes, but I'll need help.

What about Doaa? Can you still work with her?

Doaa should produce six hundred pieces.

Does Fatima produce six hundred pieces per day?

We need her too much right now, but sooner or later we'll probably need to fire her.

At 10:31 A.M., back down on the floor, Rania was approached by a tearful woman in a long black *abaya*.

"Why are you crying?" Rania asked. "Did someone upset you?"

"I'm tired."

"What's wrong?"

"I'm tired."

At 10:40 A.M., the second casualty—another woman splayed out in her chair, apparently unconscious. Once again, it was unclear what caused the fainting—the heat or a management decision. And once again the ritualistic theater played out: the gathering of co-workers, the tears and hugs, the promise that the woman would be switched to the line she wanted.

In the course of the morning, Rania headed off other potential disasters. She spotted a worker who was about to mix up the fabric tapes from two different orders—one was a dark gray, the other matte black—and alerted her to it. She searched all over the factory for a thousand missing barcode tags that had been separated from their work bundles. She puzzled over the legs on a pair of teal Tommy John–brand boxer shorts: Why weren't they matching up? Rania first blamed the worker but later decided that the mistake was made by the cutting department—a tiny discrepancy in measurement that the woman operating the sewing machine was supposed to notice, and fix.

As I followed Rania around the factory that morning—often at a jog, as she checked in on problem stations with quick, darting movements—I learned that sewing garments in an Egyptian factory isn't an exact science. There's always a piece of fabric that someone has cut imprecisely and someone else has to fix on the fly, or a tag that was left out, or a piece of equipment that wasn't properly cleaned. A worker may be pregnant, or perhaps she feels ill, or she just had a fight with her husband, any of which could reduce her daily efficiency in ways a whiteboard could never explain. A good supervisor adjusts for these flaws in the system and makes the best of the materials she's given.

On a Chinese factory floor, the operating procedure is straightforward: Bosses instruct and workers obey. I never saw an assembly line worker faint, whether for real or passive-aggressive purposes. Chinese employees don't hug or kiss each other or burst into tears in the course of an ordinary workday. The work at Delta, though, depended on a web of personal exchanges in which power relations were sometimes turned upside down. Supervisors engaged in negotiations or called in favors to get tasks done; workers complied out of loyalty or refused from spite. The fainting spells, the shouting matches, the crying, the outpourings of emotion—these were the traditional tools that women used in family settings in which they had little power, imported into a modern factory. Rania often said that the key to motivating workers was to win their love. After I spent a day with her on the production floor, I understood what she meant.

At 11 A.M., she realized that her line was falling behind because her best elastic sewer was on vacation; the Ramadan exodus had begun. Rania decided to ask a woman named Doaa to fill in on the elastic machine for a couple of days. Doaa, a tall woman with a peevish expression, had recently been named a trainee supervisor and did not like the idea of being demoted, even for two days, to sew elastic.

"Okay, I'll do it," she said. "But I have to sit at a machine that I like."

"Watch this," Rania said to me, quietly. "Now she'll be very demanding. I have to be very patient with her."

Doaa took a leisurely tour around the factory floor, while Rania, my translator, Amira, and I trailed behind her like royal attendants. She tested seven or eight different elastic machines and shook her head after each one. Following this extended performance, Doaa agreed to work at the first machine she had tried, which was on Rania's line.

At 12:57 P.M., Rania sat down in a chair behind Doaa, helping pluck out stitches on pieces that needed to be redone. She didn't have to—she was the supervisor, after all—but this was how she expressed her gratitude to Doaa. It seemed unlikely now that the line would meet its target, and Rania would lose the top efficiency rating she'd held the previous month.

I left the factory around two. The working day wasn't over yet, but I was exhausted. The deep-throated hum of the air-cooling system makes every conversation harder than it needs to be. The noise of the factory throbs and eventually settles in your brain, as intimate as a headache.

Rania was still sitting behind Doaa when I went to say goodbye. I asked her what her plans were. "I'll try to unpick all these mistakes today, so tomorrow we can start fresh," she said. I left her sitting bent over a piece of fabric, patiently undoing the errors that had been made by others.

AMONG GARMENT INDUSTRY executives, Egypt is considered one of the toughest places to do business. "It's because of the people," Ian Ross said. "They're so stubborn, and they refuse to change, and they have an opinion about everything."

He went on, "Example: Two people can crash a car in the middle of Cairo, and within five minutes there's a hundred people who have an opinion about it, whose fault it is, how it happened, what should happen next, who should be blamed, okay? The workforce here is difficult."

Every factory owner I met—male or female, Egyptian or foreign—said pretty much the same thing.

Bahia Nazim, owner of a factory in Alexandria that makes baby clothes and bed linens: "No workers: That's our biggest problem. People don't like to work. The Egyptian worker is talking on the phone all the time, or going to the bathroom, or going off to pray. They're masters of wasting time."

Hani Ibrahim, owner of a fruit and vegetable packing business in the Nile Delta: "The men may work two days a week, or they go to the *ahwa*"—that was the local coffeehouse—"or they're on drugs. Maybe it's the nature of Egyptian men: They don't want to work."

Samah El-Sayyid, co-owner of a children's clothing factory outside Alexandria: "The worst thing in this industry are the workers. Please bring me some from China!"

Many owners blamed the poor workplace culture on former president Nasser. In the early 1960s, his program of sweeping nationalizations had put much of the country's economic assets under government control. At a stroke, everyone from bank presidents to machine operators became civil servants, with guaranteed lifetime employment. Wages were no longer tied to productivity; they simply rose with the cost of living. High school and college graduates were allocated jobs in the state sector, and it became almost impossible to fire anyone.

Even though Nasser-style socialism didn't last long—his successor, Anwar Sadat, shifted the economy in a capitalist direction—workers continue to pine for the generous terms of employment that were set during his era. Employees frequently behave as if the power balance is still in their favor, and their bosses submit to this view. Several factory managers told me they were afraid to ban mobile phones from their production floors, for example, because their workers would leave en masse. One woman told me that her place of work was "like a prison" because she couldn't chat with her husband whenever she wanted (she quit the factory soon after). Nasser may be a hero to the working man, but he's also the bogeyman who haunts any discussion about what's wrong with the Egyptian economy today. "The entire economic catastrophe was created under Nasser," the chairman of a cotton trading company told me. "And we're suffering from these policies to this day."

In his book *Shop Floor Culture and Politics in Egypt*, the political scientist Samer S. Shehata describes the workplace dynamics inside two state-owned textile factories near Alexandria, where he worked as a winding machine operator in the late 1990s as part of his research. Shehata discovered ingenuity in all the wrong places. Employees prepared and ate their meals right next to the machines, "refashion[ing] old blades taken from machine tools into makeshift knives, which they use to cut up tomatoes, onions, and other vegetables," Shehata wrote. They manipulated the manufacturing process so they could work less. The typical workday had an unseemly number of breaks and interruptions that included breakfast, morning tea, midmorning tea, noon prayer, lunch, and final tea. One mechanic whose job was to repair broken machines spent much of the day walking idly from place to place with the apparent goal of never doing anything. The men—they were all men— had a catalog of ways to undermine their employers. They included "sabotage . . . pilfering, evasion and escape, shirking, forgery, subversive speech, generalized indiscipline, and the violation of factory rules."

Nowadays, most of the garment industry is private, but the lax management and low expectations that marked the state-enterprise era have persisted. A USAID study of Egyptian clothing manufacturers found disorganized sewing and cutting rooms, high worker absenteeism and turnover, and inadequate training. Egypt's clothing exports could increase by between 20 and 40 percent, the report said, if its factories were better organized. In a World Economic Forum survey of one hundred forty-one countries, Egypt ranked near the bottom for the quality of its vocational training and the skills of graduates.

At Delta, Kevin Meyer was surprised to meet workers who were unable to tell their right hand from their left and industrial engineering applicants who couldn't do basic arithmetic. "In other markets, I wouldn't have accepted any of the graduates that I've taken here," he told me. The company lowered its disciplinary standards and made a conscious decision not to fire anyone. Actions that should lead to a worker's termination—an unexplained ten-day absence, low productivity lasting for weeks on end—were excused. Meyer was blunt about his reasons: "We don't have replacements."

Yet the same executives who criticized the entrenched habits of male workers praised their female employees. Most of the women had never worked before—but when they were challenged to learn new skills and meet exacting standards, they often thrived. Hani Kassis, the chief executive officer of a company called Mintra that makes stationery and plastic products, said his factory's female workers were more dedicated than the men, with half the turnover rate.

"We don't like the men!" he told me, half-jokingly. "They have a lot more options. If a man goes to any factory, he'll be accepted. The women don't have that opportunity." It wasn't that surprising: In a society with few opportunities for women, they must work harder in order to prove themselves.

"It's a richness that nobody sees here," Hani continued. "The problem is with the thinking of men. Male factory owners assume that women don't want to work in the factory, but I don't think that's true."

The Bishara Textile and Garment Manufacturing Company, one of the country's largest makers of apparel, took that faith in female workers to its logical conclusion. In 2009, the company recruited women from farming areas, brought them hundreds of miles to its Cairo factory, trained them to sew, and housed them in specially built dormitories. The Bishara group eventually employed around a hundred fifty female workers from the Nile Delta and Upper Egypt.

"It was very, very successful," Medhat Kamal, the factory's human resources manager, told me. Compared with women who had to commute two hours to and from the factory each day, the migrants "came early and worked all day. They were more productive, they were more dedicated, and they had fewer absences." Just like that, a radical idea became ordinary. Young women traveled from their villages to Cairo, worked on assembly lines, lived in dorms, and went home once a month to see their families, and the world didn't end. The program didn't last long, though. During the 2011 revolution, the women left—not because they were unhappy with their jobs, but because their families pressured them to return home during the political unrest. After that, the Bishara company lost its contacts in the rural villages and never resumed its pioneering experiment in female migration.

For anyone who was paying attention, it was clear that Egypt was wasting a tremendous amount of its potential. If an employer took the time to recruit and train women, they would work hard and excel at what they did, and they would be loyal. "They're perfect," Hani Kassis told me. "They are the best workers on earth. But you need good management. If you control those processes well, we can be the best society on earth."

AFTER I WATCHED Rania's hectic day on the factory floor, I thought her line must have missed its production target. When my translator, Amira, and I spoke with her on the phone a couple of weeks later, though, we were surprised. Rania had sewn on the elastic machine herself for most of the afternoon, in order to get production back on track. Then she asked her line to stay two hours past closing that evening—that was another negotiation, since supervisors couldn't order anyone to work overtime. The workers met their target of six hundred pairs of boxer shorts, and Rania maintained her status as the number one supervisor in the Delta factory for one more day.

I asked her why that goal mattered so much to her.

"For the past month, we've been the best production line in the factory," she said. "So we didn't want to be beaten by someone who wasn't as good as us."

To an outsider, assembly line labor looks like drudgery. The details of the products blend together, and every day is more or less the same. Rania didn't see it that way. To her, every day was specific and meaningful; weeks later, she could still remember how many pairs of boxer shorts she had been required to produce on a certain day, or which of her workers had been absent, or what crises she had met and managed. It was staying home with little to do that made the days blend together and lose their meaning. To join the working world was to measure out time in increments, but also to become more aware of its value. "If a day goes by, I can't make it up," Rania told me. "So each day is really precious."

2

STARTING FROM ZERO

RIHAM MOHAMED GALAL SEIF EL-DIN remembers when the Egyptian garment industry was something to be proud of. The big state-owned factories that had been set up under Nasser employed thousands of people in cavernous production halls. They ran their own training centers and sent engineers to France, Germany, and Italy to study innovations in dyeing and fabrics. Their workers played on the company soccer team, frequented the company social club, and made the *Umrah* pilgrimage to Mecca on a company subsidy. A job in one of these places brought a good income, prestige, bonuses, and vacations. "It was a big opportunity," Riham remembers, "a dream come true." Her father and grandfather had come of age in this world, and from her earliest days Riham dreamed of joining them, even though she was a girl.

Egyptian cotton was the finest in the world, and it had dominated the country's exports for much of the past century. In old age, an Egyptian textile manufacturer named Louis Bishara would recall the exotic names of the cotton varieties he knew as a child: There were Karnak and Menoufi, Zagora and Sakellarides and Beheira. The landowners of the late nineteenth century spawned a powerful national mythology: of the cotton barons whose mansions lined the seaside Corniche in Alexandria, or the speculator who took his life when the market went the wrong way. As in the American South, cotton created unimaginable wealth and a distinctive idea about how to live well, as the sociologist Mona Abaza describes in her memoir, *The Cotton Plantation Remembered:*

> Cotton enabled upwardly mobile nineteenth-century landowners to [build] magnificent mansions designed by European architects in the countryside. . . . Cotton paid for the maintenance of conspicuous, lavish western lifestyles, the purchase of fashionable western drawing-room furniture, Aubussons, Gobelins, pianos, chinaware and European paintings. . . . Cotton led naturally to the transfer of fat surpluses into bank accounts in Switzerland, enjoyment of the cures of Baden-Baden, boasts of shopping in Paris and London, and the employment of French, Italian, English, or German nannies for the children.

In the countryside, cotton production was the soundtrack of daily life: the clack of the weaver at his loom, the yodeling of women picking the crop at harvest time. "You would wake up one morning and all the fields would have turned white," a journalist who grew up in a village outside Minya remembered.

The hub of the trade was Alexandria, which was home to the oldest cotton futures market in the world. Riham's grandfather set up a factory downtown in 1944 to weave fabric and sew underwear. The Seif El-Din Company for Industry and Commerce grew into a vertically integrated operation with a hundred fifty employees across two factories who knitted and dyed fabric and sewed clothes for export. When Riham graduated from college in 2000, she joined the firm alongside her father, uncle, brother, and five cousins.

In 2015, when I met her, Riham was running her own clothing factory with seventeen employees in the Merghem Industrial Zone. It was fourteen miles from Alexandria on the Cairo Desert Road—a windswept stretch of highway with garment and dyeing workshops housed inside three-story brick buildings. These structures were partially crumbling and covered in a layer of yellow dust, like an archaeological site that had been abandoned. The factories no longer ran their own training centers, and no one was going to France, Germany, or Italy to study. Riham imported all of her fabric—from China or India or other places—because the domestic production of cotton cloth had collapsed in the decades since her grandfather started his business. Almost every day, she heard about another manufacturer that had closed its doors, or an owner who had given up on sewing clothes and was buying them from China instead.

Upstairs, the production area was filled with natural light. Half a dozen young women and two older men sat at sewing machines, stitching together pieces of red cotton fabric to make a girl's Minnie Mouse shirt. On other areas of the floor, women ironed, trimmed, and packed the clothes for shipment. Riham was in her late thirties, with dark watchful eyes in a delicate-boned face and a hawklike nose that made her look keen and alert. She moved through the production stations calmly and without haste but still managed to be everywhere at once. Movement was what she craved: In this business, every second of idleness is money down the drain. The factory's vast downstairs, whose dark cement floor stayed cool on the hottest days, was empty—an unusual amount of vacant space for a small enterprise.

A breeze came off the Mediterranean, which was visible through the open windows on this spring morning. The radio played: the Quran in the morning, or Om Kalthum, or sometimes "Abla Fadila," Auntie Fadila, whose old-fashioned children's stories with talking animals and strong morals the workers remembered from childhood. Riham's factory wasn't large, but it was clean and well organized. The working day ran from eight in the morning to five in the afternoon, with a half-hour break for lunch. There was a room upstairs where employees ate. In the tiny bathroom, the plumbing worked and the floor was dry and a shard of glass glued over the sink served as a mirror. The factory's sewing machines were Korean-made, a necessary compromise between the high-end Japanese equipment that Riham couldn't afford and the cheaper Chinese versions. All in all it was a modest operation, but Riham felt good to be running things the way she wanted. "One of the reasons you start a business is that you're not satisfied," she told me.

As a little girl, Riham loved going to her grandfather's factory and would often tag along with her father and her older brother, Mustafa, on visits there. Riham would gather bits of fabric that had been left over in the cutting process, and the workers would fashion these scraps into dresses for her doll. On family vacations, their father would often detour by the factory—"I'm going to pass by for five minutes"—and linger an hour or two, testing their mother's patience but delighting the children. When Riham was older, she learned from her grandmother how to operate a sewing machine. By then, she told me, "I was saving money, because I dreamed of doing something on my own." In the late 1990s, Riham attended the University of Alexandria, where she got a degree in production engineering. She was offered a job at a large multinational when she graduated, but she was helping out at the family business at the time—they needed someone to communicate with a foreign client, and Riham speaks English and French. When that stint ended, she just stayed. "I went and worked with my uncle. It's fate," she once told me, with a laugh.

By the time Riham joined the company, her grandfather had passed away and her uncle Anwar, her father's younger brother, was in charge. He ruled with a firm hand: Riham's grandfather, in his will, had stipulated that Anwar must be consulted on every financial decision within the company, no matter how small. To Riham, it sometimes felt as if her uncle's power to stifle change came from beyond the grave. If she wanted to try out some innovation she had studied in college—techniques to improve productivity, a new type of elastic machine—her uncle wasn't interested. Whatever measures Riham introduced to make the factory function better, he would resist or stonewall or quietly undo behind her back.

"I couldn't take it anymore, because I thought that I would lose everything I had learned," she said. She quit the company after six years, joined forces with a friend in a similar situation—female, educated, family company, frustration—and set up a factory to make baby blankets and quilts. After the friend left to get married, Riham continued the venture on her own.

The only way to run a business in this country, she believed, was to start from scratch and instill good values in workers while they're young. She taught the women in her charge to sew, trim, iron, fold, and inspect a finished product for defects, and also to eat more vegetables, feel pride in their work, take responsibility for mistakes, and hold out for a young man with a steady job rather than take the first one who came along.

Why are you getting married to a person who doesn't have a job? My dear, stay at home with your father!

Don't marry this man unless he is settled in one place, and he has insurance and someone to pay him every month.

A young woman who had dropped out of middle school applied for a job at the factory. Riham convinced the girl that she should go back and get her diploma, then phoned the headmistress of a local school to make sure there was a place for her there. She urged fiancés and husbands to let women work, and gave the men tours of her factory to show that her workplace was respectable. "This country can't change until the culture changes," she often said.

Every Egyptian village has its *umda*, a local chief who resolves disputes and helps people in need, and Riham fulfilled this role here. When the wife of the factory security guard was diagnosed with cancer, Riham called up a relative, a doctor, who agreed to treat the woman free of charge. She had a system for workers who were short of cash: She wouldn't lend them anything in the first two weeks after they were paid. From the middle of the month, an employee could get an advance of up to 25 percent of her salary, but she had to return the money as soon as she got her next month's pay—this way, the workers didn't accumulate too much debt. One of her machine operators had been borrowing from her for many months, in small amounts, to help pay the hospital bills for a sick newborn.

The young women who worked for Riham frequently asked her to find jobs for their fiancés, so she had arranged work for many young men who didn't impress her at all. It didn't matter: They failed to show up, or they didn't stay. *I can't sit from eight to five each day,* they told her. *I'm not used to it.* Even so, Riham preferred to have the young men working in her factory next to their wives or fiancées rather than alone at home with time on their hands.

"Honestly, when he's sitting at home, he's making a headache for me," she said. "He's on the phone all the time: He wants to eat something! She didn't do the laundry! She didn't do this. . . ."

Riham sighed. "But they never come. Not a single one."

"He doesn't want to compromise his pride—" I began.

"It's not a matter of pride anymore," Riham interrupted me. "He lost his pride when his wife gave him money to smoke cigarettes and to eat and for his children. Where's the pride? He doesn't have any pride, *at all*!" She burst out with a delighted, high-pitched laugh that sounded like the tinkling of chimes and that, I would learn, she reserved for situations she considered hopeless.

When I met Riham, she was working as a subcontractor, which meant that she completed part of an order for a more established factory that dealt directly with an overseas client. Lately Riham had decided that she wanted to land her own export customer, which would bring her larger and more reliable orders. But her factory would have to guarantee production of two thousand pieces a day—more than triple its current output—and for that she needed more workers.

In the place where the cotton economy had lived and died, she would build an enterprise to produce clothes to a globally competitive standard and teach young women how to work hard and make something that mattered. She would turn around her corner of the Egyptian garment industry and make it something to be proud of.

FOR MOST OF the last thousand years, the production of cotton textiles has been the largest manufacturing industry in the world. The technology of spinning and weaving cotton fiber is believed to have emerged independently on the Indian subcontinent, in South America, and in East Africa. This miracle fabric that was soft, durable, and easy to clean traveled on trade routes to China, Persia, Egypt, Greece, and Rome. Cotton cloth was sent as tribute to the Aztec rulers; it was a form of tax payment in imperial China; it functioned as currency for travelers in Southeast Asia and Mesoamerica. Medieval Europeans were so fascinated by the exotic fiber that they developed a mythology around its origin, which was said to be a creature that was part plant and part animal, called the "vegetable lamb."

The signal event that turned cotton into a globally profitable commodity was the Islamic conquest. During the seventh and eighth centuries, Muslim rulers in the conquered territories promoted the wearing of simple white cotton robes as a symbol of religious purity; this act, which was meant to set them apart from the extravagance of previous kings, significantly expanded the market for cotton growers and weavers. In the wastelands of Iran, Arab entrepreneurs built an irrigation system to cultivate cotton on a large scale. Teachers in the religious schools of eastern Africa taught their students to dress modestly and imparted the skills—spinning for girls, weaving for boys—to enable them to make cotton clothing for themselves. In Europe, cotton manufacturing initially took root in Islamic Spain, and textiles produced in Seville, Córdoba, Granada, and Barcelona were later exported to the rest of the continent.

"So tight was the association between Islam and cotton," writes Sven Beckert in *Empire of Cotton*, "that most western European languages borrowed their words for the fiber from the Arabic *qutun*. French *coton*, English *cotton*, Spanish *algodón*, Portuguese *algodão*, Dutch *katoen*, and Italian *cotone* all derive from the Arabic root."

Cotton eventually dominated global commerce and drove the transition to a modern economy, in all of its deplorable and exploitative aspects. In the seventeenth century, demand for Indian calico and chintz fabrics fed a fashion craze in Europe and helped drive imperialist expansion as rival nations competed to control the lucrative business. "Cotton and colonial expansion went hand in hand," Beckert writes, "for Russia and Japan . . . Great Britain, France, and the United States, as well as marginal imperial powers such as Portugal, Germany, Belgium, and Italy."

Cotton was inextricably bound to the slave trade. Cotton cloth was commonly used to purchase slaves from Africa. On plantations in the Caribbean and the American South, raw cotton was harvested by slaves, who also formed a major market for the cheap cotton clothes that factories made. Mass production first came into being in the textile mills of Lancashire, England, and Lowell, Massachusetts. It was because of cotton that the Industrial Revolution was set in motion and modern capitalism was born.

Egypt was uniquely positioned to benefit from these developments. The Nile Valley and the Delta had some of the most fertile land in the world; by the turn of the eighteenth century, cotton growing was an important part of the economy. Around 1820, a French textile engineer named Louis Alexis Jumel, who was living in Egypt, made a breathtaking discovery. In a Cairo garden, he came across a cotton bush with fibers that were softer, longer, and stronger than any he had seen.

Mohamed Ali, Egypt's ruler, recognized the commercial potential of this find and reorganized the economy to profit from it. His government ordered farmers to grow "Jumel cotton" and distributed seeds, cotton gins, and presses. Ali invited foreign experts to supervise cultivation and passed regulations on how the cotton should be planted, tended, watered, and picked; soldiers were sometimes sent to the fields to ensure that growers followed the rules. At harvest time, Ali's agents bought the entire crop at a fixed price, shipped it to central warehouses, and sold it to foreign merchants, and in good years these receipts would account for the bulk of the state's revenue. The government organized hundreds of thousands of laborers to dig canals and build roads and dams, all to irrigate the crop and move it to market. It was a mobilization of corvée labor on a scale not seen since the time of the pharaohs.

With the proceeds from cotton, Mohamed Ali tried to turn Egypt into an industrialized nation. His government imported looms, carding machines, and spinning jennies from Europe and set up cotton mills, weaving factories, and bleaching and dyeing establishments. An Administration of Spinning and Weaving was established to monopolize every stage of production. Spinners bought raw cotton from the government and sold their finished thread back to the state at a set price. Weavers were forced to work in government factories, and private weaving became a crime.

At the height of the industrialization effort in the mid-1830s, Egypt had thirty spinning and weaving factories that employed as many as thirty thousand workers; its number of cotton spindles per capita, by one estimate, ranked fifth in the world behind Great Britain, Switzerland, the United States, and France. A French textile manufacturer who toured the country's cotton mills was impressed. "It is industry," he wrote in a report for the Egyptian government, "that makes the wealth of nations."

But what Mohamed Ali accomplished through money, coercion, and single-minded purpose didn't last long. In the 1840s, the textile machines began to break down, and the country lacked the skilled personnel to fix them. Morale among employees was low. Most of the workers had been forcibly recruited into the factories at subsistence wages, and the quality of what they produced was poor; by one estimate, half of the raw material that went into the factories was wasted through carelessness. The state's top-down control hindered development in other ways. Unlike in Great Britain and the United States and later in Japan, China, and India, the manufacturing of textiles didn't create a modern industrial base, a private sector, or a wage labor force. By the middle of the century, the government ended its monopoly over cotton production and shut down most of the factories.

Egyptian cotton manufacturing more or less disappeared, but the cultivation of long-staple cotton thrived. Jumel cotton sold on the Liverpool market for two and a half to four times the price of ordinary short-staple cotton, and at a premium over all but the best American varieties. "This twist is of superior quality," a group of British merchants in India wrote, "even surpassing that imported here from England." Between 1860 and 1865, when the U.S. Civil War cut off cotton supplies from the American South, production in Egypt quintupled. In the following decades, the country reverted to an agricultural economy dependent on a single cash crop. Economic activity was geared toward growing, processing, financing, transporting, trading, and exporting cotton, to the detriment of other productive forms of investment. By 1920, 40 percent of the land in Lower Egypt was planted in cotton.

Over the nineteenth century, Egypt was integrated into the world economy, but not as the industrial power that Mohamed Ali envisioned. The country became, essentially, a giant plantation that served the needs of the Manchester cotton mills. Meanwhile, Egypt grew reliant on imports of clothes and other manufactured goods from Europe—its domestic industry decimated, as in so many places around the world, by a global commercial system dominated by Great Britain. Egyptian cotton was still the finest in the world, but the innovation, development, and profits that accompanied its manufacture went somewhere else.

In *Cotton and the Egyptian Economy,* the historian E.R.J. Owen described two countries whose fortunes diverged at the end of the nineteenth century. Like Egypt, Japan was a country of peasant farmers who worked small plots of land. Its economy was also dependent on a single cash crop—in its case, rice. But Japan used its agricultural wealth to finance a broad program of modernization. The government took over mines and shipyards and built silk factories, cotton mills, breweries, engineering workshops, and chemical plants. It introduced compulsory education and sent young Japanese abroad to learn technical and commercial skills. It embraced innovation and subsidized entrepreneurs. In the villages, landowners broke with tradition to set up businesses, and peasant sons migrated to the cities for work.

Egypt stuck to its set path. Under the rule of Mohamed Ali's descendants, the country doubled down on the cultivation and export of cotton. Rich Egyptians invested almost exclusively in cotton or in land. In the economic boom years that followed the U.S. Civil War, tens of thousands of Europeans moved to Egypt to engage in land speculation or to set up mortgage, finance, or other enterprises that were tied in one way or another to the cotton trade. Unlike in Japan, the government had no comprehensive plan to develop modern industry nor to train its mostly agricultural workforce; education remained an elite privilege, and illiteracy rates stayed high. The few entrepreneurs who did set up factories faced all these hurdles, along with a relative lack of energy sources and raw materials. "In the circumstances, it might seem that the proper question to ask is not why so little, but why so much, industry was created at this time," Owen writes.

The continuing reliance on cotton would exact a high cost. Buoyed by inflated prices for the crop during the Civil War, the Egyptian state took out large loans to finance the digging of irrigation canals, the building of railroads, and the transformation of Cairo into a "Paris on the Nile" with parks, gardens, and palaces. The crown jewel of this public-works program was the construction of the Suez Canal, for which Egypt was the main financial backer. In 1876, faced with falling cotton prices and crushing debt, the government went bankrupt. The British eventually moved in—to protect their financial interests and access to the canal—and took over running the country for the next three decades. They implemented a free trade policy that flooded the market with imported goods and further discouraged local manufacturing. By the turn of the twentieth century, Japan was undergoing a structural transformation into a modern industrial economy. Egypt remained rural and poor.

In the coming decades, the country's elites would ask why this was so; time and again, they would try to build an economy around the beautiful cotton that a Frenchman had discovered in a Cairo garden. "Egypt is the gift of the Nile," Herodotus wrote twenty-five hundred years ago, and the country's potential has always been tied to its agricultural riches. But a blessing can turn out to be a curse, and having too much of a good thing may leave you with nothing at all.

Riham's plan to conquer the American export market began with teenage girls. In May 2015, she asked two of her experienced machine operators where she might find more workers—in the topsy-turvy world of global manufacturing, the peak Christmas season was starting. They told her there were six thousand apartments across the desert road from her factory. *Six thousand apartments, and I can't get thirty workers?* Riham thought. *This isn't right.* "Which area has the most decent people?" she asked then, since she didn't want to recruit in high-crime districts. They named the neighborhoods where they lived.

Riham visited the director of a middle school there and learned that the students' three-month summer break coincided with the winter season in the garment industry. Riham decided to hire students as interns, pay them a trainee's salary, and teach them how to sew. As a bonus, she would be shaping the values of the next generation. "I'm making a system in their heads" is how she put it. The school director told students about the opportunity, and Riham started to get inquiries at all hours on her phone.

A couple of weeks later, she arrived at her factory one morning to welcome her first crop of trainees: six young women sitting in rows of wooden chairs, downstairs from the production floor.

"My name is Riham. I hope you're going to benefit from being here today," she said, speaking quickly and plainly. "Try not to worry about anything, and you can ask any questions you want."

She continued, "Do you know the name of the factory?"

No one did.

"Textile Leaders. The name has a dream within it, that we want to be the leader in textiles. We want to do the best that we can."

She explained, in simplest terms, what a factory was for. "How do you make a blouse? It doesn't take one person; it takes many people working together. It's a system. If one person doesn't do good-quality work, the whole thing will collapse. The important thing is that we're a team, so that we can make something beautiful that you would want to wear.

"In the place where we work," she continued, "there's not one thing that's important and one thing that's less important. Everything is important. The person who removes the threads is not less important than the person who's sitting at the sewing machine. Every specific station is important for our work."

As employee orientations went, this one was unusual. Egyptian factories—like Egyptian families, schools, and society—run on hierarchy. There *are* some things that are important, and other things that are less important, and young women tend to be the least important of all. In traditional textile factories, it was common to employ young girls as assistants. They were assigned, one to each worker, like handmaids.

"She's there to serve them," Riham told me. "'Go get me some water, get me this, get me that.' If there's a defect in the piece, the worker will blame it on her. She's really there to be abused." Girls might perform menial tasks for years before being allowed to sit at a machine and learn to sew. From a financial point of view, the arrangement made no sense. It seemed to reflect the urge to recreate the factory as a family, where no one was ever alone and every person knew her place in the pecking order.

Riham wanted to overturn all of that. Her new hires would learn, from day one, every stage of the production process. They would be expected to work hard, to follow the rules, and to take responsibility for their actions (*If one person doesn't do good-quality work, the whole thing will collapse*). Everything in their upbringing, Riham believed, had worked in the opposite direction. These girls attended poorly funded public schools whose teachers asked only that they show up for class (and sometimes not even that). Their mothers and fathers cared mainly about their marital prospects; any accomplishment that didn't work toward securing a suitable husband was beside the point. "Their whole lives all they hear is: 'You have to get married, you have to get married.' That's all she knows," Riham told me. "If only we could change that culture." Inside the walls of her factory, she embarked on a radical experiment: to build a system that taught young women discipline, accountability, and pride in their work, where their families, schools, and society had failed.

Riham led her new charges upstairs to assign them to their workstations and explain the finicky details of garment manufacturing. At the point where the sleeve joins the body of the shirt, the four seams must meet in a perfect cross; a ruffle attached to the shoulder should fall half in front and half in back of the shoulder seam. In a small Egyptian factory, the attention paid to a little girl's peplum shirt—an item that might one day sell for under $10 in an American Walmart—felt miraculous.

An eighth grader named Nourhan started trimming stray threads off stacks of shirts; Habiba, thirteen years old with round cheeks, was taught to inspect ruffles and ensure that seams were straight. The girls were all between the ages of thirteen and fifteen, which seemed surprisingly young to be working eight-hour days in a garment factory, but that was a concession to local mores. Families wanted their daughters to be married and settled by their late teens, so the window for a summer job had to move up accordingly. (Egyptian law allows children as young as twelve to work, as long as their employment is for limited hours, has no harmful consequences, and doesn't interfere with their schooling. Another concession to local mores, and to poverty.)

All of the girls came from working-class towns and villages around Alexandria. Their fathers were carpenters or factory workers, and at home, money was tight even if no one said so. When school was in session, these girls attended class for three hours a day—because of overcrowding, many public schools operate in shifts. They had ambitions of going to high school and college, and they dreamed of being artists or doctors or teachers.

Samar, a slender thirteen-year-old with hunched shoulders, told me this was her first time working. Her parents had not wanted her to come, but she convinced them by pointing out that the job was sanctioned by her school. "Most of my friends wanted to work here as well, but their parents didn't allow it. I'm the only one who insisted and made it happen," she told me. She wanted to be a pediatrician. Her biggest worry was that Riham would hire young men. If she did, Samar's parents would force her to stay home.

The new hires picked up skills quickly; by early afternoon, the workers had finished the ruffled shirts and moved on to pink-striped hoodies. At two o'clock, Riham called the interns to assemble again in the room downstairs. They pulled their wooden chairs into a circle.

"How's it going?" Riham asked Samar. "Did you get bored?"

"No."

"What did you learn today?"

"I learned how to sew edges."

Riham turned to a girl named Rowan, who had been working on the single-stitch machine. "Did you find the work easy or difficult?"

"It was easy."

"There's a special sound you have to listen to from the machine to make sure you're doing it right."

"Yes, I know. I heard it."

Next up was Nourhan, who had fallen behind in trimming threads. "You! You're a problem," Riham said, in a half-teasing tone. "Why was the work accumulating?"

Nourhan, who was fourteen and had a soft round face, tried to deflect blame on to colleagues farther up the assembly line. "The other workers were too slow," she said. Riham told her to write down the workers' names on a whiteboard and keep track of how many pieces she checked every hour.

"There are many things you haven't seen yet that you'll learn," Riham told the group. "You're not going to know today what you like. Maybe today you're attached to the machine, but on other days when you work on other things, you'll see that you like them more. Will you come tomorrow?"

"Yes!"

She knew that wasn't likely. A family might travel en masse to attend a wedding or visit a sick relative, or a father would decide without explanation that he wanted his daughter home. There were many reasons for a woman to quit a factory and so few reasons to stay.

"Even if they don't spend the whole summer here," Riham told me, "I want them to leave with a dream, so they can know what they're capable of doing."

ONE HUNDRED YEARS after Egypt attempted to build an industry on Jumel cotton, the country tried again. In 1927, an industrialist named

Talat Harb led a group of investors to set up the Misr Spinning and Weaving Company. Based in the Nile Delta town of al-Mahalla al-Kubra, a traditional center of silk weaving, the company was part of Harb's plan to build a diversified industrial base with textiles at its heart. Five years earlier, Egypt had gained its independence following mass demonstrations against British rule; now at last, the country could develop modern and competitive industries, unhampered by a colonial policy that had discouraged that effort. Inside Harb's companies, all official communication was in Arabic, and only Egyptians could be in charge.

This fresh start resembled, in many ways, Mohamed Ali's doomed endeavor of a century before. Once again, one man set out to "fix" Egypt's economy through money and sheer force of will. Once again, a modern industry would emerge, essentially from scratch, on the back of domestic long-staple cotton. Once again, expensive machines were imported from abroad, and thousands of men pressed into service. By 1941, locally made cotton items accounted for 75 percent of the domestic market, thanks mostly to an import tariff that had been set up to protect the infant industry.

Yet once again, the top-down control of the industry kept it from developing in a competitive fashion. The government supplied Misr Spinning and Weaving with cotton at below-market prices; the company then sold its goods, also at set prices, to a captive market. Because the start-up costs for a textile factory are high, the Misr company had virtually no rivals—and the urge to sit in place and enjoy its good fortune was overwhelming. The firm didn't venture into export markets. It didn't train workers, develop new products, or upgrade its machinery very often.

A decade after the Misr company's founding, a confidential report by two British executives who were considering a joint venture with the firm described a disorganized operation that had almost nothing in common with a modern factory. Misr Spinning and Weaving's employees, who were mostly farmers, came and went on no fixed schedule. The factory maintained a massively overstaffed workforce in order to keep its looms and spindles running. At one time or another, the report said, the company had employed virtually every male aged eight and above living in the town of Mahalla. Only one in five of the factory's spindles was usable, and the bulk of the plant was secondhand and needed to be replaced.

In England and elsewhere in Europe, long-staple cotton was spun at high counts into luxury items such as fine underwear and stockings. The same fiber in Egypt was woven into coarse gray cloth, because that was all local consumers could afford. Some economists at the time suggested that Egypt should use its own high-quality cotton to manufacture fine items for export while importing cheap Indian or American cotton to serve the domestic market. But national pride and a strong agricultural lobby stood in the way. Even the Misr Spinning and Weaving Company, which would have benefited most from access to inexpensive cotton cloth, opposed such a measure on patriotic grounds: In a 1936 report, it called the domestic use of Egyptian cotton a "national duty."

The textile industry expanded during the Second World War, thanks to a reduction in imports and strong demand from Allied troops who were stationed in Egypt, but the sector also became more reliant on the state. The government set prices and production targets, a prerogative that it held on to after the war was over. Firms were guaranteed a set profit margin as long as they provided employment and supplied the masses with cheap cloth. The result was one of the least efficient workforces in the world. A 1947 study showed that output per person in the Egyptian manufacturing sector was a fraction of what the developed world had achieved a decade earlier: one-third the level of Britain, one-quarter that of Germany, and one-eighth that of the United States.

Over the first half of the twentieth century, Egyptians saw no improvement in their standard of living. The country's population expanded, but agricultural productivity stalled, and industry failed to step up and take its place. Egypt had rid itself of its colonial rulers, but a government run by native Egyptians wasn't doing much better at delivering economic gains to ordinary people. "The life of the rank and file," the historian Robert L. Tignor wrote, "was probably harsher in 1952 than it had been before World War I." All that hard work, money, and miles and miles of the most beautiful cotton in the world: wasted.

ANOTHER STRONGMAN, ANOTHER plan: In 1952 Nasser, a thirty-four-year-old lieutenant colonel in the Egyptian army, led a coup that deposed the royal family and eventually made him the undisputed leader of Egypt and the Arab world. With financial and military aid from the Soviet Union, Nasser tried to turn Egypt into a modern industrial state. His regime took over ownership of the country's banks, insurance and trading companies, construction and transportation firms, utilities, department stores, and larger industrial enterprises. The state poured money into chemical plants, paper mills, steel foundries, and fertilizer and textile factories. Its goal was to manufacture *min al-ibra lil-saroukh,* "from the needle to the rocket." Industrial production rose, and economic growth soared.

The early 1960s would be remembered as a golden age. The state promoted higher education as a free right, which allowed ordinary Egyptians to attend college in large numbers for the first time. Graduates were guaranteed jobs in the public sector with free healthcare, generous vacations, and paid leave, and new laws made it almost impossible to fire employees. Female emancipation was an explicit goal. "Woman must be regarded as equal to man," read the National Charter of 1962, "and she must therefore shed the remaining shackles that impede her free movement, so that she may play a constructive and profoundly important part in shaping the life of the country." Female enrollment in schools jumped, and women's work outside the home became respected and valued.

But the effort to build an industrial sector and a welfare state at the same time was expensive, and often tainted by politics. In the textile sector, for example, companies were treated like political tools rather than viable businesses. Their role, in the government's eyes, was to supply cheap clothes to the market and hand out plum jobs to political supporters—"a dumping ground for anyone whom the regime chose to employ," in the words of one historian. During the years of Soviet sponsorship, cotton fabric became a commodity that leaders traded in bulk to Moscow for wheat or military hardware or whatever they decided was necessary. "The most important thing was to export twenty, fifty, or one hundred meters of fabric, at the expense of quality," the textile industrialist Louis Bishara recalled. "It ended up being just a series of export deals between the countries." The never-ending cycle of spinning gold into dross dealt "a ruinous blow" to the textile industry, according to a later Egyptian government report:

Carelessly produced coarse yarns, spun from high-quality Egyptian cotton lint, were delivered to weavers, who in turn produced poorly woven fabrics to be carelessly bleached or printed and delivered to undemanding customers.

By the late 1960s, it was clear that the statist experiment was failing. Officials debated whether to change course or double down; in 1967, Egypt's defeat by Israel in the Six-Day War pushed the country into recession before any clear policy changes had been made. After the economic crisis, though, everyone behaved more or less as before. The government neither reformed its industrial policy nor admitted its mistakes. The textile industry clung to official support and went on losing millions every year.

Young people continued to act as if a cushy public sector job was the most desirable career option. Beginning in the 1970s, the government began to slow its pace of hiring new graduates. In 1982, the average wait for one of these positions had lengthened to ten months; by the early

1990s, it was over seven years. But almost three in four young people, in a national survey, still say they prefer government employment over any alternative, and lining up to wait for a civil service position has become a rite of passage for many Egyptians. Ghada Barsoum, an associate professor in public policy and administration at the American University in Cairo, interprets this as a desire not just for financial stability but for the respect and social status that their parents' generation enjoyed. "Talking about a parent who worked in the government as the career model to follow is common," she wrote in a paper about the continuing appeal of government employment. "The preference for public-sector jobs in Egypt has become part of a national culture . . . internalized by new entrants to the labor market that continue to seek this employer."

In Minya, I met a college student named Rania who volunteered at the organization that was helping recruit factory workers for the Delta factory. She was a senior at the University of Minya, where she was studying psychology with a focus on social work. She hoped to be a businesswoman and start her own nursery school, she told me, but in the next breath she said she would apply for a government job when she graduated.

"Everyone wishes to work in the government because it's more stable and promising," she said. Only 20 percent of her class, by her estimate, would be so lucky.

"Why do people like government jobs?" I asked her.

"It's stable, and even after you leave the job, you have a monthly pension. Some people don't even go to work; their job exists only on paper. But they still get a pension."

"But it's not interesting—"

"No one goes there because it's interesting," Rania cut me off. "They just go for the income."

She was twenty-two. Nasser had died a quarter century before she was born, yet young Egyptians continued to be pulled helplessly backward by the vision he had once had for their country, even if it had degraded beyond recognition. The message, two generations on, was narrow and pessimistic: *Stick with what you know. Don't imagine that life can ever be better than it was.* No recent college graduate aspired to a government job so she could do meaningful work, learn new skills, and get promoted, just as no one dreamed any longer of building a socialist-industrial-utopian state that would compete with the West on its own terms. What they were after was stability and a pension, and for that they were willing to perform repetitive tasks of little substance, as described in one study about female employment:

> **Typically, four or five women work in a tiny room performing clerical tasks of various sorts for the government bureaucracy. . . . These women operate copy machines, record appointments, work as cashiers, stamp documents, or type. Besides being underemployed, they seldom learn new skills at the office, where the work is usually repetitive and boring. These women complain of the tedious hours, and they occupy the time chatting, since the work itself requires so little attention. . . . It is clear to women that they are not doing truly necessary labor.**

What did a country lose when so many of its young people believed that being a low-level functionary in the civil service was the best that life had to offer? How much energy was wasted, and what opportunities were closed off? Whatever work Rania found in the private sector, some part of her would be disappointed that she had not become a *muazzaf.* The word means "employee," specifically someone who works in the bureaucracy, never mind in which department or doing what task. To be a nameless cog in the machine—that was the dream.

RIHAM'S FAMILY STORY tracked national events. In 1944, during the wartime textile boom, her grandfather set up a weaving machine in the basement of his house. He initially wove fabric from locally grown cotton, then expanded into knitting and sewing men's and children's underwear. Riham's father, Galal, studied mechanical engineering and did a government-sponsored internship at the country's largest linen manufacturer. He joined the family firm in 1965, at the peak of Nasser's industrial development drive.

As a small manufacturer, the Seif El-Din Company for Industry and Commerce was allowed to remain in private hands. But in many ways, it absorbed the culture and practices of the state-dominated industry in which it operated. Everyone on the assembly line earned a set salary and a guaranteed bonus, no matter her quality of work or productivity level. In a climate of total job security, employees became demanding and hard to please. They would finish a rush order only if they were promised extra pay; they refused to transfer to a newly built production facility, in an industrial zone outside the city, because they liked being downtown and closer to home. "Nasser made people lazy," Riham told me. "His government hired more people than it needed, so people got used to being paid without doing anything. This man destroyed everything, and we're paying for what he destroyed."

After she joined the family company in 2000, Riham tried to change the workplace culture. She initially worked in quality control and pushed workers to sew items with fewer defects, but they found her too demanding. Her uncle Anwar transferred her into production, where she again clashed with employees—and with him—when she tried to set up a system for allocating tasks. Her uncle, she felt, ran the enterprise like his personal fiefdom. He didn't have a set production schedule or a system for rewarding productivity. He didn't even have clear job descriptions. "He had an idea that everyone is responsible for everything," Riham told me. "What that means is that no one is responsible for anything. He wanted to be the only one in charge."

The real power in the factory rested with "jokers," the industry nickname for workers who can operate different kinds of sewing machines and switch identities at will. The jokers decided what a production line would make each day; if Riham's uncle wanted more, he would have to negotiate with them first. Riham pushed the employees to improve their productivity, but her uncle begged her to stop. "If we lose these workers," he said, "we're not going to get any others."

The company, as in a certain type of abusive relationship, ran on blackmail and manipulation. Her uncle appeased his employees because he was afraid they would leave, and they acted as if they were doing him a favor by being there. Every machine operator ate and drank in his or her place on the assembly line, since there were no set times or places for meals. "This was a disaster: We had rats and bad smells," Riham recalled. "They would drink tea or coffee, and it always spilled on the machines."

One day she was horrified to see an employee eating fish at her workstation. "She was eating fish at the machine, next to the clothes! *What is this? Fish inside the factory!*"

Riham castigated the woman, who threatened to quit and take five of her co-workers with her. Riham let her go. She understood that if she gave in to this worker's threat, she would always be at their mercy. But her uncle secretly talked the woman into staying, by promising that Riham, who was her supervisor, would no longer speak with her.

Riham was so angry when she found out that she stayed home for a month. "The workers can really make you cry," she said.

Her father stepped in and persuaded her to return by instituting a rule that a manager could dock a worker's pay for poor performance, but Riham discovered that when she disciplined an employee, her uncle quietly replaced the money. Sensing the divide between uncle and niece, the workers started to blame Riham for anything that went wrong in the factory. She decided to leave.

Her father was upset. "This is your money," he told Riham. "You have to run this factory one day."

"No, I don't have to run it," she said. "There are plenty of people who want to run it. It doesn't have to be me."

So she started over. She and a friend who had studied textile engineering in college pooled their savings and rented an apartment in an industrial zone. They bought five sewing machines, set up a cutting table and an ironing table, and began to hire workers.

Her father understood why she had to leave, but it pained him to watch his daughter building a new operation from scratch. "They have a factory, they have a brand," Riham told me. "He didn't want us to start from zero."

"But that's the only way to do it right? To start from zero?" I asked her.

"Yes. Because we can't start anywhere else."

Family pressure came from other places. In the eyes of her mother, Riham wasn't a twenty-eight-year-old engineer running her own business. She was an unmarried daughter whose reputation must be protected from any scandal. Like most single women in Egyptian society, Riham still lived at home with her parents. But she often worked late, because her employees were moonlighting from their regular jobs and usually showed up from five to eight o'clock in the evening. After closing time, she frequently ran other work-related errands.

"My mother was very annoyed. She didn't agree at all."

"But you didn't . . . care."

"I didn't care. At first, she came with me everywhere I went," Riham told me, switching into an exaggerated falsetto: "'You're coming home late at night, what will people say?'"

When Riham went to visit clothing shops or to buy fabric, her mother tagged along. For a while, the mother-daughter duo jointly attended a textile trade fair that was held in a resort town near Alexandria. It started at six o'clock at night and ran until two in the morning. Her mother endured this punishing schedule for a month.

"Okay," she told her daughter at last, "go, go, go!"

Riham smiled when she told me this story. Now, she said, her mother just asked what time she would be home and left out food for her.

She chose her market carefully. Egypt has a high birth rate, and demand for baby products is strong, but most of the items available on the market at that time were expensive imports. Riham developed a line of baby quilts and blankets backed by her own research. She noticed that mothers often laid their infants down on thin changing mats, so she designed a version lined with polyester fiber so the baby would not bump its head. Her products sold well from the beginning. "When I started," she said, "nearly all the market was mine."

After four years, her father lent her money to buy her current place. Although he had initially objected to her departure from the family firm, he was proud of what she had done on her own. It was an interesting example of what happens when a young woman challenges her family's expectations: In many cases, the parents back down. They may even be happy with the outcome, and what looked like strong opposition turns out not to be that at all.

THE FAMILY FIRM, the Seif El-Din Company for Industry and Commerce, is still in business. It employs a hundred fifty workers in two facilities for knitting, dyeing, and sewing. The operation is still larger than Riham's. On the day I visited their factory in downtown Alexandria, the production floor was crowded with sewing machines, but more than half of them weren't being used. In the dimly lit room, the employees, who were mostly older women, talked on their mobile phones the entire time they were working, with the devices tucked snugly next to their ears by the tight fabric of the *hijab*. There was none of the camaraderie and communication between workers that I had seen in Riham's factory.

Along a back wall, several long tables were piled high with boys' athletic shorts. Riham's father, Galal, told me that the factory had produced eight hundred dozen of these, and a sales agent was trying to find a buyer. It was a risky arrangement that might result in losses if no customer was found.

"Is it possible that he won't get an order and won't pay you?" I asked.

"It happens. There are four hundred boxes of these shorts downstairs."

Upstairs, in the cutting room, Galal pointed out a metal contraption with a long slot that was fitted against the end of a table; when a worker fed cloth through the machine, it spread the fabric on the table, smooth and ready for cutting. The spreading machine had been imported from Italy and cost $80,000. But on this day it was idle. The room's only occupant was a middle-aged woman sitting in a chair, cutting fabric by hand to sew into ribbons.

Riham had told me that her main client refused to work with her family's factory. He had found the receptionist rude and the quality of work uneven.

I asked Galal if he saw a bright future for the country's textile sector.

"Of course, we must always have hope: Without hope, we will die. And having hope is part of faith. If you don't have hope, then you even gave up on God.

"If you look back at history," he continued, "it's a wheel, and it's always turning. Sometimes you're up, and sometimes you're down."

I was reminded of many conversations I've had with older Egyptians. They came of age when their government was pouring money into economic development, and the future appeared full of promise. In the 1960s or '70s, it might have made sense to have a roomful of sewing machines and an $80,000 spreading machine from Italy. In the span of half a lifetime, that country had slipped away.

Before I left the factory, Galal handed me a stack of his brother's business cards. "If you run across any customers in America, please tell them that we make good products."

AT THE END of the interns' first day, Riham said to me, "I want you to tell me what they said. I think they'll be more honest with you than with me."

She already knew Rowan wanted to sew and had assigned her to the single-stitch machine. When she noticed Habiba staring into space rather than checking finished garments, she went over—not to reprimand her, but to move her to a different spot on the production line. After Samar, the young woman who wanted to be a doctor, begged her not to hire any young men, Riham took her aside and patiently explained that this was a normal business practice ("If you study to be a doctor, there will be young men in your classes, and you need to deal with it"). Nour's vision was so poor that she wouldn't be able to operate a sewing machine until she got glasses, but Riham hadn't told her yet because she didn't want to discourage her. Finding workers and keeping them happy was her main purpose—and that included thirteen-year-old interns who couldn't sew.

With that in mind, she was as up to date on her employees' personal lives as a gossip columnist. Elham was in her forties and childless; because the infertility was on her husband's side, he felt insecure and threatened by her employment. Amal had no children either, but her husband and his parents supported her working, although her own parents opposed it and didn't know she had a job. Sara, who was twenty, was engaged and saving money for her *gihaz*. Eman, twenty-nine and divorced, was battling her ex-husband in court for custody of their three children ("Just kidnap your son and bring him back here with you," Riham advised).

Just that morning, a former employee had canceled a training session she had planned to conduct for the interns. Her husband had forbidden her to leave their baby with her mother, she explained to Riham, for the few hours she would have spent in the factory.

"They had a big fight a month ago," Riham told me, "and I didn't want to push it." Husbands were like swamp gas. They were everywhere and nowhere, filling the air with noxious vapors of stubbornness, bad moods, and conservatism while remaining invisible to the naked eye.

Mothers were another potent force inside the factory. When Riham put out word that she was hiring for the summer, it was invariably the girls' mothers, rather than the girls themselves, who phoned to make sure the opportunity was socially appropriate. Riham was on friendly terms with many of her workers' families. When an employee named Shaimaa started having an irregular menstrual cycle, Riham instructed Shaimaa's mother to administer vitamins and take her to the doctor. She also intervened on behalf of another worker, who was nineteen and suffered from anemia and colon problems. "She doesn't eat vegetables, she doesn't eat molasses. How is she going to get better?" Riham said to me.

Her role as surrogate mother to the entire enterprise surprised me—and equally surprising was that the workers took her concern for granted. No one in the factory spoke about Riham as an especially compassionate boss. They accepted as their due that the owner of the place where they worked should know about their marital plans and their medical issues. As young women in a traditional community, they were used to being looked after and cared for, and they let their parents manage their affairs and problems even though they were adults. In a society where familial bonds were so important, it made sense that the factory would operate like another kind of family.

Riham took it all in stride. "This industry is very challenging because it depends on humans, and humans have problems. I'm trying to solve them in order to have production, but not only because of production. They're part of our society. If we want to go forward, we all have to go forward."

There were certain behaviors she wouldn't put up with, though. In the foyer of the factory, Riham had posted such a list, which hinted at how much energy a person could devote to being unproductive:

Intentionally spoiling or ruining something or stealing something from work or from one of your colleagues

Disregarding or ignoring work duties or being slow and wasting time during work hours

Intentionally giving wrong information or manipulating
    information in order to take work from someone else, or as a
    false excuse to miss work
Manipulating your boss to get preferential treatment with devious
    and dishonest methods

Emotional manipulation apparently bothered her most (although the indomitable urge to consume food next to a sewing machine ranked a close second). "I saw this in my father's factory, and I determined never to do it," Riham told me. "If there was some conflict, a woman would stand up and shout, 'I'm quitting now!' And all the others would crowd around and say, 'Oh, don't leave, stay!' So I have a rule: No shouting in my factory. If anyone threatens to leave, I just stand and say nothing."

When she first started her business, she had a hard time finding workers and was desperate to keep those she had, just as her uncle had been. "After a while, I realized that I didn't want to be like him," Riham said. "I told myself: If it's not working, it's not working. It's better to lose for a while and then to make things better, rather than to lose forever and not apply a system you believe in."

Six months after she started, the Turkish-owned factory across the street closed, and Riham hired all eighteen of its workers, gaining an entire production line at once. She decided after a month to fire one of them—a young woman who was always talking on her phone—but the others told her that they worked only as a group. Riham stood her ground, and the entire line quit. She struggled to maintain production with just a handful of employees.

A year after the mass defection, a man who did ironing for Riham told her he knew the people who had quit her factory. Their new jobs had turned out to be disappointing—low pay, broken-down equipment. They wanted to come back to work for Riham but were too embarrassed to tell her. After that, her ex-employees began to contact her, one by one.

Riham agreed to rehire them at the same salaries as before, but on her terms.

"We're not working here in groups," she told them. "If I don't like a certain person from the beginning, I won't hire her. And if after a while I decide I don't need a certain person, and you tell me that you're going to leave with her, I will get rid of you all and you won't come back ever, ever again."

The workers accepted her terms. Since their return, they had been hardworking and loyal.

The story was like a parable, with its flawed human beings and its message that redemption was possible, even after long years: the tale of the Prodigal Factory Workers, lost and now found.

"Wow," I said. "So you must have patience."

"To get what you want, yes. The way you want it, yes."

EGYPTIAN COTTON IS still the country's most famous brand, but it has little to do with Egypt itself. Almost all of the crop that's planted in the Nile Valley is exported in its raw form, because decades of mismanagement have left the country's textile companies unable to spin or weave the material to an acceptable standard. Clothing makers like Riham suffer the consequences: They import almost all their cotton and polyester fabric from elsewhere, which slows down the production cycle and limits the range of products they can make at a competitive price. Were it not for Egypt's free trade agreements with the United States and Europe, which give manufacturers duty-free access to those markets, the country probably wouldn't have a viable clothing industry at all.

The vertically integrated textile sector that Egypt has dreamed of building for two centuries—under Mohamed Ali, then Talat Harb, and finally Nasser—is fragmented and inconsequential in global terms. Egypt exports about $4.5 billion worth of textiles and clothing a year.

That figure is dwarfed by exports from China, the industry leader, which are valued at $286 billion annually. But it's also less than the comparable output for Bangladesh, Vietnam, Turkey, Pakistan, Cambodia, Sri Lanka, Burma, or Morocco.

"As a cotton producer with a substantial domestic market for final products, one might expect to see a large, competitive industry serving that market," Amirah El-Haddad, an economist who has studied the Egyptian clothing industry, has written. "And given that Egyptian cotton is amongst the world's best, a vibrant high-end export sector might also be expected. Unfortunately, neither of these is the case."

This failure to build on the country's cotton riches—and to develop a significant manufacturing sector more broadly—has had lasting consequences. For a country to rise out of poverty into the ranks of developed nations, manufacturing is critical. Japan pioneered the model in the 1960s, followed by South Korea and Taiwan, and more recently by emerging economies such as China, India, Turkey, Mexico, and Vietnam. Manufacturing introduces modern management methods to a country; it drives innovation, competitiveness, exports, and productivity growth. Manufacturing can employ large numbers of people, which helps ensure that rising wealth is distributed more equitably. Yet manufacturing in Egypt has never become an engine of growth or jobs. Today, the sector makes up 15 percent of the country's economic output. Apart from a temporary rise and fall in the 1960s, that figure has stayed the same for sixty-five years.

There's also a social dimension. In countries all over the world, the rise in manufacturing has led to an increase in female employment. In the factories of South China where I reported, young women so dominated the local workforce that they complained it was impossible to find a date (their bosses invariably said they were more careful and hardworking than young men). The growth of the garment industry in Bangladesh, in which an estimated 80 percent of the workers are female, has been associated with such trends as increased education for girls, declining fertility, and delayed marriage. In the 1990s, the emergence of labor-intensive manufacturing in Morocco drew many women into paid employment for the first time. But over the same period in Egypt, the share of jobs claimed by women fell virtually across the board, other than in the civil service.

Egypt has developed in a different direction. Its high-growth industries, which include oil, tourism, construction, and transportation, are mainly the province of men. And the past half century of globalization has also seen, in Egypt and much of the Middle East, a turn toward conservatism. Beginning in the 1970s, young men from the poorer countries in the region have migrated by the millions to work in the oil-rich Gulf States. In Saudi Arabia or Kuwait, they could save enough money to build a house and find a wife back home, but they might also absorb an ultraconservative form of Islamic belief called Wahhabism that imposes severe restrictions on women in public life. Going out into the world, it turns out, can narrow your horizons. It depends on where you go and what kind of ideas you bring back.

The story of Egypt, and particularly its women, calls into question almost everything we believe about how globalization is supposed to play out:

> *Economic development improves women's lives.*
> *Integrating with the world brings in progressive ideas.*
> *Educating girls will give them opportunities.*
> *Work is empowering.*

What if none of these things is true?

THE INTERNS SURPRISED Riham by coming back the next day, and the day after that. As spring turned into summer, her factory was flooded with orders, and for once Riham had enough workers to fill them. She paid back some of the money she owed her father and set up a bonus system. If a sewer finished eight hours' work in seven, she received an extra hour of overtime pay.

An American buyer visited the factory to assess its potential as a future supplier. "I want you to increase your number of workers," he told Riham, "so you can produce for me."

"I don't hire just anyone," she replied. "I have criteria."

The buyer turned to his companion, the owner of another Egyptian factory. "She's going to be successful."

Riham planned to buy an automatic cutting machine, which would increase her capacity; right now she was limited by how much fabric she could fold, draw patterns on, and cut by hand. She would bring in a friend who worked as a life coach to teach the interns communication and other life skills. She considered setting up a dorm and bringing young women from Upper Egypt to work and live onsite—why not? Her mother warned her against taking on such a responsibility, but Riham was looking into it anyway.

"There's a lot that can be done here," she told me. "We got a big place, because in the future we hope to invest more."

Until now, the factory's downstairs had yawned dark and empty. To me, the wasted square footage seemed uncharacteristic of a business-woman like Riham, who counted every minute and every *ersh*. Now I recognized the space for what it was: a measure of her ambition.

3

PATTERNS IN THE CLOTH

IN THE ANCIENT WORLD, EGYPT was famous for the freedom of its
women. The Greek historian Herodotus, among others, was fascinated
by them:

> Not only is the Egyptian climate peculiar to that country, and the
> Nile different in its behavior from other rivers elsewhere, but the
> Egyptians themselves ... seem to have reversed the ordinary
> practices of mankind. For instance, women attend market and are
> employed in trade, while men stay at home and do the weaving.

A woman in pharaonic Egypt possessed the same legal rights as a
man, which was as strange to the rest of the world as a river that flooded
its banks every year, like clockwork, at the height of summer. As far back
as the Old Kingdom era, which lasted from about 2600 to 2100 B.C., a
woman could live independently, contract her own marriage, buy and
sell land, file a lawsuit or a divorce, and leave property to whom she

wished. Women testified in court and sat on juries. They sued their husbands for abuse, fought their brothers and uncles over property, and disinherited children who didn't love them enough. In a "wisdom" text that dates to 2400 B.C., a father advises his son about dealing with his future wife: *Do not contend with her in court.*

Marriage was a private agreement between two individuals, and there's no historical evidence of any government-prescribed ceremony, vows, clothing, nor even a word in the Egyptian language for "wedding." The documents, contracts, and letters that have survived illustrate the range of legal rights that women enjoyed. A woman could arrange her own marriage and place conditions on her future husband's behavior. A contract between two workers in the New Kingdom, dating to around 1100 B.C., stipulated that the husband would suffer a hundred lashes and lose his claim on the couple's property if he left his wife. Marriage, other than for the pharaoh, was generally monogamous. A woman could initiate divorce on any grounds or none at all, and she would receive a third of the couple's assets plus anything she had brought to the union, and most likely custody of the children. Women in Mesopotamia, Greece, and Rome lived under the guardianship of men and didn't enjoy any of these rights. Neither do women in Egypt today.

As anyone who has ever looked at a tomb painting knows, the ancient Egyptians had a casual attitude toward sex and the human body. Clothing was often optional, which made sense in the hot climate. Sexual relations between unattached adults were considered normal, and young women were not expected to remain chaste before marriage. Female desire was celebrated in love songs and poems:

> *My heart is not yet done with your love,*
> *my little fox cub!*
> *Your liquor is your lovemaking . . .*
> *I will not listen to their demands*
> *to abandon the one I desire.*

In their very freedom, women could be threatening. In a society that valued order and stability, they were feared as a source of chaos that must be controlled, and myths and wisdom texts frequently portrayed women as temptresses who would ensnare men if they could. *Beware of the woman who is a stranger in your town,* warned an instructional text that is believed to date from between the fourteenth and sixteenth centuries B.C. *Such a woman, away from her husband, is like deep water whose depth is unknown.*

Yet women were neither veiled nor secluded, and they played an active part in economic life. On the walls of pharaonic tombs, women are depicted officiating in temples, weaving cloth, and selling vegetables in the market. Records from a workers' community called Deir al-Medina show that women traded clothes, produce, land, livestock, and slaves. The most complete pharaonic document on land tenure ever found identifies 10 percent of property owners as female. Women's chief work was to raise children and manage the household, but the range of professional trades open to them was broader than in the rest of the ancient Mediterranean world. Women worked as doctors, nurses, musicians, dancers, professional mourners, weavers, bakers, brewers, waitresses, and cooks. An upper-class woman could be a supervisor in a royal household or a priestess to a female deity like Hathor or Isis. A woman might even rule as pharaoh. Hatshepsut personally led Egypt through a long period of prosperity in the fifteenth century B.C. Nefertiti served as co-regent with her husband, Akhenaten, and many scholars believe that she ruled alone as pharaoh after his death. Four or maybe five female leaders in two thousand years isn't a lot, but monarchy everywhere favors sons, and only in recent decades have some countries in Europe repealed laws that privilege male heirs. England has had just six female rulers in the last thousand years.

In ancient Egypt, the labor that was central to women's lives was the manufacturing of textiles. They made linen cloth into garments, towels, bedding, and bandages for wrapping the dead; the material functioned as a form of currency and was buried with the deceased to be used in the afterlife. (When thieves broke into the tomb of Tutankhamun, shortly after his burial, they stole valuable linens rather than the golden objects that now dazzle visitors to the Egyptian Museum.) On the walls of ancient tombs, women harvest flax, spin its fibers into thread, weave linen cloth, accept payment for finished goods, and supervise work crews on large estates. Ordinary women probably made cloth for their families and sold the surplus for extra income, and the most enterprising ones bought looms and set up shops. The hieroglyph for "weaver" is a seated woman holding what appears to be a long, thin shuttle.

All over the world, making cloth and clothing has been women's work since the beginning of recorded history, most likely because spinning, weaving, and sewing are tasks that can be done at home in between cooking and caring for children. "Men till the soil and women weave," says a Chinese adage. In the West, the association of spinning with female virtue goes as far back as the Book of Proverbs in the Bible:

> *Who can find a virtuous wife?*
> *For her worth is far above rubies . . .*
> *She seeks wool, and flax*
> *And willingly works with her hands . . .*
> *She stretches out her hands to the distaff,*
> *And her hand holds the spindle . . .*
> *She makes linen garments and sells them,*
> *And supplies sashes for the merchants.*
> *Strength and honor are her clothing;*
> *She shall rejoice in time to come.*

Weaving becomes an expression of female ingenuity in *The Odyssey*, as noted by Elizabeth Barber in *Women's Work: The First 20,000 Years*. Penelope, whose husband, Odysseus, has been missing for many years and is presumed dead, puts off her suitors by weaving and unraveling the same piece of cloth over and over (she has pledged not to remarry until she has finished a funeral shroud for her father-in-law).

She set up a great loom in her palace
And set to weaving a web of threads long and fine . . .
Thereafter in the daytime she would weave at her great loom,
But in the night she would have torches set by, and undo it.
So for three years she was secret in her design.

The ancient Greeks imagined a person's life span as a thread that was formed by the Fates at birth. "In creating cloth, which comes into being where nothing had existed before," Barber writes, "cloth and its making are thus taken as analogs for life and birth." We may labor over a beautiful piece of our own design, or work and unwork the same piece of fabric year after year. We make the best of the materials we're given.

In the first fifteen hundred years of dynastic Egypt, weaving was women's work. That changed around 1500 B.C., when innovations like the vertical loom and more intricate designs entered the country from elsewhere. After woven items started bringing higher profits, men entered and dominated the field, although women continued to make linens for daily use. That was a new pattern in history, but one that would become familiar: When technological change comes, men frequently benefit while the women lose ground.

After the pharaonic period, Egyptian women gradually gave up the liberties they had enjoyed over several millennia. The Greek conquest of Egypt in the fourth century B.C. introduced a very different idea about woman's place in the world. The classical Greeks may have invented democracy, but they sequestered their wives and daughters at home under male supervision (Aristotle considered the female a "deformed male" who was incapable of reasoning). Under Athenian law, a wife had the same status as a child—but a son would one day come of age, whereas his mother never would. Eventually, all Egyptian women were required to have a *kyrios*, a male guardian, to supervise their affairs; a similar system of guardianship was put in place after the Romans conquered the country in 30 B.C. and turned it into an imperial province. That's another pattern in the cloth: Throughout history, cosmopolitan Egyptians have tended to absorb the customs of their more conservative colonizers and neighbors.

In the fourth century, following the religious conversion of the emperor Constantine, Egypt became a Christian country, and the official view of women became, if anything, more harsh. The writings of Pisentius, a celebrated seventh-century bishop from Upper Egypt, betray a deep anxiety about women as the source of trouble and wickedness:

> For you know that many times I have warned you, O women, concerning the commandments, but you did not pay attention and you were not ashamed and you did not stop your madness. Now also . . . I command emphatically in a great instruction in order that no woman at all go outside the door of her house with her head uncovered, nor that she lift her eyes up to the face of any strange man at all. Rather, may you go about on every occasion, O women, with your eyes turned down to the ground, your covering on all sides (of your body) in all propriety.

Even in the face of hostile laws and ideologies, women found ways to act independently and protect their own interests. Documents from the era of Greek rule show, variously, an Egyptian woman acting as guardian to her child, giving herself in marriage, and consenting to a no-fault divorce, all practices that were common in dynastic times but disallowed by Greek law. The years of Roman administration saw a widening of women's scope to manage their own affairs and buy property on a large scale (land registers from the period indicate that about one third of landowners were women). And a study of a predominantly Christian town in Upper Egypt between the years 600 and 800 features women playing an active role in the region's economic, social, and religious life. In *Women of Jeme,* the Egyptologist T. G. Wilfong describes women during this period buying and selling goods and land, traveling to nearby villages and monasteries to trade, and engaging in complex lawsuits and commercial dealings. In the moneylending business, women were lenders in a third of the transactions. Women also wove and sold cloth and clothing, as they always have.

At the beginning of the ninth century, the residents of Jeme abandoned the area, and the memory of how women had once lived there faded away. "In the centuries that followed the abandonment of Jeme," Wilfong concludes, "women had less and less opportunity to engage in the kinds of activities that they had in Jeme's heyday."

THE EARLIEST WOVEN garment found anywhere in the world comes from Egypt and dates to the First Dynasty, or around 3000 B.C. It was a linen shirt with fine pleats and a fringe along the neck opening. "The linen had been carefully pleated row upon row of tiny tucks," the historian Elizabeth Barber writes, "not sewn but simply pressed in, to give it both elasticity and a trim fit." This piece of clothing was found inside out, as if its wearer had carelessly stripped it off just a moment ago, rather than almost five thousand years before a British archaeologist named Sir William Flinders Petrie dug it out of the ground on the site of an ancient cemetery near Cairo.

We don't know anything about the shirt—who wore it, or what it was for, or who sewed the delicate pleats and the fringe along the neck with such care. It's an anomaly, because so few textiles from long ago have survived. Cloth doesn't last, and so the record of women's work disappears.

ISLAM WAS BORN in the early seventh century in the deserts of Arabia. From the start, the faith rejected aristocracy and religious hierarchy in favor of radical equality among its believers. The Quran is unique among major religious texts for containing an extended passage that asserts that men and women are equal:

> *For Muslim men and women,*
> *For believing men and women,*
> *For devout men and women,*
> *For true men and women,*
> *For men and women who are*
> *Patient and constant, for men*
> *And women who humble themselves,*
> *For men and women who give*
> *In charity, for men and women*
> *Who fast (and deny themselves),*
> *For men and women who*
> *Guard their chastity, and*
> *For men and women who*
> *Engage much in God's praise—*
> *For them has God prepared*
> *Forgiveness and a great reward.*

The Quran urges male and female believers to work together to build a just society, and it sees their labor as equal in the eyes of God: *I suffer not the good deeds of any to go to waste, be he a man or a woman: The one of you is of the other.* Even the story of human creation is gender-neutral: According to the Quran, God has "created you from a single soul, and from it created its mate," and the couple jointly disobey God and are expelled from Paradise, whereas in the biblical version, Eve is formed from a rib of Adam and bears greater blame for the fall of man. Quranic law recognized women's rights to work and to own property, and it banned female infanticide. Women were prominent during the religion's founding. Khadija, Muhammad's first wife, was a successful merchant and widow who, according to tradition, proposed marriage to Muhammad and later became an important ally in spreading Islam. Ordinary women sometimes joined the faith on their own, traveled widely, participated in community affairs, prayed in mosques, and accompanied men into battle. Women made significant contributions to the *hadith*, the accounts of the Prophet's words and deeds that guided later generations.

But there are also Quranic verses that value men over women. Chapter 2, verse 228, states: *Men are a degree above women*. The Quran later expands on the concept of male authority:

Men are the protectors and maintainers of women, because God has given the one more than the other, and because they support them from their means. . . . As to those women on whose part ye fear disloyalty and ill-conduct, admonish them, refuse to share their beds, beat them; but if they return to obedience, seek not a way against them.

Men can marry outside the faith and have up to four wives at a time, but women are restricted to Muslims and monogamy. A man can divorce his wife by repudiating her—simply pronouncing it three times makes it so—but a woman must go through the court system if she wants to end her marriage. Female inferiority is occasionally a math equation: The testimony of a man is worth twice that of a woman, and sons inherit double what daughters do.

How do you reconcile these contradictions within a single document? The Quran was a text for spiritual guidance, but it was also a rule book for governing society, and these two voices—one ethical, one legal—are often at odds. The vision of Islam may have been for human equality, but its laws reflected life in seventh-century Arabia, where patriarchal dominance and slavery were the norm. In her groundbreaking 1992 book *Women and Gender in Islam,* the Egyptian American scholar Leila Ahmed traced how judges and imams—all of them men— emphasized women's second-class status in their interpretations of Islam, while ignoring the message of gender equality. Their judgments became accepted doctrine even as they diverged from the egalitarian ethos of the Quran. In her memoir, Ahmed wrote:

> So there are two quite different Islams, an Islam that is in some sense a women's Islam and an official, textual Islam, a "men's" Islam. . . . Women in Muslim societies did not attend mosques [nor] hear the sermons that men heard. . . . It was from their own lives and from hearing the words of the Quran that they formed their sense of the essence of Islam. . . .
>
> Now, after a lifetime of meeting and talking with Muslims from all over the world, I find that this Islam [is] the Islam not only of women but of ordinary folk generally, as opposed to the Islam of sheikhs, ayatollahs, mullahs, and clerics. . . . It is an Islam that stresses moral conduct and emphasizes Islam as a broad ethos and ethical code and as a way of understanding and reflecting on the meaning of one's life and of human life more generally.

Ahmed was part of an "Islamic feminism" movement that emerged in the 1990s and argued that the subordination of Middle Eastern women came not from Islam, but from centuries of its misinterpretation by the male religious elite. The movement's historians, sociologists, and other scholars believe that equality and justice for women lie within Islamic tradition and need to be brought to light to build a more just society. "The Muslim woman has only to read the text," the scholar Amina Wadud writes, "to gain an undeniable liberation."

According to these arguments, Muslim jurists have taken certain

Quranic verses out of context for their own purposes. The verse *Men are a degree above women,* for example, appears in a section about marital obligations and, logically viewed, refers to men's greater range of divorce options rather than being a universal assertion of male superiority. Many of the rules in the Quran were concessions to the socioeconomic realities of seventh-century Arabia—sons inherit double what daughters do because men are responsible for supporting their families—but were not meant to be binding on all Muslim communities for all time. Quranic commentators sometimes cherry-picked passages to suit their vision of a hierarchical social order. Thus the verse *Men are the protectors and maintainers of women* became associated with marriage, while a more egalitarian vision—*He created for you mates from among yourselves, that you may dwell in tranquility with them, and He has put love and mercy between you*—is widely ignored.

As Islam spread beyond the Arabian Peninsula into more complex urban societies, it incorporated the practices of the conquered territories into its ideology, including their laws and customs for controlling women. Particularly influential were the Sasanians, Persians who ruled present-day Iran and Iraq until the Muslim conquest in the year 640. In their society, wives were required to pledge total obedience to their husbands and to accept being loaned out for sexual services if their husbands wanted. Practices such as female veiling and seclusion were adopted by Muslim believers as their faith spread to these new areas, even though the Quran doesn't require them (Muhammad's wives are told to stay at home and receive visitors "from behind a curtain," but ordinary women need only "draw their veils over their bosoms"). The custom among the Sasanian nobility of keeping large harems of wives and concubines, sometimes numbering in the hundreds, was also adopted by the Muslim elite. Fatima Mernissi, a Moroccan sociologist, has described the way the religion co-opted men's self-interest to expand its community as "the genius of Islam."

In the years after the Prophet Muhammad's death, the emerging

Muslim law codified a range of privileges for men including divorce by repudiation, polygamy, and the exclusive right to their offspring, all of which contrasted with more varied and fluid social patterns that had existed during the Prophet's lifetime. Pre-Islamic Arabian society had recognized a woman's right to choose or reject marriage partners, as Muhammad's wife Khadija had done. Aisha, another of his wives, was revered for her religious learning and briefly assumed political leadership in a succession struggle after the Prophet's death. But the autonomy of these women reflected traces of a vanishing social order that Islam was replacing. By the time of the Abbasid caliphate in the eighth century, women in the Muslim world had retreated into invisibility. The religious establishment—what Leila Ahmed called the "sheikhs, ayatollahs, mullahs, and clerics"—developed a body of legal doctrine to justify the disappearance of females from public life.

Omaima Abou-Bakr, a professor of English and comparative literature at Cairo University, has traced how Quranic exegetes created and embellished the idea of male supremacy over ten centuries, working the same piece of cloth over and over until it was no longer possible to see the original design. Abu Jafar Mohamed El-Tabari, a Persian historian who put together the first comprehensive commentary on the Quran in the year 883, wrote that men's position as the "protectors and maintainers of women" gave them the right to discipline them as well. Writing two and a half centuries later from Mecca, Abu El-Qasim Mahmoud ibn Umar El-Zamakhshari compared the relationship between men and women to that between rulers and their subjects. The signs of men's divine favor, he wrote, included their superiority in reasoning, determination, and strength, and their ability to write, ride horses, throw spears, give sermons, sound loud prayer calls, grow beards, and wear turbans. Ismail Ibn Kathir of Syria, two hundred years on, decided that women's disadvantage in marriage made them unfit to be leaders or judges.

The belief that nature had created men and women for different roles was another thread, and it rationalized a discrimination against females that does not appear anywhere in the Quran. Abu Abdullah El-Qurtubi, an imam from Córdoba in Islamic Spain, wrote in the mid-thirteenth century:

> It is said that men have the privilege of mind and better manage-
> ment . . . and it has been said that men have strong natures that
> women do not because men's disposition is determined by heat
> and dryness which gives them strength and hardness, whereas
> women's disposition is determined by humidity and coldness,
> giving them the characteristics of leniency and weakness.

Six centuries later, the humid-female argument had apparently been put to rest, but the biological essentialism was going strong. A "system of innate disposition," an Egyptian jurist named Mohamed Abduh wrote, designed women to care for children and run the household. Domesticity as an evolutionary trait featured in the work of Shibli Shumayyil (a doctor who claimed in the late nineteenth century that men are more rational than women because their heads are heavier) and of Sayyid Qutb, one of the main theorists of modern Islamist ideology. In 1952, four years before Egyptian women gained the right to vote and run for office, the Grand Mufti Hassanain Mohamed Makhluf, the country's most senior religious authority, issued a *fatwa* forbidding female suffrage "on the grounds of their inherently unsuitable nature." And so on and so on, across seas and centuries, *it has been said:* men talking to other men about women.

Writers and scholars in the West, of course, have also held beliefs about female inferiority. Doctors in Victorian England, for example, worried that too much education would damage a woman's ovaries and make her infertile. Misogyny is rooted in all of the world's major religions. Augustine, the most influential thinker in early Christianity, pondered the purpose of woman's creation and concluded that it was only to bear children. A Church father named Tertullian was, if possible, even more contemptuous toward women: "*You* are the Devil's gateway. *You* are the unsealer of the forbidden tree. *You* are the first deserter of the divine Law.... On account of *your* desert, that is death, even the Son of God had to die." Judaism was also deeply patriarchal and viewed women as subservient to men and unfit for religious learning or leadership. Like Islam, it allowed polygamy, concubinage, and unrestricted divorce for men.

Yet many of these early beliefs evolved over time. The Protestant Reformation, beginning in the sixteenth century, placed individual faith at the heart of Christian belief, opened up theology to competing interpretations, and explicitly saw female believers as equal in worth to men and just as likely to be "called by God." Judaism underwent a reformation a couple of centuries later, through a movement known as the "Jewish Enlightenment," that challenged the authority of the rabbinical establishment, modernized religious practices, and gave rise to new branches of the faith that supported educating women and allowing them leadership roles. For both Christianity and Judaism, these reforms were extraordinarily divisive, but they eventually led to the emergence of mainstream denominations that put men and women on equal footing.

Islam has not experienced such mass upheaval in modern times. In the several centuries after it was founded, jurists debated how to apply Islamic law and practiced *ijtihad*, or independent reasoning, to resolve questions for which there was no legal precedent. By the twelfth century, though, most of the Sunni Muslim world recognized four schools of jurisprudence—which were named the Hanafi, Shafi'i, Maliki, and Hanbali schools, after their founders (Sunnis make up about 90 percent of the world's Muslims, including virtually all the believers in Egypt). Thus major matters of religious law were considered settled, and the focus thereafter would be on conforming to established doctrine. Broadly speaking, the intellectual and political changes in early modern Europe that sparked reformations in Christianity and Judaism didn't exert the same influence on Islam. The mid-nineteenth century saw the emergence of an "Islamic modernism" movement that tried to reconcile religious faith with contemporary values. Its proponents, who were primarily from Egypt and India, sought to adapt Islamic teachings to the modern age, including pushing for women's rights and education for girls. But the movement failed to reform the religious establishment or to reduce the power of orthodox ideas.

The same four schools of Islamic jurisprudence that were recognized in the twelfth century continue to shape the lives of Sunni Muslims today. Their ideas are embedded in the legal systems of different countries, particularly on the subjects of family and marriage (Egypt follows the Hanafi school). The four schools may differ on details, but all of them reflect patriarchal interpretations of religious doctrine that were codified centuries ago. It's as if a woman living in New York or London, before getting married or divorced, inheriting or borrowing money, working, or traveling, had to consult the teachings of medieval saints and theologians to tell her how to live.

WORDS ARE ONE thing, deeds another. In the millennium and a half since Islam came to Egypt, its women have often enjoyed more freedom than the religious commentaries written about them would suggest. The seclusion of females was practiced only by the richest families, which isn't surprising when you consider the expense of maintaining separate quarters for women and employing servants to wait on them. Ordinary women went shopping, visited friends, attended births and funerals, took part in religious festivals, frequented the public baths, and pressed their claims in court. We know this from medieval writings, court records, and the letters of foreign visitors passing through. "Cairo is a very large town where many women are active in commerce," two Italian pilgrims observed in 1384. "They go to Alexandria . . . to Dimyata and all over Egypt."

The proof of women's presence in public can be found in occasional decrees that ordered them to stay home—using the academic approach of "reading against the grain," or teasing out the meanings of a text beyond what its author intended. In the year 1013, the caliph El-Hakim bi-Amr Allah banned women from the streets and markets of Cairo, and even outlawed the manufacture of women's shoes in an effort to keep them homebound. The Sultan Barsbay issued a similar edict in 1438, but it was revoked within two weeks, after the markets emptied out and merchants complained. Two years later, another ban lasted a day.

One of the most vivid accounts of medieval women behaving badly comes from Ibn El-Hajj, a theologian who lived in fourteenth-century Cairo and wrote a four-volume treatise titled *An Introduction to the Development of Deeds through the Improvement of Intentions:*

> **Some of the pious elders (may God be pleased with them) have said that a woman should leave her house on three occasions only: when she is conducted to the house of her bridegroom, on the death of her parents, and when she goes to her own grave. By God, listen to this advice of our ancestors, and observe the kind of chaos and corruption caused by women's frequent exits nowadays.**

He included a long list of female deeds that needed an improvement of intentions. The women of Cairo rode donkeys and visited parks, went boating and sunbathed on the banks of the Nile. They dressed in their best clothes when they went out, wore perfume and jewelry, spoke in tender and soft voices, argued with peddlers over prices, chatted with shop owners for hours in the hopes of getting a better deal, and joked with their male relatives and neighbors. Ibn El-Hajj believed that women should leave the house only in cases of dire necessity. They should wear long, shapeless clothing and cling to the sides of houses so that men could walk down the center of the street.

Look how these norms have been neglected in our days. . . . She goes out in the streets as if she were a shining bride, walking in the middle of the road and jostling men. They have a manner of walking that causes the pious man to withdraw closer to the walls, in order to make way for them.

Many of these women, though Ibn El-Hajj doesn't say so, were probably earning a living. Women in Cairo and other medieval Muslim cities worked as doctors, midwives, wet nurses, entertainers, mourners, prostitutes, hairdressers, beauticians, and bath attendants. They sold food, ran bakeries and coffeehouses, peddled wares door to door, and acted as brokers and matchmakers. Female merchants engaged in the international sea and caravan trade, and female scholars taught religion to students of both sexes.

"The only women who did not work were in the harem—a very upper-class elite of women," Omaima Abou-Bakr of Cairo University told me. "There is historical evidence that women were very active working at all levels."

With the money they inherited or earned, women bought and sold land, houses, shops, warehouses, and business establishments, taking advantage of Islamic laws that protected their property rights. European women would not enjoy these privileges until the nineteenth century (before then, in England or France, any asset that belonged to a woman was automatically transferred to her husband's control when she married). Wealthy Muslim women set up and managed *waqf*s, or endowments for religious or charitable purposes such as mosques, schools, and soup kitchens. Middle- and working-class women also invested in real estate: In a registry of properties from eighteenth-century Cairo, between 35 and 40 percent of transactions were in the names of women.

Women were indispensable to the manufacturing of textiles, as they had been through history. Peasant women bought raw cotton or flax, which they spun and bleached at home and then resold to weavers, in this way taking part in the largest industry in premodern times. In his book *Marriage, Money and Divorce in Medieval Islamic Society*, the historian Yossef Rapoport shows that many or most women who lived in Cairo, Damascus, and Jerusalem in the thirteenth and fourteenth centuries worked for wages. The textile trade sustained a population of widows and divorcées who supported themselves and lived independently, often staying in women-only religious houses known as *ribat*s.

"From an economic perspective, we need to reconsider women's independence within and outside marriage," Rapoport writes. "Women could not have been as dependent on their husbands as Muslim jurists would have us believe."

Although men had the upper hand in marriage, the *sharia* courts, which were administered by the state and handled a wide range of commercial and family cases, looked out for women's interests. Some schools of jurisprudence recognized a woman's right to choose her own husband and to turn down one that her family selected for her. Women from all classes could include terms in their marriage contracts to ensure better treatment from their husbands. And a woman could initiate a divorce if she agreed to pay her spouse some compensation, a procedure known as *khul* that is described in the Quran and was widely practiced. From all the available evidence, which includes *sharia* court records and biographical dictionaries, marital relations in premodern Muslim societies were more fluid and equitable than we might expect.

The scope of women's freedom varied over time. The Abbasid caliphs, who ruled in the centuries just after Islam's founding, stressed religious orthodoxy and imposed constraints on women's movements and their participation in public life. During the Mamluk period, from the mid-thirteenth to the mid-sixteenth centuries, a prosperous economy offered employment and even migration opportunities for women. A British traveler to Cairo in the early nineteenth century was surprised to see women at Al-Azhar University, the leading religious institution in the Arab world. "Contrary to the ideas commonly prevailing in Europe," he wrote, "a large portion of the votaries consisted of ladies, who were walking to and fro without the slightest restraints, conversing with each other, and mingling freely among the men." But the wheel of history was about to turn again, and it would curtail many of the freedoms that women enjoyed.

In piecing together this picture of how freely Muslim women once lived, some scholars see hope. Every age invents its own Quranic interpretation, and nothing is set in stone. But to read this long history another way—against the grain—is to feel the crushing weight of sameness. Century after century, there have been women who struggled to control their own lives and men who tried to keep them from leaving the house, seeing their friends, working, traveling, shopping, and otherwise acting like human beings. These are people who live together, raise children, and love one another, fighting the same battles for more than a thousand years.

I LIVED IN Cairo from 2011 to 2016. Egyptians call their capital *Umm al-Dunya*, "the Mother of the World," and as I got to know the city I thought the name suited her well. Cairo is like an aging woman who was once beautiful. She's still stunning in the golden light of late afternoon, but visit her in the harsh glare of morning and you'll see how the years have ruined her. She's proud, overdramatic, exhausting. Show up on her doorstep unannounced and she might embrace you, but she's just as likely to throw you out. You love her, but she drives you crazy.

"So القاهرة is female?" I asked Rifaat Amin, our Arabic teacher.

"*Taban!*" He glared at me under his thick eyebrows as if I'd just insulted his mother. "Of course! Cairo is female! Cities are female! War is female!"

The street—*taban!*—is male. Men laid down the rules for female behavior a long time ago—see Ibn El-Hajj, who railed against fourteenth-century Cairene women *walking in the middle of the road and jostling men*—and they enforce the rules now, with their eyes and their voices and their bulky bodies that take up all the available space. The men crowd the *ahwa*, or coffeehouses, that appear on almost every block. They park their folding chairs on the sidewalk and force everyone else to walk around them. They watch from the doorways of their shops. They guard the entrances to parks, clubs, and apartment buildings. The men run this military state, and they enforce its edicts on the ground—in the form of young men with guns and riot gear, who appear on the street whenever trouble is brewing.

The ten million women who live here know they're not welcome. Female students move down the street in colorfully dressed, giggling groups, but they tread fast and with purpose through what's essentially enemy territory. Two women walk and talk with their heads bent inward toward each other, as if creating a private sanctuary in public. A woman who ventures out alone—*rabbina yustur!* May God protect us!—doesn't look at anyone nor stop to take in the sights. Loitering, gazing, relaxing, and commenting while out on the street are male privileges.

As a female pedestrian in the city, I feel this tension every time I step out my door. The man with silver hair who operates the subsidized bread stand nods hello and asks about my family: It's a good start to the day. Farther up the road, a very old man delights my children by offering them lemons and inviting us to sit awhile. Another street, a different man—young, thin face, no smile—says in a low voice *Hey baby* or *What you doing tonight* or just *Fuck*, and suddenly he has forced himself into my world and my brain. *What did he just say? Why did he say that?* And then: *Did I do something to attract his attention?*

When you live in a place that pays vigilant attention to female bodies, it becomes second nature to hide yours. I'm a five-foot-four-inch Chinese American, which makes me mostly invisible in a land of larger women (maybe it's a form of cosmic justice that to be tall and blond here is the cruelest fate). Still, I wear long pants, and shirts with sleeves, and often a long sweater, even on hundred-degree days; never shorts, never short skirts, never anything sleeveless. One summer evening, I returned home from the suburb of Maadi, where many expatriates live, still in the T-shirt and skirt with a slit up one side that I had worn to a pool party. As I got out of the car in front of our building, I felt the eyes of every man on the street. I shrank into myself. *What was I thinking, going out dressed like that?* When you get unwanted male attention for a certain item of clothing, just wearing it makes you feel ashamed.

A nonprofit group called Harassmap has set up an online database for women to report sexual harassment. The cases are superimposed on a map of greater Cairo, each incident marked with a blood-red dot. They resemble angry carbuncles on an infected body, clustered in the center of the city but spreading in all directions from the new international airport to the border with Suez governorate. The map fascinates me. Why, for instance, were there three reports of harassment over two days at the embassy of Mauritius? What caused the spike in cases in the summer of 2014? If there's a logic to the map, it eludes me. People are unpredictable: They move, they change. There isn't a single type or a specific setting that makes a man more likely to grope a woman, or threaten her, or do any of the things on the site's smorgasbord of offenses, including catcalls, stalking, ogling, facial expressions, unwanted attention, indecent exposure, sexual invitation, assault, and rape. (According to a well-publicized United Nations study from the time I lived in Egypt, more than 99 percent of Egyptian women have experienced sexual harassment, a level that the report called "unprecedented.") Yet a person who humiliates or assaults a woman one day might, on another, be polite and helpful to her if she asked. Sometimes a young man looks at me as he walks toward me on the street. "*Sabah il-kheir,*" I say. "Good morning." He nods and gives the appropriate response—"*Sabah il-nour,* good morning"—and moves on without looking back. Maybe I've reminded him that he's a human being, and so am I.

I have my own map of the city. We live on Zamalek, an island in the

Nile that's close to downtown but is also a haven of tree-lined streets, embassies, and villas that date back to the nineteenth century. People know me here; they've met my husband and children. The districts of Mohandiseen, where Peter and I attend Arabic classes, and Dokki, where the girls will later attend school, feel safely anonymous, with stores and office buildings. Suburban Maadi is so tranquil it's almost American, but I've had positive encounters at the other end of the social scale too, at the Friday Market south of the Citadel where working-class shoppers buy used electronics and secondhand clothes.

Conditions in Tahrir Square, the traditional heart of downtown, vary according to the political news and time of day, like a microclimate with its own weather pattern. Sometimes I come here in the mornings to practice my Arabic; I strike up conversations with strangers who turn out to be easygoing and friendly. Once in Tahrir a young man said something rude to me. A crowd gathered, and a heavyset older woman appeared out of nowhere to yell at the offender and ask me if I was all right. *Umm al-Dunya:* Cairo's women look out for one another. On some afternoons, Tahrir feels like a carnival. Parents push their babies in strollers, and people buy cotton candy and orange juice and paint their faces the colors of the Egyptian flag. The square changes on days of political tension—now it's all young men in tight T-shirts, and the air smells of tear gas and male bodies and anger. Extending northeast from Tahrir is Mohamed Mahmoud Street, where the forecast is usually bad. Young men throw stones at the Ministry of the Interior building; as the police headquarters, it's a favored target of protesters. They hurl obscenities at me, too, because I should know better than to be here. I never go to Tahrir Square at night.

Cairo may be the mother of the world, but she looks at me through a man's eyes. If I walk down the street pushing my daughters in their twin stroller, the city loves me. I am Isis, the goddess of fertility (also, Egyptians love children, and my babbling identical twins are a big distraction). When I'm with Peter I'm ignored, and men who might have talked with me when I was alone don't even meet my eyes. This behavior is supposed to be respectful, but it creates instead a sense of complicity, as if something had happened between us that must stay hidden.

"Sexual segregation," the Moroccan sociologist Fatima Mernissi has written, "intensifies what it is supposed to eliminate: the sexualization of human relations."

Some of my diciest encounters have been in taxis. I talk to the drivers to practice my language skills and to get a sense of what people are thinking, but there's something about the enclosed space that triggers intimacy.

Sabah il-kheir!

Sabah il-nour!

Where are you from?

America.

Are you married?

Yes. I have two children. They're twins!

That's usually enough to neutralize my femaleness and allow us to move on to safe territory like the current president, why the country is a mess, and how America is secretly financing the Muslim Brotherhood in order to keep Egypt down. But sometimes I lose track of the signposts through inattention or my rudimentary Arabic. Before I know it, we've arrived in a sexually explicit cul-de-sac:

Egyptians want to have sex several times a day.

How often do you have sex with your husband?

Egyptians care about only two things, sex and food.

(Sometimes it's *Egyptians care about only two things, sex and money.* But in these conversations, sex is always one of the only two things Egyptians supposedly care about.)

When I get into a taxi in a remote area, I call Peter right away so the driver is aware that someone knows where I am. If the dreaded G-word comes up—*gins*, which means "sex"—I cut off my interlocutor midsentence. Like flipping a switch, he changes to politics or the weather or his fantasy of finding a submissive Chinese wife (if only he knew). You manage the risks as well as you can. My husband worked with a female photographer who once had a taxi driver pull off the road, drag her out of the car, and try to rape her. A person passing by heard her shouts and came to her rescue, and she was treated in the hospital for head injuries. Another woman I know was groped by a cabbie while he was driving. She managed to open her door, jump out of the vehicle, and run across many lanes of traffic to get away from him.

Egypt isn't actually a sexually segregated society. Men and women interact on college campuses and at work, on public transportation and in the street, but the belief that males and females shouldn't mix is still strong. In a national survey, nearly three-quarters of married women said their husband became jealous or angry if they spoke to another man. It comes down, again, to words and deeds. Society has changed, but the rules remain the same, as Fatima Mernissi describes in her book *Beyond the Veil:*

> **Women in male spaces are considered both provocative and offensive. Since schooling and jobs both require women to be able to move freely through the streets, modernization necessarily exposes many women to public harassment. . . . A woman is always trespassing in a male space because she is, by definition, a foe. A woman has no right to use male spaces. If she enters them, she is upsetting the male's order and his peace of mind. She is actually committing an act of aggression against him merely by being present where she should not be.**

Early on Friday mornings, I go running around the island of Zamalek with two female friends. The city is deserted at this hour—most people are still asleep, and later the men will head to the mosque for prayers—and we can run down the middle of the street if we feel like it. This is my favorite moment of the week, and the only time I feel entirely free outdoors. No one bothers us. Maybe we're moving too quickly—if a ten-minute mile can be considered fast—or our sense of purpose puts them off. We wear long T-shirts and shorts layered over running tights. Even on the hottest days, we don't show our legs.

I left Cairo in June 2016. I always vowed to Maggie and Havra, my running partners, that on my last run with them I would dress for the ninety-degree heat in a tank top and shorts, everything else be damned. But I never did. I told myself it was enough to run through the streets of *Umm al-Dunya* and to feel as if the city were mine. The truth is, I lost my nerve.

THE ARRIVAL OF the modern age closed off many freedoms for women. In the early nineteenth century, Egypt's industrializing economy decimated the cottage trades that had employed women in large numbers. They weren't welcome in the new economy. Only men were hired to work in factories that used steam power; only men received training on advanced machinery. Women were confined to workplaces that relied on animal power. They did menial tasks, like sorting cotton and hauling bricks and sand for construction.

Around the middle of the century, when the economy shifted focus to doing business with Europe, women were further marginalized. Foreign merchants moved to Egypt to import goods and trade cotton, but women were in no position to exploit these opportunities. Increasingly, they faced not only the constraints of their own culture but also new forms of discrimination imported from the West. Women could neither buy stocks nor open bank accounts, for example—both were innovations from Europe, which didn't recognize a woman's economic existence apart from her husband's. The transition from subsistence farming to cash crops also favored men. Wives had worked alongside their husbands on the family farm, but the modern system of wage labor didn't have much use for them. Men were hired as laborers on cotton-growing estates; men became salaried employees in factories and government offices. Once the man was established as the family breadwinner, women's work became, by definition, unimportant.

The historical evidence of women working in Egypt becomes thin in the nineteenth century, as doors are closed to them one by one. The practice of female seclusion spreads from the elite to the middle class. Women lose the power to include conditions in their marriage contracts to protect themselves; they rarely register property in their own names anymore. In the Nile Delta town of Hamaqa, a judge rules that a woman who eloped against her family's wishes must return home and her new husband be imprisoned, and he urges other judges to join him in combating the "immorality" of the times.

Such restrictions on female autonomy haven't always been in place. They are a reaction to the country's jarring encounter with the modern world, which worsened later in the nineteenth century with spiraling debt, national bankruptcy, and occupation by the British. In a time of displacement and change, Egyptian society turns conservative. It imposes control wherever it can, and women bear the brunt of it.

"It's a reactionary desire to hold on to a religious and cultural identity," Omaima Abou-Bakr explained to me. "And inside that, women and the family are always cultural icons. Let's hold on to that; let's not change that.

"The big ambivalence for societies like Egypt is that you are receiving modernity via colonialism," she continued. "To this day—it's been a hundred years—we're still battling to resolve that ambivalence. How do you modernize but keep your cultural identity? And we women get caught in that crisis."

After the British took over administration of the country in 1882, they overhauled certain institutions—the financial system, the military—and remodeled criminal and commercial law on the French civil code. Only in the realm of family law, which governed marriage, divorce, guardianship, and inheritance, did Islamic rules prevail. But where traditional *sharia* courts had practiced flexibility and followed regional custom in their decisions, the new British-imposed statute set a single standard. Its authors, who were mostly Egyptians trained in European-style law schools, often selected the most restrictive version of Islamic doctrine and applied it across the board. The result was drawn from *sharia,* but without the fluidity and local diversity that had been essential to how *sharia* was applied. (Egypt's Christian adherents were governed by separate legislation that was drafted by their own religious authorities.) The new family laws also borrowed elements from the European legal system, such as the subordination of women to fathers and husbands that was contained in the Napoleonic Code.

Modern Muslim states, writes a Georgetown University historian named Amira El Azhary Sonbol, oversaw "the institution of new customs labeled as *sharia* that deny previous freedoms while emphasizing earlier discriminations." As Egypt entered the modern age, two seemingly incompatible ideologies—one Eastern and religious, the other Western and secular—united to shape a conservative body of law that denied women many rights and freedoms. It has remained largely intact to this day.

In the twentieth century, an Egyptian woman could no longer contract her own marriage, set conditions on the union, or initiate a divorce without her husband's consent. A mother could not easily become her child's legal guardian if her husband died; divorcées and widows lost custody automatically when they remarried. The courts could even force a wife to stay in a marriage against her will, based on an expansive interpretation of obedience that came not from *sharia* but from nineteenth-century British law.

Just as the Industrial Revolution brought forth the male breadwinner, so it created his helpmate, the devoted housewife. The government set up schools to teach girls needlework, childcare, cooking, and laundry (too much impractical education, it was said, would distract them from "their natural avocation" of keeping house). Women's magazines appeared, and stressed the importance of hygiene and household management. The cult of domesticity blended the Victorian ideal of the selfless wife and mother with centuries of Muslim male belief in female inferiority, and even reformers bought into it. In 1899, a judge named Qasim Amin published a book called *The Liberation of Women*, in which he argued that women should be educated—so they could be better mothers and housekeepers:

> It is the wife's duty to plan the household budget . . . to supervise the servants . . . to make her home attractive to her husband, so that he may find ease when he returns to it and so that he likes being there, and enjoys the food and drink and sleep and does not seek to flee from home and to spend his time with neighbors or in public places, and it is her . . . first and most important duty to raise the children, attending to them physically, mentally, and morally.

In the early twentieth century, a small but vocal women's movement fought for their right to vote and access to education, along with the reform of laws that governed polygamy and unilateral divorce. Its leader was Huda Sharawi, an upper-class woman who had been raised in traditional seclusion but gained national fame when she removed her veil at the Cairo train station in 1923. In the following decades, most upper- and middle-class women in the cities switched to wearing Western-style dress with no veil. They entered schools and joined the workforce, although progress has been uneven. One Egyptian woman out of every three is still illiterate, and female labor participation remains among the lowest in the world. Most of the inequalities in marriage, divorce, custody, and inheritance that existed in Huda Sharawi's time remain in place today.

The crisis that confronted Egypt in the nineteenth century hasn't ended—in Omaima Abou-Bakr's words: "How do you modernize but keep your cultural identity?" One response has been to shift toward religious and social conservatism. The 1970s and '80s saw a fundamentalist revival that emerged on Egyptian college campuses and spread across social classes. The movement was fueled by Saudi Arabia, which practices the ultraconservative form of Islam called Wahhabism that considers women to be inherently sinful, intellectually inferior, and unfit to travel, work, get married, or make other key decisions in their lives without the approval of a male guardian. With its immense oil wealth, Saudi Arabia funded schools, mosques, and other organizations abroad to spread its beliefs. These efforts were aided by the mass migration of workers from all over the Arab world to the Gulf States, where they absorbed these ideas and brought them home.

This same period saw the resurgence of the veil in Egypt. Its early adopters were young women from villages and small towns who moved to the cities to attend college and started wearing "Islamic dress"—ankle-length dresses or skirts, long sleeves, and a headscarf that covers the hair and sometimes the shoulders (a more extreme version includes gloves and the full-face covering called the *niqab*). The veil signaled both upward mobility and traditional propriety. A 1982 study on Cairo University's campus found that female students who wore the veil came from less educated families than their unveiled classmates. They were also less likely to support a woman's right to work, to occupy high political office, or to have equality in her marriage. The veil has become standard attire in Egypt, and its wearing these days seems less about choice than convention.

It is the wife's duty to plan the household budget . . . to make her home attractive to her husband . . . to raise the children. These words, which were published by Qasim Amin more than a century ago, still express the feelings of most Egyptians. In a 2018 poll, fewer than one-quarter of people viewed married women's work positively; three-quarters of the respondents, among both sexes, said that male job seekers should take precedence in times of scarcity. The labor laws in most Muslim countries allow a husband, in certain circumstances, to prevent his wife from going out to work. Their rationale is based on chapter 4, verse 34 of the Quran: *Men are the protectors and maintainers of women.* Because a wife relies on her husband for support, she owes him obedience in return, and that includes not leaving the house if he doesn't want her to.

Yet it's only in the past few decades, feminist scholars say, that the definition of obedience within marriage has been stretched to deny women access to the job market. They counter with a rival verse—*To men is allotted a share of what they earned and to women is allotted a share of what they earned*—that implicitly accepts that women will work and enjoy the fruits of their own labor.

The Quran actually warns, in the opening of its third chapter, that people will try to misuse its words for their own purposes:

Some of its verses are definite in meaning—these are the cornerstone of the Scripture—and others are ambiguous. The perverse at heart eagerly pursue the ambiguities in their attempt to make trouble and pin down a specific meaning of their own: Only God knows the true meaning.

Every age invents its own Quran. Societies evolve, and words signify different things at different times. Yet so many of the book's interpreters insist that their meaning has always been the true one, going back to the Prophet Muhammad and the first community of Muslims.

History is a wheel, and we're all trying to get to a better place.

On January 16, 2000, an unusually packed session of the Egyptian People's Assembly opened debate on the "Law on Reorganization of Certain Terms and Procedures of Litigation in Personal Status Matters." Under cover of its bureaucratic-sounding title, the bill proposed a dramatic change. Nineteen years after the country ratified the Convention on the Elimination of All Forms of Discrimination Against Women, twenty-nine years after the constitution granted equal rights to all citizens, and thirty-eight years after Nasser's National Charter made female emancipation a cornerstone of government policy, women in Egypt would finally be free to divorce their husbands.

The proposal, which had been drafted by a coalition of activists, lawyers, legislators, and scholars with support from the Mubarak government, addressed a contradiction at the heart of the legal system. The country's constitution and international human rights treaties guarantee equal rights to all citizens. But inside the family—the third rail of Egyptian politics—women are subject to *sharia*-influenced laws from the nineteenth century that limit their autonomy in practice. A woman has the legal right to vote, run for office, and serve her country as its ambassador, government minister, or president. But she can't marry without a male guardian's approval, retain custody of her children if she remarries, or work or travel without her husband's consent.

She also couldn't easily end an unhappy marriage. A man could divorce his wife by repudiating her three times and registering the deed with a religious notary. He didn't have to go to court, or even tell his wife in person; she would be notified later, a practice so common that it had its own shorthand, *ba'at leha wara'itha,* "he sent her her paper." A woman had to file a court case and cite grounds for ending her marriage, such as her husband's impotence, disease, violent abuse, desertion, or failure to provide financial support. The process was so cumbersome and costly that many women chose to remain in marriages that were unsatisfactory, or even abusive.

For more than a century, reformers and political leaders have tried to amend Egypt's family laws but have made only piecemeal gains because of opposition from religious conservatives. In 2000, their strategy was to use Islamic tradition to their advantage. Chapter two, verse 229 of the

Quran lets a wife "give something up to her husband in exchange for her freedom." In a related *hadith*, the Prophet Muhammad tells a woman named Jamila Bint Abdullah that she can divorce her husband as long as she returns the garden he gave her when they married. Muslim jurisprudence thus recognizes a woman's right to divorce by *khul*, or "casting off," as long as she pays back the sum of money that her husband gave her when they married, known as the dower, or provides him with some other compensation. *Khul* was widely practiced in Egypt until the codification of family law under the British at the close of the nineteenth century. In the new proposal, which was based on historical research and approved by the grand imam of Al-Azhar as compliant with *sharia*, a woman could divorce if she gave up her dower, alimony, and other financial claims. Her husband would have no say in the matter and no right of appeal.

The discussion in parliament lasted a month. The legislation had the full support of the Mubarak government, whose advocacy of women's rights included reforming child custody and alimony laws and naming the country's first female judges. Even so, some members of the ruling National Democratic Party spoke out against the bill. Representatives from the Wafd Party walked out in protest of "this crime against Egyptian society." A statement from Ali Nasr, an M.P. from the Upper Egyptian city of Beni Suef, caused an uproar: "A rooster can have forty hens and a lion marries more than four wives, but it has never happened that a hen married two roosters." (He also walked out, after some members demanded that he apologize for his remarks.)

The crude tone of the debate shocked even veteran activists. "It was a very dirty dialogue," Azza Soliman, who watched the proceedings from the visitors' gallery, told me. She's a lawyer and founder of the Center for Egyptian Women's Legal Assistance, which was one of the bill's backers.

"I was scared of this parliament," she continued. "How can this parliament make laws for women and respect women? This is the problem."

In a book about *khul* that she co-authored, Soliman related some of the choicest bits of dialogue:

> Most parliamentarians agreed that women could not be trusted. "Their mixing with men creates marital aversion, not because a woman hates her husband, but because she loves another man."

> Mohammed Ahmed Marzouq stressed that a wife was vulnerable to seduction, or she herself may succumb to the temptation of seducing a man; in either case she would destroy the household and cause the children to go astray. . . .

> Parliamentarian Al Ghoul . . . claimed [that *khul*] would rid men of women's infidelity and save them from the violence of wives who kill their husbands and cut them into small pieces.

Many of the M.P.s predicted that women would promptly abandon their husbands and children if the law were passed (men, invariably, were portrayed as calm and devoted to their families). The implication was that every Egyptian woman was trapped in a marriage against her will, which made you wonder what their own home lives were like.

> Husny Behalou expressed his fear that many women would rush to divorce and abuse the right to *khul.* . . .

> Dr. Hermass said he believed that women would act hastily and regret the results.

> There was a lot of shouting.

> Fayez Al Tenikhy shouted: "Does she have the right to be custodian of my own children after she rejects me?! Does she have the right to live in my own flat with another man?!"

Another parliamentarian exclaimed: "Are the children not part of the rejected husband? How come she gets the right to keep them?"

"*Of course* they take it personally!" said Soliman. "Nobody can imagine that a woman could tell a man: 'I don't want you.' *Nooooo!* Only a man can say this."

Much talk centered on what Muhammad might have meant fourteen centuries ago when he told Jamila to give back her husband's garden. Politicians with no special background in Quranic exegesis engaged in it anyway:

[Some] parliamentarians claimed that the Prophet Mohamed did not decree the divorce between Jamila and Qais Ben Thabet, but rather advised Jamila's husband to divorce her. According to this logic, a judge's authority should not replace a husband's. . . .

Amin Hammad argued that [the marital home] was the modern equivalent of Jamila's garden, and a woman who is a custodian of her own children should renounce the marital home if she sought *khul.* . . .

Sayed Fath el Bab claimed that the husband should be compensated for all the expenses that he had incurred from the moment of marriage until the moment of *khul.* . . .

Mokhtar Aly Saad said that a wife who now hated her husband should return everything he had offered her. . . . This would prevent *khul* from becoming a means by which women could enrich themselves.

Both the parliamentary discussion and the newspaper coverage of it framed the issue not in terms of women's rights but on the need to preserve the family at all costs. The bill's proponents argued that the new *khul* provisions would actually stabilize households, by requiring women to pay back their dower to their husband if they divorced. *Al-Wafd* claimed the law violated men's human rights by challenging their authority at home; several papers said the legislation was a Western and Zionist conspiracy to destroy the Muslim family. Political cartoons mocked female equality, with drawings of women flirting with men while their husbands pushed baby strollers and washed the dishes. Despite the opposition, accusations of apostasy, and apocalyptic visions of a future in which Egyptian men might have to do housework, the bill passed—mainly because the Mubarak government wanted it so much, observers said.

The passage of the law was a landmark victory for Islamic feminists. They had found a basis for women's rights within their religious tradition and used it to push society in a more equitable direction. In the two decades since the law was passed, more than fifty thousand Egyptian women have used *khul* to free themselves from unhappy marriages. Neighboring countries like Jordan and Morocco have followed Egypt's example and introduced legislation that gives women the right to no-fault divorce.

Yet the *khul* campaign followed a historical pattern, in which a modification to family law places some limits on a male right, while leaving in place an unequal system that demands female obedience in marriage in exchange for financial support. That compact underlies other male privileges, such as the right to verbal divorce and to wed multiple wives, and it keeps women in a state of perpetual disadvantage. "It is at best a partial solution, helpful only to some," a political sociologist named Huda Zakareya wrote after the passage of the *khul* law. "By promoting it as a satisfactory solution, we undermine our dreams of developing an effective feminist movement."

Above all, the campaign showed how difficult change could be—that the reinstatement of a practice that had existed for most of Islamic history could be considered a victory. In the twenty-first century, an Egyptian woman can practice a right that was first described in a religious text one thousand four hundred years ago. For the first time in more than a century, words and deeds have matched up.

There shall be no sin upon either of them if the wife gives up something to her husband in exchange for her freedom. And these are the limits of God.

4

WORK STUDY

To get to the Delta factory, you drive south from Minya and take the first bridge across the Nile. The river is wide and blue here, and it glitters like a jewel in the sun. Past a crude Nefertiti statue and the unfinished Aten Museum—it's more than a decade behind schedule, my taxi driver, Karam, tells me—you continue south on the highway, between lush farms and palm trees on one side of the road and sheer limestone walls on the other. The road arcs upward, gives one last view of the broad river, then turns abruptly inland onto a parched plateau the color of ashes.

We pass what appears to be an army installation—walls, razor wire, armed guards in watchtowers. "No one knows what they do here," Karam says. That's not technically true. But in this military-run state, so much of the landscape looks like a prison camp that at some point you stop paying attention.

More rubble, more razor wire and guard towers, and here is the site of a brand-new capital city that was planned ten years ago but only partially built. Vacant and unfinished buildings litter the landscape, their missing walls and gaping windows making the area look like a bombed-out war zone, although the place is still called, with Egyptian optimism, *al-Minya al-Gadida,* "New Minya." "The governor wants to move all the government offices here," Karam tells me. I have my doubts.

The road curves to reveal another cemetery, of a more conventional kind. Hundreds of mud brick domes stretch into the distance on either side of the road, like waves in a clay-colored ocean as far as the eye can see. The tombs are arrayed in tidy rows, the Muslims in their quarter and the Christians in theirs. On the long drive out from Minya, the city of the dead is the first place I've seen that looks finished according to plan.

"That's between you and God," as Karam says. "You don't mess with that."

We keep driving, along the edge of the Eastern Desert now, to arrive at the Matahra Industrial Zone, which feels like another optimistic name for what's mostly empty highway and blowing sand. Where the road dead-ends, two men sit at a folding table and drink tea while looking out at nothing, like characters in a Beckett play. We ask them the way; they know nothing. After many inquiries, I arrive at the Delta Textile Factory, which is housed in a long, white two-story building with narrow windows.

The first time I come here, I'm taken inside and upstairs to a sight as strange as anything I've seen. Hundreds of women sit in neat rows in a vast production space, sewing. Their dresses and headscarves, in hot pink, royal blue, and gold, shimmer like a mirage in the desert. Supervisors move up and down the lines inspecting their work; cleaners with vacuum hoses circle around them, as in a precisely choreographed ballet. Such energy and order, in this landscape of broken and forgotten things: It feels like a miracle.

It took me a long time to find this place. Minya is a hundred sixty miles south of Cairo, on the long, green stretch of the Nile Valley that extends from the edge of the city all the way to the border with Sudan.

This is Upper Egypt, *al-Saeed*, the southern region of the country where the strictest forms of Islam are said to be practiced, where women rarely leave their homes and the *tha'r*, or blood feud, erupts with alarming frequency. This is the part of Egypt where one woman out of every five has never attended school and one out of four is married to her first cousin. Human behavior can take a turn to the outlandish: EGYPTIAN WOMAN REVEALS 42-YEAR SECRET OF SURVIVAL: PRETENDING TO BE A MAN was the headline on a story that came out of the area when I was there ("Egypt's president, Abdel Fattah El-Sisi, personally gave her an award for being an extraordinary mother"). Occasionally someone in the NGO world, which was centered in Cairo, would tell me that Upper Egyptian women did work in factories and run their own businesses. Others were doubtful. It felt like discussing a creature so rare, like the ibex or the snow leopard, that it might not exist at all.

"In that community, women don't work outside the home," said a participant in a female entrepreneurs' conference in a four-star hotel on the Alexandria waterfront, which was about as far from Upper Egypt as you could get without falling into the Mediterranean.

"There's not a single ready-made-garment factory in Upper Egypt," the head of a U.N. agency in Cairo told me.

But as Herodotus observed, "A man always believes his eyes better than his ears," so I took the train to Minya to see for myself. I contacted a local journalist I knew there, who happened to spot a newspaper ad placed by a factory that was hiring women. When he called the number, the person who answered the phone invited us to come by. This string of unlikely coincidences—it felt like *kismet*, a word which incidentally comes from Arabic—led me to the Delta Textile Factory, which I probably would never have found otherwise. This was one of the largest manufacturing operations in Upper Egypt, but no one outside its immediate neighborhood seemed to know about it, and I never found any mention of the facility in print or online. A $2.5 million garment factory could be built and then swallowed by the desert—just like the Great

Sphinx, which for many centuries lay submerged beneath the sands, awaiting rediscovery.

Eight miles south of the Delta factory is another site that feels just as remote. In the rock-cut tombs of Beni Hassan, which date to 1900 B.C., a series of famous wall paintings show how women made textiles in pharaonic times. Inside the tomb of Khnumhotep II, one woman roves linen fibers while another spins thread; two more sit weaving on a horizontal loom under the gaze of a female supervisor. The white of the women's dresses glows in the dim space, luminous after three thousand years.

The burial chambers are carved into steep limestone cliffs high above the Nile. When I came here with my translator, whom I will call Mai, armed security officers set upon us as soon as we got out of our taxi, like ravenous dogs that someone had forgotten to feed.

"You don't have insurance with you?" one of the men demanded, while the others pressed close and fondled the triggers of their guns.

Mai and I bought our tickets and started climbing the steps to the tombs, doing our best to ignore the policemen who panted after us for a while and then gave up. In the 1990s, a violent Islamist insurgency in this part of the country killed hundreds of people, including foreign tourists. Two decades later, visitors are still required to travel with "insurance," in the form of an armed police escort. But the last thing I wanted was their "protection," so we just walked faster.

No one else was visiting Beni Hassan on the afternoon we were there. The art in these tombs is studied by Egyptologists around the world, but almost no Egyptians come to see it with their own eyes. The swarms of police probably don't help (the security apparatus may be good at some things, but promoting tourism isn't one of them). Most of the ordinary Egyptians I've met seemed proud of their ancient history but also detached from it. Too many rulers have passed through, spouting too many different ideologies, to allow someone to feel a meaningful connection to pictures on a wall.

Even when the record of women's work is inscribed in stone, it can disappear.

By the first week of August in 2016, Delta had thirty production lines up and running. But worker absences had been even worse than Kevin Meyer predicted. Factory turnover during the recent Ramadan holiday was 45 percent—for every two workers trained, one went missing. Efficiency plummeted, and the rate of errors increased. When the month was over, many of the employees rematerialized as if they'd never left.

In August, Ian Ross traveled to Minya and called a meeting of supervisors. The Minya factory, he told them, should be run by people from Minya. The company's long-term goal was to hire local executives for all key positions, beginning with a female production manager. Every person in the room turned her head, as if by prearranged signal, to look at Rania. The factory was like a village: There was no point in hiding what everyone knew.

"I was extremely happy after that meeting," Rania told me. "I wanted to convey that happiness to people, to show that I wasn't afraid of problems." Her high profile in the factory annoyed some of her co-workers, and she wanted to prove that she was up for any challenge.

Before the gathering, Ross and Aruna Jayakody, the factory manager, had met with Rania privately and told her she was being considered for the job. But Rania sometimes got into fights with her colleagues—recently, she had shouted at a manager for supposedly mistreating another supervisor she was friendly with—and Ross had gotten wind of this.

"Be careful," he told her. "Don't make any problems, because you're a candidate for this position."

"I don't make any problems," Rania answered coolly.

In October, she was assigned to oversee three new production lines on an unfamiliar part of the floor. On the first chilly day of fall, I went to the factory to watch her work. I arrived at seven-thirty, just as one of Rania's workers came up to announce that several women were missing. Rania would have to manage three absences that day, after seven the day before. "Each girl has a different reason for not coming," she told me. "Some are getting married, and some just don't want to come anymore."

By nine o'clock, one of her lines was already falling behind. Rania conferred with the line's immediate supervisor, a woman in a *niqab* named Fatima, and together they went to see Jack, the production manager on their part of the floor. They asked him to transfer someone from another line to help them catch up.

"If you give me a worker for the Singer," Fatima pressed Jack, "I can produce five hundred pieces an hour."

Jack turned her down. Many of the lines were short of people that day, and Rania was an experienced supervisor who could manage on her own.

On the production floor I ran into Savy, a South African executive who was in charge of training. "The absentee rate in the factory is high," she said.

"How high?"

"Ten or fifteen percent, these two days. The weather is getting cooler, so families don't want their girls to go out."

She gave me a wintry smile. "They're used to treating their daughters like babies."

Jack reappeared on Rania's turf around ten o'clock, this time to ask her help. "I need someone to work on the elastic machine," he said. "I'm one person short."

Rania said she couldn't spare anyone. Jack hadn't assisted her when she asked, and now she was returning the favor.

"I could have helped him, but I'm not going to help him," she told me after he left, flashing a rare smile. "An eye for an eye."

At a quarter to eleven, Rania was summoned to the office of the factory manager. Aruna Jayakody was a soft-spoken and serious man from Sri Lanka, who looked as if he did not enjoy the work of harsh discipline. "There was no production on two of your lines in the last hour," he said. "Why?"

"There's only one girl working on the Singer, and Asmaa had maintenance on a machine for an hour," Rania said.

"Why didn't you ask Jack for a girl from Eman's line?"

"I asked Jack, but he refused."

Even as she was speaking, Aruna was already on the phone: "Send her a girl from Eman's line." The factory operated on a complicated exchange of favors and obligations, requests and refusals, but power wasn't distributed equally. Rania was so productive that the factory couldn't afford to lose her output for long. She usually got her way.

Delta continued to shed workers that autumn, and gradually I understood why. As the days got shorter, the minibus drivers made fewer stops on their routes so they could finish work by nightfall. Some of the women now had to walk long distances in the dark to get home. A newly promoted supervisor named Hind Ali said she would probably quit, even though she was one of the factory's most productive workers. "I don't want to leave, and they don't want me to leave," she told me. In a brand-new factory, it was impossible for executives to foresee every reason a woman might decide to stop working. Like the rituals of Ramadan, a change in the weather could ripple across the factory floor, setting off a delicate cycle of disturbance that no eye could see.

I ASKED A woman who worked on Rania's line why she was quitting the factory. Her name was Seham Forkash and she was in her late twenties, with large dark eyes in a strong-boned face.

"I'm leaving because I'm tired."

"But why, specifically?"

"I'm leaving because I might get married. I can't really focus—I need to plan for the wedding."

I asked her when the event would take place.

"We haven't set a date, but planning something like this takes a few months at least," Seham said. "I need more time to be able to think about the planning."

"But wouldn't it help to have a few months' more salary?" I asked. Her logic mystified me. If you were getting married in six months, it would make sense to save as much money as you could before the event. But women in Egyptian factories often said *I'm getting married in six months, so I'll quit now.*

"Financially speaking, I'm fine," Seham said. "I'm not here for the money. I'm just here because I'm bored at home, and I want something to occupy my time." Her father was the principal of a village school, and her family owned land.

"If it were up to me, I would continue to work here," Seham went on. "The environment is lovely, and I love working here. I love seeing my friends. My parents are the ones who are interfering. They're telling me I should stay at home, now that I'm going to be married soon."

When you got past all the euphemisms and evasions—*I'm tired, I'm not here for the money, I'm just bored at home*—the reason a woman left a job was almost always because someone in her family didn't want her there. Sometimes the objection came from her parents, other times her husband or fiancé. Occasionally a woman's parents approved of her employment but her in-laws didn't, or the other way around. It was dispiriting: There were so many potential arguments for restricting a woman's freedom that it was bound to prevail.

The majority of the women I met in Egyptian factories were working there despite their families' objections. And they were the successes— the ones who had worn down parents and husbands through long arguments, patient discussions, shouting. Young women sometimes stood up to their parents and won, but I noticed that wives rarely worked against the explicit wishes of their husbands. More often, they tried to bring them around. In Riham's factory, I met a woman who had lobbied her husband for two years before he agreed that she could take a job.

Two years! That struck me as excessive until I met Sahar Nasr, the World Bank's lead economist for the Middle East, who was based in Cairo. She graduated from college with highest honors and got her doctorate in economics, but she stayed home for eight years after marriage because her family didn't want her to work. The opposition came from all sides: her husband, her children, and even her mother, who had worked as a lawyer. "After my two children were in school, I made my revolution," she told me. "If you're persistent and you're determined and you believe in yourself, you can do it. But you have to fight for your rights. No one is going to give you your rights."

A few months later, in the improbable way in which things sometimes happen in Egypt, Nasr was named the Minister of International Cooperation. When I heard that she had commissioned a report on female economic empowerment, I felt like cheering. But she of all people knew the degree of opposition that women are up against.

How many others had given up fighting with their families, or not even tried to convince them, because it was too hard? Among Egyptian women in their twenties, three-fourths are unoccupied with either work or school. Female inactivity peaks between the ages of twenty-five and twenty-nine, when 82 percent of women are neither employed nor studying. (The comparable rate for men is 10 percent.)

When women stayed home, time had a way of slowing down:

I got married three years ago. I was sitting in the house doing absolutely nothing.

After I quit school, I stayed home for four or five years, doing nothing.

After I got married, I stayed home for four years. I was bored, and I had so many problems with my husband.

I tried to persuade him to let me work, but he didn't agree. That was five years ago.

I was feeling bored and suffocated sitting at home doing nothing. I'm twenty-seven.

It made sense that a woman would leave her job to take care of a newborn baby, but that wasn't why most of them quit. The impetus was usually an engagement or impending marriage. The act of severing one's connection to the workplace served a ritualistic purpose: It signaled that a woman was committing herself to marriage and domestic life. Seham was many months, or maybe more than a year, away from being married—*We haven't set a date*—but already she had to play the obedient wife, and that meant sacrificing her independence.

While Seham was speaking, I realized that we had met before. Six months earlier, I had ridden a shuttle bus with seven women from a farming village who were going to their first day of work at Delta. The women wore long *abayas* and headscarves in bright coordinated colors, as if they were on their way to a party: *We're very excited, we got up at five o'clock.* The most talkative one had been Seham. "I just want to learn," she had said. Her parents opposed the idea, but she had won them over—at least she thought so.

In 2005, Seham had gotten her *diplome,* a vocational school degree that poorer Egyptians often acquired after middle school, but she hadn't held a job before or since. Two other women on the bus shared her profile: *diplome,* no work experience, unmarried. What was it like, I wondered, to spend twelve years getting an education and then to stay home for the next ten? What happens when a woman tries to break this pattern?

After having a taste of the outside world—*I love working here, I love seeing my friends*—Seham was quitting it already. She hadn't broken any pattern, only fitted herself more closely into one that was made for her. This would be a short break, she said; her fiancé, who worked as a driver, had agreed she could find employment after they were married. I wondered when that would be, or how much time would pass before Seham came out again.

THE WORLD THESE women came from was never far from the minds of the people who ran the Delta factory. For Kevin Meyer, a major factor was geography. "Work is a culture shock for them," he told me. "I think it has to do with the farming cycle. Here in Upper Egypt, they farm for a couple of hours. When the sun gets too hot, they hide in the shade for a while. Later, they work a bit more; then they hide again. So when I tell the workers, 'You need to do this action one hundred times an hour,' they say, 'Give me a chance. I don't know if I can do it.'"

The global manufacturing cycle divides time into infinitesimal segments—one-third of a second to sew a seam, 465 minutes in a day— but many of Delta's employees had a more leisurely relationship with the clock. "You can take a break during work to go to the toilet, or to wash your face, but they basically say, 'I'm going to the toilet, and that's a good time for leisure,'" Meyer told me. In a couple of instances, he had sent a female security guard into the ladies' room to retrieve a worker who had fallen asleep.

"We're trying to get people to understand the difference between 'a break' and 'rest,'" he said. He chastised an employee he found napping at her sewing machine between tasks ("If I'm home and have nothing to do," she explained, "I sleep") and had a running argument with several others who wanted to iron clothes from a sitting position. Once I watched him approach a woman who was squatting against a pillar in the middle of the factory floor, as relaxed as if she were on the front stoop of her house.

"Get up!" he said, more irritated than angry. "You're too young to have back pain—you're not even twenty years old!"

A lot of what was wrong at work, for Meyer, could be expressed in a single word: *insha'allah*. The term, which means "if God wills it," is universally deployed in Arabic when one speaks about the future, in recognition that all things are in the hands of a higher power. But it can also feel like an all-purpose hedge against anything turning out differently than planned.

When Meyer told his instructors that a number of production lines should be ready by a certain date, the response was always: "Yes, *insha'allah*." In his mind, the phrase ruled out accountability. It gave itself room to fail. It made and revoked a promise in the same breath.

"My trainers say: 'Let's go for it, *insha'allah*,'" he said. "No! Commit to it! 'Yes, I am committing to it, *insha'allah*.'

"No! It's an oxymoron to say: 'Yes, but only if nothing happens.' You have to plan, measure, do the things you need to do to reach your target. It's just a huge gray area."

One day in his office, Meyer showed me a piece of paper with the heading "Training Performance Chart":

TRAINING PERFORMANCE CHART

COVERSEAM HEM BOTTOM

The graph, which was the proprietary information of a team of U.K. management consultants, showed the progress of a typical worker assigned to sew hems in a garment factory. On her first day, she would produce at 25 percent of a set target; that was her efficiency rate. That figure would increase over the next nine days, to 55 percent. In the subsequent three days it would stay flat, and then rise again until, on Day

Twenty, she attained the target efficiency rate of 75 percent. From that day on she should maintain that level, hour after hour, day in and day out.

The practice of measuring human movements with mathematical precision in order to raise productivity is known as "scientific management" or "work study." The field emerged in the United States at the turn of the twentieth century (its pioneers included Frank and Lillian Gilbreth, who are best known from the biographical book and film *Cheaper by the Dozen*). Industrial engineers break down any task in the workplace into individual steps, decide on the most efficient way to perform each micromovement, put the actions back together, and compute the time needed to complete the operation. To sew a one-centimeter-long seam on a piece of clothing, according to the global industry standard, should take exactly twenty-nine-hundredths of a second.

"But don't these actions take different times based on the machine?" I asked Meyer.

"No. This is the standard. This has been done using a multitude of machines in India, Mauritius—wherever there's a sewing trade happening."

"Where's the factory now, in terms of the global standard?" I asked.

"We're at forty-five percent of the standard."

"So you need to get twice as fast."

"We need to get twice as fast."

The drive for continuous improvement in the global garment trade clashes with a deeply ingrained preference to do things as they've always been done. Meyer had recently introduced an automatic hemming machine into the factory. On a regular sewing machine, a worker has to hold a piece of fabric and fold it bit by bit to sew a hem; the new one allowed her to insert the garment, fold it once, press a button, and let the machine do the rest. The employee who was chosen to be trained first—an experienced hemmer, which was probably a mistake—flatly refused to try. She cried; she couldn't learn; she threatened to quit. For the first two days of her training, she sat and watched while an instructor demonstrated the device's workings over and over. On Day Three, after much encouragement, she consented to try it out, but the old machine was allowed to sit next to her "like a pacifier," as Meyer put it. After another week of practice she had mastered the technology, and the old machine was removed.

"She actually got on very well with the machine eventually," he told me, "but after a lot of blood, sweat, and tears." According to his analysis, the automatic hemming machine should raise output by 42 percent. The British consultants might have mapped out the woman's learning curve like this:

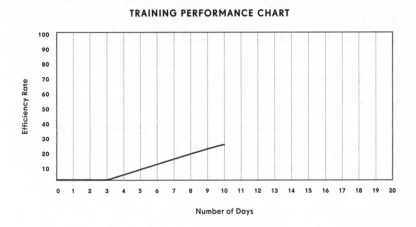

TRAINING PERFORMANCE CHART

Later that fall, the company planned to bring instructors from the U.K. to teach work study methods. First they would train Delta's industrial engineers how to break down individual tasks and redesign them to be more efficient; the next phase would be to teach those steps to workers in every department across the factory. Delta's employees might quit on a whim or vanish for a month, cry at the sight of new technology, or fall asleep in the bathroom, but executives believed they could sew to global standards that were calibrated down to hundredths of a second. The goal was to reach 50 percent efficiency across the factory by the end of the year, Meyer said, up from 25 percent now. *Insha'allah.*

AT THE BEGINNING of November, I visited Rania at home. Her village, Saft al-Sharqiya, is nine miles south of Minya, but the word "village" doesn't convey the smothering density of much of rural Egypt. Thousands of people lived in back streets with houses set so close together they blocked out the sunlight. These passageways converged on a dirt road that ran beside a milky-white canal, which apparently served as the local garbage dump. Only an occasional buffalo, snorting and galumphing along as if late for an appointment, told me that I was in the countryside. Upper Egypt, *al-Saeed*.

Rania's husband, Yasser, waited at the entrance to the alley for my translator, Magda, and me. He was handsome in a generic way—dark eyes, neat mustache—and wore a gray tracksuit and flip-flops. I was surprised to see him. Rania had told me that they weren't on speaking terms, but I guessed that they had reconciled. He led us up the road to where Rania stood in front of their home, looking regal in a teal *gallabiyya* trimmed in cream and gold, her hair wound in a tight black *hijab*. "I have been waiting for you," she said.

Magda and I sat on a couch in the front room like local dignitaries, and people came in and out of the house to meet us. Yasser's mother kissed me on both cheeks; his sister, a recent college graduate, told us she was looking for work in mass communications. Zahraa and Asmaa, two supervisors who worked with Rania in the factory, were also visiting. A few neighbors appeared and stood in a mute row inside the door, sneaking occasional glances at me like students awaiting punishment. A woman wearing a black *niqab* slipped into the room and sat down next to me. No one introduced her.

Rania and her fellow supervisors went into the kitchen to finish preparing dinner, leaving us alone with the mystery woman.

"Do you know who this is?" I asked Magda in English, under my breath.

She didn't.

"Should we talk to her?"

I turned. "What's your name, and are you from this village?" I asked the woman in Arabic.

"I'm Fatima, from the factory," she answered.

At that moment, Rania came back into the room. "Don't you know Fatima, who has the highest-producing line in the factory?" she asked me.

Everyone broke into high-pitched laughter. Magda turned to me. "She's from the Delta factory, and you didn't recognize her!"

How could I recognize her? Here's a woman who's draped head to toe in an opaque polyester fabric, with only two square inches of skin around her eyes visible. Almost everything that made her unique was hidden under her billowing black garment. How could anyone know that this was *Fatima, who has the highest-producing line in the factory?* But the *niqab* is one of those elements of Egyptian life that ordinary people rarely talk about (though politicians and academics elsewhere have ongoing debates about whether the full-face covering symbolizes subjugation, liberation, or something in between). For me, the *niqab* completely threw off the rhythm of ordinary human interactions, but just as striking was how naturally the other women regarded it.

Yasser didn't join us for dinner. Magda and I ate with Rania, her friends from the factory, and Rania's son and daughter. After the other women left, I asked Rania to explain things I had observed at her work—production targets, efficiency rates. The factory felt very far away.

Her children crowded next to her on the couch. Dina was nine, with big dark eyes and her mother's rounded cheeks. Kareem, a handsome twelve-year-old with dark bangs plastered across his forehead, would occasionally look at me and start laughing for no apparent reason. "He's never seen a foreigner before," Rania said.

I asked her what her hopes for the children were.

"I want her to be a doctor and him to be a police officer. I want them to be good and not suffer as I did."

We cracked sunflower seeds and sat in silence.

Suddenly Rania said in a low voice: "My husband took a second wife." She had mentioned this the first time we met but hadn't spoken of it since.

"How is that for you?" I asked her, just as quietly.

A quick shake of her head. *"Sab."* "Hard." Her face wore a tight, pained expression.

Rania pointed at the ceiling. "She lives upstairs. She's sitting in the next room with his mother and father."

The second wife's name was Asmaa. Yasser had married her a year ago, while Rania was staying at her father's house. He didn't even tell her about his new wife; she found out by chance, on a visit back to the village. Rania later returned home to live, primarily for the sake of her children, and discovered that Yasser and Asmaa had claimed all her wedding furniture while she was gone. The couple now occupied the second floor of the family home, with their newborn son and Yasser's parents. Rania lived downstairs with her son and daughter.

Throughout my visit, I waited for the second wife to come downstairs to meet me. I wondered how Yasser would introduce her, and what I would say, and how Rania would react. But the second wife never appeared, and nobody mentioned her name. As the evening wore on, I understood that she was avoiding us because Rania didn't want her there. It also became clear to me that Rania and Yasser hadn't reconciled at all.

Late that night, the two of them walked us down the alley toward the main road out of town so we could get a taxi. A crowd of about fifty men and boys gathered to stare at me. Finally, Yasser hustled me into a nearby house for safety, and the herd stampeded past.

The owner of the house was a friend of his and a *sheikh*, a man respected for his piety and exemplary behavior. In the dimness, I made out a man past middle age who had a long thin face and a wispy beard. "What religion are you?" he asked me.

"Christian."

No response.

"Is that good?" I prodded him.

"Yes. Christians and Muslims are very close." He seemed cheerful and good-humored, someone who was used to having people listen to him.

He peered at Rania.

"My wife," Yasser said.

"Everyone's saying that you've taken a third American wife," the sheikh replied.

The others in the room laughed. Rania didn't say a word—her face went blank, as if she hadn't heard a thing. I remembered her pained expression when she told me about her husband's second marriage. Over the course of my first long day and evening at Rania's home, this was the only time anyone else had mentioned it. How terrible that it was a joke, made by a man who didn't even know who she was.

In a photograph, Rania sits on Yasser's lap and wears a shimmering orange dress. Her eyes are deeply outlined in kohl, and she looks straight at the camera, as if challenging the viewer to step in and intercede. The expression on her face is fierce and scared at the same time. She doesn't smile.

"That was my wedding day," Rania said, when she saw me looking at the picture. It was tucked into a mirror frame in the bedroom she shares with her children now.

"But you don't look happy," I teased her.

Rania didn't say anything. I remembered, then, that she had told me her father forced her to marry a man she didn't love.

Rania has many photos of that day. Open one of her family photo albums at random, and there she is in the orange dress sitting on Yasser's lap, or posing with members of her extended family. Here are the relatives admiring the wedding jewelry, while Rania looks off in a different direction from everyone else ("I didn't care about that at all," she said). Tucked in the back of the book, there may be a baby photo of her son or daughter—but flip open a new album and the cycle begins again, the relatives, the wedding jewelry, Rania on Yasser's lap and the orange dress and the fierce look on her face. She was fifteen or sixteen then, and she's thirty now. Half of her life has elapsed since these pictures were taken, and yet she can't break free of this day and its continuing power over her.

In Egypt, marriage is widely considered to be a woman's chief purpose in life, and the source of all her fortune and happiness. Egyptian parents begin saving for the event early, the way some American parents start putting away money for college when a baby is born. The buying of china plates and bedsheets for a girl's *gihaz* may take place before she's old enough to understand that these things are intended for her. As she enters her teens, her male relatives begin to police her movements closely. Any hint of impropriety—coming home late, being alone with a man—can damage a family's reputation and hurt the marriage prospects of all its members.

Marrying young remains the ideal. The median age of marriage for women in Egypt is twenty, and nineteen in rural Upper Egypt. Marriage is the only socially acceptable path for young men and women to have sexual relations and become independent adults. Until then, almost all grown children live at home, and single women in particular exist in a twilight of suspended animation: *bored and suffocated, sitting at home, doing nothing.* In the factory world, Riham told me, she was shocked by the number of women who were married by their midteens.

"Their fathers are scared to take responsibility for the girl," Riham said. "They want to get rid of her. It's dangerous if she's single and she's at home. And it's not because he doesn't trust the girl," she continued. "It's because he doesn't trust the men—his neighbors and his family! Because they're living in a big house, all of them in the same room and touching, so he's scared for her. There's no privacy at all, and this causes problems. Even in our religion, God warned us about living this style of life. Because you're in front of him all the time—he's your sister's husband, but you're always in front of him at home. This is not right."

The preoccupation with safeguarding female virtue feels disconnected from any love for the actual female. Rania grew up with her mother and grandmother; her parents divorced when she was a baby, and her father went to work in Iraq. When she was twelve, her grandmother died and her mother remarried, and Rania's home life came to an end. According to Egyptian law, divorced women lose custody of their children if they remarry, the rationale being that a new husband can't resist the temptation of living in close quarters with his stepdaughter (grown men, like toddlers, apparently can't be expected to exercise self-control). Rania shuttled between the homes of several uncles. During her middle school years, they made her work in their construction materials warehouse rather than attend classes. "They wanted to crush me," Rania said.

After she moved away, Rania visited her mother often, and she got along well with her stepfather. But there was no question of returning home. "I only told my mom this one time, 'I want to come live with you,'" Rania said. "My mother cried hard. I never brought it up again."

She later moved in with her father, who had returned from Iraq and remarried. With his support, she enrolled in a trade school to get her *diplome*, but she clashed often with her stepmother and didn't feel comfortable living there either. When Rania fell in love with a young man from her mother's village, her father opposed the match and insisted she marry Yasser instead. It was out of spite, Rania believed, to show her that he was in charge.

"Yasser came and proposed, twice," she told me. "The first time, I refused. When Yasser came again, my father obliged me to accept him."

"How did he oblige you?" I asked her.

"Yasser convinced my father. When the father is convinced, that's it. You can't say anything."

Rania's mother didn't attend the wedding. Once again, local custom intervened—a divorcée, the villagers said, shouldn't enter the home of her ex-husband, his brothers, or anyone in his family, even on the day of her child's wedding.

I've studied Rania's wedding photo, trying to read the expression on her face. She was about to marry a man she didn't love, and her mother couldn't be there to support her. She was the only person who loved Rania unconditionally, but at all the important junctures in Rania's life—where she would live after her parents' divorce, whether she would go to school, or whom she should marry—her mother had been absent. The men of the family had made these decisions, and Rania's happiness was not their main concern.

When she was young, she told me, she dreamed of being a police officer or a doctor one day. Over more than a year that I visited Rania at home, I saw a lot of her personality in her daughter. Dina was nine, whip-smart and strong-willed. When I gave her and her older brother a set of Legos, they quickly figured out how to put the pieces together. Dina commandeered the instructions and moved quickly through the steps, ordering Kareem to locate this piece or that and grabbing it from his hand when he found it. Unlike her shyer brother, Dina asked me questions and remembered the things I told her, like the names of my daughters and the fact that we were building a house in America.

On one of my visits, I came with a new translator, Mai, who was a literature professor at a university. When Mai introduced herself as a teacher, Dina asked, "Are you the teacher for Ariel and Natasha?" I could see she was trying to fit the pieces of my life together. "Do you have a maid to cook and clean for you?" she inquired on another occasion. She always wanted to see pictures of my daughters and asked whether our house in America was finished.

"Come and see it," I urged Dina and her mother once.

"But you'll have to pay for the tickets," Rania said, allowing herself a small smile.

"That's fine."

"Maybe we'll go and we won't come back."

When I asked Rania what she envisioned for Dina, I was struck that she said the same thing she had once wished for herself: *I want her to be a doctor.* That was a dream, like going to America, that no one remotely expected to come true. In a few years, Dina would have to put away childish things and start preparing herself for marriage.

IN THE EARLY morning while it's still dark and the call to *fajr* prayer has yet to sound, Rania awakes and puts the kettle on. When the water boils she washes up and gets dressed, then eats a breakfast of bread and jam. She takes her time applying makeup—foundation, blush, heavy kohl around the eyes, blue eye shadow, and red lipstick—and winds a *hijab* tightly around her head, inserting pins at precisely calibrated intervals. She puts on a black parka and touches up the fingernails of one hand with cherry-red polish, waving it briefly in the air to dry.

"Ready?"

As we leave by the side door, I notice that she has laid out the children's clothes and backpacks for school. A buffalo who lives several doors down pokes his head out, as if to check the weather for his morning commute. The village is dreamy and gauzy at first light, and the air smells fresh. Even the plastic bags floating in the canal look beautiful.

Rania stops at a corner shop to buy snacks. She's at a crossroads, with villagers coming at her from all directions. An old man herds his sheep, and young men in *gallabiyyas* walk by singly or in pairs. Women shuffle past, wearing loose *abayas* and plastic slippers. Rania looks sharp against the backdrop of the village, her outlines clearly defined. She's the only person in sight wearing Western-style clothing, and certainly the only woman with a fresh manicure and a black handbag.

The company shuttle leaves at 6:27 A.M.—*The bus won't wait for you*—and fills with passengers as it moves along the agricultural road. You can spot the Delta workers from a long way off. They stand at the side of the road in small knots, apart from their neighbors. They're wearing vivid-colored dresses and full makeup, and even their posture is different: Erect and alert, they board the bus and head to work, leaving the village behind.

These images are deceiving, though. A woman may go out into the world, find work, earn money, and develop skills she never imagined that she would have. But her status at home may not change at all, since her family doesn't value those things. Study after study of Egyptian women has shown that working outside the home doesn't bring them more power within it. Their society regards female labor as an act of desperation, not emancipation. "It's considered a luxury to be a stay-at-home mother or housewife," Rania Salem, an assistant professor of sociology at the University of Toronto, told me. "That is the cultural ideal."

In her studies in rural Minya and elsewhere, Salem found that wives who worked didn't enjoy more equitable marriages or greater influence at home. Authority still derives from traditional sources. For single women, the best guarantee of being listened to by her husband is to bring a large *gihaz* to the marriage. For wives, it's giving birth to a son.

When I reported among female factory workers in South China, I found that their work experience in the city overturned the village hierarchy that placed them at the bottom. After a young woman went out to work, she had to fend off contradictory instructions from her parents: *Don't switch jobs. Send more money. Get married. Come back.* The clamor of poor advice usually stopped once she started wiring money home. She might learn new skills, jump to a better job, or start a business; at home she began to voice her opinion about whether her father should buy a motorcycle or her younger sister stay in school. These women still married relatively young, typically by their midtwenties, but they chose their own partners and set up households without input from their parents. They changed, and they *obliged* their parents to accept it.

In other countries and historical eras, industrialization has liberated women from social constraints. For young women in nineteenth-century France, domestic work in the cities provided an opportunity to save money and move up the social ladder. Places as disparate as India, Mexico, and Bangladesh have seen empowerment follow women into the workplace. In Egypt, women's work has had none of these effects. Because the end goal is predetermined—to marry, quit, and become a homemaker—there's neither the time nor the space to imagine a different outcome. If a young woman gets a job so she can buy bedsheets and kitchenware, then working only reinforces the message that her fate lies in domestic life.

In a village called Abu Hinnis outside Minya, I visited a garment factory that combined vocational training with paid work. A hundred thirty young women, all between the ages of sixteen and eighteen, worked here. On the afternoon I went, around fifteen teenage girls were sitting at sewing machines. Their eyes followed me around the room, bursting with curiosity and eagerness.

"Most of the girls are engaged," the owner, Hani Raway Yusef, told me. "Usually they get engaged in the first or second year of high school, and they get married in the third year."

"What happens after they get married?" I asked.

"They just stop working."

The focus on a domestic future can keep a woman childlike and ignorant. In the Delta factory, I met an eighteen-year-old named Noura Ali. She had a soft face with acne-scarred cheeks. An intricate design drawn in henna, probably from a wedding she had recently attended, covered the backs of her hands and reached up her arms like a spiderweb.

"I spend my whole salary on my *gihaz*," she told me, even though she had recently ended an engagement and had no marriage plans. When I asked her what she was buying, she rattled off items like a savvy housewife. She already had china dishes, bedsheets, cups and bowls for the microwave, cooking bowls, and utensils. She still needed a mixer, an iron, carpets, an oven, and a refrigerator.

"I'll keep working until I buy all the things I need," she said.

"How long will that take?"

"One year. And then I'll quit this job."

"Wouldn't you want to continue working, to save more money?"

Her eyes widened. "What for? What am I going to do with all this money?"

The Islamic injunction that men should provide for their families, while women's money is their own, tends to diminish the work that women do. Even when a woman contributes to the household finances, she and everyone around her may pretend that's not the case. "Working in the factory, it doesn't feed you," a young man in a village outside Minya said about his sister's employment, which he opposed. Wives claim not to care about the money they make, or they say they spend their wages on clothes or things for the children or the kitchen, as if these are frivolous items of no importance. In fact, a national survey found an astonishing one out of every three employed women earns the same or more than her husband. Especially in economically depressed rural areas where men often work sporadically, or not at all, it's clear that women's work matters more than anyone would admit.

Women erase themselves instinctively, but sometimes the process is deliberate. In Riham's factory, I met a woman whom I'll call Dina. She was in her thirties, with a pale, pretty face. She had worked in garment factories on and off since her late teens and was here now because her husband's job didn't bring a steady income. "A lot of men don't want their wives to go out," she explained, with a quiet smile. "My husband and I are very supportive of each other."

About a month later, I was back in the factory and happened to speak with Dina again. "The last time we talked," she said, "I told you that I was working to help my husband. When I went home that night and told him about the interview, he said: 'No! You're working because you want to, not because I need your support.' So I would like to ask you"—that gentle smile again—"to please remove that line. I don't want to make my husband cross and angry."

IN *Between Marriage and the Market*, an ethnography of working-class Cairo in the 1980s and early 1990s, the anthropologist Homa Hoodfar writes that women have pragmatic reasons to embrace the traditional marriage model that requires husbands to provide for them. The country's economic deterioration and the contraction of the bureaucracy have left women with few attractive job prospects. Tasks like cooking and laundry—which were once the painstaking work of many hours—have been simplified by modern appliances, which has had the perverse result of devaluing domestic labor and making wives more financially dependent on their husbands. Women jealously guarded this domain, Hoodfar observed, and ridiculed men who tried to help them with the housework. Playing up their roles as wives and mothers is their best option, she concluded, even though the women acknowledged this wasn't what they imagined for themselves.

Far from questioning the basis of the sexual division of labor, women actively participated in reinforcing it by appealing to tradition and Islam. . . . In the face of social change, which had devalued their economic functions in the household, women were desperately trying to protect what opportunities they had.

Some of the women in Hoodfar's study hid their jobs as maids or handywomen from her and pretended to be full-time housewives, which was considered more respectable. Wives sometimes found that their husbands contributed *less* to the family finances after they started working. "To prevent this," Hoodfar wrote, "they adopted strategies such as . . . not revealing the amount of their income, or, as a last resort, leaving the labor market." Women rarely challenged the ideology of female dependency head-on. It made more sense, from their point of view, to manipulate the system to their advantage.

In the 1960s, the Nasser government's policies produced the first generation of career women who enjoyed some financial independence and contributed materially to their own marriages. The decline of his welfare state cut short the social transformation it set in motion. Sadat's presidency, in the 1970s, did enact a law to increase female representation in parliament; it also tried, unsuccessfully, to grant women greater legal protections in the case of divorce. But his Open Door economic program did damage to women in the long run. Because these policies fueled inflation and a demand for consumer goods from abroad, they set a new standard for expensive trousseaux and lavish weddings that Egyptian families have been struggling to meet ever since. Today, women are once again reliant on their parents to negotiate and pay for their marriages, which can cost many times a family's annual income.

Women were prominent in the 2011 revolution that ended the thirty-year rule of Hosni Mubarak. The videotaped plea of an activist named Asmaa Mahfouz, who urged her fellow citizens to join her in protesting the regime, went viral and was credited with bringing thousands of protesters to Tahrir Square in the demonstration's first days. At its height, according to one report, a quarter of the million protesters in the square each day were women. But advancing women's rights was never one of the revolution's stated goals, and the uprising didn't spark a broader discussion about how to correct the gender inequalities in Egyptian society.

The economic crisis that followed the revolution actually hurt women more than men. In the aftermath of the protests, female unemployment jumped to 24 percent, compared with 9 percent for men. And the political instability of that era exaggerated the fear that surrounds women and girls even in the best of times. Husbands urged their wives to quit their jobs, and fathers pulled their daughters out of school. In the face of societal turmoil, people retreated into their homes and did what was expected of them.

In the end, the Arab Spring further eroded women's position in society. For not the first time in Egypt's modern history, a disruptive event—a failed industrial revolution, colonial incursion, political upheaval—pushed people into a defensive posture. Amid so many reversals in policy and changes of regime, there's one entity that can be counted on. The 2011 revolution did nothing to change that most conservative of institutions, the Egyptian family. It just made it stronger.

"THIS IS GOING to sound terrible," Ian Ross said to me one day, "but to me, the girls who are most empowered are the ones who are divorced."

I agreed with him. Divorcées might be the most liberated women in Egypt. They had freed themselves from the belief that a woman's purpose in life was to get married; they were living, breathing proof that her existence need not revolve around a man. Divorced women made up around a third of the workers at Delta—their disproportionate presence, in itself, was evidence of an autonomy that other women lacked.

Over the two and a half years that I reported in Egyptian factories, I encountered only one woman who had a concrete plan to change her life circumstances. Doaa Mohsen, who was twenty-eight, worked as a security guard at Delta. On the day we met, she was wearing an electric-blue dress. She had full round cheeks, cheerful brown eyes, and a strong handshake.

"I was married, but not anymore," she said as soon as she had introduced herself. "Do you have a groom for me?"

"From China, from America, from Egypt?" I teased her.

"Absolutely not from Egypt!"

While she was still in college, she explained, she had married a man who was her mother's cousin. The couple had two daughters, but their relations deteriorated. Doaa's husband sometimes disappeared for months at a time; at home, he would stand by while his mother or sisters bullied her. Yet he wouldn't file for divorce, Doaa said, because he didn't want to pay alimony and child support. Finally, she divorced him by *khul*—but at a high cost. She forfeited her rights to the part of the dower her husband had not paid yet, and to any future maintenance. In addition, she relinquished property that legally belonged to her, including furniture, kitchen appliances, and the gold jewelry he had given her when they married.

She also left her children. By law, Egyptian mothers get custody of their children in a divorce and fathers are required to pay child support, but the courts are often too weak to enforce these provisions. Doaa moved back in with her parents, but they didn't have the space or the money to take in her kids as well. Unless she ceded custody of her daughters to her husband, she figured that he wouldn't contribute anything toward their upkeep.

The day after Doaa filed for divorce, she got a job at a factory and enrolled in a continuing education program at the University of Minya to get her college diploma. She worked days and attended class on weekends, studying for a degree in social services. After graduation, she planned to do social work or to pursue her Ph.D. and then teach.

She had no intention of getting married again. "I've tried the single life and the married life, and I prefer the single life," she told me. "I believe that a woman without a man can do anything she wants."

Doaa and Rania, the two women in the Delta factory I got to know best, were like two halves of the same insoluble puzzle. Each was a strong-willed woman trapped in a bad marriage, but their stories had played out in reverse. Doaa had regained her freedom and self-respect, but at the cost of losing her children. Rania got to watch her son and daughter grow up but was humiliated every day by her husband living with another wife in full view of her children, her family, and her neighbors. Whenever I spent time with Rania at her home, I found myself wondering why she didn't get divorced—until I met Doaa, a woman who had done just that. Which choice would I have made?

The common thread in their stories was a society that punishes women who try to find happiness for themselves. She can remain with a man she doesn't love. Or she can risk losing her property and her security, and sometimes her reputation and her children as well, if she wants something else in life. Rania had grown up motherless because of this impossible choice. Now Doaa's children would too, in a cycle of loss endlessly repeating.

The girls were seven and six. Doaa hadn't seen them in two years, but she was working with them in mind. She hoped that the decisions she was making now—to study for her degree, to live independently without a husband—would shape her daughters into women who would one day stand up for themselves.

"When my daughters grow up and ask about me," she told me, "I want them to know what I've done, so they can be proud of me."

5

MAIDEN VOYAGE

YOUNG PEOPLE FLITTED IN AND out of Riham's factory, their inner turmoil all but stamped on their foreheads. A new arrival named Mohamed
complained that everyone listened to American-influenced pop songs
while they worked instead of the Quran. "What do they want, to turn
this place into a discotheque?" he asked Riham. He lasted two weeks.

A sixteen-year-old showed up asking strangely specific questions.
*What's the price of gold? How many bedsheets do you need when you get en-
gaged?* She left after a month to get married—annoying Riham, who
had correctly predicted the girl would stay just long enough to earn
money for her engagement.

"She thinks marriage is fun," Riham told me. "She gets to shop at the
market and buy nice things and be a lady." She shrugged. "After three
years, she'll come back divorced. That's fine."

At heart Riham was an optimist, persisting in tasks that might drive
an ordinary person to despair. She challenged housewives with several
young children, or teenage girls in their first jobs, to produce work to a

high standard in a society that didn't ask that of them. She dared to compete with China, where workers on massive factory floors sewed apparel to fanatically precise standards. She asked her employees to take pride in their work.

"Look at what he's doing," she said to me one morning. One of the sewers was standing up and putting a protective cover on his Singer machine.

"He's finished his work and he's putting a cover on the machine, even though I didn't tell him to do this," Riham said. "He cares for the machine—he feels a connection to it. That's what I want to build."

When I used to speak to workers in Chinese factories, I was struck at how disconnected they were from the things they made. Running shoe uppers, liquid crystal displays, or mobile phone parts: These were just interchangeable bits and pieces in a vast, impersonal manufacturing machine. Riham's workers didn't see their products like that.

"When you're sitting at a machine, you're creating something bigger," a teenage intern named Nourhan told me, in her second week on the job.

A woman in her forties named Elham, who had worked in export zones for more than two decades, said she loved sewing on the assembly line. "When the factory is working well and I see the finished product, it's something as smooth and beautiful as playing the piano," she told me.

The wages that Riham paid—between $120 and $160 a month for an ordinary sewer—weren't especially high for the industry. But she offered her staff set hours, limited overtime, and a salary that wasn't whittled away by all kinds of fees and deductions. In the factory world, one day off a week is standard, but Riham observed two-day weekends. She wanted her employees to spend time with their families and remember what they were working for.

"I don't call my workers names, I don't cut from their salaries, and I have fixed times," she said. "If a worker wants a larger amount of money, she'll fit in somewhere else. If she wants to be treated like a human being, she'll be happy here."

Striking a balance between treating workers fairly and running a viable business wasn't easy, and the women didn't necessarily appreciate the effort. During the late spring of 2015, in the middle of handling a large export order, Riham lost two of her most experienced sewers. An employee named Maha wanted to take two days off to bake biscuits before a holiday. Riham told her to wait a week until they had shipped out the order, but Maha refused and left.

The departure of Elham, the woman who had compared assembly line work to playing the piano, was also unhappy. One day, Riham told me, Elham was tired and wanted to take a nap next to her machine over her lunch break. Riham wouldn't allow it, and the woman quit on the spot.

When she returned a few days later to collect her pay, Elham complained about how Riham had treated her. "In our old factory, we used to eat and drink tea next to the machine, but you said we can't do that," she said. "We listened to you, but now you say that we can't sleep next to the machine either."

"You're a grown-up," Riham replied. "If you don't like the system, you should come tell me, finish the work that's in your hands, and then leave. But leaving like this isn't appropriate. If you ever think about coming back here to work, don't."

After this, Riham put more faith in developing her younger employees, like the interns she had just brought into the factory. If she caught them early, she believed, she could teach these young women to value loyalty, hard work, and the community she had built. "The best workers are the ones you train," Riham told me. "The money you spend training them is more than compensated for by the length of time they stay and work for you. They're trained here, they make friends here, so they feel like this is family."

———

THE MOST PROMISING employee in the factory was a young woman named Sara Adel. She was twenty and looked as if she belonged on a college campus somewhere—wide smile, long hair in a loose ponytail— but the sharp scissors that hung from a string around her neck warned that she meant business. Sara was sitting at a table on the far end of the production floor when I met her that spring. Her job was to trim loose threads from shirts before they were packed for shipment.

"I like the work," she told me. "I've learned how to be productive." She had a *diplome* in computer technology. Her father worked in the factory too, as a sewer on the Singer machine.

Her greatest regret, she said, was that she hadn't continued her education.

"Why didn't you?"

"Because of my fiancé." He worked as a minibus driver in Cairo. After the wedding, Sara would quit her job and join him there. It would be impossible, she explained, for her to juggle both work and family obligations once she was married.

I asked Sara if this was her choice or her fiancé's.

"It's my decision." She smiled. "I would beat him up if he prevented me from working."

When I visited the factory a month later, Riham had begun to train Sara in quality control. Her new job was to spot flaws in the finished garments, then trace them back to the workers responsible and direct them to correct their mistakes. Soon afterward, Sara was promoted again, to the position of "lineman," in which she was in charge of maintaining the flow of production on the assembly line. When Riham had to attend a three-day management conference in Alexandria, she deputized Sara to oversee the operation in her absence. When Riham returned and told her what she had learned, Sara asked to borrow her notes so she could study them too.

I was surprised that Riham was becoming so dependent on Sara. Wasn't she leaving soon to get married? "The turnover in this industry is very high," Riham explained. "She has been here two years. If she stays another two years, that would be fine."

Every morning now, Riham set the day's production schedule—which pieces needed to be sewn, in what order, and by whom—and Sara kept track of each person's output and amended the plan as needed. She learned how to motivate employees who were older than she was, including her own father.

"The point is, the worker needs to feel that her work is important," she told me. "And why she needs to move from one place to another, to help the rest of the line to move forward.

"At other factories," she continued, "people just give orders. But here, things are different. We need to feel that we're all a team, that we're all important, and everything we do is important," she said, unconsciously echoing what Riham had told the interns earlier.

I asked how she liked her new job.

"I've benefited a lot from this role—I can see how all the stages of production work," Sara said. "Coming into the production hall, sitting with all the workers and seeing how they work, is a big adventure."

"Does this change how you see your future?"

"Of course I've changed. My aim has changed. Now I feel that I need to develop and do things at a higher level."

"What about your plan to get married?"

"Getting married will definitely affect my plan," Sara said, and she seemed to deflate a little before my eyes. "If I weren't engaged, I would have gone on to do further studies in production. But now that I'm engaged, I can't do it."

I asked her if she might adjust her plans. Wouldn't it be possible to continue working after marriage?

She shook her head. "I know my abilities. I won't be able to do both. I'm annoyed, but I don't know what to do about it."

Sara would get married, quit her job, and move to Cairo. I asked her about her plans half a dozen times, and the answer was always the same.

THE CAPABLE YOUNG women who worked in Riham's factory took for granted that maintaining a job and a household after marriage would be impossible. *I know my abilities,* Sara had said. *I won't be able to do both.* An employee named Rahma used almost identical language: *I won't be able to manage both the house and work.*

Even in their own families, there was evidence that that wasn't necessarily true. Rahma's mother had worked both before and after marriage and was now employed full time as a sewer at the El-Nasr Clothing and Textiles Company, one of the country's largest garment factories. Sara's mother was a college graduate who had operated her own nursery school for many years. She sold the business to raise four children but returned to the workforce later, after Sara's older brother died. "I noticed that when she went back to work after Ahmed's death, she was psychologically depressed," Sara told me. "Work was something that helped her."

Women have been working in Alexandria's garment sector for seventy years. Riham's family firm started employing them in 1954, when it set up its sewing side of the business. "Since the start of this industry, ninety percent of the workers have been women," her father, Galal, told me. "That was the general atmosphere."

Well-to-do couples sometimes ran a business together and shared in the design, manufacturing, and selling of clothes. In 1967, a Greek Egyptian woman named Flora opened the Bettina Boutique on Sherif Pasha Street, which was then the most fashionable avenue in Alexandria. Her husband owned a factory that made a smooth woven fabric known as tricot, and Flora designed women's clothes for the cosmopolitan set.

She's in her seventies now, still glamorous with her wavy blond hair and shapely Sophia Loren–style sunglasses. "I had a loyal clientele, many of them foreigners," she told me. "They were Jews, Italians, Maltese, English, Greeks. Alexandria used to be something different.

"I was very famous," she recalled. "Everyone knew me as Madame Bettina."

Among some well-off families, it was considered acceptable for a woman to run her own business, and these pioneers passed on what they learned to their daughters' generation. When Riham started working after college, she became acquainted through her family network with an older production engineer, who trained her to spot and fix mistakes on assembly lines. "She taught me almost everything I know," Riham told me. A friend's mother, who ran her family's pajama business on her own after her husband died, showed Riham how to cut fabric and took her to trade shows. The female co-founder of another firm supplied Riham with materials and embroidery free of charge.

But women from the working class, with no family business to enter, often had to challenge their relatives head-on if they wanted to work. In a 1981 study of female employees at two factories outside Cairo, the sociologist Barbara Ibrahim found that the decision to get a job initially caused conflict within families. Wives fought with husbands; daughters challenged their fathers. One of the women explained to Ibrahim how she hid her employment from her social circle in order to protect her reputation:

> We told the neighbors that I was going to school and so I had to carry some books with me each day. . . . In those first years the buses drove us right to the entrance of the production rooms. We ran inside so that no man would see us and begin talking about us. But among ourselves, we knew that to work was not shameful.

It was notable, though, how quickly these attitudes changed. Half of the women who took up factory work in the late 1950s or early 1960s, Ibrahim wrote, had families that strongly opposed the move; by the mid-1970s, only 14 percent did. Parents started to see a daughter's employment as a net gain. It brought income to the family and also expanded a young woman's social network and marriage prospects. Ibrahim concluded, "The message ... seems to be that the positive benefits of female employment now outweigh the once-salient social costs."

But just as women's employment was on the verge of becoming entrenched, it went in the other direction. Egyptian society turned conservative in the 1980s, helped by the spread of fundamentalist ideas from the Gulf. At the same time, the public sector stagnated, and prestigious positions at state enterprises became rare. Women continued to work in the civil service, but the jobs brought lower status and less money than they once had.

Working women had gained society's respect in a single generation, and now they lost it again. In her study of working-class Cairo, the anthropologist Homa Hoodfar found that men who married in the 1970s hadn't opposed their wives' being employed. But their counterparts in the 1990s did—in their eyes, the salary that came with a wife's job no longer compensated for her absence from home. All the college-educated women in the neighborhood, Hoodfar observed, worked for a living. Their daughters all said they would prefer to stay home.

In Alexandria, the Bettina Boutique closed in 2000. "The culture changed, and more women started to be veiled," Flora told me. "I couldn't make veils or Islamic dresses. It's not my work—I don't like it. Every age has its own flavor. If you don't understand it, you can't do this business."

By then, most of her foreign clientele had moved away. Sherif Street was no longer fashionable, and the city that was once known as the Bride of the Mediterranean was slipping into obscurity. In the intervening years, Alexandria has continued to suffer from government mismanagement and poor-quality construction, and it has also become a center of religious conservatism. From the Corniche, you can still take in the wide, thrilling arc of the Mediterranean. But the buildings that line the waterfront are decrepit, with peeling façades and gaping windows—

gloomy sentinels of their own decline. You can walk down to the long sandy beach and swim in the blue-green waters, but almost nobody does. It's considered shocking for a woman to wear a bathing suit in public.

"Downtown used to be a very stylish area, with lots of Greeks and Italians," Flora's daughter Nadia told me. She's tall and striking like her mother, with the same air of imperious chic. "But it changed. Now people are wearing flip-flops there."

I spent an afternoon talking to mother and daughter in a small home furnishings shop that Nadia owns. The women smoked Marlboro Reds and finished each other's sentences.

Of course, we prefer the sixties and the seventies. Everyone was so open then.

The country was more beautiful.

If you watch the old movies, you can see how beautiful our country was. Like Paris.

Egypt had gone backward. The two women weren't really sure why or how it happened, but they accepted it as the inevitable order of things. "If you ask anyone in any country, they'll always say that they prefer the past," Nadia said. "It's natural."

I wanted to tell them it wasn't true. In some places in the world, things move forward and people's lives get better. I have rarely met anyone in China, for instance, even among those in their sixties or seventies, who expressed a desire to go back to the way things were. But I didn't say anything to Flora and Nadia. It would have been too sad, and they probably wouldn't have believed me.

A FEW WEEKS after the interns joined the factory, Riham invited a college friend, a life coach named Radwa El-Sheikh, to come speak to them. Riham wanted her summer hires to learn more than how to trim threads or sew a straight seam. In her vision for a better society, teenage girls should think about what they wanted from life and be brave enough to communicate those ideas to other people. If their families and teachers were incapable of instilling such values, Riham would do it in their place.

"I studied something called coaching, which means that if you're in one place and you don't know how to get somewhere else, I'll teach you," Radwa told the interns in the factory's conference room one morning in June 2015. She was small, with delicate features, but everything about her projected assertiveness—her feet planted firmly apart, her rapid speech, her neon silicone bracelets printed with inspirational words: *Share. Laugh. Love. Leadership.*

"I want you to ask whatever you want to ask. Stop me, ask me to repeat myself, tell me you don't understand. I'm giving you permission. Don't you always want to talk?" On a large sheet of paper she had taped to the wall, she wrote: *No one stays silent.*

After some hesitation, the members of the group started to speak. They were between the ages of thirteen and fifteen—still children, and yet I felt as if they were living through the final phase of an experiment designed to teach young women how to suppress themselves.

I don't know myself. I can't see my role or my purpose. At home I have no opinion—I do what they want me to do.

Why does a person want to please other people more than to please herself?

Sometimes when I talk a lot, people misunderstand me, so I decide not to speak at all.

I please people. I please my sister, I please my friend.

I told her I'm free. And she said: "Don't say that—it's a very bad word! It means you don't care about the people around you."

A thirteen-year-old named Samar, who had told me that she wanted to be a pediatrician, spoke up. "Sometimes my mom tells me, 'If you speak too much, you annoy the people in front of you.' Sometimes I say the wrong word."

"What do you mean, the wrong word?" Radwa prompted her.

"Something that annoys the person in front of me. So my mom tells me, 'Don't talk,' and that really annoys me."

"So what's the solution?" Radwa asked. "Your mom's solution is not to speak at all."

"Yes. That's not a solution, and it makes me really angry."

Rehab, who was fourteen and came from the Upper Egyptian city of Qena, said that her father had arranged her engagement to a cousin when she was eleven. She didn't like her chosen fiancé—"I stayed with him for three months and I hated him" were her words—but Rehab's older brother insisted on the match. Their father was in poor health, he warned her, and might have a heart attack if she went against his wishes.

Rehab stopped eating intermittently as a form of protest. Over a few months, she fainted several times and checked in and out of the hospital. One day, her father asked her why she was so tired. She told him she hated her cousin and didn't want to marry him, and her father called it off.

"I'm free, *al-hamdulillah*," Rehab said.

Rebellions like hers were rare, though—mostly the girls internalized the values their parents taught them. When Radwa asked them to list the personality traits in their friends that they most admired, they described someone with perfect manners who never upset anyone. Their ideal, to my eyes, was a human being whose inner life had been squeezed out of her, like a sponge.

I like that she is polite.

What do you mean by polite?

She doesn't raise her voice in the street. She doesn't shout at her mom. She looks polite—her manners are polite.

Her manners are very respectful.

What do you mean by respectful?

She doesn't raise her voice.

Is it really bad if we raise our voices?

Yes, against older people.

What if that older person is wrong?

God will judge him.

I was struck at how different these girls were from teenagers you might meet elsewhere, and later I asked Radwa about my impression. "At fifteen, they would start to question social norms," she said, about young people in the United States or Europe. "Here, they're not questioning social norms at all. They're just accepting it, and judging whoever is not."

She continued, "When we ask them to describe their best friend, they say: 'She's well-behaved, she dresses properly, she doesn't raise her voice.' This isn't the same as 'I have fun with her, she understands me.' The lack of awareness is very striking." The pressure to conform to the family's expectations was strong, and possibly growing stronger, she believed. She had counseled people in their twenties who broke off relationships in order to marry the person their parents wanted.

I asked Radwa what she thought would happen to these girls. Would they one day challenge social norms if they had to, or just go along with what was expected of them?

"There are three here—Samar, Rehab, and Nourhan—they are strong. The others will resist in their own way. Habiba will convince herself that this is what she wants. And Noura is convinced that she doesn't have the right to want." Radwa continued, "Definitely four hours is not enough. The reason I wanted to come and talk to them is this: I want them to know that there's something else in life. So at least they know."

EDUCATION SHOULD BE one way to empower young women. Egypt has built thousands of schools over the past few decades, especially in rural areas, and the country has dramatically reduced a gender gap in enrollment. Ninety-one percent of Egyptian children now complete elementary school, and girls graduate in higher numbers than boys.

By any measure of actual learning, though, the system is in terrible shape. Rapid population growth and chronic underfunding have pushed educational facilities to the breaking point. One out of four school buildings has been deemed unfit by the government, which includes structures that lack working toilets, windows, or doors, or those on the verge of collapse. Students may crowd fifty or sixty to a classroom and attend school in shifts, so that a typical day lasts only a few hours. Only one-third of middle schools in Egypt operate on a full-day schedule, according to a recent study by a Cairo University professor; the most ill-equipped institutions, the report found, "encouraged families not to send their children and to keep them at home." Once a model for the Arab region, the Egyptian educational system is now one of the worst in the world. It was recently ranked 130th out of 137 nations by the World Economic Forum.

Rather than invest time and money to fix the public school system, the government has allowed an informal for-profit sector to develop in parallel. Egyptian families spend more than almost any others in the world on private tutoring—between 20 and 30 percent of household income, according to one survey—often just to ensure that their kids pass from one grade to the next. Many teachers double as private tutors to supplement their income, frequently instructing the same students in the same course materials they're supposed to cover in their regular classes. It's common for an instructor to pass only those students who are paying her and to fail everyone else, and several interns in Riham's factory described this reality in matter-of-fact terms. An eighth-grader named Habiba told me that she had flunked math the previous year because she hadn't enrolled in her teacher's tutoring session for that subject. All of her classmates in the same situation also failed.

"How did you do in your other classes?" I asked her.

"I used to take private lessons with all the other teachers, so I passed."

"So that's the key factor?"

"Yes. It's a must."

If education, as the American reformer Horace Mann said, "is a great equalizer of the conditions of men," the Egyptian model only reinforces the inequalities.

In the early 1990s, an anthropologist named Hania Sholkamy studied child-raising practices in an Upper Egyptian village. On a return visit ten years later, she discovered that not a single child in the community had benefited from school as a path to social mobility:

> **The views expressed by children show school as an experience that frustrates many girls and which intimates to them a sense of failure and futility. None of the twenty-five children that I originally worked with have gone on to a path different from the one to which they were destined. None of them have had a door opened by school.**

The promise of education plays out in the lives of lower-class Egyptians, particularly young women, like a cynical con game. In the 1960s, the Nasser regime built a national network of technical high schools as part of its industrialization program. Graduates were assigned jobs in the public sector, and millions of young men and women gained entry into the middle class. But their numbers soon swamped the system. The bureaucracy became overstaffed, and the quality of education deteriorated; finally, in the 1980s, the government phased out the jobs guarantee.

Yet women from poor backgrounds continue to stream into these institutions to get their *diplome*, even though the reason the schools were created no longer exists. One study, shockingly, showed that getting a *diplome* confers no economic advantage over remaining illiterate.

"These are the women who are unemployed at very high rates—fifty, sixty, seventy percent," Ragui Assaad of the University of Minnesota told me. "I call them trapped. They're in village settings where there are very few jobs to be had, but they cannot go to where the jobs are."

He continued, "They can still educate their kids, they're better mothers, and they have later marriages. But they're a trapped workforce."

Despite these failings, the government has made no effort to revamp the system or close the schools. A study by a political scientist named Moushira Elgeziri concluded:

Technical education is offered, not for educational or professional reasons, but rather on social and political grounds—to ease the burden on higher education and as a safety net to ensure at the same time that those who have been deprived of entry into university are not out on the streets.

When I reported among Chinese factory workers, I found that most of them had emerged from a similar network of vocational high schools. In China, as in Egypt, the system has been criticized for providing poor-quality education to a rural underclass. Yet once these women started working, they quickly figured out the skills they needed to get ahead, and the country's nine-year compulsory education system had given them solid literacy and numeracy skills to build on. Many of the workers enrolled in commercial schools to study English, or computer technology, or the basics of mold design—knowledge that would bring them higher salaries in direct relation to the skills they acquired.

But if the pursuit of self-improvement through study feels like an evangelical calling for so many Chinese, it's not nearly so widespread in Egypt. Parents send their sons to school to prepare them for the labor market, but education for daughters is a social marker—a sign, like polite manners, that a young woman has been raised well and will make a good wife and mother. In her research in Upper Egypt, Sholkamy noticed that wealthier families kept their daughters in school longer as a way to reflect their social status:

> Kahareb has failed her [middle] school final year for the last
> three years, but her parents keep her in school anyway. . . . Kaha-
> reb's father works for police intelligence and has a large land
> holding. His connections and his position of power brings him
> much income and status. He is adamant that Kahareb should
> stay in school until she passes, then he will keep her at home.

Even for women who work, learning can feel unmoored from any
purpose or sense of satisfaction. In the maintenance shop of the Delta
Textile Factory, I met a nineteen-year-old named Yasmin Ashraf Abu
El-Magd, who monitored the supply of sewing machine needles. She
had a technical high school diploma in art and was studying calligraphy
at a government institute in her spare time. When I saw her again a
month later, she was planning to enroll in a computer science program
next.

"I want to have many certificates," Yasmin told me. "I had a diploma
in arts, now calligraphy, next computer science. It would be good for my
CV and my future."

She studied computers for a year but dropped out—"It's quite expensive, and I'm not very interested in it"—and wavered between going
back to it, resuming her art studies, or beginning an unrelated five-year
course in engineering. Yasmin was a troubling but typical case of what
sociologists call "diploma disease," which can be traced, like so much of
the pathology in the Egyptian system, to the failed promises of the
Nasser era. His jobs program had guaranteed work to anyone with a
high school or college diploma. Even after the policy was abandoned, it
left behind a labor market oriented toward rewarding credentials rather
than skills or productivity. It's a major reason that the quality of the
workforce is so poor.

Over the past few decades, the government has made progress en-
rolling girls in school. I met women in their thirties and older who had
never learned to read and write because their parents didn't see the point

of educating females. Those sentiments are rarer inside Egyptian families these days. Now it's often the young woman herself who decides to drop out because she sees education as a waste of time. Rehab, the young woman who had starved herself to get out of an unwanted marriage, quit school after seventh grade to work in Riham's factory.

"My parents didn't want me to drop out, but I didn't feel I was getting educated," she told me. "I wasn't learning anything." And who was I to tell her otherwise? Everything she said rang true.

THE ONLY WOMAN I met in Riham's factory who didn't seem to be conforming to family expectations at all was Mona, a nineteen-year-old who ironed and inspected finished garments. She was tall and heavyset, and she prefaced almost everything she said with the word *adi*, which means "it's normal."

Adi, *I'd just spend time in the kitchen, tidying everything up, and surfing the internet.*

Adi, *I might stay online for a couple of hours, take a break, and then go back.*

She was dead-set against getting married if it meant giving up her freedom. So, nothing *adi* about that at all.

Mona was from Aswan, in the far south, and she had moved to Alexandria with her family in the eighth grade. She wanted to continue her education, but her former school hadn't issued her the papers that would have allowed her to transfer somewhere else. She took private lessons on her own for a year—again, not *adi*—but she had trouble staying motivated and quit. She stayed home for four or five years, doing nothing.

"What did you do at home during this time?" I asked.

"I was doing nothing," she repeated.

What does it mean to do nothing? Mona described a typical day for me.

I used to stay up until six in the morning, then wake up in the afternoon. During the day, I'd do the laundry and the ironing. In the evening, I'm sitting with my mobile phone in my hand, communicating with friends and surfing the internet. *Adi*, it's normal.

Eventually she started teaching at a nursery school and then found a job in Riham's factory. She began working there while her father was away on business. When he returned and expressed his disapproval, Mona told him that she had already been hired and might as well continue. The feigned-innocence defense—*I'm already doing this, is there a problem?*—was surprisingly effective. In a village near Minya called Tayyiba I met a woman whose husband bought her a sewing machine so she could mend the family's clothes. He objected when she started sewing *abaya*s for other women in the village. "I have this machine," she told him, "so I might as well work." The wonder was that women didn't use such tactics more often. When they insisted on doing things their way, their families often caved in.

Mona and I chatted for fifteen minutes without her once bringing up the subject of marriage. Finally, I asked her point-blank: "Do you want to get married?"

"Frankly, no. I don't want anyone asking me 'Where are you going? When are you coming back? Don't work, don't do this, don't do that.' I don't want anyone giving me orders and controlling me."

A couple of months before, a young man who was the relative of a friend of Mona's had expressed interest in her. Through her friend, Mona relayed her terms: "I want to work. I don't want anyone to control me." That conflicted with her would-be suitor's main condition—that she not have a job—and the negotiation ended before it began.

When Mona related the conversation to her parents later, her mother was upset that she had turned down a marriage prospect so abruptly. "Why? It's not right!"

"It's okay," Mona said. "He's just a man, and he's gone."

"If I'm ever going to marry someone," Mona told me, "he has to let me work and to do the things I want to do."

"Have you ever met a man like that in Egypt?" I asked her.

She bit her lip. "No."

"Do you think there are men like that in Egypt?"

Another silence. "I don't know."

IN THE FALL of that year, Riham's factory saw another new arrival: her brother Mustafa, who took a leave from the family firm to join her. He took charge of the financial and legal aspects of the business, leaving her to focus on day-to-day production.

Both brother and sister had grown up going to the factory—"We would always go in with my father and play with everything," Riham recalled—but they had ended up at opposite ends of the business. Mustafa's specialty was knitting and dyeing fabric, which relied on large, expensive machines that were operated by a few workers. He had no experience and little patience for managing teams of garment sewers, with their infinite capacity for mistakes.

"My brother left his company to join me, but he doesn't see this as very promising," Riham told me. "He told me that we should import ready-made garments from China instead."

The two of them frequently clashed over how she treated her employees. Recently, Riham told me, she had needed twenty-five T-shirts to be embroidered by another factory. A fourteen-year-old employee had sent out the backs of the shirts instead of the fronts, by mistake, and Riham had to absorb the cost of the error. Mustafa wanted to dock part of the girl's pay as punishment.

"You're not severe with them," he lectured Riham. "You need to cut their salary when they make mistakes."

"The girls working here are fifteen and seventeen years old," his sister answered. "They're girls—they're still learning. If their work isn't good, we can train them. Or we can yell at them, and they'll leave."

She was still struggling to find enough workers. "There is a lot of work, but no employees," she told me one morning in October. The interns had helped a lot in the summer, but now they were back in school. Riham had contacted an employment agency and was also looking into applying for outside funding to train her workers.

Later that fall, Mustafa would go to China to attend the Canton Trade Fair. He planned to order a shipping container filled with children's clothes and accessories. If the items sold well, he would scale up the import side of the business. That was his solution to the headaches of Egyptian manufacturing—outsourcing much of the task to the Chinese.

Like Riham, Mustafa loved the factory world. "We have two factories. I built one of them in 1993," he told me. "It's like my own son." But he was more hardheaded than Riham. It was too difficult to find good employees in Egypt, he believed, and too much work to train them from scratch. He also lacked her stomach for risk. He had only taken leave from the family firm rather than quitting it altogether. I couldn't help thinking that Riham had bet her future on the new business; Mustafa joined later, after it was already established.

Riham was undeterred—she continued to train her young workers and correct their mistakes. "I'm going to get workers," she told me. "It will take time. I'm doing this for the next generation."

EVENTS OUTSIDE RIHAM's control solved her worker shortage issue, even as they created new problems. As the year 2015 drew to a close, the global clothing market slowed, and new orders to the factory dried up. Heavy rains around Alexandria caused flooding, which led to power cuts and the temporary shutdown of some manufacturers, including the one that Riham produced for. When I visited her factory on a gray day in November, the workers were moving slowly and mechanically through their tasks, as silent as sleepwalkers. The production floor felt empty now that the interns had gone back to school.

"This year, there are financial problems worldwide," Riham said, as a massive clap of thunder crashed outside. "We've never stopped like this. It's even worse than the chaos after September 11."

She considered her options. The baby quilts and sleep sacks that she designed for the local market did well, but being a small manufacturer was a disadvantage. Even if buyers liked what she made, they preferred to place their orders with larger factories that offered a complete range of infant products. The export market, even more than the domestic one, demanded scale. Manufacturing for an overseas customer required covering the up-front costs of buying the fabric, dyeing it, sewing it into garments, shipping the order across the Atlantic, getting it through customs, and delivering it to the client. Only after the clothes passed inspection there would the manufacturer get paid. The process, from start to finish, took between six and eight months and required an amount of working capital that Riham didn't have.

Mustafa attended the Canton Trade Fair in early November and bought a container's worth of children's goods, as he had planned. "In China, they are running," he told me. "Here, we are sleeping." Importing was more profitable than manufacturing, he said, but he wouldn't know how much more until he got the items through customs.

Riham took advantage of the lull in business to do some housekeeping. She trained a young woman she had recently hired. She and Mustafa also drew up a statement of their long-term goals for the company:

Vision: Achieve a sustainable growth through the following:
- Managing profit in parallel with quality
- Being a great place to work where people are inspired to be the best they can be

One weakness in her operation, Riham knew, was that she didn't delegate enough. She hired a younger cousin, a college student studying commerce, to visit retail shops and build relationships with their owners. After he went to five stores without making a sale, he got discouraged and quit.

"It's hard work," I said.

"It's hard work, because I'm doing everything myself," Riham said. "I know this isn't the way to grow, but everyone I know is like this—doing everything themselves." Outside the factory windows, a steady rain began to fall. "There's no system," Riham continued. "We don't feel like we can delegate. This was the problem in my father's factory; I don't want to do things this way. I want to build a system, but there's not a single person I can trust." Now she was going down a long list of stores, updating phone numbers, cold-calling owners, and introducing her products to them.

"It must be hard to sit and wait for people to call you back," I said. As a journalist in Egypt, I had found that people rarely returned calls or even answered their phones. Over three decades of reporting in Asia, Europe, and the United States, I hadn't encountered such a widespread aversion to picking up one's phone anywhere else. Was it self-importance, apathy, fear of the unknown? It was a major reason why it was so hard to get things done.

"Oh, I'm not waiting for anyone!" Riham answered. "I don't expect anything. God will provide what he provides, and whatever is in his plan will be right for me."

Even during the slow season, she didn't reduce her workers' hours, and she didn't let anyone go. It was too hard to find and train employees, so she held on to the ones she had and paid them in full, even if they spent much of the day looking out the window. "I don't want them to feel unsafe."

In December, her factory introduced a fleece pajama shirt and started selling it to local retailers. Then catastrophe struck: The hem on the garment turned out to be the wrong width, and stores started sending the shirts back. They were unsellable in their current state, and Riham's factory was out £E5,000, or around $640.

The workers were accustomed to throwing their finished items in a communal pile so that it was impossible to trace whose handiwork was at fault. Riham realized that she needed a better system. "From now on, we'll each be responsible for one operation," she told her employees. "And if you make a mistake, I'll deduct it from your salary." Among those she singled out for criticism was Mona, who had been doing quality inspections on the pajama shirts and should have noticed the error.

The next morning, Mona came in to tell Riham that she was leaving.

"Why?" Riham asked her. "You don't want to take responsibility for your own actions?"

"No. I prefer to stay home and not to take any responsibility." Two other workers also quit because of the new policy.

In her family factory, Riham remembered, her father and uncle hadn't believed in punishing or firing anyone. "They always say, 'They're poor people, it's not their fault, I don't want to cut off his bread,'" she told me. "There's no punishment and no system. At the end of the month, workers are supposed to get something cut from their salary if they need to be punished. But they'll always beg and get it back." The employees played on their bosses' sympathy, and the bosses gave in. It was like the worst kind of parenting, but practiced on adults instead of four-year-olds. Riham's own policy, which her brother had criticized, was to fire people only for negligence or dishonesty; any subpar work, she believed, could be solved by giving an employee more training or moving her to another part of the floor. Now she saw that if she wanted to make her workers accountable, she would have to be stricter. Between the lax management model of her family's business and Mustafa's harsher methods, she was trying to find a middle way.

Riham eventually figured out how to salvage the shirts with the faulty hems, but it was too late. Winter in Egypt doesn't last long, and no one wanted fleece pajama shirts anymore.

It wasn't just the financial loss that bothered her. As a small manufacturer, Riham had limited opportunities to win the trust of her buyers. "When they see me selling pajamas for two or three seasons, they'll trust me again," she said.

In February 2016, I visited Riham at the Nelly Kids Fashion Fair, a twice-yearly exhibition of children's goods in Cairo. She had told me her business suffered because her product range was narrow. Now, displayed on the back wall of her exhibition booth, were all the new items she had designed over the last two months to rectify that. There was a Minnie Mouse shirt and matching shorts, infant onesies and blankets with appliqués of monkeys, soccer balls, and dump trucks. Tank tops in vivid primary colors were her concession to Egyptian village style— "They want a piece that's cheap and colorful"—but I also noticed stylish zebra-print pajamas and *Frozen* nightgowns in unusual shades, like peach and mint. "I went to the wholesaler and he said, 'What are these things? I can't sell them. Take them away, take them away!'" Riham said. "But I can't design things that aren't to my taste."

Her new line marked a bold push into the domestic market. Riham's baby quilts and blankets, which were displayed on the left side of the booth, had always sold well. But in the past three years, factories that made children's sleepwear had significantly cut into her sales by producing similar items or importing them from China or Turkey. This was the first time that Riham had designed such an extensive collection of more than thirty items, in an effort to compete with her larger rivals head-on.

On the far wall were the goods that Mustafa had brought back from China. On display were colorful bedsheets, novelty pillows in the shape of cupcakes and monsters ("I tried to produce these pillows but it was a

disaster"), and cloth diaper covers with adjustable snaps and an antibac-
terial bamboo lining ("I didn't even try"). The diaper covers were neatly
folded and hung in a grid, five pieces across and five down with space
between each one, like paintings in a gallery. Nothing like them was
available in Egypt, and on the first morning of the fair they were getting
a lot of attention. Riham was selling the diaper covers for £E59 apiece,
around $7.50, with strict orders from her brother not to give discounts.

A man who owned a store in Cairo approached and asked questions
about sizing and prices. He left abruptly—it was time to pray—but
promised to place an order when he came back. "He likes the diaper
covers and, thank God, he doesn't think they're too expensive," Riham
told me. "He wants to buy the whole collection."

But the Chinese imports weren't going to be the savior that she and
her brother had hoped for. Several weeks earlier, the government had
imposed tariffs of between 20 and 40 percent on many imported goods;
the new policy was intended to help local manufacturers and conserve
the country's shrinking foreign reserves. In the future, anyone who
wanted to bring products into Egypt would have to register with the
government and provide proof of his legal status, trademark registra-
tions, and other certifications. The measures were announced while
Riham and Mustafa's shipping container was en route from China to
Egypt, somewhere on the Pacific Ocean. The Egyptian government, to
everyone's surprise, could move fast when it wanted.

Directives rained down on Riham like an unexpected squall at sea.
Items that had been tariff-free when she bought them had become,
overnight, at least 20 percent more expensive. The import of diapers was
now banned, customs officials told her, and she had to explain over and
over what a diaper cover was before she changed her mind and called
them "plastic underwear" instead. The taxes on different categories of
merchandise changed, and changed again, and Riham struggled to con-
tain the damage. When the ship with her goods finally arrived in port,
she hired a young man to sneak on board and stick new labels on the

crates, in accordance with the amended rules. He was caught, and she had to pay an additional £E11,000 in fines.

"After my brother paid all the import taxes, he just sat there and didn't say anything," Riham told me. "Finally he said, 'I'm broke.'"

Because of the unexpected tariffs, the items would bring in little profit now. Her Chinese suppliers weren't interested in the government's complicated registration process, so Riham and Mustafa's maiden voyage into the import business was likely to be their last. Under Nasser, the government had confiscated private businesses and micromanaged the economy for more than a decade. Sisi-style governance was more like a hit-and-run accident—appearing out of nowhere to do damage, then vanishing again.

I said I had heard that the rules were supposed to help domestic manufacturers like her.

"I don't mind the rules, just tell me in advance so I can plan for them, not when my goods are already in port!" she said in exasperation. "But the government employees have no brains in their heads. They don't generate any goods on their own, so they try to get their hands on yours. They need to take all the government employees and throw them into the sea and find new ones." She laughed her high-pitched, silvery laugh.

As I walked around the fair, which occupied two floors of Cairo's exhibition center, I was struck at how much energy had been expended in making the exact same things. There was an occasional display of children's jeans or sundresses, but nine booths out of ten featured pajamas and tank-top-and-shorts sets in flimsy, colorful cotton. They were presumably knockoffs, and the same cast of characters appeared over and over, a slate of Saturday morning cartoons on repeat: Elsa, Anna, Mickey, Snoopy. Elsa, Anna, SpongeBob SquarePants.

When I visited a village near Minya called Abu Hinnis, I met a woman who wove palm leaves into baskets to earn extra income. That seemed enterprising, until I met many other women engaged in making the same shallow basket, of the same size, for the same price. The younger women in the village, working from home, stitched identical pairs of toddler pants that sold for pennies apiece. The preference for the familiar and the consistent ran deep. Sons followed their fathers into trades, a custom that was common in pharaonic times and is also prevalent today. People stuck to set paths, even the ones that led to bad outcomes. The government tried to develop a textile industry and failed, tried and failed, and tried again. Young women go to school, stay home, get married, and have children, and the cycle begins again.

"People here refuse change, in everything," Riham told me. "When you bring in something new and sell it, they'll come to you and ask, 'How many did you sell? What did people want to buy?' and then go and do the same thing."

"When you show them something that's before their eyes, they accept it," she continued. "When you show them something new, they panic. Everyone does pajamas. Even I am doing pajamas."

"Why?" I asked.

Pajamas were inexpensive to manufacture and needed no special technology, she explained. "It's easy. We're lazy."

On the last afternoon of the fair, I stopped by Riham's booth again. I expected to see a crush of customers—things in Egypt tend to happen at the last minute—but I found Riham sitting alone with her brother. Her new product line hadn't done well; it turned out that customers preferred to stick with suppliers they already knew. She had received fewer than half the number of new orders she had gotten at the same exhibition a year ago. The Chinese diaper covers were selling well, but they were a nonrenewable resource.

Bahia Nazim, an older woman who had organized the exhibition and was a mentor to Riham, had come by to see her. "People are saying that you're doing well with your Chinese imports," she said. "But think—you're not going to import again, so you need to think about what you're going to do." She urged the younger woman to go out and see what was missing in the marketplace and to fill that niche, rather than just copying everyone else.

I remembered how proud Riham had been when she showed me the products she had designed. Now, sitting under the harsh white flood-lights of the exhibition hall, she looked tired and drained.

"Are you disappointed that your new line didn't sell?" I asked her.

"This is my second year to try and enter the pajama business," Riham said. "Last year was my first try, but people told me I had only a few samples, so they wouldn't place orders with me. This time I made a larger collection, and they told me, 'We place orders with only a few companies.'"

She would have to rethink her business model yet again, she told me. "This is my second try, and I didn't succeed. I think God is telling me that I should do things differently."

6

DOWNTOWN

ABOUT TWELVE MILES OUTSIDE MINYA, the Nile makes a wide loop to the east before eventually settling back into its northward flow. The village of Bayyadiyya sits at the bend in the river, as if hiding in the crook of someone's elbow. The appearance of shelter is deceiving, though: Hemmed in by water on one side and desert on the other, Bayyadiyya has never had enough farmland to go around. In the 1980s, residents began leaving town to look for work. They went to the Gulf States, primarily, but occasionally as far away as Europe or America.

The émigrés started to return home for good in the 1990s. The successful ones bought land and built houses on the town's main streets— three-story structures with wrought-iron balconies and gilded accents, often painted in the gaudy colors of seaside cottages, like yellow or aquamarine. Businesses sprang up to feed the appetite for luxury. Bayyadiyya has more than thirty car dealerships, several gold shops, and quite a few fancy hair salons. "Everything became expensive," people say when remembering this era of sudden growth.

On the dirt roads leading into town, old men herd their goats, and children and chickens scatter in the dust before approaching cars. But Bayyadiyya isn't really a village, in the traditional sense of a rural settlement more or less cut off from the world. More than twenty thousand people live here—most of them not in spacious villas, but in brick and concrete houses that crowd close together in narrow alleys. Money flows in freely, along with ideas about how to live. Between 50 and 70 percent of the town's young men are said to be away from home at any given time, and almost everyone has a relative somewhere else. Bayyadiyya feels not much different from the *ashwa'iyyat* of Cairo, the dense unplanned neighborhoods where the poor live, but plucked from its urban surroundings and set down amid fields of garlic, arugula, and sugarcane.

"It's not a town, it's a city," a woman named Mona Hafez Abdel-Maseeh told me. She's a friend of a friend of a friend of my translator, Amira, or some connection equally distant, who has come to meet us in a district they call "downtown Bayyadiyya." Mona is thirty-four and slight, with intense dark eyes and fine features. She's wearing a black blazer and matching pants, so that initially I took her for a professional woman from the city. Later I learned that she grew up here and works in the village as a nurse. Other than a short stint in Cairo, she has never left.

Mona brings me to visit a tailor. In his tiny street-front shop, he sews *gallabiyya*s for the men of the village. The other sewing workshops around here are closed today, she says apologetically, because the government inspector is supposed to come by. Anyway, Mona is more interesting than the man she has brought me to see.

WHEN MONA WAS six, her father went to sign her up for school. Mona could already read, and write her parents' names, but her father couldn't afford to pay the £E40 enrollment fee. There was probably more to the story, because Mona remembers her mother getting mad at her father when he came home without her registration papers.

A few years later, Mona enrolled in a literacy program that was run by two Catholic priests (her family, like most of the residents in the village, is Christian). Girls typically took such courses just long enough to learn how to read and write, and then stayed home until suitable husbands could be found for them. A priest named Sameh Farouk noticed that Mona and her friend Noura were promising students, and he encouraged them to continue their studies.

The two girls graduated from middle school and transferred to the trade high school in the district capital of Mallawi, which was seven miles away. No young woman from the village had ever gone so far away for the sake of her education. They weren't included on the school's attendance roll, nor were they given marks because they were so much older than the other students, but they took their final exams just the same. "If you're holding pen and paper, don't let anyone laugh at you," Mona remembers a villager telling her.

She was twenty-four when she finally got her *diplome*—by then, most of her peers were married with children. Mona turned down several proposals; for a while, she considered becoming a nun. Eventually, the Catholic church hired her and Noura to teach in the same literacy program they had once attended.

About a year before I met her, Mona happened to mention to a fellow passenger on a train that she was interested in nursing. The man told her about a training course in Cairo that was run by the Coptic Orthodox church, and Mona applied and was selected for the six-month program. After she graduated, she returned home to Bayyadiyya. Her mother was suffering from diabetes and other illnesses, and Mona used her nursing skills to care for her before she died.

In this sequence of events, she saw God's hand at work: the chance meeting with the stranger, the intercession of the church, and the unexpected gift of time and the knowledge to attend to her mother in her last months of life. Neither of her parents had gone to school, but her mother had believed fervently in Mona's education.

"If you saw her at my graduation, you could feel how proud she was," Mona told me. She pulled out the gold cross that hung around her neck and held it in her palm, as if testing its weight. "She gave me this necklace that day. She encouraged me a lot—she always said I would be a doctor."

It's more common now for girls from the village to attend high school or even college. About ten years ago, a few women went to Cairo to work as housemaids. They were initially looked down upon— "the man who would allow his daughters to go out to work was doing a very shameful thing," Mona said—but the women eventually became breadwinners for their families and their deeds were accepted, even praised.

"There's a traditional saying: 'A girl cannot walk alone,'" Mona told me. Then she said, quickly: "But now it isn't that way. I go everywhere alone."

After we talked to the man with the tailoring shop, Mona said she would introduce me to some female shop owners she knew, but first I had to finish the bottle of soda she had bought for me. "If you don't drink the whole thing, I can't get married," Mona teased me, and I forced down most of a sixteen-ounce bottle of 7-Up. I didn't want to jinx her marriage prospects.

FOR ALMOST HALF a century, Bayyadiyya has been producing one thing the rest of the world wants. Men have been leaving town since the 1980s to do manual labor in the resorts of South Sinai and the Red Sea or in neighboring Arab countries like Saudi Arabia, Libya, and Kuwait. They may stay away for years, and it's common for a woman to say that her husband is *misafir*, traveling. Bachelors who do well abroad can find wives when they return; the migrants who are already married usually spend their earnings buying land or renovating their homes.

Decades after people started going into the world and bringing back the money they made, Bayyadiyya is still fundamentally poor. There are few jobs, and no local industry. When migrants return to the village, they tend to spend their money on status-enhancing purchases such as houses and cars. They buy large-screen televisions, refrigerators, and washing machines. This type of conspicuous consumption inflates prices—*Everything became expensive*—and redefines what it means to live well, even as it makes that life unattainable for those without access to well-paying jobs in other parts of the world.

If the returnees invested instead in businesses or factories, that might stimulate the local economy, but the thinking here runs in another direction: What would be the point of being successful if you still had to work so hard? So the economy stagnates, everything gets more expensive, and soon a new cohort of men goes out again.

So much movement, so little change: That's the failed development model of Bayyadiyya, and of Egypt, and of many other places in the world that have experienced globalization's disappointments. A country needs strong leadership and smart policies to benefit from opening to the outside world. It needs measures to attract investment; its companies must find their competitive niches; its workers require training and skills. A country lacking these advantages is more likely to be pummeled or exploited in its encounter with global competition. Egypt is the largest source of migrant labor in the Middle East, with around eight million men living and working away from home. Their earnings keep many families afloat, but the money hasn't been channeled into more productive forms of investment and entrepreneurship, and it has brought little lasting benefit to the economy.

In a revealing study, the economist Rasha Qutb traced the impact of remittances from abroad on Egypt over nearly four decades and found they actually had a *negative* impact on growth. Because the money is primarily spent on housing and consumer goods, it tends to drive up imports and inflation without bringing about productivity gains or structural improvements in the economy. The influx of cash can also have the psychological effect of reducing motivation to work among migrants' family members, Qutb found. "Those who receive remittances can become highly dependent on the 'easy money,' which may encourage them to reduce their work efforts or participation in the labor market," she writes. "Such attitudes reflect a 'moral hazard' problem that can negatively affect growth rates."

Seen from the perspective of the village, migration raises expectations for a better life even as it puts that life out of reach for many people. Women suffer twice over: They can't travel overseas for work, but they're burdened by the newly expensive rituals of marriage that migration has brought home.

"In the past it was very simple to get married," Mona told me. "You needed a few plates and cups, a manually operated washing machine. Now they have to get an automatic washing machine, a refrigerator, an iron, an oven, and three sets of everything. In the past when a girl got married, she could live with her family; now she has to have her own house."

Like the weather, the soaring cost of marriage is a favorite topic of conversation in Bayyadiyya. "We have a problem: People are always observing each other," Rizkallah Nouh, the pastor of the Evangelical Church, told me. "If someone gives fifty grams of gold to his wife, everyone talks about it. It becomes a kind of competition." He estimated that it takes £E200,000, or more than $22,000—about four years of an average rural family's income—to get married. The bride's family contributes kitchen appliances and her trousseau, and the groom pays for an apartment, furniture, gold jewelry, and the wedding celebration. Families may save money for years, send members abroad, or sell their land or livestock to cover the cost.

"People always have a way, except the very poor," the pastor said.

"The poor people just have God with them, and they just live in one room." He laughed, but in a gentle way.

WHEN I LIVED in China, I found that migration has a liberating effect on young women. In cities hundreds of miles from home, they earn significant wages for the first time and make their own decisions about work, money, dating, and marriage. In Egypt, it's mostly the men who leave. They go to some of the most male chauvinistic countries in the world, pick up reactionary ideas, and bring them home. Misogyny, it turns out, is contagious.

One study of Egyptian households found that the wives of returned migrants give birth to one more child, on average, than women whose husbands never went abroad—which suggests that husbands bring back conservative views about family, including the importance of having more children. In Jordan, a similar survey concluded that having a family member spend time in a conservative Arab country makes his female relatives more likely to drop out of school and less likely to have a job, to possess freedom of mobility, or to support women's equality. The ideal life path for a Bayyadiyya woman is to get engaged at sixteen, marry at eighteen, and start having children right away, preferably boys.

Even from thousands of miles away, men retain their dominant position in the home. A migrant worker's wife may have more interactions with schools, police, and government offices when left on her own. But her husband, from afar, has many options to undercut her authority. He may set up a private bank account, invest his savings without telling her, or contribute less to the household than he used to. He can continue to exercise close surveillance over his wife, usually through his family members.

Hind Ali, an employee in the Delta factory whose husband worked in Cairo, told me that the customs in her village prohibited a woman from leaving the house or wearing bright colors as long as her husband was "traveling." "I have to ask him by phone for permission to go out," she said. "If I go out somewhere without telling him, his family finds out and tells him. He'll call and start shouting at me."

The influx of cash income from migration can relegate women to a position of greater dependency within the family. Surveys in Egypt show that following a husband's departure, a wife is more likely to drop out of the workforce. This seemed to hold true in Bayyadiyya ("They're all busy with Viber and Facebook," Mona said of migrants' wives, referring to two popular social media platforms). The central importance of migration has strengthened the belief, already deeply rooted, that a woman's place is in the home.

Migration gives Chinese women the chance to live a different life. Egyptian men, it turns out, are happy with the one they have.

THROUGH MONA, I got to know some of the female shop owners of Bayyadiyya. Most of them were in their thirties and single. They belonged to a group they called the Nile Young Ladies, which met Sundays after church to discuss their personal concerns. "We're talking all the time about our husband, even though he doesn't exist," Mona said, and laughed.

Samia Farah Youssef ran a tiny store that sold toiletries and hair accessories. She had started working as a teenager to support her elderly father and then, after he died, she used a small inheritance to open the shop in 2010. The villagers were in favor of the venture, Mona told me, because the family was poor.

Samia was thirty-one. "You can have her *bi-balash*," Mona joked— "for free"—when Samia told me her age. She was so old, by village standards, that she couldn't hope to ask for anything from a prospective groom.

A neighbor named Afaf Ramses Makram was in even bleaker circumstances. Her father had abandoned the family when she was a girl, and they had relied on a subsidy from the church to get by. Now Afaf worked in a shop supporting her younger brother and sister, who were both married but had no income.

She met me in the front room of her house, which had a packed dirt floor and one piece of furniture—a narrow wooden bench, on which we all sat in a row. Afaf was strikingly pretty, with high cheekbones and long honey-colored hair. She had a partially paralyzed leg that she dragged behind her when she walked.

I asked her if working in the shop was difficult.

"No, not at all. Quite the opposite."

"What do you like about it?"

She broke into a smile. "That I'm selling."

When Afaf told me she was thirty-two, no one joked about whether anyone could get her *bi-balash* or any other way. Her disability made it unlikely that she would marry.

On another day, Mona took me to the shop of a woman named Seham Salah. Her place was wide and open to the street, much larger than Samia's, with its merchandise set out neatly on racks. The store sold hair ties and clips, makeup, shampoos, creams and lotions, and fluffy stuffed animals.

"When I started, I had only these two shelves," Seham told me, marking a spot with her finger on the back wall of the store. She had a cheerful round face and stood with her head held high, and her bright eyes glittered behind thin gold-rimmed glasses. She was gregarious and talkative and seemed a natural fit for her line of work.

Seham had opened the shop three years before, after persuading the priest of her church to rent her the space at a discount. A neighbor's husband introduced her to wholesale traders in Mallawi, seven miles away; Seham traveled back and forth by minibus and brought back whatever she thought would sell ("My arms hurt so much from carrying things"). If a customer wanted something that she didn't have on hand, Seham would take the bus to Mallawi to buy it, even though the cost of transportation wiped out any hope of a profit. Her business revolved, perhaps inevitably, around brides. They bought cosmetics, shampoo, lotion, and perfume—everything they needed to look beautiful on their wedding day.

Seham showed me a fat orange tube of mascara, with the words *Colossal Volume* printed on it in silver letters. "I charge eight pounds for this. In the hair salon, it might be sixteen."

A vial of perfume: "I sell it for twelve pounds. The hair salon sells it for twenty or twenty-five."

There were six hair salons in the neighborhood. Brides used to buy all their beauty products from them when they got their hair and makeup done. Young women still made wedding-day appointments at the salons, but now many of them stopped by Seham's store first to stock up on everything they needed.

"So did they lower their prices because of competition from you?" I asked.

"No. The hair salons have their own customers, and they don't care," Seham said. "I don't mind selling lots of products at a low price. They would prefer to sell one product at a high price." I had always imagined that doing business in Egypt would be exhausting. With thousands of mom-and-pop shops and many layers of intermediaries, the markets struck me as fragmented and inefficient. And so they were, but Seham saw opportunity there.

For most of her life, her abilities had gone unnoticed. She was the second of six children, but she didn't go to school like her siblings. When it was time to register, her parents couldn't find her birth certificate; by the time the piece of paper was located two years later, Seham was considered too old to start first grade. Like Mona, she later took literacy classes run by the church and obtained her *diplome*.

When Seham was twenty, her mother died of cancer and left her the head of the family (an older sister had already married and left home). Seham took care of her four younger siblings and sold homemade bread and cheese for extra income. Her youngest brother, Amgad, was only eight when their mother died. "He's like my son—I raised him. Now he's an engineer, and he's married."

When the oldest of her three brothers wanted to wed, Seham sold a piece of the family's land to help pay for it. The gold jewelry that was supposed to be for her own marriage, a gift of a necklace and bracelets from her parents, was spent instead on installing indoor plumbing in the family home. "My sister's husband took my gold and sold it, and used the money to pay for household expenses," Seham recalled. "I never even saw it."

After her brother's wedding, Seham wanted to go to Cairo to be a nun. Her second brother intervened and asked her to help him get married too. In other words, would she sacrifice more years of her life so that he could have a better one?

Seham agreed. This time, she sold two pieces of land that her father had left her and gave the proceeds to her brother. In return, he promised to build and furnish a three-story house that they would share, with the top floor reserved for her. He built the house but minus a third story, then took the money she had given him to go into business instead.

"I just let it go," Seham said. "I knew he needed the money."

At the age of twenty-six, with all three of her brothers settled in their own homes, Seham left Bayyadiyya. She joined the nuns of the Santana Church in Cairo. "I thought it would be a more peaceful world, very quiet, away from human desires and manipulation and control over other people. But I found out it was the same. The head of the nuns wanted to control other people."

Her younger sister was having conflicts with her brothers and their wives, and the nuns ordered Seham to go home to take care of her family. Seham resented this—"They never tried to understand me or to find out what kind of painful journey I'd been on"—but she returned to support her sister and stayed on to help her get married. Seham later moved to Cairo and joined a different church, but it didn't work out. She returned to Bayyadiyya again, maybe for good.

Her store earns £E300 a month, and sometimes double during holidays; Seham either saves the money or buys more inventory. No one in her circle of friends is an entrepreneur—"Working in sales is not good work for a woman"—although lately a few of them have expressed interest in joining her. A local businessman offered to buy her out and let her work in whichever of his shops she wanted, but she turned him down. She likes having the freedom to close up whenever she wants so she can stop by the church.

I asked Seham about her plans for the future.

"She wants a man," Mona interjected, teasing.

"No, no, no!" Seham said. She wished to renovate and expand the store. She was taking lessons on an electronic keyboard from a neighbor; she had a good voice, she told me, and sang in the church choir. She planned to enroll in the continuing education program at the University of Minya to study music, with a focus on piano. "What gave me courage to pursue this dream was working by myself here," she told me.

Seham had spent so many years and all of her inheritance in service to the marriage economy of Bayyadiyya. In helping her four siblings to get married, she had probably forfeited her own chances. She was thirty-seven—almost two decades past the time she should have wed, according to local standards—and now she made a living selling products to help younger women look more alluring on their wedding day. These were the decisions she had made, or you could say that she'd had no choice at all. A woman is expected to tirelessly sacrifice and to want nothing for herself.

As we left Seham's shop, Mona seemed to be thinking the same thing. "There's a sadness inside them, because they know they'll never be allowed to love," she said. But later I wondered: Was Mona talking about the women she had taken me to meet, or about herself?

IT TOOK ME a while to register that everyone I was meeting in Bayya-diyya was Christian. "The whole village is Christian," Mona explained. "There are only about a thousand Muslims living here."

"Are there villages that are entirely Muslim?"

"There's a village called Rayramun that's all Muslim, but we never go there," she answered. "We just pass by, but we've never gone inside."

"How far away is it?"

"Ten minutes."

I asked Mona if she knew someone who could take me around Rayramun, but she was alarmed. "If you go there, you'll get beaten."

Officially, Christians account for 10 percent of the Egyptian popula-tion, and in cities they tend to mix with Muslims in schools, govern-ment offices, and the workplace. The divide is stronger in rural areas. "We face south, they face north" is how a Coptic Christian woman de-scribed the line of demarcation in her village between Christian and Muslim neighborhoods. Upper Egypt has traditionally been home to large numbers of Christians, and occasionally you will find a village, like Bayyadiyya, that is almost entirely Christian.

Disputes between the two groups occasionally flare into violence, especially during times of political tension. In 2011, in another part of Minya, two Muslims were killed and Christian-owned homes and shops set on fire, after a disagreement that started over a speed bump. More than a dozen churches were burned in 2013 during the unrest that followed an army massacre of Muslim Brotherhood supporters in Cairo. (An incident around this time, in which people from Rayramun cut off the road to Bayyadiyya and threw stones at residents' cars, was behind Mona's warnings about visiting there.)

As a Christian village, Bayyadiyya has a history of foreign influence that sets it apart from the surrounding countryside. American Presbyte-rian missionaries set up the village's first educational institution, a school for girls, in 1904. Several decades later, a Jesuit priest who had been educated in France started organizing schools for farmers' children. The Catholic Church founded the literacy program that Mona and Seham attended; today it operates fifty-three schools in Upper Egypt that serve more than thirteen thousand students. Religious organizations have built roads, improved sanitation, run health clinics, organized vocational training, financed microcredit, and worked to stamp out practices such as female genital mutilation and early marriage for girls.

Bayyadiyya has five Coptic Orthodox churches, two Presbyterian churches, a Catholic church, an Evangelical church, a Plymouth Brethren church, an Assembly of God church, a Methodist church, a Faith church, and a Baptist church. The Catholic Church taught Mona to read and write; the Coptic Church later trained her to be a nurse. The Catholics rented space to Seham to start her shop, and they supported Afaf and her brother and sister after their father abandoned them. The state isn't a significant presence in the village: In six visits I made to Bayyadiyya over two years, I never met a single official. A public elementary and middle school opened in 1997—ninety-three years after the Presbyterians arrived—and there's still no government-funded high school.

"We're a rural village in Upper Egypt, and we're Christian. We're marginalized," one community leader told me.

The active presence of churches is a boon for women, because they provide a socially acceptable reason for them to leave the house. When Malaka Refai, a project officer with Catholic Relief Services, set up a program to promote interfaith cooperation among youths in a Minya village, she discovered that it was much easier to recruit Christian women. "They were already very active in the church," she told me, "so their families were used to it." She found less of a community built around the mosques, so young Muslim women have a harder time convincing their families to let them go out.

Yet the more time I spent in Bayyadiyya, the more I was struck at

how much the place had in common with Muslim communities I had
visited. The Presbyterians had set up a school for girls in 1904, but what
had that brought the women of the village a century later? Mona and
Seham had still missed out on their elementary school education and
spent years trying to catch up. Mona was still teaching basic literacy to
women; the program she had attended twenty years earlier was going
strong. Young women still married early—a single female past the age
of twenty was considered "expired," like a bottle of milk that has gone
bad—nor did they migrate or work in significant numbers. Studies of
rural Egypt have shown that Christian women have greater mobility
than their Muslim counterparts. But by any other measure, such as their
decision-making power at home or their attitudes toward gender equality, there's no difference.

   "It's a different kind of patriarchy" is how Mariam Boctor, a Christian woman who briefly worked for me as a translator, explained it. Unlike in the West, the evolution of Christianity in Egypt was not
accompanied by the growth of personal freedoms, and certainly not for
women. The Coptic Orthodox Church continues to prohibit divorce in
most cases, and it preaches the importance of female virtue and submis-
siveness and the wife's role as spiritual guardian of her family. In recent
decades, the spread of secular ideas associated with modernization and
the West, plus the rise of Islamic fundamentalism in Egypt and throughout the Middle East, have further added to the Church's sense of being
under siege from all quarters. "The stronger the Islamic brand of fundamentalism," a historian named Mohamed Afifi has written, "the more
defensive and fundamentalist the Copts became in a clear reaction to
what they considered a threat to their very existence as a community."

   In a Christian village called Abu Hinnis, across the Nile from Bayyadiyya, Mona took me to see a priest she knew named Timouthaous.
He was a tall man with a flowing beard, who wore a long black robe and
a necklace with the distinctive cross of the Coptic Church—square,
each arm ending in three points. We met him in the side room of a

church on the town's main plaza. Every so often a child would dart into the room, kiss the priest's hand, and withdraw without making a sound.

He didn't have much time, he told my translator, Amira. What did I want to know?

I asked him about the history of Abu Hinnis. We went back to the first century and the travels of the Holy Family, monasteries, priests, martyrs, the Arab conquest, more martyrs. Timouthaous had a big round floury loaf of bread in his hand, and he offered me a piece as he talked.

I refused politely, not wanting to deprive him of his lunch.

"You're supposed to take it," Amira told me in a whisper. "It's a blessing, and you just refused it."

The Long March of martyrs resumed, and I cut in hastily. "How is it that the whole village is Christian?"

"It's the work of God," the priest said, smiling serenely. "It's because the land is preserved with the blood of the martyrs and the lives of the saints."

"What if a Muslim family wanted to live here?"

"It has never happened, and I don't think it will."

Later he asked me what religion I was.

"Christian," I said.

"Which denomination? Catholic? Protestant?"

My mind raced. I had met a lot of Copts and Catholics in town—it was probably best to stick with something more obscure.

"I'm Protestant," I heard myself say, for the first time ever.

"Ah." And then, in halting English: "Martin Luther."

"Martin Luther," I agreed.

He turned his attention to Amira, who nodded and kissed his hand as if she were a fellow Christian instead of a Muslim, just as I was pretending to be a Protestant and not an atheist. In the face of patriarchy—the living, breathing, hand-kissing kind—we crumpled. A couple of fakers.

———

THE LIVES OF Christians in Egypt, whether they care to admit it or not, have been shaped by the larger Muslim society. During the era of Ottoman rule, Coptic officials, merchants, and craftsmen sometimes registered their marriages and divorces in *sharia* courts, even though this went against Church law. Some high officials went so far as to recognize polygamy as an accepted practice, which gave rise to a violent schism within the Church and two competing popes (the conflict was resolved in the seventeenth century, and today's church doesn't allow polygamy). On the question of inheritance, the Coptic Church explicitly follows the Muslim model—thus sons get double what daughters do, a practice that is observed by Christian families in Bayyadiyya and elsewhere. The devaluation of women, which has been pushed through centuries of selective interpretation of Islamic texts, has become part of everyday social practice. Women's work is to marry, bear children, and stay home. That division of labor holds true whether you're a Muslim or a Catholic or a Copt—as long as you're Egyptian.

One afternoon I visited the pastor of the Evangelical Church in Bayyadiyya, who brought the principal of the middle school to meet me. We were joined, I was surprised to see, by a foreign woman. Sister Cecilia Vanzon was a Dutch nun of the Order of the Sacred Heart who had lived in Bayyadiyya since 1980 and worked on women's issues.

Girls no longer marry at the age of twelve or thirteen, she told me, and the practice of female genital mutilation is on the decline. Families now send their daughters to school, although women don't usually work unless they went to college and can get government jobs in the city.

"Nobody hires someone with just a *diplome*," agreed the principal, whose name was Ayyad Habeeb Abdel-Quddous. "Unless you have a craft or open a hair salon."

"So what's the point of getting a *diplome*?" I asked. "Isn't it just a waste of time?"

"It's better than nothing," Ayyad said. "At least she can read and write. In the future, she can teach her kids how to do that."

"If she goes to the doctor, she'll understand what he tells her," Sister Cecilia added. "When she has kids, she can help them with their homework."

"I don't disagree with the importance of women learning how to read and write," I said. "I would just hope that after eleven years of school, they could do more than that."

Sister Cecilia looked at me patiently. "It's a village. Don't forget."

She was fluent in English, but she had lived in the country for so long that she kept switching automatically into Arabic to talk to me. Like the churches in the village, she was, above all, Egyptian. Bayyadiyya has been open to the outside world for more than a century. But at the end of a day, it's a village—or a city—in Egypt. *Don't forget.*

THERE ARE STILL many women in Bayyadiyya who can't read or write. Most families enroll their children in school, although a small number keep their daughters home to help with the household chores. A more pressing issue, as I had found when speaking with the interns in Riham's factory, is the poor quality of the education. In Bayyadiyya's elementary school, children crowd fifty to sixty in a classroom and attend for four hours each day. "A student may be in sixth grade, but he can't write. So he fails," Ayyad, the local principal, told me. At the middle school level, 10 percent of the class—around a hundred kids—drops out each year. The boys go out to work, and the girls mostly stay home. Without pressure to find a job and earn a living, young women are prone to forgetting what they learned.

Mona has taught in the Catholic Church's literacy program in Bayyadiyya for fourteen years. When she started, many of her students were women in their teens and twenties who, like her, never had proper schooling. Some of them just wanted to be able to write their names, while others learned "more than you ever expected."

"My thinking is: Don't give me a fish, teach me how to fish," Mona said. "I want to teach them how to do things, to share the knowledge I've learned." Over the years, she estimates, she has taught three hundred women to read and write.

Most of her current students are in their forties and fifties, as illiteracy is being stamped out among younger generations. Even though the demographics are encouraging, there's a long way to go. The fact remains that one in three women in Egypt can't read or write, and the figure is higher in rural areas. Mona had quit teaching the year before when she found a job working as a nurse in a lab, but a group of young women showed up at her place of work one morning and begged her to come back. Now she teaches four mornings a week on top of her nursing job and gets a small stipend from the Catholic Church.

One evening, I asked Mona if I could meet some of the women she taught. Her supervisors in the church would never approve a visit from a foreign journalist, she said, so she just picked up the phone and called one of her students. Half an hour later, we were hurrying through the darkening streets of the village. In the front room of the student's house, around twenty women had assembled, sitting on the floor to wait for me.

My kids are in third, sixth, and eighth grades. They used to ask me how to do their homework. That made me want to come take this class. Now I know how to write my name, my father's name, and the numbers. I can dial a phone number.

My son has a medical issue that requires frequent visits to the doctor. Now I can read and write enough to do calculations and also pay bills. There was a problem on our bill in how the electricity was measured, and I discovered it and corrected it.

I've been to literacy school, but I never learned how to read and write until I started Miss Mona's class. The teachers weren't very good, and I had to stay home once I got married.

They were the wives of farmers, many of whom were working abroad. I was surprised at the range of ages. Despite what Mona had said, a fair number of her students were young. One woman was twenty-four, with two children; another had four kids and wasn't certain how old she was—"maybe thirty or around thirty-two, I don't know." Several of them nursed infants as they spoke with me. As usual when I encountered a group of Egyptian women, I was struck by their confidence and force of personality. But I could also see past that to the ways society had failed them.

I wanted to learn with Miss Mona so I could teach my kids. I have three boys who are in second, fifth, and eighth grades, and a little girl who is two months old. Hopefully, I'll enroll her in school and give her the best education.

One woman raised her hand and said she had been studying for five months "so I can teach my kids." She continued, "We have a saying here: You should get educated when you're young, or you'll be an old maid." She wouldn't give her full name, only her initials: S.S. "My brother's in America, and I'm afraid he'll read this," she explained, and everyone laughed.

My translator, a young woman named Magda, urged me to say something to the students in Arabic.

"You have a lot of courage," I told them, speaking slowly, as I picked my way through the linguistic minefield to land safely on the words I knew. "Even though you are not that young, you are still studying. That is good."

"Is there still hope for us?" an older woman in the back of the room called out.

"*Taban!* Of course."

It was undoubtedly beneficial for these women to know how to read and write; now they could support their children in school, pay their bills, and navigate the healthcare system. But I was struck by how not a single woman said she wanted to learn in order to improve herself or to get a better job. The education of women is seen in the narrow context of helping others and fitting into a socially prescribed role. You become literate in order to help your kids, just as you work in a garment factory so you can get married.

Is there still hope for us? So many things would have to change before the students in Mona's class could make the most of what they had learned. Opening to the world was not enough. The residents of Bayyadiyya were already connected to the world beyond their village through migration, trade, and social media networks. But that exposure hadn't translated into more progressive ideas about marriage, family, and lifestyle—quite the opposite, it introduced a taste for lavish weddings and brought more pressure on women to conform to their traditional roles. In Bayyadiyya I met a woman whose brother worked in America, yet she had never gone to school.

It's better than nothing.

It's a village. Don't forget.

I was irritated when Sister Cecilia said that, because I felt that the women here deserved so much more. But she was the one who had lived and worked in Bayyadiyya for forty years, not me.

UNUSUALLY FOR A single woman, Seham lives alone, in a house down an alley near her shop. The front room has matching Louis Quatorze–style high-backed chairs and a tile floor in a checkerboard pattern—it's a space to impress visitors, a common feature in Egyptian homes. The black-and-white tiles stretch through a hallway to the kitchen and bathroom at the back of the house. In between these two areas is a sort of vestibule. It has a bare cement floor and a narrow bed pushed against one wall, as in a monk's cell.

The house doesn't belong to Seham. Her brother built it with the money that Seham gave him after she sold her land. He later sold the house to one of their sisters, who has four children and works as a lawyer in the larger town of Mallawi. On occasional visits home, she meets clients in the room with the fancy chairs. Seham's share of the house is the patch of cement floor with the bed.

Her older sister had attended the same literacy class as she, but one day an administrator at the school noticed her intelligence and had her transferred into the regular educational system, which put her on the college track. Seham's younger sister also attended university, partly with Seham's help. Both of the sisters married and had children. Seham was stuck in between. She had missed out on her schooling; then, after their mother died, she had been responsible for her younger siblings as the oldest child still living at home. These seemingly small accidents of chance and timing had shaped her life—like ripples in a pond, spreading in wider and wider circles until they filled her entire horizon.

I once asked Seham if she thought about how her life was so different from that of her sisters.

"I've thought about that a lot," she answered. "I attribute that to luck. I believe in luck, I believe in fate."

"So what is your fate?"

"I'm the kind of person who moves forward all the time, in order to develop myself. I'm satisfied with my fate, with whatever God gave me. When I sit with my sister, I don't feel there's any difference between her level and mine."

If their mother hadn't died, Seham probably would have married and followed a conventional path. Now she considered herself too old to wed, although she sometimes had offers. An older widower had proposed marriage, and so had a man more than a decade younger than she was. Seham said no to both.

"Why would someone who's twenty-six be interested in someone significantly older than him? What is it that forces me to marry someone like him? I'm independent, I earn my own living, I have my own place. I don't see the need to force myself into circumstances that are awkward for me," Seham said. "I'm already an adult—I know what's right and what's wrong. I don't think I'll find the right man who will understand this mentality and be able to accept it. I'm too old to be controlled by anyone."

I first met Seham in early 2016. In November of that year, her business suffered when the government devalued the Egyptian pound ("Everyone's complaining about rising prices, and no one's in the mood to buy things"). By the next year, sales were recovering and her profit was double what it had been eighteen months earlier. Seham bought a refrigerator and a new TV for her home. She expanded the line of cosmetics she carried, and planned to start selling women's and children's clothes.

Out of difficult circumstances, she had built a life. She ran her own business; she supported herself; she lived independently. She had immeasurably improved the lives of the people around her, often at the cost of her own happiness. She was the living embodiment of the biblical injunction *Love thy neighbor as thyself.*

But she also reminded me why female enterprise and female success don't translate into greater respect. In the eyes of her community and her own family, Seham was a woman without a husband, children, or a home of her own. No one wanted the life she had. Her hard-won freedom and accomplishments had come out of hardship, and people counted themselves lucky not to be in her place. Other studies in rural Egypt have shown that women who live on the margins of society—who come from lower-status clans, or are especially poor—enjoy greater freedom of action. But the community remains blind to what they do.

On one of my last visits to Bayyadiyya, I noticed that Seham wasn't wearing her gold-rimmed glasses anymore. She had given up her dream of studying music, she told me; she'd heard that the continuing education program at the University of Minya was being canceled. Seham took the money she had been saving and spent it on laser eye surgery instead.

When she wasn't working in the shop, she volunteered helping older people in her church. Their adult children were often away or busy with their own affairs. "I think human relations are changing," Seham said. "People are more focused on their own interests and their own families, on making things better for their children, that's it. The family bonds that were strong in the past aren't so strong anymore. Even the bonds between sisters aren't as strong as they used to be."

Seham frequently brought the older members of the community to and from church services, to take part in activities and celebrate their birthdays. All her life she had looked out for other people, and she was used to living that way.

Mona was offered a job at a government hospital in Cairo. It was a good opportunity, with excellent pay—£E3,000 a month, or almost $340—but she turned it down. She had to stay in Bayyadiyya to look after her elderly father. Like Seham, she had spent her adulthood caring for others—teaching illiterate girls to read, working as a nurse, tending to her dying mother and now her aging father. Egyptian families were large, and the quality of healthcare was poor. There was no end to the number of people who needed help.

I moved back to the United States in the summer of 2016. On a return visit, I went to Bayyadiyya—it was my first time there in a year— and met up with Seham, who told me the news: Mona was married and pregnant and living in Cairo.

Her new husband was a driver. The couple had met through a friend of his who was a student in Mona's literacy class. Both men were illiterate. Mona's husband was a year younger than she was and had a leg that was partially paralyzed from childhood polio.

"Was she happy to move to Cairo?"

"She married of her own free will," Seham said, as if I had asked a different question. "Her family didn't agree to the marriage. They saw him as unsuitable, because he's uneducated and has a partially paralyzed leg. But Mona insisted, when she saw how much the man was devoted to her and how badly her family treated him." The family had eventually agreed to the match.

"Didn't Mona worry about marrying someone who wasn't educated?" I asked.

"She was aware of the difference between them, but she thought: 'I'm thirty-five or thirty-six, he's more convenient than someone who might come along, like a widower who is much older.' Mona wanted to have her own space. She wasn't very comfortable living with her siblings."

I was surprised and taken aback at the news—that Mona, who had worked so hard to educate herself and to pass on her learning to others, had married a man from the village who could neither read nor write. *Don't give me a fish, teach me how to fish,* I remembered her saying. I had assumed that she was too committed to her independent lifestyle to give it up: *I go everywhere alone.* But there were circumstances in her life that I didn't know about. She wanted to marry and have children. Her relations with her family were probably complicated, even though she had never mentioned a word of it to me. Getting married, it occurred to me now, was the only way a woman could free herself from the endless chain of responsibility for other people—to claim her own life, even as she tied it to someone else's.

She had been inching toward marriage the entire time I knew her, and she had been telling me so, in indirect ways. I just hadn't paid attention.

If you don't drink the whole thing, I can't get married.

We're talking all the time about our husband, even though he doesn't exist.

You can have her for free.

She wants a man.

There's a sadness inside them, because they know they'll never be allowed to love.

Mona had quit her job, Seham said, because she was pregnant.

"But will she work afterward?" I asked.

"Oh, yes. Mona is the kind of person who can't stay home."

Through my translator, Mai, we contacted Mona to see if she could meet with me when I returned to Cairo. She initially sounded enthusiastic, but then called me back to cancel our appointment. She would be traveling, she explained, and couldn't see me after all.

It seemed likely that her new husband had interceded and prevented her from meeting me. Whatever personal liberty Mona had enjoyed in the village didn't carry over to her new life in the city. Like so many of the young men from her hometown, Mona had succeeded in leaving Bayyadiyya at last. But also like many of her compatriots, who went to Saudi Arabia or the United Arab Emirates or Kuwait, she was discovering that freedom in the wider world wasn't as she had imagined it to be.

Mona is the kind of person who can't stay home, Seham said.

I have to believe her, because Mona is gone.

7

EXCESS MOTIONS

AFTER I DECIDED TO REPORT in Upper Egypt, a friend of a friend introduced me to a young woman named Walaa, who worked as a translator at the Olympic Training Center in Cairo. We met at a downtown mall to discuss the possibility of working together—which died as soon as I mentioned my desire to travel to rural Minya.

"Why do you have to go there yourself?" Walaa asked. "Can't you get this information from other people?"

I explained that talking to people was what a journalist did. Besides, I wanted to go.

"You should travel with a man at all times, to be safe," Walaa said firmly. Her family would never let her go to Upper Egypt with me, she said, but if her mother came along it might work. "Even to meet you today," she continued, "I needed to get permission from my mother. Just like your daughters need your permission to go somewhere."

But my daughters are four, and you're twenty-five.

It was when Walaa started giving me career advice—"You need to sell your book on the internet"—that I decided to wrap up our meeting as fast as I could. It was infuriating to deal with someone so closed-minded and sure of herself—but in another way, it was also enlightening.

To SOME EXTENT, Walaa had a point. There were risks to traveling around the Egyptian countryside, although it wasn't my modesty that I worried about. Egypt is a militarized police state, run by an ex-director of army intelligence who came to power following a coup. The streets bristle with military hardware: Tanks and troop transport vehicles guard intersections, conscripts finger the grips of their assault rifles like prayer beads. As a woman, a foreigner, and a journalist, I felt triply conspicuous; outside Cairo and Alexandria, I couldn't easily slip under the radar. Minya had been the site of violent attacks during an Islamist insurgency in the 1990s, and there were occasional clashes between Muslims and Christians. Foreign visitors, and journalists in particular, were supposed to travel under police escort at all times, which sounded as appealing as taking a reporting trip with Walaa's mother.

Over two years of going to Minya, I gained an education in how the security apparatus works. A woman in her late twenties named Amira El-Raghy, who had worked as a researcher for *The Economist* and other news organizations, accompanied me as a translator on my first half dozen trips. Then she moved to Italy to study costume design, but she introduced me to a friend and fellow translator whom I'll call Farah. Farah later went abroad to pursue a degree in heritage development, but she in turn put me in touch with her sister Mai, who was a college literature professor. So I was passed from one capable young woman to the next, all of them engaged in deeply humanistic pursuits while living under a regime that cared nothing about such things. These women used stealth or persistence, as warranted; they practiced charm; they played dumb. They were not above assuming the role of the helpless woman if it might help them, but they also stood up to the police, asked impolite questions, and navigated the bewildering jumble of the government bureaucracy. This is how you get things done in a system that's designed to thwart you. If you're Egyptian, you do it every day.

On my first visit to Minya in October 2015, Amira and I checked into our hotel and then headed out to eat lunch and meet a woman who owned a clothing shop. As we left the building, a police officer posted at the entrance stood up from his chair.

"I should accompany you," he said, but he sounded uncertain.

"Why?" Amira asked.

"You're in Upper Egypt."

"This is Upper Egypt—isn't it safe here?" Amira asked, her brown eyes as large and innocent as a puppy's. "Why do I need anyone to accompany me?"

He hesitated. Outsiders weren't supposed to wander around Minya by themselves, but he was young and probably unaccustomed to dealing with foreigners, especially such single-minded ones. He seemed friendly and eager to appease us (the prospect of having to follow us around on such a hot day might also have been a deterrent). Amira had no trouble wearing him down. He took our phone numbers and let us go.

The next morning, we ate breakfast early (another key to outwitting the security apparatus, which prefers to sleep in) and breezed down the hotel steps into a taxi, before the lone policeman at the door had time to get out of his chair. We traveled by cab, minibus, and finally pickup truck to the village of Bayyadiyya. Back in the city by midafternoon, Amira discovered twenty-two missed calls on her phone from someone her caller ID identified as *Ashraf, Informant*. This turned out to be the stocky policeman in a tight-fitting khaki uniform who was waiting for us at the hotel. He was furious. Because of us, Ashraf had been forced to start his informant work very early—"He's been here since nine o'clock," the receptionist told us, smothering a giggle. He had lied to his boss and pretended he was with us all day, to avoid getting in trouble.

In the interest of relationship building, we agreed to let the cops accompany us to visit a children's clothing retailer named Mister Baby (no one else seemed to see the absurdity of traveling in an armed convoy to interview someone about baby clothes). The police detail went ahead, and Amira and I followed in a taxi. Our driver, ignorant of the high-stakes security operation under way, stopped to pick up a young woman for the extra fare. At a roundabout, our police escort must have noticed that our number had mysteriously increased. He halted his car, rushed over, and opened the front passenger's side door.

"Get out!" he shouted, waving his weapon.

"What's going on?" the young woman asked, terrified. We apologized and told her she should leave right away.

After we arrived at the shop, Amira berated the officer for scaring the woman. The man refused to back down. "She knows perfectly well what's going on," he responded.

I wondered if all my future reporting in Minya would be as dramatic as my journey to Mister Baby, but in fact I never traveled with an armed escort again. On later trips, I would write out on a piece of paper that I didn't need police protection while I was in the city; this, along with my signature and passport number, worked like a magical incantation to keep the authorities at bay. Once I stayed at the Armed Forces Hotel, on the advice of a local factory executive who assured me that a military-owned establishment wouldn't have police on the premises, since the two institutions were rivals. It was a solution that could only have come out of the head of an Egyptian, and it worked just as he said. But the place was far from downtown, and deserted—who besides me wanted to spend the night with the armed forces? I never stayed there again.

Occasionally, the police let me know they were keeping tabs on me. Once when Amira and I checked out of our hotel the day before our reservation ended, the officer posted there asked why we were leaving early ("Of course, they know everything about us," Amira said). Another time, a cop at the hotel let slip the name of a remote agricultural road that we had been on earlier in the day, which suggested that we were being tracked by our mobile phones. But the police never disrupted my reporting; as far as I know, they didn't talk to anyone I interviewed. They seemed to have decided that I wasn't worth the trouble.

Over time, Amira and I learned to make our handlers useful: When life gives you dried onions, make *koshari*. One evening we wanted to return to Cairo but didn't have train tickets. The police officer at our hotel told us to look up a colleague of his when we got to the station. The 6:45 to Cairo was sold out, his friend told us, but the last compartment in first class wasn't full. He waited with us on the platform until the train came and then escorted us to two empty seats in the No. 6 car, exactly where he had said they would be. I tipped him £E15, and Amira and I enjoyed air-conditioned comfort all the way home. There's nothing like turning the security state to your advantage.

IN MY TWO years of traveling to Upper Egypt, I was amazed at how much reporting could be accomplished under a repressive regime. For the same reasons that the Egyptian government had failed to build a manufacturing sector or reform its educational system, the security state was less than airtight. You could often talk your way into places you wanted to go, with the police always a step behind. And if they caught up to you they could be disarmingly human—friendly, or inexperienced, or just not wanting to be bothered. But they held the power, and they could deploy it at any moment.

In early 2016, during the time I was making regular trips to Minya, an Italian Ph.D. student named Giulio Regeni was found dead in a ditch outside Cairo. His body showed multiple stab wounds, broken bones and teeth, and cigarette burns; an Italian autopsy report said he had been repeatedly tortured over the course of four days. Regeni had been researching independent trade union activity among Cairo's street vendors, which might have led state security to target him as a trouble-maker and a spy. Italian prosecutors have charged four members of Egypt's security services in absentia for Regeni's killing, which drew condemnation from around the world. The Egyptian government has never allowed a full investigation into his death.

The murder of Giulio Regeni served as the crudest type of warning to the journalists, scholars, activists, and aid workers who practiced in areas that the government didn't look kindly upon. You made rational-izations to yourself: Cairo street vendors were politically sensitive, while garment workers in Minya were perfectly fine. But at any moment, the human decency you took for granted could transform into something so brutal that it couldn't be understood or explained. No incantation could protect against that.

One theory that circulated after the killing was that it was less a deliberate act than a case of gross incompetence. In the general atmo-sphere of hysteria about foreign spies and terrorist networks, some police officers might have detained the young man and then over-stepped their bounds, with no idea of what it meant to brutalize a foreigner to that extent or how disproportionate their actions were. The police I had met on my reporting trips were mostly lazy and inept, and that made them absurdly lax in my eyes. But it could also make them dangerous.

Regeni's murder showed a lot about the nature of the police state under Sisi—mostly absent, then suddenly present. It could appear sloppy and somewhat ridiculous until the moment it beat a person to death and snapped his neck in two. I stored this knowledge away and hoped I never had to use it. My own incantation: Garment workers in Minya were perfectly fine.

———

THE DELTA FACTORY was doing better than fine. When I visited for the first time in February 2016, two hundred fifty people worked there; two months later, their number had doubled. By August of that year, the company employed nine hundred workers on thirty production lines, hitting the goal marked on Kevin Meyer's office calendar only a few weeks behind schedule. Efficiency climbed from 20 percent at the beginning of the summer to approach the 50 percent that Meyer had targeted, with a generous helping of *insha'allahs,* by the end of the year.

In the spring, every production line had lost an average of six people per month—that worked out to a turnover of 25 percent. By September, that figure had been cut in half. So many of the employees who had quit returned that Delta began turning people away, like the ones who had disappeared for long periods without telling their supervisors. "It's stabilized a lot quicker than I anticipated," Meyer told me. "It's put me in a position of strength, where I can choose who I want to hire. If we still had the twenty-five, thirty, forty percent turnover, I couldn't have done that."

In order to retain workers, Delta was moving quickly to resolve any potential problems. When some employees complained about overly long commutes, for example, the company expanded its fleet of buses. Meyer also sensed a subtle shift in mindset among the workers. People now had to be persuaded to leave their jobs, whereas before they had needed reasons to stay. In six months, female employment had turned from a fraught personal choice into something ordinary.

The next step was to shape the workforce to global efficiency standards. Every new supervisor, trainer, and industrial engineer underwent something called the Personal Profile Analysis, which required a person to read through a checklist of twenty-four sets of adjectives and select in each case the term that best and least described her. Through her chosen forty-eight descriptors ("brave," "happy," "domineering"), an individual could be mapped onto a chart with four quadrants labeled Dominance,

Influence, Stability, and Compliance, and slotted into the job that most suited her.

One day in his office, Meyer showed me diagrams of different personality types—it was human behavior expressed in zigzag lines, like stock prices.

PERSONALITY PROFILE TYPES

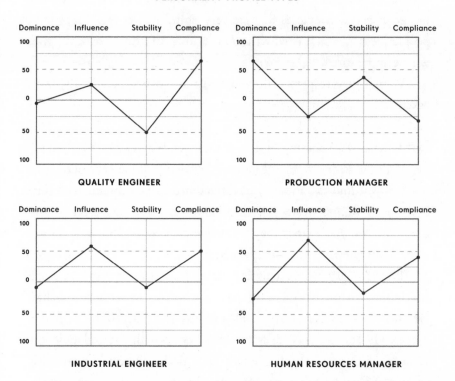

QUALITY ENGINEER

PRODUCTION MANAGER

INDUSTRIAL ENGINEER

HUMAN RESOURCES MANAGER

"If a person scores a medium-to-high dominance level, a very high influence level, a low stability level—meaning that person is a really focused person who wants to work with one or two tasks at the same time—and is a very compliant person who sticks to the rules, that person falls within the realm of human resources," Meyer explained. "Because for HR you need to be a little bit forceful, but you must have very high influence with people and be able to persuade them to do things for you. You don't need to work with twenty different things at the same time. And you need to stick to the rules, because HR is all about compliance."

Industrial engineers were high in Influence, he continued, because they had to communicate with people at all levels of the company and convince them to work in a different way. Production supervisors tended toward Dominance. "Very driven, very forceful, very intense, because he has goals and deliverables that are very tight," Meyer said. "He's not a people pleaser, which is why the *I* is so low. And he'll break the rules whenever he can."

"Which type of person do you find the most of here in Egypt?" I asked.

"What do you think?"

My head was spinning. "High-dominance people," I guessed, thinking of all the strong women I had met inside Egyptian factories.

"No, you find the most in quality control. I just interviewed three brand-new women yesterday. They came across as very assertive and dominant, or that's what they wanted me to think. But as soon as I started interviewing them, they faded."

The Personal Profile Analysis is based on the work of an American psychologist named William Marston, who categorized human behavior into types based on how people perceive and react to their environments. He laid out his ideas in a 1928 book with the indelible title *Emotions of Normal People* (though he is probably best known as the creator of Wonder Woman). Marston and other psychologists adapted his theories for clients like United Studios and General Motors, at a time when technology seemed capable of mastering all the complexities of the human mind. (Another Marston invention was the lie detector.)

I thought about the Personal Profile Analysis while I watched Rania working. It seemed to me that a successful supervisor needed all the qualities that were ranked on Marston's lists: She must be "brave," "happy," *and* "domineering." Dominance was a given, but she also had to Influence others into helping her when it wasn't part of their jobs, to have the Stability to do many things at the same time, and to Comply with rules and standards.

PERSONALITY PROFILE TYPES

Dominance	Influence	Stability	Compliance

PRODUCTION MANAGER

Was it statistically possible to rank high in all four categories? Were supervisors really superheroes? That seemed to be the only way to turn out six hundred pairs of boxer shorts every day whose legs matched and whose seams lay flat and whose tag fell exactly in the middle of the waistband.

IN THE MORNINGS when women arrive at the Delta factory, they hug and kiss each other as if they've been apart for months or years rather than just one day. A thirty-four-year-old supervisor told me that she thought of the young women on her line as her daughters; they gave her Mother's Day gifts and shared a cake on her birthday. Rania said something similar: "I'm just like their mother. I'm the one who protects them." She insisted that production problems on her lines be addressed only to her, as a way to protect her charges from bullying.

She had worked at Delta for seven years and formed deep alliances.

At the front of the production floor were the three lines she had been supervising in the first months that I knew her; having improved them to the level of target efficiency, she handed them back to the factory. Now she oversaw three lines of trainees at the back of the floor, but every morning she stopped by her former neighborhood to say hello, like a policeman walking his beat.

The factory's use of Rania as a troubleshooter—take a problem line, turn it around, move on—meant that a large number of people on the floor felt loyal to her. When she was short one worker on the Singer or the Flat Lock machine, she frequently turned to one of her former lines for help. If a woman who had once worked for her felt mistreated, she would ask Rania to intercede (some crying or fainting might be involved too). Maybe the way people looked out for one another did resemble the dynamics within a family, although Rania's use of the term surprised me. Her own experience with kin had been almost entirely negative. No one—not her father, her uncles, her husband, or her mother—had stood up for her when she needed to be protected. "You have to win people over with love," Rania said about the new family she had founded.

At 7:44 one morning in November 2016, Rania was knee-deep in trouble by the time I arrived at the factory. Two of the workers on her lines were absent, a third had just completed training, and a fourth had recently fallen down some stairs and needed to go home at once. The young woman stood, tall and pale and listing like a ship in need of repair, while several supervisors argued over who would replace her.

Before eight o'clock, Rania had already clashed twice with Jack, the production manager—once over the employee absences and another time over missing chairs. The two of them lobbed words at each other like bombs.

I don't have any more people.

Work with what you have.

The line will stop.

Rania mentioned to me, in a low voice, that she suspected a quality control worker was purposely trying to make her look bad by entering the wrong production numbers into a computer. "Someone is playing games," she told me. "I could make a scene, but I'm going to handle this discreetly." As she rose in the Delta hierarchy, she was acquiring more enemies and getting drawn into more turf battles.

Around nine-thirty, Rania started quarreling with a packing department head named Asmaa. Delta was running a health and safety training program for its employees, and every department had to send several people. Rania had dispatched one of Asmaa's workers—a sorter named Shaimaa—without checking with Asmaa first. Missing a worker could lead to lost productivity, so supervisors constantly haggled over girls like housewives at the vegetable market. This particular negotiation escalated into a shouting match that could be heard all over the floor.

I'm not going to give you anyone! You have three girls, and I don't have any!

Well, you're from Denshway!

Are you saying I'm from Denshway?

Denshway was a village in the Nile Delta that had been the site of a famous clash between Egyptian residents and British soldiers in 1906. Somehow, in the intervening century, calling a person a native of that place has turned into an insult of the worst kind, although no one could explain to me why this was so. I never met anybody who was actually from Denshway, so I still don't know.

The drama unfolded like a performance art piece all over the factory, as Rania went first to the women's changing room and then to the cafeteria in search of Shaimaa, who was unfortunate enough to have become a pawn in this power struggle. Rania finally found her sitting at a table, with her shoulders slumped and eyes red from crying, and led her down the corridor of executive offices to speak with Mohamed Hanafy, the personnel manager.

In a factory full of strong-willed women, Mohamed was the rare mild-mannered man, like a Nordic stranded on a Mediterranean shore. He had a paler complexion than most Egyptians—milky pallor, light blue eyes—and he always spoke in a calm voice, with a perpetual air of surprise at the emotions spilling out all around him.

"Why is she crying?" he asked, when he saw Shaimaa.

"Asmaa yelled at her," Rania said. "She shook her and took her bag."

A few minutes later, Asmaa herself burst through the door, looking tall and imperious, and threw herself into a chair with her arms crossed. She sighed loudly and then lit into Shaimaa. "You're so slow, that's why I have to bring other girls to work with you."

Kevin Meyer walked into the room to use the photocopier, and Mohamed explained the situation. "When it comes to sending a girl, we must maintain the hierarchy structure," Meyer said, to no one in particular. "If Rania sees someone who's free, that's fine, but she must communicate with her supervisor. The problem is not with production; the problem is with communication."

In five minutes, he had resolved a conflict that had eaten up almost an hour and a lot of energy. "Okay, it's over now," Meyer concluded. "Let's get back to work. *Shukran*. Thank you."

Later, he told me that Rania's perceived promotion above the other supervisors was causing conflicts. "Technically, Rania and Asmaa are equal. But there's a perception that because Rania has three lines below her, she has been elevated to a higher status. She sees it, and other people see it—"

"I'm sure I don't help being here either," I interrupted.

"It's not just you. Whenever management comes, there's just a little more interaction with Rania than with other people. She's always in their face. She has this tendency to break the rules," Meyer continued. "She gets the job done, there's no two ways about it, but she tends to pull rank, and that gets people's backs up."

I once asked Rania what her shortcomings as a manager were. She looked blank. It was the first time she had been stumped by one of my questions.

"Are there any?" I asked, and she laughed.

"My mind is working around the clock," she said at last. "If I can't think of ways to improve efficiency, maybe that will be my downfall."

The day that Rania fought with Asmaa, I decided that her degree of Dominance was through the roof, but that maybe her *I*, Influence, needed work. She still fit Kevin Meyer's description of the ideal supervisor: *He'll break the rules whenever he can.*

THE PRACTICE OF work study breaks down every task on the assembly line into a string of codes. To sew two pieces of cloth together, for example, requires five steps: A worker picks up a piece of cloth with one hand, picks up a second piece of cloth with her other hand, puts the two pieces together, then repositions first one hand and then the other hand to hold the pieces correctly for sewing. In the lingo of work study: GET GET PUT GET GET. She aligns the chest pocket on a shirt: GET PUT GET. She brings the material to the sewing machine's foot, the forked metal plate that holds fabric in place: PUT FOOT. In the 1970s, a British company named GSD Corporation Limited (which stands for "general sewing data") published these codes for the sewing industry, identifying thirty-nine basic motions used in garment manufacturing and calculating the optimal time to perform each one.

In the fall of 2016, Delta began training its instructors and industrial engineers in the methods of work study. The students met at the company's Cairo headquarters, in a conference room with a large U-shaped table and the inevitable display of men's boxers and briefs on the wall (never in my life had I spent so much time looking at undergarments). The instructor, a man named Dylan Shannon, was from the U.K., and the class was conducted in a mix of British English, broken English, and technical gibberish. I could manage the first two idioms but was hope-less in the last.

> Me personally, I prefer to use an MG2T where possible because it's cheaper and takes less time. Sometimes it's worth changing the workplace layout to facilitate being able to use MG2T rather than an MG2S.

> MAPE is very rarely used. In the majority of cases, the MAP codes are used when adding it to the FOOT.

> It's the same motion sequence as MAPE but the degree of diffi-culty of the GET is harder.

The students watched a series of videos starring a woman with a fluffy blond perm and bright red lipstick, who performed sewing opera-tions in a factory somewhere in England circa 1985. "They used the same video when I was doing GSD training," Shannon, who had cropped silver hair and was in his forties, said. "I think they're making a new one."

> My first Golden Rule is: An MG2T or MG2S must always be fol-lowed by a FOOT if you are sewing.

> Golden Rule Number Two: To add a label, always use MAPI.

Occasionally through the fog of MAPEs and FOOTs, I grasped some-thing essential:

> You're going to look at the detailed motions within a job. You're going to look at things in far more detail than you ever thought possible. And you'll all be asking: "Why are they doing it that way?"

Despite appearances, work study isn't meant to make employees work as fast as they can. The goal is to remove the individual from the process and to establish a sequence of motions that any worker, in any factory, on any day, can follow consistently without feeling tired. *Measure the job and not the operator* is the industry mantra. Fatigue is factored in: The operator of a single-needle lockstitch machine is allotted 9 percent of her work time to recover from her labors. A button sewer gets 5 percent. Allowances are made for those working under continual eyestrain (2 to 4 percent), or at especially monotonous tasks (4 percent) or high temperatures (5 to 6 percent). There's a tendency to look at a human being as an assemblage of body parts, as in the 1957 book *Introduction to Work Study*, which remains a bible in the field:

Use of the human body
When possible:
1. Motions of the arms should be symmetrical and in opposite directions and should be made simultaneously.
2. Hand and body motions should be made at the lowest classification at which it is possible to do the work satisfactorily.
   Class 1: Pivot is knuckle; body member moved is finger
   Class 2: Pivot is wrist; body members moved are hand and fingers
   Class 3: Pivot is elbow; body members moved are forearm, hand, and fingers

The students in the Delta class were nothing like the disembodied selves featured in work study training manuals. Mona Abdel-Monem, who had trained workers inside Delta for fifteen years, was compact and energetic and had a wide toothy smile. A recent college graduate named Rania, whose degree was in archaeology, had warm brown eyes and a sharp sense of humor. After a week of GET PUT and PUT FOOT lectures, the students were given Canon handheld video cameras ("I think after this training is finished, we need to keep these cameras for ourselves,"

Rania said). Their assignment was to analyze the production of Calvin Klein boxer shorts in Delta's Cairo factory.

"Welcome to hell," Mona joked, as she entered the vast production space crowded with sewing machines. She and her classmates spread out in pairs to film each stage of manufacturing, checking off items on a list as they went ("close waist elastic," "attach label at center back"). Mona took detailed notes but found time to encourage the workers too.

"When you're sewing one, you can prepare the next one," she told a young woman who was sewing a zigzag seam into a waistband.

"I'm new here," the woman said, not looking up from her machine, "and I'm scared of making a mistake."

"You must always be thinking of being quick, my dear." Mona smiled and pinched the woman's cheek playfully.

Back in the classroom, the engineers replayed film one of them had made of a woman sewing ("attach gusset to front and back"). They offered withering critiques:

> The way she does it at the end saves work for her, but it creates more work for the next person.

> This is their workspace, but there's no space to put anything. Every place has bags, bags, bags. She has no place to work.

> At the end, she tosses the work on a pile. The next worker will have to sort it out again, but she doesn't care.

"Personally, I've never seen it that bad," Shannon said about the woman's sloppy workstation, now immortalized on video for all time. "But she's very good at sewing."

After the engineers completed the course, they would remake the working procedures inside Delta—breaking every task into parts, pinpointing wasted seconds and excess motions, and redesigning the process to be more efficient. They would teach workers the new method and require them to stick to it.

Work study isn't widely practiced in Egypt—Delta's executives didn't know of any other company doing it—but it struck me as a searing laser treatment applied to the national disease, which Egyptians themselves often described in two words: *mafish nizam*, "there is no system." People slept late, they skipped meals and missed appointments and didn't answer their phones; there seemed to be a collective paralysis that prevented institutions from setting rules and following them. Individuals might be gifted and work hard, but there were few systems in place to reward personal industry, promote intelligent people, or put good ideas into practice. So much effort was wasted, or replicated, or came to nothing, and the failure started from the top. Egypt is frequently described as a police state, but up close it often feels as if there is no state—just a handful of strong personalities improvising their way through the disorder without a coherent long-term plan. Policies that were patently good for the country's development were endlessly discussed without ever being put into practice (in its economic management, according to one study, the gap between official policy and actual performance is greater in Egypt than in any other country in the region). All of which explains why the country has no significant manufacturing sector, why a child can go to school for six years but still not be able to read, and why the police in Minya couldn't be bothered to get out of their chairs and then later lied to their superiors about it. *Mafish nizam.*

Delta's new regimen, as Kevin Meyer explained it to me, would apply mathematical rigor to every endeavor. It would cancel out cultural differences—*men are in charge of women, I'm only doing this for fun, insha'allah, insha'allah*—and the makeshift nature of Egyptian life, to build a system identical to one you might find in Mumbai or Manchester. From the first time I met Meyer—in the parking lot outside the

Minya factory, where Amira and I were waiting for a shuttle bus back to Cairo—he was evangelizing about the possibilities.

"The idea," he said, "is to make the cost accounting in a factory in Minya the same as the cost accounting in a factory anywhere in the world."

"Good luck with that," Amira said, her intended encouragement coming off as sarcasm instead.

Growing up in Johannesburg, Meyer had no inkling that his future lay in such an esoteric field. The youngest of eight children and a mediocre student, he finished high school and stayed home for a year, doing nothing. One day, his older sister took him to the children's uniform factory where she worked and found him a job doing packing and odd jobs. He hated it—"I was always saying, 'Why are you doing it this way? Why don't you do it another way?'" After six months, an executive in the industrial engineering department offered to have him shadow her around the factory for a few days ("They were doing time studies and motion analysis and all this stuff I didn't understand at all"). The department director was a British man named Richard Ellis. He noticed Meyer and assigned him to write a three-thousand-word essay on what he had learned.

That was on a Thursday. Meyer labored over the piece all weekend and handed it in the following Monday. At the end of the workday, Ellis called him into his office.

"I told you to write an essay that was three thousand words long," the director said.

"This *is* three thousand words," Meyer responded.

"Count it."

He did. "It's three thousand words exactly."

"That's the type of people that we want," Ellis said. "You're starting tomorrow." And so he was hired—a young man who, against all odds, had grasped the importance of being precise.

He started as a junior work study officer while attending classes at night to get his diploma in industrial engineering. In his first six years on the job, Meyer wore shoes, slacks, a dress shirt, and a tie to work every day. "It was a good training ground. I'm not sorry that I went through it that way." His story was straight out of Benjamin Franklin and Horatio Alger and a thousand self-help manuals: Correct your external behavior, and you'll become the person you want to be.

EVEN IN A world designed by industrial engineers, not everyone performs exactly the same. Delta ranked its lines every month based on four criteria—on-time delivery, defects, efficiency, and attendance—and awarded bonuses according to those ratings. In November 2016, the company announced a plan to identify and reward high-performing individuals for the first time.

A little after eleven o'clock one morning, executives and supervisors met in the conference room of the Minya factory to hear about the new incentive scheme.

"The trends are good," Kevin Meyer said, pulling up a slide that showed factory efficiency ranging between 45 and 60 percent. "Now we're going to go one step further and measure each and every operator." From now on, he explained, employees would use an electronic barcode system to track every piece of work they completed.

At 11:46 A.M., the electricity cut out. A deep sigh passed through the building as the machines shuddered into silence, like dying beasts. Disruptions to the power supply were fairly common, and Meyer continued speaking in the now-dim conference room—about internal balancing, production sheets—without missing a beat. An executive read out the names of ten supervisors who would test the program first.

Rania immediately raised her hand. "Why did you choose those ten lines? The five lines in the back could use it more." She was pushing for the lines she supervised, which were in the back of the factory floor, to be included. If there was any chance to raise productivity, she didn't want her team missing out.

Meyer picked up on this. "Rania, I understand what you're trying to do," he said. "We need to implement it slowly, okay? If we go big and we don't get the correct information, the system will fail and people won't trust us."

He wrapped up the meeting and told supervisors to spread the word. "Forty thousand hours, that's the goal for this month. We must not drop from that."

I went back downstairs with Rania. The power was still off, and the production floor was pulsing with excitement. While I had been in the meeting, the rest of the Delta Textile Factory had transformed into a giant block party. Untethered from their work routines, the women gathered in large circles—talking, laughing, and singing. The ceiling lights flickered on one moment and off the next; at every instance, the workers erupted in cheers. Periodically a rumor would wash over the crowd—*The buses are coming! They're leaving now!*—and people would rush for the exits to see if their transportation home had arrived yet. There wasn't a manager in sight.

I strolled around the factory talking to workers at random.

Coming here has changed me. I love meeting new people and seeing new things.

I like my supervisor. If she leaves, I'll leave.

I don't have any plans for the future. It depends on the guy I marry.

By two o'clock, the women of Delta had gone wild. Groups of workers sang and clapped, whooping and ululating on the production floor. They crowded around me, clamoring to take my picture and screaming *What's your name?* in English, over and over. A woman came up and boldly touched my hair. They formed a circle with me at its center and yelled out questions:

Which place has prettier girls, Cairo or here?

We need seven hundred grooms! We're all spinsters!

I sat down with Rania and Magda, my translator, and a few of the other supervisors, and the crowd surrounded us. They sang a song that expressed the greatest joy they could imagine, which is the song of a woman on her wedding day.

Around two-thirty, the workers started to leave. The buses had finally arrived; electricity still hadn't been restored, and no more work
would be done today. The final words from Meyer's presentation—*Forty
thousand hours, that's the goal for this month*—were still in my head. That
day on the floor, I understood the immense task that Delta had set for
itself: to build an orderly system where none had existed before. I saw
how fragile the effort was, and how quickly it could break down. And I
grasped the value of implementing work study in a place like this. It was
easy to ridicule the program's "scientific" aspects—the fractions of seconds saved, the tendency to view human beings as body parts. But work
study was a framework upon which to establish a factory that could
compete with any other in the world, and bring training and wages and
a community to women who had none of those things. Following these
principles, a factory could survive and even thrive in this inhospitable
zone on the edge of the desert where almost nothing seemed to take
root.

Rania remained seated and appeared to be in no hurry to go anywhere. I asked her to tell me the lyrics of the song the women had
been singing. She spoke slowly, playing the words over and over in her
head:

> *When he met me, he held my hand,*
> *My son, my son, he held my hand.*
> *O* tamiya, *o* falafel,
> *And estrangement is difficult to bear.*
>
> *Put your hand in mine and let's walk like Upper Egyptians,*
> *And if they ask you, tell them this is my lover,*
> *Hold your waist to my waist,*
> *And if they ask you, tell them this is my bride.*
>
> *Put your shoulder to my shoulder,*
> *And if they ask you, tell them this is my wife.*
> *He held my hand, he held my hand.*

The floor was almost empty now. Rania finished and looked at me with a smile.

IN DECEMBER, THE workers began sewing a Lacoste-brand T-shirt, whose long symmetrical seams down the front made for a more difficult product than boxer shorts. The following month the company started making the shirts for Tommy John, another major client. Delta was at full strength—almost a thousand workers, producing at 45 percent efficiency—and growing fast. When I visited in February 2017, cardboard crates were stacked ten high and every which way; they snaked between the assembly lines, like mazes constructed by children. I peeked inside a box: Avia-brand nylon and Spandex bike shorts, another new item. More pairs of shorts hung on garment racks, already wrapped in plastic and ready for their Middle American debut. The *Women's XS Solid 7 Captivate Short,* the attached price tag said, would sell for $9.86 at Walmart.

At every workstation was taped a photocopied sign:

- MAKE HAPPINESS A HABIT.
- LIFE IS HOPE WHO LOST HOPE LOST LIFE.
- BEAUTIFUL LADIES CLEAN THE MACHINES 4 TIMES PER DAY.
- I'M HAPPY TO WORK WITH NICE PEOPLE LIKE THIS.

"Work is going well. You can feel the energy," Savy, the executive in charge of worker training, said when I saw her on the floor. The place was buzzing: It was rumored that the governor of Minya would visit that day.

A skinny, sullen-looking young man named Ahmed, who worked in Personnel, tracked me down. The governor was scheduled to arrive at eleven, and I should make myself scarce before then. "I'm not supposed to show my face either," Kevin Meyer told me. The dream of self-reliance died hard, and so an Israeli American company managed by British, South African, and Sri Lankan executives had to tie itself in knots to look like an Egyptian company run by Egyptians (Chinese American journalists apparently also ruined the illusion). By a stroke of luck, the Sri Lankan factory manager was absent that day, so Atef, a tall, stooped, shy Egyptian man who ran the quality control department, would pretend to be in charge of the entire factory.

The bike shorts were a big step forward for the Minya operation. Making boxers, Meyer explained to me, is simple: Sew the front and back pieces together, attach an elastic waistband, repeat. On biking shorts, the elastic is concealed by fabric, and there are many more pieces of cloth to stitch together. This particular design for Walmart had a hidden pocket inside the waistband, and extra-thick seams that were sewn on a triple-stitch machine, and many other steps—twenty-two in all, double what was required for men's underwear.

"We went through hell with that style," Meyer told me. "There was a lot of pain and shouting and screaming and crying and tears." Half a dozen machine operators quit their jobs. Friendships ruptured, including the relationship between Rania and one of her supervisors.

"She's quite a strong character," Meyer said. "She put pressure on them and they couldn't cope with it."

"Who was the supervisor?" I asked.

"Fatima."

I was surprised—Fatima was the woman in the *niqab* whom I had met at Rania's house. "I thought they were good friends."

"That was my impression as well. But Rania was put in a new position and was under pressure to deliver. She had to push and still maintain the friendship, and one of the two had to give."

It said a lot about the complexity of worker relations that in a factory of almost a thousand people, someone at Meyer's level would know the state of friendship between two line supervisors. He and Savy had personally overseen the retraining of Fatima—she had been moved to another part of the floor—and persuaded most of the women who quit to come back. Delta was meeting its hourly production targets for the bike shorts, and Walmart had increased the size of its order.

When I got home, I checked out the Walmart website. There they were: *Avia Women's Active 7" Captivate Training Shorts*, selling for $9.86 a pair ("perfect for your active lifestyle"). Under the product description, I was startled to see many of the features—"flat elastic waistband," "hidden inner pocket," even "assorted colors"—that precipitated such grief and drama on the Minya factory floor. The shorts had gotten three reviews, each one awarding the product five stars. *Love these shorts for biking and working out!* one customer wrote. *I love how they fit on me and how cute I look working out,* said another.

The comments made me think about the vast distance between the women who sewed these garments and the ones who ended up wearing them. In what world, I wondered, might someone like Rania need to wear a pair of Spandex bike shorts, or worry about *how cute I look working out?* That was a paradox of globalization: It linked two worlds but left them impossibly far apart.

AFTER COMPLETING THEIR training, the industrial engineers at Delta began to implement work study techniques inside the factory. They began with the packing department, whose workers assembled three-packs of boxer shorts for shipment, one each in black, white, and gray. Their previous method—but *mafish nizam,* there is no system—had been to dump several boxes of the shorts on a table and grab what they needed from the pile at random. The engineers filmed the process, analyzed it ("Mr. Kevin, this is a complete mess!") and reorganized the work area. They put three boxes of shorts, one of each color, on every table. A packer could take one pair in each color, in sequence, and develop a rhythm as she worked.

"I assume the workers liked that better?" I asked Meyer.

Of course not; they fought him every step of the way. "This is going to take longer!" was their initial reaction.

Productivity fell the first hour, as the workers adjusted their movements, and they eagerly told Meyer so: "See? It didn't work." The second hour, they filled as many boxes as they had under the old method ("but it's the same!") Over the next several hours, their rates improved steadily until they were packing eight boxes an hour instead of the original four. "This actually works!" a supervisor said in astonishment. At the end of the day, all the employees agreed that the new system made them more productive than they had ever been.

"How did you do it?" Meyer asked the packers.

"I don't know."

The governor of Minya never made it to the factory. But something more consequential was happening inside Delta. On that day, Meyer told me the company had decided to buy a piece of land behind the current facility, more than doubling the size of the operation. They would erect a second building, which could house between seven and fifteen production lines and additional warehouse space.

"So that's a huge vote of confidence in Minya, right?" I asked. "It means that this is working."

"Yes, it is. However, it puts us through exactly the same pains we just went through."

"You've got to do it all over again."

"We've got to do it all over again," he echoed. "We're looking at the surrounding villages again, promoting the factory, getting new recruits, between three hundred fifty and five hundred people."

"What's the time frame?"

"Three months."

"Three months?" I was in shock. "Wait!"

"I said, the building will be done in three months, and then we can start the recruitment."

Over the past year, I had watched Delta executives hire more than seven hundred women and turn them into productive workers in the face of high turnover, family opposition, resistance to new ideas, fainting spells, screaming matches, and a great deal of—to use one of Meyer's favorite expressions—"blood, sweat, and tears." Now their reward would be to do it all over again. "I think I'm going to cry," I said.

"I'm going to cry."

He was flying to South Africa that afternoon for an extended home leave—"I need a break"—but he would return in the spring to build out the new operation. This time it would be easier, Meyer predicted, because experience had taught Delta that the most trainable workers lived within ten miles of Minya. Proximity to urban life was necessary, the executives concluded, to shape a worker who respected the demands of the clock, who would come to work on time and adapt to the production schedule. Beyond that cutoff, village customs and village time kicked in, making the transformation too hard. *Ten miles*—that was the distance between the modern world and whatever it left behind.

RANIA DIDN'T SHED much light on her falling-out with Fatima ("How did you know about that?" she asked suspiciously when I inquired about it). To her, all conflict was personal, and anyone who disagreed with her must be flawed or disloyal. Fatima was ungrateful and forgot how Rania had helped her rise; Fatima was lazy and pushed her work onto the other supervisors. "I'm friends with everyone in the factory," Rania said. "Except Fatima." She mentioned that her lines were ranked first, third, and fourth in the factory. The message was clear: *Good riddance, I'm better off without her.*

The competition to be the most productive line in the factory seemed to be gaining urgency. If there was a delay in getting materials, Rania would give the available work on all three of her lines to her friend Zahraa, to help her hold her number one position even as Rania's other lines fell behind (manufacturing, apparently, worked like the Tour de France, in which some team members sacrificed themselves so that another of them could win). Hind Ali, another supervisor I had gotten to know, told me that her line planned to work overtime that weekend. "We want to keep our number one position until the first of the month," she said.

What was behind the cutthroat quest for supremacy? The factory handed out prizes like teacups and kettles to the top lines, but these felt like extras. "The gift is symbolic," Rania told me. "It's the honor that matters." Perhaps the contest was a way for the workers to replicate the dynamics of rural life that were so familiar to them. In the village, bragging rights were based on small distinctions in circumstance: *My family has land. We don't need the money.* Status, in the factory world, came down to minute differences in efficiency—the gap between winner and runner-up was less than one percentage point. But coming out on top mattered a great deal, even though the numbers had no meaning to anyone outside the factory walls.

Being Delta's star supervisor brought pressure, Rania told me. "They say it's easy to reach the top of the mountain," she said. "The hard part is staying there." On the morning of the governor's no-show visit, I watched her clash with employees in the factory warehouse over batches of black thread, then fall into a conflict with the man who headed the electrical department. She complained to him that the machine that heated steam for ironing was taking too long and putting her workers behind.

As the two of them argued, Asmaa, one of Rania's supervisors, came up and reported that she hadn't produced a single pair of shorts in the past hour because of delays with the steam machine. Asmaa was small and pale and usually looked harried. This morning she had a pencil tucked behind each ear, which made her appear doubly stressed.

Rania checked her phone: It was almost eleven. "When did you come to me with this problem?" she asked sharply. "You should have come earlier, not ten minutes before the hour is finished."

"Should I go and get the manager?"

"Yes, go get the manager."

Rania turned her attention to a young woman who was ironing. Nisma was eighteen, with a slender freckled face and slightly protruding front teeth, and something of a rescue case. Delta had intended to fire her, until Rania interceded and agreed to take charge of her. Now Nisma refused to take orders from anyone else.

Rania held up a pair of boxers with one hand on each side of the waistband, pulled the fabric taut, and laid it on the ironing table. "Hold it on two sides, put it down, iron it."

Nisma put a pair of shorts on the table and began to iron carelessly, using one hand.

Rania tried again. "Straighten it from the bottom, then stretch it." She smoothed out the fabric before ironing first the front of a pair of boxers, then the back. "Your turn."

Again, Nisma slapped down the iron and pushed it around without bothering to smooth out the fabric. I had never seen anyone convey such apathy in the act of ironing.

Rania looked at the ceiling. "God, please make her work!" she intoned dramatically.

As we walked away, Rania told me, "They were going to fire her."

"Is she getting better?" I asked doubtfully.

"Even if she doesn't get better, I'll keep training her."

That was the saving grace of Egypt. The streets and buildings were falling to pieces and almost nothing worked right, but people showed a remarkable generosity toward one another that was striking, especially in a poor country. This behavior seemed partly tied to the Muslim faith, which emphasizes charity and a person's obligation to help the less fortunate. Rania could shout at the electricity manager or snap at Asmaa but also take time to carry someone like Nisma, who was surely not helping her hourly productivity.

I remembered, from my earlier visit, how Rania had encouraged the young deaf woman who was learning to sew on the elastic machine. During the time I reported at Delta, she had been one of three deaf workers I came across. In every case, the others went out of their way to accommodate these particular co-workers. In her factory outside Alexandria, Riham employed an intellectually disabled young woman named Shaimaa, who did simple tasks like trimming threads and hardly ever spoke to anyone. *If we want to go forward, we all have to go forward,* Riham had said. That sentiment held Egyptian society together and made life bearable.

In the course of the day, Rania stepped in at various stations to speed things along—ironing waistbands, running the motif presser. The steam machine was fixed, and production picked up. At one point, I spotted Nisma in tears—"She said her arms hurt," Rania told me—but later she was ironing shirts one after another in a steady rhythm, her mouth slightly open with effort.

Rania's lines all hit their targets. It was a day without a crisis, in contrast to all the other times I had followed her around the floor. When I went to say goodbye, I realized that she hadn't gone to the production manager once all day to beg for a replacement worker.

"You must not have any absences today," I said.

"No, actually we do." Asmaa was missing two workers, and Zahraa two as well, but the team had become so good at managing things that I hadn't noticed.

"So you're better at line-balancing?"

Rania shrugged. "It became easy."

THE SECOND TIME I went to Rania's house, she killed two ducks in my honor. This takes place early in the morning: Say a prayer, then use a sharp knife to lop off the head quickly so the animal doesn't suffer. By the time I arrived with Magda, my translator, Rania was soaking the birds in boiling water and plucking their feathers into a metal basin. She lent us *gallabiyyas* to wear so the blood wouldn't splash on our clothes.

"Kareem, come here." She set the boy to work pulling the feathers off one duck, although he found it difficult going ("it's much harder than chickens"). Later, Dina came over and held a slippery piece of the meat tight with both hands, so that Rania could chop it in half with a butcher knife whose blade came perilously close to her daughter's fingers.

In the winter of 2005, I had witnessed an almost identical scene in a Chinese farming village. Chen Meirong, the mother of a young migrant worker who I was writing about, crouched on the kitchen floor pulling feathers out of a chicken—the same basin of scalding water, the bright red blood—while her youngest daughter watched from the doorway. "The children refuse to do this work," the mother told me. People in rural China accepted that the younger generation would leave the village, first to attend school and then to work. They would live in a city and shop at a supermarket and never need to know how to pluck feathers from a duck that their mother had raised and had killed that morning. In Egypt, children still do these things. No one expects village life to come to an end or that sons and daughters will have to learn a vastly different set of skills than their parents.

Soon after I arrived, Kareem came into the house from the side door carrying a baby boy in his arms.

I was surprised. "Who is that?"

"Mahmoud."

"Whose son is he?"

"He's my brother."

A few minutes later, the baby's mother entered the room to scoop him up. As soon as she left, Rania turned to me, her posture stiff and vigilant. "That's the second wife."

Asmaa was young and slim with arresting dark eyes, and she wore a *gallabiyya* in a vivid shade of purple. She came in and out of the house several times in the course of the day. We were never introduced, and we didn't exchange a single word. I was curious about her and how she had ended up here, but I never found the occasion to ask her. I sensed that even acknowledging her humanity, in Rania's eyes, would have seemed a betrayal.

Yasser showed up and said hello, then returned with a ladder to fix a flickering lightbulb over the door. He and Rania chatted and laughed about something; later, I saw Rania go into the space between the houses to ask Asmaa a question. You couldn't say the three of them had reconciled, exactly—it was more like an uneasy truce that was holding for the moment.

Over six hours Rania plucked, cleaned, disemboweled, boiled, fried, and roasted the two ducks and also shelled peas, peeled carrots, stewed chickpeas with tomatoes, boiled rice, and tossed a salad, while talking to me at the same time. Yasser fiddled on the ancient computer in the living room—"He's trying to impress us by watching a foreign movie," Magda whispered—and then played a soccer video game for two hours. He went out and returned with a can of Stella beer for me. I declined, out of respect for Rania and the conservative mores of the village. Yasser sat down and poured out half a glass and drank it by himself.

The dinner was delicious. As on my first visit, Magda and I ate with just Rania and her children. Partway through the meal, Yasser passed through, piled a plate high with duck and bread, and retreated to his part of the house.

After we ate, Rania sat with Magda and me to snack on sunflower seeds and look through her wedding albums again. At one point, Asmaa came in to ask Rania something.

When the younger woman had left the room, Rania suddenly took a handful of sunflower seed shells and flung them after her, as if she were casting an evil spell.

She looked at me. "Oh, Leslie."

"Oh, Rania."

She shook her head and laughed and sighed, all at the same time.

———

THE CHILDREN ENTERTAINED themselves with the board game Connect Four, which I had brought them. They played at breakneck speed, each person totally focused on getting four checkers in a row without paying any attention to what his or her opponent was doing. When it was Rania's turn, she studied the board and deliberated before every move. She always won.

Yasser told me that around 40 percent of the people in the village had gone abroad to work. The conversation turned to where they would travel if they could.

"I'd like to go to Sweden, because it's beautiful there," Yasser said. "Or Greece."

Rania was sitting on the couch, peeling a bowl of carrots that she held in her lap.

"Where would you like to go?" I asked.

She bit her lip and shook her head quickly, an expression I had come to know. It meant *This isn't something I want to talk about.*

"I don't want to go anywhere."

As RANIA GAINED experience in managing three supervisors and their lines, she found ways to further boost her numbers. She had struggled to get enough workers before, but now she made do with fewer. Zahraa's line, the undisputed leader in the Minya factory, had twenty-six people at one point. Rania reduced that to twenty and planned to knock off two more (the extra workers were sent to other assembly lines). The strategy was simple math—the fewer the people doing the work, the greater the productivity per worker—but the risk lay in being caught short of a crucial person at the wrong time. Rania moved employees around and stepped in herself when needed. Production, to her, was like a complicated symphony with all the parts playing continuously inside her head.

When I visited the Delta plant in August 2017, a large gold-plated trophy sat at the head of one of her lines; once again, her team had achieved the highest efficiency rate in the factory. Production was still going full tilt. Boxes of finished garments were stacked in the yard outside the factory, and construction of the new plant was about to start. The company was planning for audits by two major clients, Nike and Columbia.

At the end of the workday, I waited for Rania at the factory entrance; my translator, Mariam, and I were to go home with her that evening. The workers passed by in a continuous stream, chatting and shouting, with joy and relief and exhaustion in their faces. A few women recognized me, from my year and a half of visiting the factory, and came over. *She's still upstairs. She's coming.* The workers were used to seeing me in the company of Rania—I had become part of their village.

Mohamed Hanafy saw me as he walked past. "Who are you waiting for?"

"Rania."

"She's finished," he said. "She'll collect her pay. Today is her last day."

"What? Rania, the supervisor?" I was shocked.

"She was making big problems in the factory. I'll tell you about it, but not now."

RANIA APPEARED AT last, looking troubled. We got on the company minibus, and she sat in the back row with Zahraa and spent most of the trip talking on her phone. When we got to her home, she put some pieces of duck to cook on the stove and then sat down with Mariam and me in the living room. Yasser joined us. On the couch was a twenty-one-piece dinnerware set that Rania had won for overseeing the best line in the factory. It was still in its box, unopened.

Rania started talking about a man in the factory named Khaled, the head of security and "a shady character," who sometimes phoned women after hours to flirt with them. Rania had ordered him to stop calling her—"I shouted at him and made a scene"—and that angered Mohamed Hanafy, who had good relations with Khaled. Mohamed already resented her, Rania said, because she stood up for her workers and sometimes challenged him.

Yasser sat next to her, his expression one of total attention mixed with incomprehension. There was something about him—his short neck, his meek smile—that made me think of a turtle. He was slow, stubborn, patient.

"Who is this Khaled?" he asked.

I was struggling, too. Mohamed Hanafy, as Delta's personnel manager, was in charge of almost a thousand workers. Rania was one of thirty supervisors in the Minya plant. Was it really possible that he feared her so much that he had pushed her out?

Several times when she had been absent from work to run errands, Rania continued, the rate of defects on her lines had gone up. The factory manager had also accused her of "making trouble" with two women, but that couldn't be true, because she hadn't even been present at the time he said she was. Her account of her own firing was terribly garbled. Events in the workplace seemed all mixed up in her mind, and one detail followed another and another, until I couldn't figure out which ones were important. Maybe she didn't know either.

The story ended with Rania stopping a Delta executive as he left the factory that afternoon in his car. "Give me some time, and we'll contact you," the man told her.

"So should I come in tomorrow?" she asked.

"I didn't say that."

"Should I not come in tomorrow?"

"I didn't say that either. Give me some time, and we'll contact you."

Now it was evening, and no one had called. "I'll just wait and see what happens," Rania said.

Yasser objected. "If you just wait and do nothing, then it won't go your way." He turned to me. "Leslie, can you intercede in her case?"

I told him I didn't have any authority inside the factory, but I would try to find out more. I was struck by Yasser's concern. He listened to his wife and tried to understand her position. Even though he couldn't offer much advice, it was clear that he took her work seriously and even respected what she had accomplished. That was more than you could say for many Egyptian husbands.

"The problem with this country," Rania said, "is that when someone has power, they always use it to get what they want."

Asmaa didn't appear all afternoon. I assumed she had been warned to steer clear of Rania on this of all days. Finally, late at night, the door to the living room opened and she entered carrying her baby. I noticed that whenever she made an appearance, she held her son in front of her like a talisman. He was her armor, the sole proof of her worth in this household where she had so little status.

"*As-salam alaykum,*" she said to me in greeting. She deposited the little boy on the floor, where Rania's children were playing with the set of Legos that I had brought, and then vanished like a spirit. The baby, Mahmoud, had a round face and pale brown hair in corkscrew curls.

"*Shaklu wihish,*" Rania said. "He's ugly. Even though they try to make him look nice." She made a face at the baby, who started to cry.

She was back on speaking terms with her husband; even Asmaa was being allowed to show her face downstairs. The adults in the household were managing the delicate act of appearing civil to one another. Rania had apparently decided to take out her unhappiness on one-year-old Mahmoud, the family's weakest member.

"SHE CREATED A lot of problems in the factory," Mohamed Hanafy said, when I met him the next morning. "This is just the latest one."

"What kind of problems?"

"She forced two girls on her lines to make Sexy Call to a driver."

"Make *what?*"

"Sexy Call."

"Make *what?*"

The term, in English, had entered the Egyptian Arabic lexicon a couple of years earlier, when a man was taped bragging to a woman over the phone about his sexual stamina. The recording went viral on YouTube, and, in the inexplicable way in which things happened in Egypt—or was this just a social media phenomenon?—the man became a celebrity. The Sexy Caller enjoyed a brief acting career, appearing in commercials and even a television serial that aired during Ramadan.

According to Mohamed, Rania had ordered two women who worked on one of her lines to make Sexy Call to a company driver whom she disliked. Rania recorded the conversations for future blackmail purposes. The matter sounded frivolous, not to mention bizarre, but it scared the company's executives, Mohamed said. The two women who made the calls were Muslim, both of them married; the driver was Christian. Sectarian violence had started over less.

"Do you know what that would do?" Mohamed asked, looking at me to see if I understood. "That could close the factory."

Rania had initiated other plots against her enemies inside the factory, he continued. She urged two workers to file a complaint against a manager, claiming that he was verbally abusive. She filmed a female employee sitting next to a driver as supposed proof of her promiscuity. (Sex and videotape were her favorite weapons, by his account.) Both Mohamed and the factory manager had warned Rania that she would be fired if she continued trying to hurt people she didn't like. "The workers are terrified of her," he said. "Where does she get this sense of her own power?"

He acknowledged that Rania was a good supervisor, and he sympathized with her marital situation (of course, there are no secrets in a clothing factory). "I know that Rania has a difficult life at home, I know this," he said. "Maybe she treats people badly because that's how her husband treats her. But how can I keep a supervisor if she treats workers like that?"

He continued, "There's something wrong with her mind. A normal person doesn't do this. Whatever dirty thing is in the factory, she's involved in it."

AFTER I SPOKE with Mohamed, I went down to the factory floor. It felt strange to be there without Rania. I found Zahraa and asked her what she thought about the accusations.

"I don't want to say bad things against her, because she's my friend," Zahraa said. "But there are these very conflicting reports, and I don't know what to believe."

"But this work is so important to her, isn't it?"

"The job is very important to her, both psychologically and financially."

"What do you think will happen?" I asked.

"It's very difficult to predict what she'll do."

She was Rania's closest friend inside Delta, and I had expected her to rush to Rania's defense. But Zahraa didn't tell me that Rania and Mohamed Hanafy had never gotten along, nor that he wanted her gone. She didn't mention Khaled's late-night phone calls, or the defective work, or the hours that Rania had taken leave from the factory, or anything else to corroborate Rania's jumbled list of grievances. Instead, she said that the conflicting accounts left her uncertain whom to believe. Reading between the lines, I had to assume that the charges might have merit.

BEFORE I LEFT Rania's house, she asked me: "Leslie, will you still come to the factory when I'm not there?" I assured her that I would come see her wherever she was.

But after speaking to Mohamed Hanafy, I realized that I had misunderstood her question. Rania hadn't asked: *Will you still come see me when I'm not at the factory?* She had said: *Will you still come to the factory when I'm not there?* It was as if she couldn't conceive of the Delta plant being interesting to me if she no longer worked there. Or maybe she was testing my loyalties, trying to see if I would choose the factory over her.

I had spent more than a year watching Rania rise inside the factory world, and the way it fell apart—the sudden firing, the ugly accusations—was shocking and painful to learn about. But the suggestion that she had been instigating power games of some kind didn't come as a surprise to me. She was good at cultivating allies and building her network, but she could turn on people with startling vindictiveness. That shouting match with Asmaa, the packing supervisor—that had been Rania's effort to move in on a competitor's turf and control one of her workers, I saw that now. Her friend Fatima, the supervisor, couldn't produce bike shorts fast enough, so Rania turned against her. The factory, in her eyes, wasn't a group of people moving toward a common goal; it was an arena in which everyone competed fiercely for supremacy and only one person could win. Rania seemed constitutionally unable to see things from another person's point of view, or to judge her own actions critically. When I'd asked her about her shortcomings as a manager, she hadn't known what to say. It was likely that she had no idea why she had been fired.

A subsequent factory investigation would prove to be agnostic on the issue of Sexy Calls. Nobody could say for certain whether the Calls had occurred, or who had prompted them. But what Rania had been guilty of doing, time and again, was inciting members of the Delta workforce against her enemies, as Mohamed had described. Some months later, when I reached Kevin Meyer at his home in South Africa, he corroborated that Rania had tried to manipulate production to benefit herself and hurt her rivals. His reaction to the whole affair was similar to mine: "It's a pity, because she's great."

Mohamed Hanafy had said: *Maybe she treats people badly because that's how her husband treats her.* Rania often spoke about the factory in family terms—she was like a mother to her workers, she won their loyalty through love. But Egyptian family dynamics can be poisonous. Several generations often live together under one roof, because of long tradition and short finances. Family members are unable to speak openly about what makes them unhappy, so they may resort to subterfuge or manipulation to get their way. Petty fights can turn into full-blown feuds that drag on for weeks or months, and everyone takes sides.

Since she was in her teens, Rania had shuttled between three families, and in each one she had been treated badly. On her mother's side, her uncles had forced her to work for them and showed her no love. In her father's family, her stepmother was a bully and her father forced her to marry someone she didn't care for. Her own husband had betrayed her by marrying a second wife without telling her, making Rania the laughingstock of the neighborhood. At every stage in life, she had been hurt and humiliated by someone stronger than she was.

It was no wonder that, once she found herself in a position of power, she played by the same rules.

WHEN THE ANTHROPOLOGIST Homa Hoodfar studied marriage in working-class families, she discovered that interviewing husbands in the presence of their wives often led to fights between the couple:

> Five interviews out of nine resulted in severe family disputes primarily because husbands and wives did not agree on the limits of men's financial responsibilities. . . . When I interviewed the ninth husband it ended up in such a fight that I dropped the idea of interviewing the men but continued to talk with them informally and ask their views.

All families fight. But much of the strife in an Egyptian household stems from the imbalance of power that is a structural feature of the marriage. A husband is expected to financially support his family; in return, he enjoys authority over his wife as well as the right to repudiate her or to take multiple spouses. If this arrangement was once meant to ensure that women were taken care of, today it seems custom-made for conflict. Marriage is a zero-sum game, with most of the power concentrated on one side.

Married couples, Hoodfar observed, often had very different ideas of what a husband owed to his wife and children. Men typically provided food, clothing, and housing but regarded anything beyond that as an extravagance. A husband might occasionally pay for a household appliance or medicine, but this was considered a gift for which his family should be grateful. One man had purchased an electric washing tumbler, an old-fashioned device for washing clothes, years before; he brought this up whenever he and his spouse quarreled over money, as proof that he had done more than his share. Wives struggled to pay for doctors' visits, household goods, and the children's education out of the allowances their husbands gave them. If women had jobs, they sometimes bought these things on their own to avoid arguments.

Married men invariably hid their true income from their spouses, Hoodfar found, as a way to assert their status and keep their wives off balance. Women sometimes put money into a *gamiyya,* a type of savings club common in Egypt, without telling their husband. Wives who ran small businesses almost never asked their partner for help.

As one woman said, by nature men have sticky fingers and would develop an appetite for the few piasters their wives earn. Another woman said if something came up and she could not attend to her business, she would ask her children or a friend to take over. If they could not help, she would simply close the business because, as she said, once men take over, that is the end of your business.

Each side ascribed the worst motives to the other. Husbands complained that their wives were greedy and demanding; wives saw their husbands as selfish. And these were couples who were still married! "On closer observation," Hoodfar wrote, "the basis for the bitterness seemed to be the unwillingness of husbands to share information about their incomes and actual personal expenses."

The conception of marriage as blood sport is built into the institution. When the parents of a young woman negotiate a union with her future husband, her status as the weaker party is foremost in their minds. Their aim is to protect their daughter, as much as possible, from future exploitation. A bride's parents may demand that he give her a kilogram of meat each week, or pay a certain amount for clothing or household expenses; negotiations may cover whether the woman will use contraception during the first year of marriage or only after a child is born. The document known as the *ayma*, which lists the wife's assets, is intended not just to let her reclaim these goods in case of divorce, but to remind her husband and his family of her worth.

Domestic quarrels tend to multiply as other relatives get involved. Sometimes issues of honor are at stake, and sometimes they're not. A brother may insist on chaperoning his engaged older sister everywhere to protect the family's reputation. A mother may come to blows with her grown daughter over the number of teacups in her trousseau. A mother-in-law may take a saucepan from her daughter-in-law's home without asking her. A sister-in-law may rearrange the furniture in her brother's apartment because she prefers it that way. Since so few women work outside the home, they can focus a great deal of time and energy on these battles.

Almost all the divorced women I knew in Egypt cited family interference as a cause of their marital breakdowns. Hind Ali, a supervisor inside Delta, told me that her husband's mother complained whenever she went out to work or to visit her own parents; Hind's husband tended to treat her much worse if his sisters were around. The mother-in-law of

Eman Abdel Hamid Mohamed, who worked in Riham's factory, complained about her so much that finally Eman stopped visiting her.

"He's the son of his mother," Eman said about her husband—which,
from her point of view, was the worst thing you could say about someone.

A lot of domestic warfare is rooted in the tenets of Islamic law. The
male privilege of polygamy, for example, reminds a wife that she can be
replaced anytime by another, thus pitting women against each other as
rivals for male attention. The Islamic requirement that a man support
his sisters, if needed, creates a different arena of conflict between female
relatives over a family's resources.

The greatest obstacle to conjugal harmony is the exalted status of the
mother-in-law—in many of the stories I heard, the family matriarch
seemed to regard the marriage of her adult son as an existential threat.
"The close link between mother and son is probably the key factor in the
dynamics of Muslim marriage," the scholar Fatima Mernissi writes.

> **In a traditional setting the mother's involvement with her son . . .
> goes so far as to prevent his being alone with his wife. A husband
> and wife cannot be together during the day without being con-
> spicuously anti-social. . . .
>   The triangle of mother, son, and wife is the trump card in the
> Muslim pack of legal, ideological, and physical barriers that sub-
> ordinate the wife to the husband and condemn the heterosexual
> relation to mistrust, violence, and deceit.**

In her book *Avenues of Participation: Family, Politics, and Networks in
Urban Quarters of Cairo*, the political scientist Diane Singerman writes
about household disputes, many of them driven by women, that she
witnessed while doing her research. In a section of her book entitled
"Bonds of Discord," Singerman describes a young woman who accused
her older sister of wanting to hurt, rob, and possibly kill their father to
gain control of the family's produce business ("the wholesale fruit trade

can be quite profitable in Egypt," the author comments). Fierce combat in another family centered on which of three sisters-in-law spent the most time at the mother's apartment, cooked more food for her, or bought the most expensive gifts for the grandchildren.

No slight, never mind how petty, goes unnoticed. Singerman writes about a marriage engagement that collapsed after a young man turned down his future mother-in-law's request to put several bags of pasta in the trunk of his car. The older woman took his refusal as an insult and refused to attend the fiancé's brother's engagement party, then finally decided to go but slipped on the stairs on the way, cutting her forehead and successfully attracting all of the attention at the event ("despite suffering a serious wound," Singerman writes, "tactically she had won that round"). The engagement was eventually called off, and the "pasta incident" was cited as proof of the groom's unsuitability.

Is all this really necessary? The economist Amartya Sen invented the term "cooperative conflict" to describe the way families present a united front to the world but compete among themselves for advantage; to some extent, domestic strife is the rational outcome of individuals trying to advance their own interests. But the power struggles inside families and marriages can be damaging, not to mention exhausting, and they shape patterns of behavior that are hard to change.

Egypt's divorce rate is rising—in 2021, there was one new divorce for every 3.5 new marriages, which works out to a divorce rate of 29 percent (ten years earlier, the figure was 17 percent). But the vast majority of people remarry, so that divorced adults living on their own make up less than 2 percent of the population. With one or several failed marriages behind them, almost everyone jumps right back into the fray. What would you have if you didn't have family?

THROUGH THE SPRING and summer of 2017, the industrial engineers put the principles of work study into practice on the assembly lines in

Minya. Their job, essentially, was to persuade workers to do things in a different way than they were used to. On the morning I visited, there were two of them—the recent college graduate, Rania, whom I had met during the training course in Cairo, and her colleague Sahar. They were both earnest young women armed with clipboards. "We know the operation by heart," Sahar told me, "but we carry these so they take us seriously."

The task at hand was sewing a V-neck on a T-shirt. The workers were supposed to use a vacuum cutter on the sewing machine to snip the thread after they were finished, but it was an unfamiliar technology, and air from the cutter might blow the thread around. Many of them stuck to using scissors, even though it wasted material and took longer—two-thirds of a second longer, according to a video analysis that Sahar and Rania had done. The workers weren't convinced.

"My supervisor told me to do it this way," a young woman named Batta told me. Three days after being instructed to use the vacuum cutter, she was still resisting. "Using the vacuum cutter will increase the air pressure, so I'd rather use scissors."

"What do you think of their efforts to teach you the correct way?" I asked.

"I don't agree with this. It will make it harder for my colleagues as well." On an adjoining line, a worker named Nima didn't believe that sewing a stitch a different way would increase her hourly output by 40 percent. "I can do it faster the old way," she told me, before adding reluctantly, "but the new way is the correct one."

When I lived in China, I met young women who made critical life choices minute by minute: Jump to another factory, learn a new skill, break up with a boyfriend, return home, go out again. I watched transformations take place over a year or two, although usually it took less time than that. Farmers' daughters became factory workers and then reinvented themselves as office clerks, salespeople, purchasers, production managers, marketers, even English teachers. They learned how to type and use computers; they studied etiquette and public speaking; they bought high-heeled shoes and straightened or colored their hair. They earned money, dated who they wanted, and talked back to their fathers.

So consuming was the new life that they almost forgot about the old one. "Seeing the self I used to be," a young woman named Lu Qingmin wrote me after she read my first newspaper article about her, "I realize that I have really changed."

In Egypt, I learned that change is hard. People mostly stick to the roles they were born into, and that's true even for young women who would seem to have the most to gain by breaking free. China is the exception; Egypt is the way things tend to happen all over the world. But it's useful to remember that for most of the modern era, China was considered a hopeless case. When Mao Zedong died in 1976, China was an agricultural nation with a large population, widespread poverty, and a hidebound culture that seemed impervious to change. Well into the 1990s, jokes about the poor work ethic and terrible customer service were common among foreign visitors ("We don't serve many dishes here, and all of them are bad," I remember a restaurant waitress telling me in 1991, on my first trip to the country). China's transformation may point the way forward for other nations—and it shows, above all, that nothing is predetermined.

China and Egypt are among the oldest continuing civilizations in the world, with histories that stretch back to ancient times. But China in the twentieth century broke with its past on three separate occasions— once with the 1911 revolution that ended dynastic rule; again in 1949, when the Communists broke the back of the feudal system; and once more in 1978 when Deng Xiaoping introduced economic reforms that let farmers sell part of their harvest on the open market. Food production soared; markets and factories started to pop up all over the country. For the first time in decades, it made sense to leave home and try your luck somewhere else. The Chinese economy that grew out of that era is one that rewards private enterprise and personal initiative.

Young women and men at every level of society are comfortable taking the risk of jumping to a new factory, a new profession, or a new city, in the faith that it will pay off. In 2003, her first year living in the factory city of Dongguan, Lu Qingmin sent home $420, which was almost double what her father would earn that year from selling pigs and cotton. The money she earned enabled Qingmin to gain clout at home and to start saving for a new life. Such small acts, writ large, have driven the country's economy to grow more than 9 percent every year over the past several decades, and built a middle class that numbers seven hundred million people. The welfare state is gone, and almost no one misses it. China today is a different country than it was half a century ago.

Egypt, over the twentieth century, has also cycled through a succession of governments—starting with the kings descended from Mohamed Ali, to Gamal Abdel Nasser and his successors, to the Muslim Brotherhood, which held power for a year following the 2011 revolution, and the current military-led regime of Abdel Fattah El-Sisi. But the underlying social and economic structure hasn't changed. The welfare state hasn't been replaced by a dynamic capitalist alternative; the government and the military remain powerful players in the economy, along with a handful of well-connected businessmen. Egypt's manufacturing base remains weak, and the economy has grown at less than half of China's pace. Young people still aspire to the security of a government job, as their parents and grandparents did. The risks for a young woman to leave her farming village and join the modern economy are just as high as in China, but the payoff is far less.

China has some factors that have enabled rapid change. One is geography. When the economy began to boom in the 1980s, the growth was centered on cities and factories along the coast. Young people frequently traveled hundreds of miles, from their villages in the interior, to find work; because of the distance, they typically returned home once a year to see their families. A young woman's decision to *chuqu*, or go out, forces a dramatic break with family. It liberates her from traditional expectations that she marry young, have children, and stay home.

In Egypt, human habitation is confined to the Nile River Valley, and towns and cities are arrayed along this narrow corridor like beads on a string. Work is a short commute away—an hour's bus ride, maybe two at most—and everyone returns home at night. Family, to a young Chinese worker, may be the voice on the other end of a phone line coming from hundreds of miles away; for her Egyptian counterpart, it remains her everyday reality, reminding her of how she should behave. "I was the first girl in the village to go out to work," a young woman in Bayyadiyya once said—which temporarily threw me, since for me the phrase meant traveling across the country, as the Chinese did. Then I realized that she had just walked down the road a few blocks.

The force of religion in everyday life in Egypt, an element that's missing from Chinese society, can also make it harder to change. Women have always stayed home and obeyed their husbands, the conservative Muslim believers say, and they've marshaled centuries of Quranic exegesis to justify their arguments. It's not true, in fact: Middle Eastern women in the past sometimes enjoyed more rights and a higher rate of economic participation than they have today, and the Quran contains as many arguments for female equality as against it. But a teenage girl in an Upper Egyptian village, say, is in no position to challenge such claims made by those in power to suit their own purposes. As the historian Afaf Lutfi al-Sayyid Marsot writes:

> When countries seek to industrialize, they need women's labor. . . . Religion is brought in as a clincher to induce women to go out and work by accentuating those interpretations that praise the work of women and the equality of the sexes. Once the need for women's labor is gone . . . women are told to stay home, raise children, and serve their males; and then religion brings out those passages that accentuate the role of women as nurturers and housekeepers.

In China, people can imagine a better life. The national obsession to *rushi*, "join the world," is born of a system that rewards self-improvement and builds expectations of a brighter future. Individuals *want* to change because they know it will bring opportunity—they're just not sure yet what form it will take.

The Egyptian system fosters, instead, a breakdown of the imagination. In an unpromising socioeconomic environment, people tend to focus on the costs of change rather than the benefits. To engage with the outside world, especially as a young woman, may bring risk, criticism, or even danger. So individuals talk themselves out of taking chances.

It doesn't feel safe to go to another factory. I know Riham's factory already.
My parents don't want me to work here anymore.

I don't think I'll continue working here for long. The winter is approaching.

If I got promoted, it would be less comfortable for me, and I wouldn't like it.

There's little faith that landing a poorly paid job may lead to a better one, or that taking a class may impart the skills or confidence to change one's direction in life. In an uncertain world, as scholars frequently point out, it may be rational for a woman to stick to society's rules—to rely on a man for sustenance, to lock herself into marriage early—but where does that leave you? In China, I knew a young woman who talked her way into half a dozen jobs that she wasn't qualified for, and another who changed her identity from assembly line worker into manager of twenty such workers in a year, and yet another who went straight from being a penniless student of English to a highly paid teacher of the language. None of these developments was rational either.

The transformation of China over the past several decades was possible because of economic policy, geography, and history. But it also needed millions of individuals who broke the rules that school and their parents had taught them. They could envision a different way to be, and the imagination is where change begins.

———

WHEN I ASKED Delta employees if they talked about their jobs with their families, they always said no. Even if they were proud of what they had accomplished in the workplace, at home their employment was treated like a secret, almost a shameful thing. Getting promoted to a supervisory position didn't make a woman more likely to leave her house without her husband's permission, and achieving a 70 percent efficiency rate couldn't prevent your mother-in-law from complaining about you to the neighbors. It was easier and smarter to stay quiet.

"When I get home I'm just so tired," Hind Ali told me. "I make a separation between my home life and my work life."

Venture ten miles beyond the city, Delta executives had told me, and it would be too hard to shape the people you found there for the modern workforce. Ten miles was roughly the distance between the Israeli-American-owned factory where Rania had learned the garment trade, impressed foreign executives, and fostered her dream of becoming a production manager, and the home where she cooked elaborate meals, raised her children, and accepted the humiliation of a polygamous marriage. Now she was home for good—but in another way, she had never left at all.

8

THE WEIGHT OF A DREAM

ONE THING ABOUT RIHAM—SHE MOVED fast. When I first visited her factory, a security guard would open the gate to let me in. He was a young man who moved like an old one, as if every action caused him pain and must be performed at half speed. He never smiled, and there was a world of hurt reflected in his dark brown eyes.

"I hired him because he's Aswani, and people from Aswan are supposed to be honest," Riham said. The first time he lied to her, it was over a worker who was unhappy and subsequently left the company before Riham knew anything about it. Later the man tried to extract money from her for medical treatment for his wife, who might or might not have cancer. He complained that Riham didn't respect him—and that was true.

"He should have the keys to the factory," she told me, "but I haven't given them to him because I don't trust him."

"So, are you going to try and change him?"

"I'm not going to try and change him. I'm going to replace him."

When I stopped by a week later, a young woman opened the gate. The man's final offense had been to pick a fight with Riham over his right to monitor the workers' attendance. "It turns out that he didn't spend much time in Aswan," Riham said, as if that explained everything.

After her clothes sold poorly at the industry exhibition in early 2016, she retooled her operation. With exports to the United States and Europe still slow, and with importing from China no longer an option, Riham focused on manufacturing for the domestic market. This was a piecemeal business—five hundred shirts was considered a large order—and it required retraining her workforce. An export operation like Delta's relied on specialization, and a worker might sew the hems on identical pairs of Calvin Klein boxer shorts for weeks on end. But for the local trade, Riham needed "jokers"—the industry term for workers who could operate any machine and switch on a dime, depending on the needs of production. She taught a young woman named Naglaa, who had previously worked on the Overlock machine, how to operate the Collarette and hemming machines as well. Sara continued to oversee production but also learned to sew so she could pitch in when necessary. If a worker finished her sewing allotment for the day, she might change to inspecting garments instead.

Working in this way required planning and concentration—it was like doing several jigsaw puzzles at once. A longtime employee named Amal mistakenly sewed on a collar that was too large for its shirt (she was talking on her mobile phone and didn't notice). Another time, she attached two sleeves to the same side of a blouse. Sara noticed the mutant garment on her way to the bathroom, and the two women got into a heated argument, shouting over who was to blame, and throwing half-sewn pieces of clothing at each other across the production floor.

"It's Sara's fault," Amal told Riham afterward. "She should have checked it."

"Each stage is the responsibility of the person doing it," Riham said.

"You're responsible for each stage of work that you do. If you don't like the style of this factory," she continued, "you can go work at a factory with a hundred machines and talk on the phone all day long and do the same thing for days or weeks or months. But here with me, you take the phone out of your ear and learn a new style of working."

"Okay," Amal said.

"Now," Riham told me, "before she does anything, she asks."

On a day that I visited in March 2016, the factory was juggling production of an orange polo shirt, a child's pajama top, and a baby's onesie. The size of each order was tiny—fifty, or sixty, or a hundred pieces—and Riham employed only eight workers now, which was half the number she'd had when I first visited her a year ago. It felt like a diminishment: The ground floor of her factory still remained empty, and now some of the machines on the second floor sat idle too. Cut off from the world, Riham was trying to survive on the small piece of earth left to her.

But her team was busy, and for the first time in a year she paid off some of the debts she had incurred when she set up the business. Recently, she had traveled to Saudi Arabia with her family on an *Umrah* pilgrimage, and production continued without a hitch. That was good news, because there were other changes. Riham was getting married.

SHE HAD KNOWN Ahmed for five years. They were in the same circle of friends and had volunteered together working with children in a Nile Delta village. He was an engineer by training, like her, and ran a company that supplied the construction industry. Ahmed was short and heavyset, with dark brown eyes in a kind, crumpled face. He had liked Riham for a year but had been too shy to speak up.

One evening, Riham had arrived home carrying a bunch of flowers. "Nice bouquet" was her father's comment. "Who gave it to you?"

"A friend."

"Oh, a friend. Is he married?"

"No."

"Why not?"

"I don't know."

"Go find out: *Why isn't he married?*"

Some time later, Riham told her parents that Ahmed would like to meet them. "Tell me what terms you've agreed to," her father said, "so that I can agree to everything!"

On the appointed day, Ahmed showed up at the apartment alone— this was unusual, but his father was sick. He praised Riham as a respectable young woman and talked about his family background, his work situation, his apartment and income. Riham sat with her parents and brother but, as was the custom, remained silent.

"He was very nervous—he looked like a baby chick," she recalled. "I think my father was nervous, too. He didn't say a word."

Mustafa assumed the role of Grand Inquisitor. The family's main request was that the couple move into the building that Riham's family owned, so that the parents and adult children could all live in adjoining apartments. Among wealthy families in Egypt, this is a common arrangement. "We'll bring food over if you like, or you can drop off your kids with us," Mustafa said. "But we really want you to live in the apartment below ours."

Ahmed agreed. His family had the same setup.

Suddenly, Riham's father spoke up. "What are you going to do about being overweight?"

Oh no! Riham knew this was a sensitive subject for Ahmed, who was trying to slim down. She broke protocol: "Father, I like him like this!"

"You like him like this?"

"Yes!"

"Okay!"

She was forty years old, and her mother had been preparing for this event for a long time. When Riham was still in college, the family had purchased for her a set of the porcelain dishes and dinnerware that are an essential part of a bride's *gihaz*. They had bought special cutlery from Saudi Arabia, water glasses and tea glasses, two grills, bedsheets, and cookware, some of which had been in storage for so long that it was obsolete. "My mother bought a lot of things I can't use, like metal pots," Riham told me. "No one uses metal pots now. She was buying towels, lots of towels. She bought scissors and cutting knives. This is the culture here: Even if you don't have room for everything, you can store it at your neighbor's house." She usually accepted these gifts from her mother, then quietly gave them away.

After the engagement was formalized, another negotiation began— this one, over furnishing the new apartment, was even more drawn-out even though technically everyone was on the same side. Riham's father, Galal, wanted the couple to buy a large coffee table, a wall unit for the TV, and a chiffonier—a tall chest of drawers for the bedroom. Riham pointed out that her closets already had drawers. She didn't want the coffee table, nor the wall unit, nor the Louis Quatorze gilded wood chairs that her father favored. Galal imposed on Mustafa to take Riham shopping, but he proved a turncoat and took his sister's side in everything—which wasn't surprising, since his own home had an empty spare room that their father had been trying to get him to furnish for twelve years.

The longest-running argument was over the *niche*, a cabinet whose sole purpose is to display the pieces of the wedding china. Many Egyptian households have multiple *niches*—one for the mother's set of dishes and one for each unmarried daughter's—and they are considered as essential to family happiness as a large-screen TV or the floor-length curtains that have to be washed several times a year by hand. "I don't like it," Riham told me. "You have to polish it all the time, and every time you polish, you have to take every piece out and put every piece back. We save our time in order to do better things than this, I hope."

There wasn't a polite way to say it. "I don't want the *niche*," she told her father.

"Why?" He was shocked. "This is wrong! People will come and say that there's a missing part in the room!"

"I don't want it, I don't want it! Plus I don't know if there will be space for everything."

"Have you seen the living room? There's plenty of space!"

Galal appealed to his future son-in-law. "She doesn't want the *niche*," he told Ahmed. "Try to persuade her to get the *niche*."

"Actually," Ahmed said, "I don't like the *niche* myself."

The wedding of Riham's brother more than a decade earlier had been extravagant ("My mother panicked and ordered a lot of food, sheep, turkeys") and the family had so many leftovers that they filled a truck and distributed the food in a poor neighborhood. Riham wanted a modest celebration—a small reception, a wedding dress she designed herself—but she frequently overheard her mother discussing elaborate party venues with the maid or other members of the family.

"This is their culture," Riham said. "But people don't have money to spend on these things anymore, so they need to change."

"Are you trying to change the culture?" I asked her.

"I'm going to live the life I want to live."

THERE ARE A hundred and twenty-nine pieces of tableware in a bride's *gihaz*. I learned this fact not from Riham but from her number two in the factory, Sara. When we met, she had been engaged for two years and was working hard to buy everything she needed—living room furniture, bedsheets, towels, her winter and summer wardrobes, the Chinese.

"The Chinese?" I repeated. "What's that?"

Sara told me that *Seeni*, which means "Chinese," refers to the set of porcelain dishes and dinnerware that a bride brings to the marriage. "It's been that way since my mother's and grandmother's time. When you say *Seeni*, everyone knows what that is."

I didn't, and so Sara explained to me what a Chinese was.

Twelve teacups and twelve matching saucers
Twelve coffee cups and twelve matching saucers
Twelve dinner plates
Twelve salad plates
Two large serving bowls

She stopped—"I can't remember all the details"—then went on:

One sugar bowl
One big teapot
One small teapot
Twelve glasses
All the kitchen utensils

Brides usually had forty or sixty sets of towels and bedsheets, which Sara thought was excessive. "I'll buy ten high-quality sheets, and that's enough for me now." One of her neighbors had three daughters, the youngest still in elementary school, and she was already stockpiling kitchen and bedroom linen for them.

"It's very complicated," Sara said. "There's huge pressure on people to buy all these things."

She was marrying her cousin Murad, who was six years older and drove a minibus in Cairo. They had met for the first time several years ago, when he visited Alexandria with his family. Their second encounter was at his sister's wedding, where they talked and got along well. At their third meeting, during another family gathering, Murad pulled Sara's father aside and said he wished to marry her. He outlined his work and financial situation, and her father asked a lot of questions: *How long is your current job contract? How much money have you saved?* (Sara wasn't supposed to be present, but she stood behind them and heard everything.) Together they read the *fatiha*, the opening verse of the Quran, which represents an informal agreement to marry.

The families met a few months later to hammer out the terms. Murad would pay for an apartment plus most of the furniture and fittings, carpets, and curtains. He asked that Sara not work after they married. Since she was still attending school, she and her family agreed.

The negotiation almost broke down over kitchen appliances. In Cairo, the bride's family are supposed to buy them; in Alexandria, where Sara lived, these are the responsibility of the groom. Murad's family felt that their son was already contributing enough and suggested the two sides split the cost. Sara's father objected. Finally, he reached across the intercity divide—just over a hundred miles, as the crow flies—and said he would buy a washing machine. After that, Murad's family agreed to pay for everything else.

"If he hadn't said that, I don't think things would have worked out," Sara said, of her father's peace offering.

She graduated from trade school a few months later and took a job at Riham's factory to earn money for her *gihaz*. She enjoyed working more than she expected and rose quickly—even though she was one of the youngest employees, she became Riham's deputy. But Sara had promised her future husband that she wouldn't work after marriage, and it was too late to reopen the subject now.

OVER THE YEAR 2016, Sara oversaw production in the factory while also preparing to get married, which seemed like another full-time job that was far more stressful than the one she already had. She joined one *gamiyya* after another. These were informal savings associations in which a group of people, who were usually acquaintances or colleagues, would commit to paying a fixed amount of money each month into a common pool, then took turns pulling out a lump sum on a rotating basis. The *gamiyya* was an enforced savings program and an interest-free loan rolled into one, and it had been in widespread use in Egypt for centuries. Sara belonged to one *gamiyya* whose required contribution was £E400 a month, about $50, and a larger one jointly with her father to save up to buy living room furniture. "Until now we've spent forty thousand pounds, and we're not done yet," she told me.

In March, she began taking the train to Cairo every month to oversee renovations of the new apartment. Her father, mother, and younger brother made the trip with her, and more family were involved on the other end. Sara's biggest headache was her fiancé's oldest sister, who had strong opinions about how the furniture in her brother's new place should be arranged. "He'll say, 'Marwa says we should put the vase here,' and I don't agree," Sara told me. "There are always people whose job is to make life more complicated for others."

In May, the women in the factory started a *gamiyya* to help Sara buy winter clothes. She still couldn't say for sure when she would get married. She wanted to pay off some debts, and her to-do list was long.

"Would it be terrible to set a date for the wedding if you didn't have, say, carpets?" I asked.

She looked at me with a slight smile on her lips. "I don't know," she said at last. "I don't know what to think about it."

"They aren't raised to think like that," my translator, Amira, said to me in English.

I was struck by the fact that both Riham and Sara were getting married, but Sara was accumulating many of the same things Riham was trying to give away. The difference, I realized, was one of class. Fluent in English and French, Riham belonged to the country's small elite—in her world, women enjoyed more freedom to work and travel and to live as they pleased. For a working-class woman like Sara, stricter standards applied. There was no benefit to flouting the rules.

By the middle of June, most of the furnishings in Sara's apartment were ready, although the walls still needed painting. She thought she would marry by the end of the year. I spent four hours in the factory one day and watched her rushing from one station to another, picking up finished piles of work and distributing new bundles to the workers. Finally I asked if she could spare a few minutes to talk, and she came to rest for the first time all morning. "We have too many orders that we needed to finish today," she said, by way of apology.

Her full days in the factory contrasted with the stasis that awaited her. After the wedding, Sara would withdraw from the working world to live among objects that had been the focus of so much negotiation and strategizing and hard work. These were more beautiful new things than she had owned in her life or would ever own again, and yet her preparations felt somber to me, almost like the activity that surrounds a death. You call friends and relatives, you decide on the guest list and the music and the flowers, and it distracts from the reality of what's coming.

"I feel that I'm going to be home alone," Sara said, when I asked her thoughts about her upcoming marriage. "I don't know how I'm going to get used to being alone at home all day."

"How are you going to fill your time?"

"I don't know."

THE EXORBITANT COST of marriage has been the subject of commentary in this part of the world for a long time. On a visit to Cairo in 1332, the Syrian historian Khalil ibn Aybak El-Safadi witnessed the wedding of an Emir's daughter whose trousseau was carried by eight hundred porters and a hundred mules and consisted of cushions, chairs, silver and copper utensils, trays, earthenware pots, rugs, blankets, mattresses, clothes, jewelry, and eight hundred thousand *dinars'* worth of gold. Ibn El-Hajj, the fourteenth-century theologian, observed that a Cairo bride must have three wooden *dikka* chests, one each clad in brass, copper, and silver. The burden fell hard on poor families, who sometimes relied on charity to marry off their daughters. In one instance from late medieval times, an Egyptian merchant provided trousseaux for twelve hundred brides.

In the modern era, the cost of marriage increased dramatically after

Egypt's economic opening in the 1970s. Sadat's Open Door policy de-regulated imports, which stimulated the buying of appliances, electronics, cars, and other consumer goods; overnight, what had been considered luxuries like TVs and washing machines became basic necessities. Migrants returning from overseas invested their savings in new houses or apartments, and owning a home became another prerequisite for marriage.

The political scientist Diane Singerman traces the impact of this one-upmanship in a working-class district of Cairo. A family that had married off a daughter with two rooms of furniture in the early 1970s found that they needed three rooms' worth by the end of the decade; the nominal price of these items, over six years, had jumped sevenfold. The average cost of marriage, by 2012, had risen to ₤E62,000, or approximately $10,164. That's the equivalent of the wages of an ordinary worker laboring continuously for eight years and three months, if he saves every penny he earns.

"Young men generally expect to devote five or ten years of their lives to the process of capital accumulation before they can marry," Singerman writes. "They plan their education, career path, and love life around this financial campaign." For most Egyptians, getting married represents the largest capital investment they'll make in a lifetime.

Singerman describes her astonishment while watching a family's youngest daughter examine her still-incomplete trousseau one morning in the family's attic:

> She began opening box after box of kitchenware, noting what she still needed to purchase. The quantity of goods was staggering. . . .
> These items had been purchased over a period of five years by the mother and her older daughters. . . . During the exhibition of the trousseau, mother and daughter argued briefly over whether this daughter would receive all these items when she

married in the near future. The mother yelled at her daughter that she was incredibly greedy and certainly did not need twenty-four teacups or thirty coffee cups, for example. The mother thought she might use some of the items for the trousseaus of the next generation—her granddaughters, who were now approaching puberty (the eldest granddaughter was thirteen at the time; the youngest, two and a half).

Over the past several decades, men and women have been marrying later. But this does not reflect an erosion of traditional values. Young people are delaying marriage because it takes so long to acquire all the goods they need; making a good match, in a time of economic uncertainty, is more critical than ever. The extravagant investment in marriage reflects deeply conservative thinking about a woman's place in society. A bride will need all of this furniture, appliances, bedding, and fine china because she isn't expected to work again, and the couple will soon have children to provide for. "They have to start as perfect as possible," as one mother put it, "because there is no other chance to improve their living standard later." Sara was working like crazy; Sara would quit her job when she married. These two things were connected.

Some scholars see this accumulation of household goods as economically rational. It's a form of forced savings, and it's the main way that families transfer wealth to their daughters. In Egypt's inflationary economy, they point out, durable goods like refrigerators tend to keep their value, and they also bring their owners status in the eyes of friends and neighbors.

Yet it's impossible not to see waste behind the massive sums that are spent ensuring that a young woman has the same matched set of furniture and the same one-hundred-and-twenty-nine-piece *Seeni* as everyone she knows. Money that could have been used to further an education, travel to a new place, or start a business is instead turned into coffee cups and serving trays that are stored in attics and basements across the country. These items may represent security to a young woman, but they also set exceedingly narrow terms for what her future looks like. The goal, for the family and for the country, is always to replicate what already exists.

How does it feel to be a teenage girl who is greeted every day by a shelf of her wedding china, reminding her of her purpose in life? Maybe she can ignore it for a while; in Riham's factory, I was struck by the aspirations of the summer interns to be doctors, teachers, or engineers. The father of one of them, a man named Mahmoud Ibrahim Ahmed, who also worked in the factory, told me that his oldest daughter wanted to be a doctor or a lawyer, and his second daughter an artist. The girls were fourteen and twelve, and their mother was already buying things for their marriage.

"I agree with their ambitions, and I support them in their education," Mahmoud told me.

"Would the girls marry and then continue their studies?" I asked, thinking that it takes many years of schooling to become a doctor or a lawyer.

"It's mainly her decision. If she wants to get married and continue her education, I support that, but it also depends on her future partner."

For a girl growing up in this society, a career was like a brightly colored toy that served to delight and distract her while she was young. Sometime soon, these plans would start to seem fanciful when weighed against the treasures that were being stored, in closets and attics and other rooms, for their sake.

THE EXPORT MARKET stayed slow, and in the summer of 2016, Riham began to see the effects. Workers who had been laid off from their jobs in the country's export zones showed up at her factory gate looking for work. One morning, a young woman appeared unannounced while

Riham was overseeing a large order for a demanding new client. She sized up the candidate in seconds, like an emergency room doctor in triage mode.

"How old are you, and what's your marital status?" Riham asked.

"I'm married but separated, and I'm twenty-seven." The woman didn't know how to operate a sewing machine, although she had worked in garment factories for years.

"How come you stayed so long and you didn't learn how to work on the machines?" Riham asked.

"I wanted to, but they didn't let me. And because I got married, I wasn't that focused on learning the machine."

"She's not going to come," Riham said flatly after the woman left. "In this career, if she's twenty-seven and she hasn't learned the machines, it means she doesn't want to learn. Maybe she was there to get married."

That was a good guess. When a young woman takes a job in an Egyptian factory, it's unlikely that she's concerned about learning the business, improving her efficiency, or expanding her skill set for the future. No—she wants to meet someone to marry, that's the only future she can see. If she's already engaged, then she's doing a different set of calculations, as she mentally transmutes every month's wages into bedsheets, dishes, and Chinese cups.

She quits her job and gets married. If things don't work out with her husband, she might return to the factory in a few years—divorced, with a child or two. Perhaps she starts taking her work seriously, and tries to improve herself and develop her skills because her livelihood depends on it now. But for young women in Egyptian society, the dream of marriage blocks out every other possibility. Only when she fails at the one task she has been assigned in life is she allowed to think about herself, for the first time.

I met Amal in November 2015, when she was working as a sewer in Riham's factory. She was twenty-three, with soft rounded cheeks and dark eyes. She quit a couple of months later, then reappeared the following spring, newly engaged and ready to start earning for her *gihaz*. "She got engaged, so she has to work," Riham told me. "That's the only reason she's coming."

Amal's fiancé drove a taxi. He had approached her at a friend's home—he was her friend's half brother—and they talked for half an hour. A week later, he came to her house with his parents and proposed marriage. Over forty-five minutes, the families hammered out the details of furniture, carpets, and curtains. Following local custom, Amal wasn't present during the negotiation. She learned the outcome when she was called into the room and the two families said the *fatiha* together.

"So half an hour is enough time to get to know someone?" I asked her.

"I felt comfortable talking to him. I didn't feel that way with the person I was engaged to before."

She had broken off an earlier engagement, and so had he. That was one of the things they talked about the day they met. He also objected to the way she dressed, so she put away her jeans and casual tops and adopted the *abaya*, a long loose dress that covers the entire body and is typically worn by older women from traditional backgrounds. He didn't want her to work after marriage or to leave the house by herself, though he would make an exception so she could visit her mother. "When you find yourself feeling bored, I'll take you out," he promised. She agreed to everything.

"But what if you want to go out with friends?" I asked.

Amal shook her head. "He doesn't allow me to go out by myself."

"Why?"

"He comes from Upper Egypt."

"Where in Upper Egypt?"

She corrected herself: He was from Alexandria. He just *thought* like someone from Upper Egypt.

"It's fine for me," Amal said. "I'm a loner—I like to stay by myself."

In the next breath, she said that she had friends both inside and outside the factory.

"So you won't see any of these friends anymore?"

"This friend of mine is married," she said slowly, as if recalling a memory from a long time ago. "I used to go see her after she was married. I don't know if people will come to see me after I'm married."

"So people can come to see you, but you can't go out?"

She nodded.

I asked Amal if she agreed with these ideas.

"I like him and he's a good man, so I would accept anything he said."

I HEARD VERSIONS of this story many times. There was the fleeting glimpse of a young woman, at a gathering or on a balcony or even in a photograph, then the brief conversation between strangers, the snap decision to get married, and the meeting of the families to hash out terms. No one who took part in these interactions seemed to find it strange that a negotiation over a washing machine and kitchen cabinets could take longer than the decision to spend a life with another person.

Romance follows this frantic timetable because there are so few socially acceptable ways for men and women to meet. Any encounter is precious, every opportunity must be seized: If you don't act now, your next chance might not come for many months. Arranged marriages aren't common anymore, but modern unions haven't changed in the sense that couples often marry without knowing much about each other. Among the divorced women I met, a common thread was that the man they wed turned out to be completely different than he had seemed. (The discovery of a husband's "secret life," which might include an outside relationship or a propensity for physical violence, is a frequent cause of divorce, according to one study in Cairo.) That could happen to anyone, but it was definitely more likely if you chose to spend your life with someone you had just met.

You could say that Egyptian courtship is stuck in medieval times, but that would be a misrepresentation of practices between the ninth and nineteenth centuries that gave women greater power to set the terms of their marriages than they enjoy today. Throughout this period, young women and their families could attach conditions to their marriage contracts to protect themselves. A frequent stipulation was that a wife could divorce her husband if he took another wife or a concubine, but these documents might also spell out that a husband couldn't drink wine, stay away from home for a long period, beat his wife, nor could he prevent her from working, visiting her family, seeing friends, going on pilgrimage, raising her children from a previous marriage, or wearing what she pleased. The pledges were legally binding, and a man who violated them would have to grant his wife a divorce with full financial rights, if she chose. An Egyptian woman's right to set such terms—like her ability to initiate divorce down the line if she wished—disappeared at the end of the nineteenth century, when the British imposed a more rigid set of statutes governing family law.

Today, would-be brides are allowed to add conditions to their marital contracts, but they seldom do, for fear of causing tensions or rupturing an engagement. Women rely on informal promises. Many of the wives I talked to said their fiancés had agreed that they could continue working or complete their schooling after marriage, but a husband doesn't suffer any penalty if he breaks his word. In the 1980s, a group of activists drafted a new marriage contract that would help wives assert their rights to employment, education, travel, marital property, and divorce, but they gave up in the face of opposition from the religious establishment.

Historically, negotiating the terms of marriage beforehand gave women some protection in a union that was inherently unequal. Today, it's often the man who imposes conditions, as a way of asserting his will in a relationship that's already strongly skewed in his favor: *Don't take a job, don't wear those clothes, don't stay out late.* In the Delta factory, a young woman named Yasmin met her future husband when he spotted her picture in a friend's photo album and arranged to chat with her online. After they got engaged, he asked her to pray more, to return home earlier, and to adopt conservative dress. Like Amal, she went from jeans and shirts to the *abaya* and a long, cape-like head covering that concealed her neck and shoulders and flowed halfway down her torso, like a nun's wimple. ("The next time you see me," she joked, "I'll be wearing full *niqab*.")

Even Riham worried that getting married would compromise her freedom to live and work as she wanted. Ahmed seemed decent and open-minded, but people could change or turn out to be different than they appeared. Uncharacteristically for her, she wavered. She said a special prayer for those who are at a crossroads and face a difficult choice:

O Allah, if in Your knowledge, this matter is good for me both in this world and in the Hereafter, then ordain it for me, make it easy for me, and bless it for me. And if in Your knowledge it is bad for me both in this world and the next, then turn me away from it, and turn it away from me; and ordain for me the good wherever it may be, and make me content.

Amal's choice was clear. A few weeks after telling me about her engagement with the man she had known for thirty minutes, she broke it off, took her final month's pay, and quit the factory. "We tried to get her to stay," a friend and fellow employee told me. "But now that there's no husband, she doesn't want to work anymore."

IN OCTOBER 2016, Riham got married—right on schedule, and on her terms. About a hundred guests attended the signing of her marriage contract, which was held in a rented hall with an open-air garden. The day before, Riham and her family had prepared two hundred fifty meals and distributed them to workers and residents in her and Ahmed's neighborhoods. "You give a gift to God," Riham explained. "It's a good way to start a new life."

Several weeks later, the government devalued the Egyptian pound by 50 percent against the dollar, in an effort to stabilize the economy and shore up the country's foreign currency holdings. At one stroke, Riham's domestic garment business became untenable. Because the industry relies on imported raw materials—almost all cotton and yarn come from overseas, as do goods like polyester stuffing for quilts—a weaker currency means higher costs and a more expensive final product. "You can go one year without buying clothes," Riham said. "All people's money will go to eating and private lessons." She abandoned her carefully designed business model—domestic market, small orders, jokers—and started working as a subcontractor for exporters again.

One morning in November, Riham showed up at the factory to oversee a rush order for girls' tank tops. Her leg was in a heavy cast—she had broken a bone in her foot while on her honeymoon in Lebanon—and she moved with the aid of a metal walker, like an elderly lady. For two hours, though, she was in military commander mode, giving orders, asking questions, naming names.

Naglaa, you're working carelessly. If you don't be careful where you're putting things, they're going to catch and get torn.

Rahma, I want you to work faster.

Mustafa, in two and a half hours, you've finished only two baskets. It should have taken less time.

Can you hear me, Mona? I'm trying to tell you what to do.

"Do you always criticize everyone when you first come in?" I asked.

She laughed. "This is my job: You are the outside eye. In the morning when you come in, you see things with a fresh eye. After a while, you don't see them anymore."

To suit the more demanding export schedule, she had changed up her worker policies yet again. First, she bumped up salaries. Ordinary sewers now earned £E1,000 a month, about $65 at the new exchange rate, but she now required everyone to work six days a week instead of five. Employees who finished their work ahead of time would get a bonus, but those who fell behind would have money deducted from their pay. In the first month, four workers received bonuses and one was penalized. In Riham's long evolution toward asking more of her employees, this was another step.

"So you're not being nice anymore," I observed.

"I wasn't appreciated for being nice, so I started to take my rights."

Being married forced her to be more efficient. Every morning, she prepared breakfast for herself and Ahmed and tidied up the apartment before arriving at the factory by eight-thirty. She could no longer work as late as she liked in the evenings, and her weekends were filled with family obligations.

On the other hand, marriage also brought emotional support from a partner who understood her world and spoke her language. When Riham worried that the lighting in her factory was too dim, Ahmed studied her workspace, did some research, and found her replacement lights at very little cost. "He's not like normal Middle Eastern husbands," Riham said. "He's proud that I'm working, and that I have my own business. He wants me to rise up.

"He's different, and this is why I chose him."

SARA'S WEDDING WAS delayed. The same devaluation that upset the factory's operations also wrecked her carefully calculated marriage budget. Furniture she had already ordered became more expensive; a set of kitchen cabinets, which she had bought for £E5,000, jumped 30 percent in price by the time she went to pick them up. She canceled some purchases and kept others but had to renegotiate everything. "Now we have to go back and buy things all over again," she told me. The wedding that was supposed to take place at the end of 2016 was pushed back to the following spring.

Over the winter, the young woman named Rahma who had worked in the factory for a year started to take over Sara's responsibilities. By the time I visited in February 2017, it was Rahma who was talking to Riham every morning, Rahma who was assigning employees their tasks and adjusting targets as the day progressed. Sara sat at an Overlock machine sewing a little boy's T-shirt—she had become an ordinary worker again. "I'm supposed to leave right before Ramadan, so someone else needed to be trained," she explained. Her wedding was now scheduled for June.

"Are you excited?"

She shrugged. "It's a nice change. It's a new life."

Riham later made it clear to me that this was a demotion. "Right now, Sara is just passing the time," she said, with a severity that surprised me. "She's not concentrating anymore. She's not giving; she just wants to take. It's better to put her on one machine, so I can keep track of her."

"She's also being very negative," Riham continued. "I'll say, 'Do ten thousand pieces,' and she'll say, 'We can't do this.'"

When I had met Sara for the first time two years before, she told me it was her decision to stop working after marriage. "I would beat him up," she had joked, if her husband kept her from doing what she wanted. Now I knew that wasn't true. She was leaving not because she wanted to, but because of a promise that had been made to her fiancé, Murad, while she was still a schoolgirl.

She had gained so much experience, she told me, through overseeing production and learning how to manage others. "You can't have just one way of talking to people," she said. "You need to talk to different people in different languages. I really like this field and I would like to continue working in it."

"Do you think you will?"

"I don't think so. I would love to, but my husband wouldn't be happy."

For the first time, Sara told me how she had challenged him directly on this issue. It had been about a year ago, she said.

"I have good experience working, and I enjoy it, and I'm qualified to work wherever I want," she had told Murad. "Especially the place where we'll live, there are a lot of small factories and I can find work there."

Murad said no. His sister had worked briefly as a secretary in a medical clinic, until he made her quit.

"I didn't let the women in my family work," he said. "Why would I let you work?"

"When I tell him I want to work, he gets offended," Sara told me. "Even if I tell him it's because I want to do it for myself and that I enjoy the work, he thinks it means I'm worried that he can't provide well for us."

"Do all Egyptian husbands feel as he does?"

"Yes. I have no idea why it hurts their pride so much. It's not like I'm going to work in a bad place."

Murad sounded as if he would make a good husband. He was working hard to give his future wife a comfortable home, with all the furnishings she was supposed to have. Sara valued his sense of responsibility and his ability to plan for the future; it was a quality they shared and one that drew them together. But Murad was fundamentally unable to take in what Sara was trying to tell him. I was struck by what she had said—*You need to talk to different people in different languages*—and how, consciously or not, she had described her own predicament. Sara was a woman who worked because she wanted to, and she had dreams and ambitions that had nothing to do with a man. To her future husband, she was written in a foreign tongue.

"What do you think about this society, where men have so much control over women?" I asked Sara.

"It's because men have always been the source of money, so they think this gives them authority over everything," she said, a construction that was lifted straight out of the Quran: *Men are the protectors and maintainers of women . . . because they support them from their means.* "They're also concerned that their wives will get too tired. So out of providing her with comfort, or at least that's their excuse, they don't want her to work. I can't do anything about it. I can't do anything to change it."

Then she continued, unexpectedly, "But the thing is, women accept it. So that actually allows men to impose their ideology over women, because we let them do it. In my case, I tried to convince him, but I failed."

Every time I talked to Sara, I was struck by her intelligence. On that day, she was fully honest with me for the first time—about her wish to continue working and her husband's opposition, and what she thought about a society in which this conflict played out, over and over, and almost always ended the same way. Maybe it was because this phase of her life was coming to a close that she was finally open about how she really felt. Her *gihaz* was ready, her apartment was furnished, and her life's work as a wife was about to begin. She was twenty-two, and the time for being sunny and upbeat and making jokes about beating up her husband was past.

OVER AND OVER, I watched women diminish themselves to satisfy a man. They ended friendships; they gave up work they enjoyed and were good at; they dressed and behaved in ways they never would have chosen. Sometimes women explained the male impulse for control as an expression of love, but more often they said this was just how men were. Even if a woman was more educated than her partner or worked in a higher-skilled job—which was common, since young men frequently worked as drivers or security guards—it didn't make for a more equitable relationship.

It was infuriating to watch these makeovers-in-reverse, to see how easy it was for a man to take a woman and reduce her to something less than she was. I didn't know these particular men, but I had encountered many others like them. A young man I sometimes met for Arabic language practice was displeased when I mentioned that I didn't cook breakfast for my husband every morning. A member of a government committee to draft a new constitution spent much of our interview making obnoxious propositions ("You must agree to marry me, or bring me a wife"). So many times, an Egyptian man had taken offense at something I said—an observation about his country, for example—when the same words out of my husband's mouth would have been accepted or even welcomed. They loved to lecture me on subjects, like the American media or America's foreign policy toward Egypt, that I understood better than they ever would.

Every time a woman gave in to a man, she fed into the immense wellspring of Egyptian male superiority, which was an inexhaustible resource if ever there was one. In Sara's words: *We let them do it.* However brazen their demands, women usually felt compelled to go along with them. Sara tried to persuade her fiancé to let her work after marriage. But when he said no, she gave in. It was acceptable, in her world, for an engagement to end over who would pay for a washing machine, but not over a woman's desire to work. There's a significant body of scholarship explaining why this behavior makes cultural sense. The country's weak economy, the decline of the government sector, and the move toward religious fundamentalism have all made women more vulnerable. Surrendering what little power they have in exchange for a man's protection may be a rational choice.

But a counterargument could be made: When a woman does go against traditional expectations, she often gets her way. Riham had quit her family company, started her own business, chosen the man she would marry, and furnished her apartment as she liked. At every stage, her parents had not necessarily agreed with her choices, but they had gone along in the end (even about the *niche*). Her upper-class position gave her more leverage, but I had also encountered young women from working-class families who took jobs without a father's permission, then used a range of strategies—which included secrecy, delay, or winning over a family member as an ally—to hold on to what they had. Social barriers that appeared to be rigid actually fell all the time. Seen from this angle, the wonder was that women didn't challenge them more often.

One of the workers who passed through Riham's factory was a young woman in her late teens whom I'll call Noura. She had striking dark eyes in a slender face, and an air of preternatural calm that contrasted with a violent family history. She had never gone to school and was rarely allowed out in public, because her father was afraid she would get involved with a young man and disgrace the family. Her father had spent time in jail for killing a man in a fight—inadvertently, he said— and he sometimes beat Noura and her mother. On the day that we met, she pulled back the edge of her *hijab* to show me a round, reddish scar the size of a quarter, where her father had knocked her forehead against the floor. After two of Noura's previous engagements ended, her father told her to work for her own *gihaz* because he refused to pay for anything anymore.

"I'm really afraid to get engaged to someone who will turn out to be like my father," she told me. Both her grandfather and uncle were "very savage," and her two younger brothers were starting to show abusive tendencies as well. "I want to find someone different from him, but I don't know if such a person exists."

Three weeks later, Noura got engaged. A young man named Alaa who worked in a neighboring factory spotted her at a restaurant, grabbed her mobile phone and dialed his own number, then called her later that day to propose marriage. She was surprised, but he was as insistent as a pop song. "It just feels that you're the one I'm looking for," he said, and finally these words won her over.

There were conditions, naturally. She shouldn't work after marriage. She wasn't to go outside without his permission. And she must never hang laundry on the balcony, in case someone saw her.

"You trust me," Noura said. "Why do you ask me to do these things?"

"I want you as you are," he responded. "I don't want you to wear makeup. I don't want you to dress up or even to wear nail polish. I want you to be like a soldier." Noura agreed to everything.

"I feel that he's also the one I'm looking for," she told me the next time she saw me, repeating the young man's words as her own. "He understands me very well. He discusses everything, he's calm, and he doesn't shout at me."

I was so shocked I didn't know what to say. In a few weeks, Noura had gone from *I don't know if such a person exists* to *He's the one I'm looking for*. She had sworn not to marry someone who was controlling like her father; now she had capitulated, without a struggle, to a suitor who sounded like a carbon copy of him. It made sense, I realized, for women to defy their fathers while bending over backward to accommodate fiancés or husbands. A young woman had to believe that her future mate understood and respected her more than her father did, even if the two men held the same ideas.

Noura smiled at my bewilderment. "Every time you come," she teased me, "you're confused."

"But last time you told me you might not ever marry, because you worried that every man would turn out like your father."

"He's very different from my father," she said. "He's not aggressive and irritable all the time; he's very communicative and understanding. He demands a lot of things of me, but he doesn't shout at me." Nothing about the encounter with Alaa sounded promising, but I could see how a suitor who made unreasonable demands without yelling might count as an improvement in her eyes. Not long afterward, Noura quit the factory, most likely to join her fiancé in his place of work. Riham wasn't in touch with her anymore.

Women go out of their way to justify male authority over them. One reason they prefer to wed older men, the anthropologist Homa Hoodfar observed, is that it's more palatable to obey someone with greater life experience rather than a young man with very little. A seventeen-year-old female student told her:

> I would never marry someone of my own age, education, income, or social stature. . . . The problem is that in our society men like to think they are wiser than women, though if they are equal in age and education it is always the woman who is more clever, as you can see all around you. On the other hand, according to our religion a wife has to obey her husband. . . . Therefore, it is better for a woman to marry someone who is older, more educated, who has much more experience in life than she has, and so it would not be illogical for her to obey him.

Marrying up is a way for a woman to rationalize her second-class status rather than to object to being put in that position at all.

There are women who are working to change this situation. Azza Soliman, the lawyer who helped draft legislation two decades ago giving women the right to no-fault divorce, runs an NGO that is currently lobbying to rewrite the country's family law. Soliman is married to a Dutch photographer who lives in the United States ("I like this part-time marriage!"). Talking to her, and to her small circle of activist colleagues, was like catching a glimpse of the Nile after trekking many days through the desert. But women like her were rare, and they almost always came from the educated elite. It wasn't reasonable to expect an ordinary woman to be a revolutionary in her own family. *I can't do anything to change it,* Sara had said. She was one of the few women I knew who had tried.

Working in a garment factory, I realized, was a suitable preparation for the rest of life. You're assigned to sit at a station, and you do the work that's handed to you, and everyone around you is doing the same thing. We make the best of the materials we're given.

WHAT DOES REBELLION look like? Mona, the young woman in Riham's factory who had told me she wouldn't marry if it meant losing her freedom, had a standard set of questions for any potential suitor her parents introduced to her.

"What do you ask them?" I wanted to know.

"Adi," she said. "It's normal."

How old are you?

What kind of work do you do?

Do you want to stay doing the same thing for the rest of your life?

If those queries didn't scare them away, she had others.

What's your plan for life?

Do you smoke?

"What's the wrong answer?" I asked.

"If he answers 'I don't know, I don't have a plan, I'm satisfied with where I am now and I don't want to do anything else,' that's not the answer I like," Mona told me. She was tall, and her face wore a habitually gloomy expression. I felt a twinge of sympathy for the young men on the receiving end of her interrogation.

I asked if the young men had questions for her too.

"Usually they're not important questions," she said.

What do you like?

What do you not like?

What do you like to buy?

Mona wasn't like most of the young women—like Amal, or Noura—who drifted in and out of Riham's factory with only marriage on their minds, but still she struggled to find a purpose. She quit the factory in November 2016 ("I felt suffocated"), then rejoined the following spring

("Actually, I felt even more suffocated at home"). Her return to the workforce was more or less happenstance. I had called Mona at home asking if she could meet me at Riham's factory to talk. She agreed, and then decided on the spur of the moment to start working there again.

"When you called and asked me to meet you in the factory, that encouraged me," she said. "I talked to Riham, who said she would be happy to have me back." In a life with little direction, she was looking for signposts. My phone call had seemed to be one.

Being back in the flow of work revitalized her. "I wake up early, I go to sleep early, and I have energy. I have discipline in everything in my life." She joined two different *gamiyya*s and was saving money to buy a sewing machine, and she talked about starting her own clothing factory one day. "This time I've made this decision that I'm staying for a long time. I'm not going to leave."

When I saw Mona a couple of months later, she had changed course again. "I gave up on that idea," she said, when I asked if she was still saving for a sewing machine.

"Why? Was it too hard to save that much money?"

"It's not hard to save money. I just decided I didn't want to save anymore for a future plan. I don't want to plan anything."

"What made you decide this?"

"Just me—by myself."

I didn't doubt that the young men she was meeting were hapless, or inarticulate, or that they lacked a plan for life. But the same things could be said about Mona. She had an eighth grade education, and she wasn't a very valuable worker. She lacked Sara's quickness or Rahma's steadiness: sometimes Riham made exasperated comments about her carelessness and her lack of drive. Mona said she wanted to buy a sewing machine and set up her own business, but she never moved closer to these goals. I learned later that she didn't know how to sew.

Like the heroine of an Edith Wharton novel, Mona was trapped—unwilling to accept the socially prescribed role of wife and mother but unfit for anything else. She valued her liberty, but turning her back on society's expectations hadn't made her free. It made her marginal and invisible, a person with no definable place among everyone she knew. So Mona drifted, unable to express what she wanted. There was no one among her family or friends who understood her, no one to encourage her, no one who had pursued a dream of her own and could show her the way.

The last time I saw Mona, she was stationed at the front of the production floor trimming stray threads off finished shirts, just as she had been when I met her more than a year before. That was the day Sara told me that she had tried and failed to persuade her future husband to let her keep working. Noura had already followed her new fiancé to another factory. Amal had given up on hers and left.

I asked Mona what she planned to do with the money she earned, and she said she had no idea. She had quit the factory and returned, found a dream and cast it aside, and no one would ever know. *Adi*, it's normal.

9

FREEDOM

ON ONE OF THE FIRST days of fall in 2016, I met Doaa Mohsen at the front gate of the University of Minya. A new semester had just started, but the campus was serene and quiet on a Friday morning, which was the beginning of the weekend according to the Islamic calendar; the wide boulevard that ran in front of the school was almost empty in both directions. Doaa and I sat down in a café opposite the entrance and drank tea. She had round, slightly pockmarked cheeks and brown eyes that appeared sometimes merry and sometimes sad. She spoke in a low and even voice, as if she were lulling a child to sleep. A breeze picked up and riffled the fringes of her headscarf.

I had met Doaa in the spring, on my initial tour of the Delta factory. My first encounter with Rania took place a couple of visits later, and over the next year and a half I followed the courses of these two lives. Each was an ambitious woman and a mother of two children. And each had been stuck in an unhappy marriage, although events had played out in very different ways. I watched how Rania suffered by remaining with a husband she didn't love. Doaa had divorced her husband about two years before I met her. From her, I learned what it meant to break free.

Unlike Rania, Doaa had a fairly humdrum job as a security guard. Stationed at the entrance to the Delta production floor, she checked the bags of workers going in and out of the production area to make sure they hadn't stolen anything. But she led an unusual parallel life as a college student. She was now in her third year in the University of Minya's continuing education division, which was open to midcareer students who had never finished college. The program represented a rare second chance in the world of Egyptian education, but it suffered from many of the system's broader failings. Only one out of ten students, by Doaa's estimate, actually attended class, which took place on weekends to accommodate people's work schedules. Most of her classmates relied on study notes that were distributed by the professors; they showed up only for exams. Failure rates, unsurprisingly, were high, though there appeared to be no clear guidelines for what one needed to do to pass. "I had a friend who failed a class again and again, and she didn't know why," Doaa told me.

The students were equally in the dark about the government's plans for adult education, and there were periodic rumors that the program might tighten entrance requirements or even shut down. Applicants to the university from the vocational education track were no longer being accepted, Doaa had heard; with no information available, she had developed her own elaborate theory as to why. "Some security officers who were quite low-level got into a fight with high-level people, and the high-level people got mad at the low-level people. That's why they changed the rules." Given the black box of Egyptian government policymaking, where the security forces held so much power but didn't necessarily behave rationally, her explanation seemed as plausible as any.

Doaa was majoring in social services—"I like talking to other people and listening to their problems"—and she hoped to find a position as a social worker or a teacher after she graduated. Inside Delta, she had recently participated in a weeklong health and safety training program, which certified workers to handle first aid and other emergency situations. Even this humble detail worked its way into her career ambitions. "This certificate is worth a lot," she told me. "I can get a job with this."

"Would you want to work in human resources inside Delta?" I asked her.

"*Insha'allah.* I could work in Delta—that's my preference—or open my own office as a social worker. I could work at school or with a professor. There are a lot of options. I'm not ruling anything out."

We spoke for more than two hours, and the time for Doaa's next lecture came and went. "Aren't we going to make you late for class?" I asked.

"Oh, not to worry. My second class was canceled because the professor didn't come today."

"Does this happen all the time?"

"No, not all the time." She thought for a minute. "The same thing happened last week. It's the beginning of the term."

I would have thought a professor might make a special effort to show up for his own class, especially at the start of the school year. But this was Egypt: *Mafish nizam,* there is no system. Other places might have absentee students, but where else could claim so many truant teachers? The rules changed without warning, and matters like the academic calendar and class schedules seemed to be decided roughly five minutes before they happened. All of the disorganization helped explain why, in the two and a half years that I reported inside Egyptian factories, Doaa was the only woman I met who had a coherent plan to educate herself and change her life.

THIS WAS HER second try. Doaa had finished her third year of studying law at Beni Suef University when she got married. Her husband, who worked at a state-owned tourism company, had promised Doaa and her parents that she could complete her studies and get her college diploma. After the wedding, he changed his mind.

"Why didn't he want you to study?" I asked.

"There's no specific reason. He would just tell me, 'There's no reason for you to continue.'" To maintain peace between his family and hers, Doaa lied to her parents and pretended she was still in school.

The man she married was her mother's cousin and the oldest son in his family, both of which suggested reliability. But it didn't turn out that way at all. As the only male child, Doaa's husband had grown up spoiled and used to doing what he wanted, while his mother and sisters cleaned up after him. He frequently went away on long business trips, leaving Doaa with almost nothing to live on. Her husband's mother supported her, especially after their two daughters were born. "My mother-in-law took care of him, and now she was taking care of me and my kids as well," Doaa said. But the woman was also an intrusive presence. She often entered Doaa's apartment without asking, or took her pots and pans, or forbade her to leave the house until she finished her chores.

When Doaa was pregnant with their second child, her husband objected to a hospital delivery. It would be too expensive, he complained, even though the medical bills for their older daughter, who was born by Caesarean section, had been paid by Doaa's father. Instead, Doaa gave birth at home, with the help of an aunt who was a nurse. After the baby was born, Doaa fainted and lay in bed for more than a week, unable to eat or drink much. At the ten-day mark, her husband's younger brother visited and was alarmed at her deathlike state—"my lips were yellow, which is a bad sign"—and insisted that Doaa be taken to the hospital. It turned out that the scar from her previous C-section had torn, and she had been bleeding internally for days. She was given medications, and eventually pulled through. The doctor told her she was lucky to be alive.

"After that incident, my family started to hate his family," Doaa told me. "I did too." The final rupture came when her mother-in-law removed the gas pipes from her apartment and sold them without telling her. Doaa was so upset that she stayed in her bedroom for three days, then got into a violent argument with her husband's sisters and his mother. "It's either me or her," Doaa overheard her mother-in-law telling Doaa's husband. That was an easy choice: He called a taxi for his wife and daughters.

"Where's your suitcase?" her mother-in-law asked, as Doaa was walking out the door. "You haven't packed your things. Don't you know that you're not coming back?"

Doaa took her children to her parents' house. When her father called her husband to attempt a reconciliation, he didn't even answer the phone. That night, Doaa sent her daughters home again. Unless the children lived with their father, she knew that he wouldn't pay an *ersh* for their care, and she couldn't afford to raise them herself. The little girls were seven and six. She patted them on the back and said goodbye, and told them it was better this way.

The next day, Doaa hired a lawyer and filed for *khul,* the no-fault divorce that has been an option for women since the new law was passed in 2000. She got a job at a crystal factory outside Minya and enrolled at the university. She later jumped to a clothing factory, and then to Delta—it wasn't her ideal position, but the wages covered part of her tuition, and her parents paid the rest.

Doaa knew only one other woman who had split with her husband through *khul.* Most marriages ended when a husband repudiated his wife, which didn't require the involvement of the courts. If the man didn't agree to a divorce, then *khul* was the only way a woman could free herself without the time-consuming litigation of filing for a fault-based divorce. But it required a financial sacrifice on the woman's part, and the community as a whole frowned on it.

"People have a negative view of *khul* because it's insulting to the man," Doaa told me. "When women ask for it, they have to give up their financial rights. It's as if they're saying, 'I'm willing to give up everything in my life just to get rid of you.'"

She sometimes spoke with other divorcées in the factory and encouraged them to return to school and rebuild their lives, as she was doing. Most of them were traumatized by their failed marriages and barely able to stay afloat. "When I speak to them about furthering their education, they say they're just trying to work as hard as they can to support their children," Doaa told me. "They don't have time for anything else. It has done huge damage to their personalities."

The part of Doaa's story that made the deepest impression on me, though, wasn't the way she finally left her husband but how long she had stayed. Her story wasn't that he had abused her for years and then she walked out on him. No—he failed to provide for her, mistreated her, and almost killed her through negligence, and she still stuck with him for seven years until he kicked her out. Even so, many people in her circle thought she should have remained in her marriage. In a society that valued family above all, it was impossible to comprehend why a mother would give up her own children.

Of all the women I met in Egyptian factories, only Doaa was a recognizable type from my China reporting days. She came from an ordinary background but was improving herself through education; she could imagine a different life from the one she had been born into. Doaa had broken free of what society expected of her, but that liberty had come at the highest possible price. For a woman in this society, freedom could be only a consolation prize, the thing you got after you lost everything that really mattered.

"Psychologically, it took a huge toll," Doaa told me, her voice still low and calm. "I regret that I kept silent for so long, but I also regret that I spoke up. Either way, I am to blame."

No one I spoke to seemed surprised at the country's surging divorce rate. "This is a trend in Egypt: Women can't take it anymore!" Alia El-Mahdi, an economist at Cairo University, told me heatedly. Both of her daughters were divorced.

Men, naturally, had a different explanation. "The men see beautiful women on TV and become dissatisfied with their wives," Ali, an Upper Egyptian man in his thirties who worked for a news agency in Cairo, told me. He blamed the national mania for soap operas—starting with *The Bold and the Beautiful* in the 1990s, and more recently with productions from Turkey—for the high rate of marital dissolution and many other social changes. Young girls now had private lives, teenagers dated in secret, and housewives no longer cooked elaborate meals from scratch. It was all, according to Ali, because of the astonishing lifestyles people had seen on TV (which definitely made me see the Ewings, the Carringtons, and the Forresters in a more positive light).

One thing that was beyond dispute, even to the Alis of the world, was that men enjoy the lion's share of privilege in a divorce. Through the right of repudiation, a husband can end his marriage at any time without entering a courtroom. Until the law was changed in 1985, he didn't even have to inform her of what he had done (now, in what must count as progress, he's required to tell his wife within thirty days).

On the other hand, a woman can end her marriage only through the legal system. She may petition for a fault-based divorce, but that requires evidence and often eyewitness testimony of the harm she suffered from her husband; the litigation can be expensive and drag on for years. Filing for *khul* is quicker, but it entails forfeiting the right to future financial support and submitting to several months of compulsory mediation. This can be as unpleasant as it sounds: Many family court arbitrators consider it their job to persuade wives to return to their husbands, no matter what the circumstances. The assumption that a woman is too irrational to make her own life choices is built into the legal system, since a man can quit his marriage whenever he feels like it, no counseling required. A senior member of the National Center for Judicial Studies, a government body that trains judges, said in a 2004 interview:

The question of settling divorce should be in the hands of the wiser party, and that is the man. Men are wise, which is why they

do not have to go to court. Islamic law would consider the wise
wife an exception, and you cannot generalize an exception.

Both the law and the way it's practiced deter women from seeking
divorce. Because the Egyptian legal system doesn't recognize joint marital assets, a couple's home and any property they acquired during the
marriage are usually registered in the man's name; separating from her
husband may impoverish a woman or even leave her homeless. Following a divorce, husbands are required to return the property their wives
brought to the marriage and also to pay the part of the marriage dower
that they still owe, as well as alimony and child support. But the courts'
inability to enforce these rules—again, *mafish nizam*—often lets men
off the hook. (Eighty-eight percent of women, according to one study,
gave up their claims to marital property when getting a fault-based divorce through the courts.) Whatever the method of divorce, custody of
the children goes to the mother by law. Yet many women who pursue
khul give up that right voluntarily, as Doaa did, because they can't afford
to support their kids on their own. Others remain in unhappy marriages
because the cost of leaving is too high.

Divorce hasn't always been so hard on women. During the medieval
and Ottoman eras, divorce was freely practiced in the Middle East and
accessible to both sexes, the historian Yossef Rapoport writes. About
one-third of marriages in fifteenth-century Cairo ended in divorce, according to his analysis, a surprising figure that far surpassed the rates in
Europe or China at that time. Women initiated the splits as often as
men:

The majority of divorces in Muslim society were neither unilateral repudiations nor judicial dissolutions, but consensual separations. . . . These settlements were always initiated by the
wife, who would ask her husband for a divorce in return for
monetary compensation. . . . Divorce was rarely a one-sided
affair.

Women usually gained custody of the children and often served as
their legal guardians if their father died; among both sexes, remarriage
was common and free of any social stigma. The four schools of Islamic
jurisprudence often differed on specific points, because they were drawn
from traditions in different parts of the Muslim world (judgments made
according to the Maliki school, for example, tended to be more favorable to a wife's alimony claims). Women used this inconsistency to their
advantage, often suing for divorce according to whatever legal tradition
gave them the best chances. After the codification of family law in the
early twentieth century under British rule, all the flexibility went out of
the system, like a balloon deflating. Women lost the right to contract
their own marriages and to set the terms for them. They could no longer
initiate divorce nor easily become legal guardians for their children.

The successful passage of the *khul* law in 2000, though, has encouraged reformers to take on a century-old legal framework that continues
to treat women as childlike dependents. In September 2017, a member
of parliament from Upper Egypt named Abla El-Hawary proposed a
comprehensive new marriage law drafted by several women's rights organizations that were involved in the reintroduction of *khul*. Among its
provisions were that women and men would have equal access to divorce and an equal share of the marital property. A woman whose husband planned to take a second wife would be granted an instant divorce,
if she chose, and divorced mothers would retain custody of their children even if they remarried. In Doaa's case, such a law might have given
her the financial security to keep her children even after a divorce.

I asked Gawaher El-Taher, a director at the Center for Egyptian
Women's Legal Assistance, which of the proposed changes are the hardest for legislators to accept.

"*Kul,*" she joked. "All of them." She continued, "We had a meeting
with twenty parliamentarians. The two articles they had severe objections to were the ones on matrimonial assets and restrictions on polygamy."

"Is that what you expected?" I asked. "That those are the articles the male parliamentarians would feel most strongly about?"

"Let me tell you something," her colleague, Nada Nashat, interrupted. "Anything that reduces the man's power regarding sex or money definitely brings objections. That's it—that's the bottom line." The bill's supporters are continuing to meet with members of parliament and other organizations to try to ensure its passage.

For now, female-initiated divorce is limited to the truly desperate. Only the worst circumstances would give a woman the courage to say, as Doaa put it: *I'm willing to give up everything in my life just to get rid of you.*

A FEW WEEKS into the new semester, Doaa received an unexpected phone call: A relative of her ex-husband's told her to prepare a copy of the *ayma,* the list of items she had brought to her marriage. By law, her husband should have returned these things—which included kitchen appliances, two rooms' worth of furniture, and gold jewelry—when they divorced. Doaa had sued him two years before, and a court had ruled that he should return her property and be jailed for six months, but nothing had come of it.

What finally broke the logjam was enforcement of another kind. At the funeral of a family member, Doaa's uncle had approached her husband's family and told them to return all of her property. "Doaa's father is staying silent about this, but I'm not going to," he said. "If her brothers get involved, my sons will get involved. It will become a huge family fight, and I'll take the side of my sons."

The sister of Doaa's ex-husband overheard these threats and was frightened. Her loyalty was naturally to her own brother. But she was also connected to Doaa's family, through her marriage to one of Doaa's cousins. If a fight broke out between the two families, she would be caught in between. She and her mother pressured her brother to capitulate.

Doaa got her property back. It included money from the sale of her wedding jewelry, along with appliances, utensils, a dining table, and bedroom and living room furniture, so many items that she had to rent a small apartment to store all of it. She met with her ex-husband, in the presence of a relative serving as their intermediary, and told him she would like to see her daughters once a week. Under duress, he was more cooperative than he had been in a long time.

"You should have told me from the beginning," he answered. "I wouldn't have said no."

The following Friday, Doaa's brother went to pick up the children from their father's house. Doaa waited at home. She hadn't seen her girls in two years and she had bought them new clothes for the occasion, slippers, hairbands, and snacks for their day together. She was surprised to hear shouting from the stairwell and ran down to see what was happening. Her daughters were out on the street, screaming and crying. They refused to enter the apartment building where Doaa lived.

"You took all my father's furniture!" her older daughter, Nuseiba, who was eight, yelled when she saw her mother. "What else do you want from me?"

With her brother's help, Doaa brought the girls upstairs. At first, Nuseiba sat by herself and refused to speak to her mother. Her younger sister, Asinat, cried and implored her to behave. When their aunt called, Doaa overheard her daughters address the woman as "Mama" over the phone.

"Why do you call her that?" Doaa asked.

"Because you left us," one of her daughters said. "We didn't have anyone else."

"There's only one mother, and that's me," Doaa said. "She is your aunt."

She explained to them that she and their father didn't get along and wouldn't be getting back together. The girls would continue to live with their father, but from now on they would spend every Friday with her.

"I didn't leave you," Doaa told her daughters. "I'm working, and I'm working to improve myself. I'm studying. I didn't get remarried."

Gradually she won back her daughters' trust, and the three of them made plans for the next week's visit. Doaa would be preparing for her midterm exams, so all of them would study together. Then she planned to bring the girls by the Delta factory so they could see where their mother worked.

The next week, Doaa waited for her daughters at home, when again she heard noises on the stairs. It was a repeat of the previous visit—her brother struggling with the children, the screaming in the street—but this time the girls didn't even make it upstairs.

Doaa guessed that her mother-in-law was telling her daughters lies about her. "The girls probably went back and told her that I'm working and studying, and she probably got jealous," she told me. Doaa's ex-husband heard what had happened and offered to bring the children by again. For a third time, the girls shouted and made scenes, this time for half an hour, until their father took them away.

In the factory cafeteria, during a break from work, Doaa took out her phone and showed me photos of the day she spent with her children. They were skinny and long-legged and as vivid as dragonflies, in their brightly colored winter coats of purple and sea green. In some of the pictures, Nuseiba perched on the edge of the couch and steadfastly refused to look at her mother, with a sulkiness that any parent would recognize. She's furious and she hates you, but after a while she calms down or forgets what she's mad about.

Doaa didn't have the luxury of waiting. After her daughters screamed at her for two Fridays in a row, Doaa decided: no more Fridays. By law, she should have custody of her children and be paid monthly child support. But all the power lay on the side of her ex-husband and his relations, and she was too exhausted to keep fighting them. The return of

Doaa's furniture had averted open warfare between the families, but it could start up at any time and suck her children into its whirl.

"What will you do now?" I asked her.

"I'm not going to try anymore," Doaa said. "I don't want to lose the girls, and I don't want them to be torn between their father and me. I don't want to damage them psychologically."

She was silent for a while. "When they grow older, they'll understand."

In Riham's factory, a woman named Eman Abdel Hamid Mohamed tried to explain to me how she and her husband were related. He was her first cousin, the son of her mother's sister. At the same time, his sister was married to one of Eman's brothers, and a cousin of his had just wed her youngest brother. "I have five aunts, and all the children are married to each other. It's *salata*," she said of her family arrangement—a salad.

The most famous practitioners of kin marriage were the pharaohs. In certain dynasties, it was common for brothers to marry sisters, and sometimes fathers their own daughters, in order to concentrate power within a single royal lineage. (The second ruler of the Eighteenth Dynasty, Amenhotep I, is believed to have been the product of three generations of brother-sister unions.) Marriage between first cousins is explicitly permitted in the Quran, and the preference for marrying within the clan has persisted, with surprising resilience. One in every three marriages in Egypt is between blood relatives, a figure that has held steady since the 1960s—and which includes President Sisi, who married his first cousin. The practice is most common in rural Upper Egypt, where almost half of all marriages are between kin, but it extends across regions and classes. A union between paternal first cousins is traditionally considered the ideal match.

Like the ancient pharaohs, extended families believe that intermarrying their offspring will consolidate the wealth and status of the clan. The evidence for this claim, though, is mixed; a study of married women in Egypt found no consistent correlation between greater land ownership and higher rates of kin marriage. There is some proof that for a woman, marrying a relative is cheaper: Since the two families already know and trust each other, she can bring fewer assets to the marriage without losing face.

The abiding preference for kin marriage reflects, above all, a deep instinct to keep things as they are. Even young people cling to the known and familiar. A survey of Egyptians in their twenties and early thirties found that almost all of them had been introduced to their partners through relatives, friends, or neighbors. Very few of them, unlike in the West, married someone they met on their own through school or the workplace. Only one out of five young women said she would risk marrying a man her family didn't know. From a young age, boys and girls are raised with the expectation that they will wed someone in their circle of familiars. The political scientist Diane Singerman observed these dynamics in her study of a Cairo neighborhood:

> **Far more flirting, sexual innuendoes, and physical relationships appear to occur within the household than outside of it. . . . These intrafamilial relationships often have an explicitly sexual aspect to them. . . . A young boy can grow up in almost constant contact with a cousin who lives in the same building or neighborhood, and subsequently marry her. People always tease young teenagers about which cousin they will marry, and it is obvious that attractions develop between relatives.**

Like the need to accumulate goods for one's trousseau, the preference for marrying within the family is founded on pessimism about the future. For a young woman, being wedded to a relative instead of a *gha-*

reeb, a stranger, is supposed to give her more leverage in the event of future conflicts with her husband and in-laws. It's also a type of insurance against abandonment. A man is less likely to leave his wife, the argument goes, if she's also his cousin. These bleak scenarios would seem to reflect how powerless many women feel as they enter marriage, and how little faith they have in what comes next.

Eman, the worker in Riham's factory, was twenty-nine years old with arresting dark eyes in a long slender face. Originally from the Upper Egyptian city of Qena, she had been in love with her cousin for five years before their marriage. But that wasn't why she accepted him. "The first reason I married him is because he is my relative," she told me. "I wouldn't have married him if I didn't know him very, very well."

One of the things she knew very, very well was that he was very, very lazy. He had worked with her brothers in construction, installing floors in apartments, but he was a day laborer in the literal sense. Sometimes he would work for just one day and then take the rest of the month off.

"He didn't want to work," Eman said. "He wanted to have a job where he would feel accomplished and powerful."

"What kind of job did he want?" I asked.

"It wasn't anything specific, that's the problem. I made fun of him: 'Do you want to be a government minister?'" Eman has sharp opinions that she doesn't mind sharing. Her tongue, as the Egyptians say, is long.

"So you married him even though you knew he didn't like to work?"

"Yes, it's a problem, really." Eman laughed. "I wouldn't advise this for anyone else. I won't let my daughters do this."

After the wedding, her husband continued to be an unreliable earner, but he also refused to let her work. Eman complained—loudly—to her mother about their poor living conditions, and she clashed so much with her mother-in-law that her husband asked her to stop visiting his family. He started to have spells of crying and confusion and consulted a traditional healer, who told him his wife had put a curse on him. The couple endured separations and reconciliations and the births of three children, but they eventually divorced. Over the two years I knew Eman, she and her kids lived with her parents while she pursued a bewildering number of legal cases to force her husband to return her furniture and pay child support. The courts usually ruled in her favor, but their judgments—jail time for her husband, thousands of pounds to be paid for the children's care—remained on paper only. "I will never get all the money that I'm owed from him," she said.

I asked Eman if anyone in the family had interceded on her behalf.

"Everyone is busy in their own house and minding their own business, and they don't care about me," Eman told me. "Some of them also say it was my choice from the beginning to marry him, so they want me to take responsibility for my own actions."

That was the flip side of being embedded in the family structure: Often, relatives don't want to get involved in individual disputes because it might instigate a broader conflict. In Doaa's case, the threat of wide-scale domestic warfare helped her get her marriage property back. But her close ties to her husband's family probably exacerbated tensions, and the same was true for Eman. Women may marry relatives with the hope of gaining leverage in the marriage, but a study by two sociologists found that they have significantly *less* decision-making influence than women who wed outsiders, maybe because they're more likely to be under the thumb of their in-laws.

The suffocating bonds of family is the subject of the Egyptian director Mohamed Khan's 2013 film, *Fatat El-Masna* ("Factory Girl"). It tells the story of a young woman named Hayam who falls in love with her supervisor in the Cairo garment factory where she works. As Hayam becomes the target of rumor and gossip, the attacks on her reputation are led by her mother, while her aunt becomes her strongest defender. Eventually, Hayam is cleared of wrongdoing and is welcomed back into her community. Oppression and liberation, judgment and absolution, all have come from within her own family circle.

An extended family might be united against the world, but most of the time the attention of its members is turned inward. For women especially, the family—with its mothers and mothers-in-law, sisters and daughters and aunts and nieces and cousins—*is* the world. All of the harm and suffering they fear from strangers, they end up inflicting on each other.

IN HER LAST year of college, Doaa was drawn into a new blow-up inside the Delta plant. A friend of hers named Aya, who worked as a nurse in the factory's clinic, got into a fight with Mohamed Hanafy. He was the personnel director whom I had thought of as perpetually mild-mannered. But clearly I was wrong, because in the course of a shouting match with Aya, he was said to have slapped her and then been chased down a hallway by some workers. Finally, the manager of the factory and a security guard came to his rescue and helped him get away. Doaa had heard her friend's screams for help and supported her version of the story. As workers in the factory took sides, some people started to suspect Doaa of being more deeply involved than she said she was.

"The minute I talk about it, everyone assumes that I know more and that we planned the whole thing in advance," Doaa complained.

Both Mohamed and Aya lost their jobs over the incident, but employees continued to discuss the details. In the close environment of the factory, rumors bloomed, like hothouse flowers, into conspiracies. What exactly was the relationship between a senior executive like Mohamed, who was in his thirties, and a single woman more than a decade younger? Why had they been fighting? Some people said that Mohamed had been obsessed with Aya for a long time. Others speculated that Aya cooked up the whole story, though no one could say why.

The departure of Rania, several months earlier, had also divided the workforce. "Some people disliked Rania because of her manners, and they were happy that she left," Doaa told me. "And some people were upset, because they know she has children and needs the money. The whole factory is hoping she can find work again."

I commented that the factory felt like a family, and Doaa agreed without my having to explain what I meant. "Yes, there are a lot of personal problems—feuds, revenge, jealousy. People like to take revenge and backstab one another."

She had seen her older daughter, Nuseiba, again. After hearing through friends that her ex-husband had a new wife, Doaa decided to visit her girls at school to make sure they were okay. As soon as Nuseiba was brought into the headmistress's office, she started to yell at her mother. "What brought you here? I don't want you. Go away!" She kicked Doaa and spat at her. She believed, erroneously, that her mother had gotten remarried.

The school administrators were shocked at the girl's behavior and tried to calm her down. They urged Doaa to come back to the school on another day to help Nuseiba work through her emotions, but Doaa was exhausted. "Right now, I'm really burned out," she told me. "Especially the way my daughter treated me at the school, it really discouraged me." Afterward, her ex-husband learned about the meeting and called her up to yell at her; in the background, Doaa could hear her ex-mother-in-law shouting insults. Her daughters were now living with their father, their new stepmother, and their grandmother. The household dynamics were likely even more fraught and complicated than they had been in Doaa's time, a cycle of dysfunction endlessly repeating.

As soon as she got her college diploma, Doaa planned to enroll in a master's program. The cruelties she had suffered in her marriage seemed to have made her more determined to succeed. Maybe the same mysterious alchemy would work on her girls and somehow help them escape the turmoil in their lives and become different people than everyone around them.

"The most important thing is that they're growing up financially secure, and that they're getting an education," Doaa said. "Maybe one day they'll get their master's degree, just like me, and look up to their mother and say, 'My mother finished her education. She got her master's degree, and she got a job.'"

She continued, "Sometimes growing up with one parent absent actually makes a child stronger. That's how I see it, that they'll grow up strong and able to stand up for themselves."

10

EGYPTIAN MADE

BEFORE I MOVED TO EGYPT, I had an image of the country in my mind. It was full of accomplished women, I believed, and was progressive and cosmopolitan in ways that many Western observers didn't care to admit. I was mostly wrong. I did meet talented female lawyers, activists, economists, social scientists, filmmakers, and journalists. They were often fluent in English, and French or German as well; they worked and traveled freely; they had been raised to believe that a girl could do anything she wanted. Many of them had attended private schools and universities that prized command of a foreign language over competency in formal Arabic, with the result that they spoke my language, but barely their own. In a country that had more than a hundred million inhabitants, they made up perhaps 1 to 2 percent of the population. They reminded me of the tiny figures that you see in the distance in a Breughel painting, far removed from the concerns of ordinary folk.

The other Egypt is where a woman's right to continue her education, hold a job, or leave the house is in no way guaranteed, and 92 percent of men *and women* agree that males make better leaders. In the chocka-block density of Egyptian cities, the two worlds exist in proximity, and the poor often live among the rich as their cooks, cleaners, and maids. But they might as well inhabit a foreign country.

Educated people sometimes spoke about the lower class, especially the women, in ways that exaggerated their backwardness ("Women in Upper Egypt don't leave the house, ever!") But there was also a tendency to erase features of this group that they found embarrassing. Men no longer object to their wives working, I was told by a college student named Rania, who volunteered with an organization that worked with women in Minya. "We're in 2016. People are more enlightened," she said, less than an hour after she and I visited villages where many of the women told me a father, brother, husband, or fiancé wouldn't let them get a job.

A woman named Marie Louis Bishara, a vice chair in her family's clothing business who served on the government's National Council for Women, was astonished that I knew a factory worker who lived unhappily with her husband and his second wife. "But a woman like that can get divorced," she said, "and apply for government funds for maintenance for her children."

I said that divorce was expensive and difficult. A poor woman might have nowhere to go if she left her husband, and her family—

"Please give me her number," Marie implored, ignoring everything I had said. "I would give her a job in any one of my factories."

Among a younger generation of educated women, I noticed a reluctance to engage in the subject. I sensed that they were tired of the Arab-woman-as-passive-victim conversation, and the way that it has been used by the West to criticize Middle Eastern societies. Maybe, like my younger self, they didn't want to be boxed in by the fact of their gender. "You can't isolate the problems of women outside of the larger issues," a young female filmmaker told me, which didn't seem true at all. How else do women gain rights if they don't explicitly push for them?

In the 1950s, the Nasser regime granted women the right to vote and to run for office, and it vastly expanded their educational and employment opportunities. The Sadat and Mubarak governments set up organizations and passed laws to promote women's rights, in both cases deploying their wives as high-profile advocates. But the administration of Abdel Fatah El-Sisi is different. Female empowerment isn't high on his agenda, and his wife is almost never seen in public. The government declared 2017 to be the Year of the Woman, but apparently only a specific type of prominent and successful female was worth celebrating. A two-day conference featured a pioneer in nanotechnology who lived in Germany, a scholar of textbook translation (Switzerland), a professional handball player (France), and several government officials who made *Forbes* magazine's list of the most influential women in the Arab world. *Et voilà!* "This conference should change the course of Egyptian women," an organizer promised, "who need opportunities and have a lot of potential."

Improving the lives of ordinary women is the work of dozens of nongovernmental organizations around the country. They typically run training and development projects in individual communities, but these aren't designed to bring about change on a larger scale and may even convey the message that salvation comes only from the outside. "This is a big problem with NGOs: After two years, they finish the program and they don't do any follow-up, and the people they work with are unemployed again," Fatima Metwally, who helped the Delta factory recruit workers, told me. "The women don't get involved in the project, and they never take action to change their own reality." It's possible, from the perspective of the village, to take a cynical view. A philanthropic outfit comes to town and the villagers join a sheep-raising cooperative, or they start growing vegetables on rooftops, or they recycle. When the program's term ends, the organizers leave, the funding dries up, and everything returns to its original course, like a branch of the Nile that, having been temporarily diverted, is recaptured by the great river once again.

Over five years of living in Egypt, I came to see the unequal position of women, and everything that flows from it, as the most pressing problem facing the country. Purely from a pragmatic standpoint, it's a colossal waste of money for a poor nation to educate millions of women and then fail to put them to economically productive uses. And the outsize power that men enjoy, in marriage and at home, carries over into how they behave in public. When a prominent man—a judge, or a talk show host, or a member of parliament—belittles women's abilities or makes misogynistic comments, he usually gets away with it, just as he does at home with his mother and sisters, or his wife and kids. (For a century, Egypt's authoritarian rulers have styled themselves as benevolent fathers to the nation, relegating citizens to the role of children.) The dynamics inside the family—with its power imbalances, its infighting, its clannishness—shape how men and women behave in factories and offices, committees and political parties, and the wider world.

BETWEEN 2013 AND 2015, I spent a year and a half observing the workings of an Egyptian news website called *Mada Masr. Masr* means Egypt, and *mada* is an Arabic word for "span" or "range," and the organization emerged as a rare independent news source in the aftermath of the 2011 revolution, as Sisi consolidated power. Almost everything about the newly founded group challenged the country's status quo. Its editor in chief, a woman named Lina Attalah, was only thirty; she led a team of mostly female reporters, whose average age was twenty-five. The staff wrote articles, in English and Arabic, that questioned the regime's policy of stamping out dissent in the name of its "war on terror." *Mada* reporters investigated the government's suppression of political opponents and its attempts to rewrite history in its favor. They brought a critical eye to constitutions, elections, trials, sectarian conflicts, economic developments, arts and cultural events, and the workers' movement.

The company had high ambitions for itself: Its co-founders wanted to do away with hierarchical structures and give employees ownership and an equal voice in key decisions. They granted me full access to document this experiment in democratic management. My purpose, as it evolved over many months of reporting, was to study how an Egyptian organization might break with tradition and operate as a functioning democracy, against the backdrop of a state that was failing at the same task.

Most of the *Mada* reporters had worked at an English language newspaper that shut down earlier that year, for what they believed were political reasons. Some of them had been friends since college; others had met during the heady days of the 2011 revolution. These shared experiences had bred intense loyalties to one another that they compared to being in a family. "When you decide to be an activist, to go into progressive politics, you need a community of people to talk to," Lina told me. "We go to these people to form an alternative family." Like Riham in her garment factory, Lina was the matriarch—knowing which reporter had stayed up too late the night before, bringing a plate of turkey to a sick colleague for Thanksgiving dinner.

But as in the factory, familial relationships could contribute to drama. In early 2015, I watched as *Mada* became embroiled in an internal conflict over a reporter named Mohamad Adam. Raised mostly in a farming village one and a half hours' travel from Cairo, Adam wrote about police recruits and Muslim Brotherhood members with insight and sympathy. He could also be volatile and difficult to work with. As the recently named editor of the Arabic language part of the website, he struggled to maintain a consistent production schedule and sometimes clashed with his colleagues. Two of the company's translators quit, citing disagreements with him. A meeting between Adam and several editors to resolve these issues turned combative ("He screamed at everyone, and everyone screamed back" is how Lina described it).

Yet Lina's decision to demote Adam back to being a regular reporter polarized the *Mada* staff. Adam's supporters accused Lina of betraying a longtime friend and behaving like an authoritarian leader. Any such demotion should have had collective approval, they pointed out, though in fact the company's own regulations didn't spell out how to handle such cases. In the months afterward, the *Mada* team met and agreed on measures to evaluate individual performance, in order to head off future disputes. Against all odds, I wrote, the group was figuring out how to make democracy workable.

After I finished writing my story, I contacted Adam, who had left *Mada* to take a job at a human rights organization, to check some facts in the sections about him. He demanded, in an email, that I either include his version of events or not write about him at all. "I want to delete this chapter from my life," he wrote.

Two days before the piece was to be published in *The Guardian* newspaper, Adam wrote me again. I was juggling a lot of things that day and didn't respond right away. His threats stacked up in my email box, like bricks in a barricade:

If you won't reply in 5 hours I'll start contacting your editor.

call me

now

I phoned Adam. I told him that I had rewritten parts of the story to reflect his point of view more fully, but I wouldn't erase a conflict that had been central to *Mada*'s evolution over the last year. His response was to deploy the tools that men have always used against women. He made accusations and threats, in a voice that drowned out mine. He shouted that I was trying to destroy his career, and that he was going to sue me. "I'm going to get you thrown in jail" were his final words. Then he hung up.

By the time my article ran (headline: THE NEWS WEBSITE THAT'S KEEPING PRESS FREEDOM ALIVE IN EGYPT), the entire *Mada* staff had turned against me. My piece depicted their venture in positive and sympathetic terms, but the reporters were solely focused on what they perceived as an attack on one of their own. "The article is rude and the writer is rude and the writing is rude and the content is rude," a reporter named Omar Said wrote, in an email to me and all the *Mada* employees. Various members of the staff attacked me for being "not respectful," "reckless," "unprofessional," and "silly." I was accused of precipitating a scandal and a moral crisis, and of engaging in "character assassination of a young man who is still beginning his life." I was reminded, "Sometimes some shyness is good." Separately, a reporter named Maha ElNabawi asked me to take out a lighthearted line in my story in which I quoted her saying that her mother didn't know the appropriate shoes to wear to a protest march, "as this quote will certainly destroy our relationship," she wrote me in an email.

They were all journalists committed to free speech and democratic principles. Yet when confronted with an account of themselves that was factually accurate but not to their liking, they behaved like the regime they opposed: They closed ranks and made personal attacks. In Egypt, the binary view of the world starts at the top—if you're not with the state, you're against it, and whoever doesn't fall into line is an enemy. This was how Rania operated inside the Delta factory. The *Mada* staff were college-educated professional journalists, but at the end of the day they lived by the same rules. Of the many reporters and editors I had gotten to know over a year and a half, not one stood up to defend my work or my professional ethics, and nobody expressed concern that Adam had threatened me. I didn't belong to their tribe.

My article described how a group of young people was making democracy work in practice—on a small scale, they changed Egypt. Publishing the story taught me the opposite lesson. Change is hard, whether on a national or a personal scale, and in the end the two are closely connected in ways I hadn't appreciated before. *Mada* was an organization that demanded transparency of its country's leaders but frequently fell short of that goal itself. Members of an inner clique, which included

Lina and those she trusted, drove the discussions at staff meetings, while people in the outer circles might be in the dark as to what had happened or what was even being talked about. A disagreement over one topic might actually be a fight about something else entirely, as in a long series of emails over whom to invite to a staff breakfast that was in fact, I learned, about employees' hostility toward Adam. "We were trying in subtle ways to hurt each other," Lina explained.

Afterward, I remembered things that people at *Mada* had told me that had barely registered at the time. Lina had been punched and dragged through the street by police on the first day of the 2011 protests, but she lied to her parents and said that she had tripped and fallen in her office. Many of the other reporters hid their participation in antigovernment demonstrations from their families, so as not to upset them. The desire to challenge one's parents clashed with a deep-seated need to please them, and the tension between these two courses of action hummed under the workings of daily life, like a low-grade generator whose sound you no longer heard. Naira Antoun, a news editor, said the dynamics inside *Mada* sometimes reminded her of "a dysfunctional family that won't give anyone any space." Lina was "like the mom," she told me. "You always want her approval more than anyone else's, but you know she'll always love you."

The family's influence is greater, and sometimes more pernicious, than people want to acknowledge. Home is where Egyptians become comfortable with a host of negative behaviors—the ways in which men bully women, and relatives engage in feuds as a proxy for honest communication, and young people absorb in their bones that the most terrible thing isn't deception or hypocrisy but causing any hint of a scandal. College graduates who had stood up to Mubarak's soldiers and tanks crumpled before their fathers and mothers, and a journalist would ask another to censor herself rather than ask why her relationship with her mom could fall apart over a newspaper quote. This kind of behavior wasn't a trivial matter: The urge to preserve family peace, even at the cost of honesty and principle, ensured the survival of the system as it was. You can't destroy the patriarchy and still try to make your parents happy.

How does it change? Since the 2011 uprising and the repressive military rule that followed, liberal activists and journalists like those at *Mada* have pushed to limit state power, draft just laws, and build democratic institutions. But many of the ills of Egyptian society are rooted in personal behaviors that are learned inside the family. Eradicating these will require a different kind of work: questioning how they were raised and having uncomfortable conversations with those they love most. And suppressing the instinct to blame outsiders for their problems. In Egypt, most problems are Egyptian made.

ON MY FOURTH visit to Rania's home in November 2017, I noticed changes as soon as I walked in the door: A new double bed, a fresh reed mat lining the floor. "*Mabrouk!*" I said. "Congratulations!" Her bedroom at the back of the house now contained a refrigerator pushed against the far wall. "It's new," she said, opening and closing the door for me, like a game show host showing off a prize.

Mabrouk!

Mabrouk!

After she returned home a couple of years earlier, following her separation from Yasser, Rania found that he and his second wife, Asmaa, had sold the refrigerator and moved her bedroom and living room furniture to their own part of the house. They also took her TV, her dishes, and even her combs and brushes. Rania had since bought a replacement television, kitchen appliances, and the double bed for the children, all on installment with her earnings as a supervisor at Delta. *Mabrouk!* It was customary to visit a bride after the wedding to admire her newly appointed home, but this felt like a grotesque reversal of the ritual—an inventory of all the items that had been taken from Rania, one by one, after she was replaced by someone else.

When she first married, she told me, she and her husband lived in the main part of the house with his parents. After their kids were born, Yasser had a falling-out with his father—"*Adi*, it was a normal fight"— and the young family moved over to this side of the property, which at the time had been a stable for the family's goat and buffalo. Rania spent her savings and her wedding jewelry—"I was selling one piece of gold after another, until I sold my wedding ring"—to help renovate the space, lay tile, install water and electricity, and buy furniture. Now she was purchasing many of these things a second time. She had worked at Delta for eight years, and the bulk of her earnings had been spent acquiring the same household goods over and over. Success in the working world hadn't brought her greater status at home, and all the time she had been working so hard just to stay in place.

"Did you hear that Mohamed Hanafy left the factory?" Rania relayed details of the fight between him and the nurse, Aya. "I'm very happy."

I hadn't seen her since her dismissal from Delta three months before, and I asked her about Mohamed Hanafy's charges against her: manipulating workers to file false complaints, spreading rumors about her enemies, Sexy Call.

Rania frowned and shook her head impatiently. *Tzk, tzk:* She clicked her tongue against the back of her teeth, the way Egyptians do to signal negation or disapproval. "He is a great inventor. He used to be very jealous when you showed up and went to talk to me rather than him."

"So Hanafy made up all these stories because he was jealous of you?"

"He was trying to create any kind of problem for me, to get me fired."

Rania had gone back to the Delta factory once to pick up her severance pay of £E13,000, around $740, which had mostly gone into her recent household purchases. She had approached the factory manager about returning to work, but he turned her down. Now Rania was hoping to join a new garment factory, run by a Cairo-based NGO, that was scheduled to open in Minya in the new year.

I asked her if she would do things differently next time, to avoid the kind of personal conflicts she'd had at Delta.

"Yes, I need to work on that."

"How?"

"In the new factory, I want to be more alert and on my guard, so I'll be aware if someone's plotting against me."

"But do you feel that you were also at fault?" I pressed her. "Did you contribute to your own difficulties in any way?"

"From my side, I was naïve," she said. "I blame myself. For not being on my guard." In any garment factory there would always be people who were out to get you, she told me. "It's an all-female society," Rania said. "It's commonly said that clothing factories never lack for problems." In her analysis—*It's an all-female society*—she was glossing over the fact that the person who had supposedly ousted her was a man.

YASSER WAS GIVING us no peace that day. He sat on the couch and tried to inject himself into the conversation. He fiddled on the computer, couldn't get the internet to work, bickered with Rania about it ("Why don't you go get it checked?" "Don't talk to me that way"), tried to look me up online, partially succeeded ("Did you work for *The Wall Street Journal*?"), and asked me the difference between Google and email. He seemed to be trying to get my attention, and he was driving everyone crazy. Even after we moved into the kitchen when Rania started cooking—I had never seen Yasser go back there—I sensed that he was continuing to monitor us.

"Maybe we should go see what he wants," I told my translator, Mai. I wondered whether he was finally going to tell this foreign woman, who kept coming over to his house to ask his wife nosy questions about her work and her firing and her dissatisfactions with her husband, that she was no longer welcome.

"We have some artifacts," he announced, as soon as Mai and I entered the living room. "Would you like to go see them?"

"No," I said. "I don't want to get involved in that."

He assured me these weren't archaeological treasures from Beni Hassan, the pharaonic era tomb site dating to 1900 B.C. where he worked as a security guard. "They have cameras everywhere on the site and it would be impossible to steal anything. These are just artifacts some of my friends have dug out of the ground."

"No, really, I don't know anything about it," I repeated.

"How about I give them to you to go sell in the United States?" Yasser asked, apparently failing to register how little I wanted to be thrown into an Egyptian prison for trying to smuggle antiquities out of the country.

"I work as a journalist," I said. "This just isn't something I do. I'm sorry."

Later, we assembled at a low table in the front room to eat a delicious meal of roast duck and many side dishes, which I knew from past visits had taken Rania all day to prepare. Yasser sat on the bed and peered at the TV while we ate. He had never sat down to a meal with us.

After dinner, the baby Mahmoud was delivered into the room, so quickly that I didn't catch sight of his mother. He was bigger and more alert than the last time I had seen him. He could walk and sit up on his own.

"He's grown up a lot," Rania commented, but she couldn't resist a dig at the toddler. "They shaved off his curls to try to make him look better, but it's no use."

"He's cute, just like his mother," Yasser goaded her.

The older children took turns putting bits of chicken in Mahmoud's mouth. Once he bit into a spicy piece and started to cry. "Stupid!" Rania snapped at him.

When he fiddled with the knob on a speaker and pulled it off, Rania swiped him to one side with her arm. "Stupid!" she said again.

Her son and daughter helped clear away the dinner dishes and then pulled out the Legos I had given them. They showed me structures they had put together and kept carefully intact: a house with a picket fence, a Chinese-style palace. Kareem was working on a skyscraper, but Mahmoud kept trying to knock it down.

"You destroy things, just like your father," Rania said to the little boy. "He only knows how to destroy things."

"I destroy things only to build new things," Yasser responded.

"Oh, so new things are better?"

"Yes, new things are better."

The uneasy three-way truce I had observed on my last visit hadn't lasted. Yasser and Asmaa had a fight, so for a while Asmaa spent her days with her mother-in-law while Yasser returned home only at night to sleep. At an earlier point, Asmaa had had a falling-out with her in-laws and moved into Rania's side of the house for four months ("but she wasn't grateful for what I did for her, and she didn't thank me and always tried to make problems for me"). Relations between Rania, Yasser, and Asmaa were in constant flux, alliances forming and shattering and rearranging themselves like light flickering across troubled water. Now Rania and Yasser were speaking to each other, but only in the language of barbed comments.

It was always bad, but different kinds of bad.

Debase a woman by bringing in another one.
—Moroccan saying

THE FIRST COMMUNITY of Muslims, according to tradition, began to practice polygamy following the Battle of Uhud in 625, when the deaths of so many men left numerous widows and orphans without a means of support. The single verse in the Quran that permits men more than one wife at a time—"If you fear that you shall not be able to deal justly with the orphans, marry women of your choice, two or three or four"— appears in a passage about the need to protect the inheritance of those left fatherless. Men who couldn't treat multiple wives equitably should abstain from the practice, the text continues, and then asserts, some pages later: "You are never able to be fair and just as between women, even if it is your ardent desire." Thus polygamy emerged to serve the community's need at a unique historical moment, and under such circumscribed terms that some scholars believe it was never meant to be practiced widely, or at all.

How did an injunction to treat female orphans with compassion turn into a blanket assertion of male sexual license? In the years after the death of the Prophet Muhammad—who in his lifetime had thirteen wives, many of whom he married to consolidate political alliances—the Islamic conquests transformed the region, bringing immense wealth to cities on the Arabian Peninsula and fueling a trade in women who had been captured in battle. Keeping large harems of slaves and concubines became the norm for the upper class. El-Zubayr, the brother-in-law of Muhammad's wife Aisha and one of the religion's early followers, was said to have left a thousand slaves and concubines when he died. These practices continued into the Abbasid era, which lasted from the eighth to the thirteenth centuries and was distinguished by repressive attitudes toward women. The scholar Leila Ahmed describes one man during this period who, after receiving his inheritance, purchased "concubines and other objects" the way one might buy a lamp or a sofa for a new home. "The words *woman,* and *slave,* and *object for sexual use,*" she writes, "came close to being indistinguishably fused."

From the start, people have understood that requiring a woman to share her husband with someone else can be harmful and degrading. Muhammad himself was said to have strongly opposed the decision of his son-in-law Ali, who was married to his daughter Fatima, to take a second wife.

I will not allow Ali Ibn Ali Talib and I repeat, I will not allow Ali to marry another woman except if he divorces my daughter. She is a part of me, and what harms her, harms me.

The historical records are full of men who dread the cruelties that await their daughters. In a letter that dates to the Abbasid period, one man wrote in condolence to a friend whose young daughter had just died. "We live in an age . . . when he who weds his daughter to the grave has found the best of bridegrooms."

Polygamy was a frequent cause of failed marriages, to judge from court records of the Ottoman era, and it was often listed in marital contracts as automatic grounds for divorce. Two pioneers of the Egyptian feminist movement in the early twentieth century, the political organizer Huda Sharawi and the writer Malak Hifni Nasif, endured the same agony of marrying a prominent man only to learn, after the fact, that he was already married. In *Women and Gender in Islam,* the scholar Leila Ahmed observed:

Pain figures in the lives of the women who throughout this century have devoted themselves to the cause of women. All suffered directly from the system in place, whose destructiveness to women . . . was explicitly set at naught, regarded as immaterial, when measured against the pleasures of men.

Reformers have been trying to stamp out polygamy for more than a century. Sharawi and other activists presented a petition to the first Egyptian parliament, in 1924, to limit the practice; two years later, a committee of scholars also recommended that the government impose restrictions. In 1945, the Ministry of Social Affairs proposed that any man wanting to marry a second wife must apply to a *sharia* judge who would assess his financial suitability first. The Nasser government twice prepared legislation, in 1960 and again in 1966, that deemed polygamy to be an injury to the first wife and thus automatic grounds for divorce. Sadat, in 1979, tried to sneak the same stipulation into law by presidential decree. A 2004 draft by the National Council of Women called for fines and other "harsh sanctions" on men who married second wives. All of these attempts, in one way or another, ran up against the wall of religious orthodoxy. Polygamy is in the Quran, is permitted by *sharia,* and was practiced by the Prophet Muhammad and his companions. It is, in the words of one fundamentalist sheikh, "the holiest of our holies."

Polygamy isn't common in Egypt today. Fewer than 3 percent of married women have co-wives, according to government statistics, although the numbers can be higher in rural communities. In her fieldwork in an Upper Egyptian village in Aswan, an anthropologist named Kirsten H. Bach found that 10 percent of marriages were polygamous. "The practice of polygamy has not been modified by education," she wrote, "but is found among illiterate farmers as well as among teachers and diploma holders and among elderly men as well as among relatively younger men." The custom was also prevalent in Rania's village, and three of her uncles had married second wives. "That's the custom in Upper Egypt," she said. "It's always been that way here, since before I was born."

Even when it's not practiced on a wide scale, polygamy can have damaging effects on a society where it exists, always, on the edge of possibility. It offers a vision of a marital union that's highly transactional and defined by sex. Rather than a pledge between two people who intend to spend their lives together, marriage becomes a crude tool to ensure that men's physical urges are satisfied. Polygamy can operate, like an unspoken threat, to keep married women in line. The anthropologist Homa Hoodfar observed that men invariably said a husband who was happily married would never take a second wife, implicitly blaming women for their own predicament. Some young wives, she wrote, worried constantly about being deserted by their husbands. They regarded their own fertility as a kind of weapon: Have several children, and your husband will be too busy (or too exhausted) to start another family. Polygamy is a perpetual reminder to women of how little they deserve. Almost all of the women Hoodfar talked to said they would remain in a polygamous marriage if they had to, as long as their husbands continued to provide for them.

The right to marry multiple wives—"two or three or four"—under any circumstances is one more way that men have manipulated Muslim tradition to suit themselves. Polygamy is "a means by which men make themselves valuable," Fatima Mernissi observed, "not by perfecting any quality within themselves, but simply by creating a competitive situation between many females." That was true around the year 623, when Muhammad took the young Aisha bint Abu Bakr as his third wife. It was true in 1892, when Huda Sharawi discovered that her husband already had a wife and three children, even though he had signed a marriage contract that committed himself to monogamy with her.

And it was true in 2015, when Rania's husband, Yasser, married a second wife. He and Rania hadn't been getting along, and she had lived most of the previous two years at her father's house. He thought she had left him for good, and he was mad about that. Marrying another woman was a snap decision, the way you might impulsively throw away someone's possessions after a fight.

"I just did it to spite her," Yasser told me. "To make her angry."

To his surprise, Rania came back. After hearing from her children that their father's new wife sometimes locked them out of the house, Rania grew worried about their welfare and decided to return. But now there was a second wife and, more important, a new baby, in the house; what Yasser had done couldn't easily be undone. In his relations with both his wives he had all the authority, but in terms of the pursuit of happiness, he seemed as powerless as everybody else.

"If I'd known she was coming back to me, I wouldn't have married someone else," Yasser said. "She has every right to be upset." But it was too late now.

I HAVE COME early to Rania's house, a little after nine in the morning, hoping to get answers to all the questions I haven't been able to ask because we've never been alone. Yasser, unfortunately, is already up and about, but after a final heroic effort to engage me in archaeological pillage—"Do you want to buy artifacts?"—he retreats to the living room.

Rania has bought a live fish from the market. It's black and shiny and slippery like an eel, writhing between her hands as we talk in low voices in the kitchen.

What was your childhood like? Do you have siblings?

She was one of the most impressive people I had ever met. She was so bright and talented but also flawed—and so intent on pursuing what she wanted that she couldn't grasp how she appeared to others or all the ways in which she was undermining herself. She fought ferociously to be ranked first in her place of work, but accepted without question a family system that put her value at close to nothing. For all the things I knew now, I still didn't understand why this had to be so.

Is it typical that a mother has to leave her children when she marries?

"Adat wa taqalid," Rania answers. "Customs and traditions. This is usually the case in Upper Egypt: When a woman remarries, she leaves her children behind."

With a turn of her wrist, she lops off the fish's head, then lays its body in a metal basin and slices it lengthwise. The creature's innards spill out, and blood spreads in red blossoms on the water.

What do you think about such traditions? Do you agree with them?

Rania pauses. By some miracle, I notice, the fish is still moving. It slaps its tail back and forth against her hand.

"I don't know what to say. I think it's really unacceptable for children to live with another man, because he might mistreat them."

If you were to remarry, would you take your kids with you?

Tzk tzk. "Children here carry their father's name, so obviously they have to be physically close to their father."

Would you consider getting a divorce?

Tzk tzk. "The kids have to be here among us both, to protect them psychologically. I don't want them to go through the same thing I went through."

You're very assertive at work, but at home you're not. Does work translate into changed behavior at home?

Tzk tzk. "There's no connection between the two personalities. I'm one person there, and another person here. You give every place what it deserves."

We eat dinner in the middle of the afternoon, because I have to catch an evening train back to Cairo. It's as delicious as any meal that Rania has made for me: fried fish, spicy chicken drumsticks, a tomato and cucumber salad, and rice. Her children join us, but as usual at mealtimes, Yasser has disappeared. Asmaa and her baby don't show up at all, so I won't have an opportunity to say goodbye to this woman I've seen many times but never spoken to. "It's like she doesn't exist. It's like she's air," Rania said once about Asmaa, and that defined my interactions with her too.

Maybe relations between the members of the family have recalibrated once again, and shifted into some new and complicated combination I can't grasp. I think about Tolstoy, who documented so many unsatisfactory marriages including his own, and understood all the ways in which two people can be miserable together. *Every unhappy family is unhappy in its own way.*

AFTER YASSER'S FAILED venture to sell artifacts that might or might not have dated to the pharaonic era, Rania tried other things. For a while she raised chickens and sold them to other villagers. She spent several months going door to door collecting water and electricity payments, but her boss turned out to be a Muslim Brotherhood member who objected to employing women as bill collectors and forced her out ("He refused to give me the bills, so I had nothing to do"). Briefly, she sold clothes. The new garment factory in Minya had opened but she decided against working there, for reasons that weren't entirely clear. The transportation was inconvenient, or she didn't want to walk home alone at night, or she would be bored because none of her friends worked there.

Her new plan was to wait. Ian Ross, the CEO of Delta Egypt, was opposed to her return, but Rania had heard that he might soon be leaving the country for good. Once he was out of the picture, she would approach the factory's management again. Maybe his replacement, whoever he was, would be amenable to hiring a supervisor with almost a decade of experience in the garment industry, who knew everything there is to know about sewing a pair of boxer shorts, and who was hands-down the most effective employee the Delta Textile Factory had ever seen.

THE LAST TIME I visited Delta at the end of 2017, everyone I had known well was gone. Rania had been fired, and so had her nemesis, Mohamed Hanafy. Kevin Meyer, after working on projects in South Africa and Haiti, was moving to Vietnam to oversee the construction of a new manufacturing facility for Delta there. Once again the company would be recruiting among a rural population, and executives would apply what they had learned in Egypt. This time, Meyer told me when we spoke by phone, new hires would be taught basic English so they felt more comfortable bringing up concerns with their managers. "You tend to select supervisors because they can sew and all of those things, but communication is a big part of the supervisor's job," he told me. A factory like Delta, or any well-run organization, operated under a clear set of rules, modifying and correcting and discarding these as it went. Human beings were messy; even minor adjustment was hard. The factory learned and applied lessons from its mistakes, improving itself with every iteration in a way that a person never could.

Delta was running at 55 percent efficiency compared to the global standard—that was a new high for the Minya workforce, and it put them on par with their more experienced counterparts in Cairo. A two-story building was under construction that would employ eight hundred new workers and double the scale of production. In a foreign investment landscape that was as parched as the scrubby desert outside, Delta was a rare success, and the local government pointed to it as a template for other investors. "They're doing very well. It's a model to follow," an industry executive named Mohamed Kassem told me.

I walked around the factory floor with Sahar Ragab, a slender, dark-haired industrial engineer I had met on a previous visit. She and a colleague were teaching workers a new way to expose the thick, raised seams on the boxer shorts they were sewing. Rather than stretch the fabric four times with their hands, once for each seam, Sahar showed them how to hold the fabric differently so they needed to pull it taut only twice.

"I want to open the seams in the old way, because then I can check and see each one," a worker told her.

"How about you do that every five pieces? But try to do it the new way for the other four?"

By reducing her number of motions, a worker could shave three seconds off the time required to sew a pair of shorts, Sahar estimated, which would significantly increase productivity over the course of a workday. Delta was implementing these time-saving measures line by line—first for the products it made for Calvin Klein, then Walmart. Eventually, the manufacturing of every single item would be rational and standardized, in service to a Platonic ideal of perfection that always seemed to hover just over the horizon.

"Do you see other problems with how she's doing the operation?" I asked Sahar.

"Yes, but we need to do it step by step, so we don't overwhelm her."

Yasmin, the young woman who had joked about adopting the *niqab* the next time I saw her to please her fiancé, had moved from managing needles in the maintenance department to overseeing quality control on a production line. She planned to marry in a year and a half and attend university to study engineering. Hind Ali, another supervisor I knew, had won the factory's top production prize twice and recently been handed a line of brand-new recruits. The young women had started at zero efficiency but were now up to 40 percent. "The line is new and they're still being trained, but things will come," Hind said.

Some months later, I would speak to Ian Ross on the phone, and we would talk about Rania's downfall. He wasn't sure about the Sexy Call accusations, but he said that Rania had tried to organize work stoppages and other measures to get people she didn't like fired. "She was trying to build her own power base inside the factory, and we couldn't allow that," he told me. "It's a shame, because she could have built a career here." The company's favored candidate for the position of local production manager was now Mona Abdel-Monem, an energetic trainer I had met during the work study course. Her superior education and experience made her a better fit for the position than Rania had ever been.

It was cold in the factory that morning. I wandered at loose ends, feeling as if I had gone to a party expecting to see good friends but instead found people I barely knew. I was used to spending entire days there, making the rounds and checking in with familiars at different stations. Now that the place was populated with strangers again, the Delta Textile Factory appeared to me as I had first seen it: a vast space with hundreds of working women who had found function and pattern, refuge and order. A clean, well-lighted place. It had materialized before my eyes at the moment I wished for it, as ephemeral as Brigadoon. I felt lucky to have found it when I did.

As I was getting ready to leave the factory, Sahar came and found me. By her calculations, a worker who sewed and stretched out the seams according to the recommended method could finish one piece in a minute and fifty-seven seconds, which was nine seconds faster than the old way. She had clocked four workers with a stopwatch and averaged their times together, and this was the surprising and satisfying result.

She wanted to show me the numbers on her clipboard before I left the factory, as if this was the thing that mattered most. Maybe it was.

11

HARD MONEY

IN FEBRUARY 2017, ONCE AGAIN, I went to the Nelly Kids Fashion Fair to watch Riham selling summer clothes in the dead of winter. Her booth was smaller than the year before, but I was surprised to find her in a good mood and doing a brisk business across her entire range of products. "They're not taking one or two items, they're taking several items," Riham told me, in between waiting on customers. "Taking one item means the buyer needs something that he can't find elsewhere. Taking lots of items from your collection means he likes your product."

Her buyers were small shop owners, mostly men, who didn't necessarily have much expertise about infant needs. In a society that had more female entrepreneurs, they might not have been in the baby clothes business at all. A man wearing a navy blue sport coat offered gratuitous advice—"I think it's better if you're more specialized"—and a burly man in owlish black glasses marveled at the fact of a nursing pillow ("You're really spoiling the mothers!"). Two stern-looking men with scraggly beards, who were from the Delta town of Beheira, asked Riham how much they should charge customers for each bamboo-lined diaper cover ("That's up to you"). These Chinese-made undergarments still got the most attention, but Riham also had a knack for designing products to suit the local market. She made her nursing blankets extra large to conceal a breastfeeding mother front and back. That seemed like a no-brainer in a culture that placed such emphasis on female modesty.

As soon as the exhibition was over, Riham planned to place orders to dye more fabric, now that she felt confident that the demand was there. "Lots of customers we lost in the last two to three years have come back, because Mister Sisi closed the import option," she said.

Riham was on intimate terms with this man, who lived in the distant Presidential Palace in Cairo but seemed to turn her life upside down every time he changed his mind. Her once-promising Chinese diaper business had been ended by Mister Sisi's sudden announcement of import tariffs the year before. His abrupt devaluation of the Egyptian pound nine months after that had killed her domestic sales and cast her back into the export market. Now, for a change, Mister Sisi's policies were working in her favor: Turkish- and Chinese-made products had disappeared from stores, but Riham suspected that this welcome development was temporary too. "We Egyptians can read what he's thinking," she said, lowering her voice and switching to the idiom of conspiratorial certainty in which many Egyptians are fluent. "He's thinking like Gamal Abdel Nasser and trying to control everything. But after a while, he'll be forced to open the markets."

She had made another big bet on the domestic business. Recently, she and Mustafa had bought two circular knitting machines to produce custom fabric for local clients, which represented a significant move into the upstream end of the textile business. The shiny machines took up residence in the factory's vast downstairs that had been vacant for so long, like down payments on a more stable future. Two new employees operated the equipment around the clock, in shifts. They were the first young men Riham had hired into the factory.

She was asking more of her longtime workers—six-day workweeks, penalties for sewing mistakes—and cutting less slack with customers, too. At the fair, a middle-aged woman in bright red lipstick and a beige *hijab* came up to Riham's booth. "I'd like to take some free samples," she announced.

"My brother is now in charge of finances, and he says we can't give away samples without paying," Riham responded smoothly. "Anything you want, you have to pay for."

"Why are you doing that?"

"Things are not going that well, so we're not willing to manufacture things and then give them away."

The woman glanced around the booth and walked away, looking unhappy. She owned a large shop in one of Cairo's oldest malls. Riham had initially given her favorable terms—generous discounts, easy returns—but now that she was established, she could be tougher.

"In the time I've known you, you've become more demanding of both your workers and your customers," I said to Riham.

"Yes." She smiled. "It's time to be like this." We both laughed.

She had an aggressive new hiring strategy. The largest garment maker in Alexandria was the El-Nasr Clothing and Textiles Company, which was known colloquially as Kabo. The firm had been one of the crown jewels of state industry in the Nasser era, but now it had privatized and was laying off workers. Riham had joined a *gamiyya* of Kabo employees with an ulterior motive. Every month, a supervisor came by to collect Riham's payment and to share the news and gossip from inside the company. Through this channel, Riham met three workers who had recently quit Kabo, and she invited them to come to her factory for a trial run.

You take opportunity where you find it, even if it means feeding off the wreckage of Mister Nasser's failed socialist state. It was time to be like this.

THE OBJECT OF Riham's devoted attention is sixteen miles from her factory, in a working-class neighborhood in downtown Alexandria. An outside visitor to the Kabo compound must first get the attention of a receptionist sitting behind a small window with metal bars, an arrangement that feels a little like going to see someone in jail. Up a tiny elevator—three people are a tight fit—to the third floor, down a long hallway with a faded maroon carpet that has seen better days, you enter the improbably spacious office of Amr El-Sharnoubi, the current chairman and managing director of the enterprise.

Established in 1940, Kabo was merged with two other garment firms and nationalized in the early 1960s. For decades, the company occupied a privileged position selling socks, pajamas, and underwear in a protected market, and its workers enjoyed generous benefits and lifetime employment. Kabo was privatized in 1997 through a stock market listing. After that, it bled money continuously, at one point cycling through five chairmen in four years as each one looked for a way forward in a competitive market.

El-Sharnoubi was named to the top post in 2009. "They couldn't find anyone else to run the company," he joked when I met him. He wore a crisp white shirt with a navy blue blazer and spoke English with a British accent; beside his desk, the television was tuned to the BBC, with the volume turned low. He smoked Marlboro Golds throughout our interview, referred frequently to a typed sheet of numbers, and kept an eye on the news ("*What* is happening in Virginia?") He had the polished and brusque manner of a banker in a hurry, which is what he was before he started selling underwear for a living.

Beginning with his Wall Street–style corner office, El-Sharnoubi's task is to build a modern enterprise on an antique foundation without wrecking the edifice altogether. He has closed some of Kabo's retail stores and opened others, reduced inventory, and restructured everything from when the firm pays down debt to how it rents cars. The company built a new factory and hired people in their twenties to work there, based on their sewing experience and productivity. In the older downtown plant, its employees are at least a decade or two senior to the new hires, many of them holdovers from state enterprise days. "People have been working here for twenty, thirty, forty years," El-Sharnoubi said. Kabo employs mother-daughter duos, and extended families, and the occasional worker who's occupied with tasks only one or two hours a day.

El-Sharnoubi has offered early retirement to, or in some cases fired, the least productive workers in an effort to improve efficiency. The Kabo factory employed twenty-six hundred workers when I visited, which was half the number it had when El-Sharnoubi came on board. But change in Egypt, even the type engendered by impatient bankers, doesn't happen very fast. Nasser-era labor laws still on the books make it hard to fire employees, since they require proof of egregious behavior and approval by a government committee. One factory boss told me he sometimes transfers unwanted workers to another department and cuts their bonuses, until eventually "they know they're doomed and have no future with the company." This is essentially passive-aggressiveness elevated to a management style. Just as I had seen at Riham's place, the employer often plays the role of village *umda*. In addition to offering government-sponsored insurance, Kabo maintains an emergency fund to help staffers through a medical crisis or a death in the family. Employees who are about to be fired beg to stay on, because their families need the money. "It's more like we're running a community service than a company," El-Sharnoubi told me.

"Where does this sense of social responsibility come from?" I asked. "Did it start under Nasser?"

"It's an Egyptian thing. Even before Nasser, you would find wealthy people looking after the poorer ones. Like in the village when anyone got married or got sick, a wealthy family would pay for them. It's in us— there's a lot of charity in our religion," he explained. "I'm not saying everyone is good like that. But it's there."

Relations between labor and management fell apart during the 2011 Arab Spring uprising, when the country saw an unprecedented number of strikes and mass protests. In many sectors of the economy, workers rose up in solidarity with the Tahrir Square demonstrators and to demand better treatment in the workplace. Employees might ask for double or triple their current salary, or call for top bosses to be fired. Inside Kabo, workers went on strike and presented El-Sharnoubi with a list of twenty demands. After negotiations that might last ten hours, the workers' representatives would end up refusing El-Sharnoubi's terms, he told me. They accused him of reneging on promises he had never made, and they attacked him for supposedly stealing money that was meant for employees. He was hanged in effigy. After that, he began to move through the factory with armed soldiers for bodyguards. Once, some of the strike organizers released snakes and scorpions on the Kabo factory floor in an effort to terrorize their co-workers who hadn't joined the strike.

As with many factory owners I had met, El-Sharnoubi's experience of the revolution was marked by turmoil and chaos in the workplace. "Those three years were like nothing I'd ever seen before," he recalled. "It brought out the worst in the Egyptian people. You treat these people as if they are your family, and then they take advantage of that. You do a lot of good and a lot of charity, but at the end of the day they don't appreciate anything."

"Why are people like this?" my translator, Farah, asked quietly.

"They have envy and hatred and anger," he answered, and his voice turned quiet too. "Along with poverty. Along with stress."

Kabo's policy had been to pay the base salaries of employees even when they went on strike. Eventually the board decided to withhold those wages, and after two months the protest ended and production resumed. Kabo now has a hundred people on staff to enforce security. "If you don't have a good security operation in a company, in this country, you'll be out of business," El-Sharnoubi told me. "We're descended from pharaohs. We need a strong leader." Or, as Riham had described her own evolution into a tougher boss: *It's time to be like this.*

THE BUSINESS OF mass-producing garments in factories attracts a surprising number of people who presumably have more glamorous occupations to choose from. I have met individuals who speak multiple languages, who studied finance in London or design in Paris, and are now engaged in producing humble items like pajamas or underwear in remote industrial zones where the wind is always blowing and sand settles into every crack and crevice. They like being part of a national industry that, even in decline, touches the lives of millions of people. The alchemy that happens every day on the production floor—fabric goes in one end, and finished clothing comes out the other—feels satisfying, even magical. Cotton, which was considered a miracle fabric when it was discovered five thousand years ago, is still the stuff of dreams.

On the far northwestern edge of Cairo's sprawl, Fadel Marzouk runs the Giza Spinning and Weaving Company. Making textiles and clothes has been the family business for more than sixty years ("I'm proud to say that I'm third generation! Usually, in most countries, the third generation quits!"), though the line of succession hit some snags. His grandfather's spinning and weaving business was nationalized—in other words, confiscated—by Nasser in 1964. His father left the country for the United States, where Marzouk was born, in New Jersey, then returned in the late 1970s to build a brand-new business from scratch. Starting from zero.

"So even though Nasser had taken away his family company, he had the faith to come back and start over?" I asked.

"Nasser was already dead, and there was a new president," Marzouk answered cheerfully, as if to say *Even dictatorships deserve second chances!* "As usual, Leslie, everybody comes back to his origins."

There's a sense of idealism, even patriotism, behind many of these private ventures. In the 1980s, a diplomat named Mohamed Kassem was posted in Washington, D.C., as Egypt's commercial attaché. "I was entrusted with building our exports, and I failed miserably," he told me. He quit the foreign service, returned home, and set up a company to help American clothing brands manufacture in Egypt while lobbying the government for export-friendly policies. Kassem had recently joined a real estate consortium to build textile industrial parks in Upper Egypt, starting with Minya, and he hoped to attract Chinese investment to the venture. As with El-Sharnoubi, the tools of his trade are pieces of paper dense with data. In his office, he gave me his investor pitch, with charts showing Egypt's export growth, tax incentives, and the low cost of labor. Africa, the last frontier.

Without meaning to, I sighed.

Kassem stopped talking and looked at me. He smiled. "You feel frustrated."

I laughed. "And I'm not even Egyptian."

"What years did you live here?"

"From 2011 to 2016."

"So you saw it all."

Kassem had done business in China, and we talked for a while about the two places. Both countries have people who work extraordinarily hard. But China has policies to promote industrial development and investment, along with geographic and social mobility and a good education system. Individual efforts are rewarded, and the country grows. China has *nizam*, a system—too much of one, perhaps, but you don't miss it until it's gone.

"I just feel like Egypt has so much human potential, but the system doesn't encourage that potential to grow," I told Kassem. "You see individual stories that are so impressive, but it doesn't become a national movement. So it's very frustrating," I said. "But you're Egyptian—you know this."

"I know. And I appreciate your feelings."

El-Sharnoubi also started out in government, evaluating state-owned enterprises for privatization. He later worked in corporate finance for Citibank and then in private equity. He had sat on the Kabo board for years as it ran through one leader after another, before finally being named to the top job himself.

The company has been turning around, on a modest scale. It became profitable in 2014; in 2017, when I talked to El-Sharnoubi, the company earned $1.8 million on sales of more than $26 million. That's of course peanuts in the global garment industry, not to mention the corporate finance universe. I asked El-Sharnoubi if he thought joining Kabo had been the right career choice.

"I'm not making as much money as in investment banking, but it's okay," he said. "Every year, at the end of the year, I would sit down and say: 'What did I do this year? What did I do that was good?' When I was a banker, I made a few deals, but there was nothing satisfying about that." Satisfaction, he discovered, comes from real things—dealing with workers, products, markets, brands.

WHENEVER I SPENT time watching Riham at work—when she corrected a worker whose stitches weren't exactly one-fourth of a centimeter long, or fixed a collar that was too large for its shirt, or struggled to complete an order when the materials had been delivered to her days late—I couldn't help thinking *There must be an easier way.* Many others apparently feel the same. A study of entrepreneurial activity around the world ranked Egypt forty-first out of forty-nine countries. Fewer than 7 percent of adults are engaged in running a new venture; a mere 2.6 percent head more established businesses.

The aversion to private enterprise is a long-standing feature of Egyptian life. In the late nineteenth century, as the economy grew on the back of global demand for Egyptian long-staple cotton, commercial activity in the country was dominated by foreigners. The Greeks were moneylenders and exporters, food traders and hotel operators. The Syrians concentrated on the retail and wholesale trades, the Armenians ran the cigarette industry, the Italians worked as artisans, and the Jews handled finance, operated department stores, and served on corporate boards. The expatriates often had education, business experience, and capital that native Egyptians lacked, but they dominated even workaday trades that didn't require particular advantages. "Boot-mending, as well as boot-making, is almost entirely in the hands of Greeks and Armenians," the British consul general Lord Cromer wrote. "The drapery trade is controlled by Jews, Syrians, and Europeans, the tailoring trade by Jews."

Wealthy Egyptians bought land. Real estate has always been a mark of status, and a powerful class of landowners sat at the top of the social pyramid and shaped government policy to their benefit. During the cotton-fueled economic boom of the nineteenth century, property was the preferred investment: Whatever profit was earned from land went into buying more of it, or into related industries such as financing and mortgages, land reclamation, and urban development. It was possible, during times of speculative frenzy, to double the value of one's outlay in just a few months.

The twentieth century saw the emergence of a wider range of business owners, but with a distinctive cast. They tended to run large, heavily capitalized operations that traded off their *wasta*, or connections, to make money. In the early 1960s, the Nasser regime nationalized most of the private sector, but it relied on certain businessmen to help implement its industrial development plan and granted them lucrative contracts and other privileges in return. Sadat's partial liberalization of the economy in the 1970s expanded this class of "parasitic entrepreneurs," who exploited their ties to the regime to make fortunes from government contracts, import licenses, and other forms of preferential access. Mubarak maintained this policy of co-opting businessmen as allies, most flagrantly in the case of Ahmed Ezz, who ran one of the largest steel manufacturers in the Middle East while serving as a top official in the ruling National Democratic Party. Anger directed at such well-connected tycoons was a driving force behind the 2011 uprising. On the eve of the revolution, a survey by Cairo University found that Egyptians considered "businesspeople" to be the most corrupt of any sector in society.

The familiar image of the entrepreneur as a small, nimble player in a ruthless market has nothing in common with the Egyptian man of *bisnis*, who tends to be politically connected, risk-averse, and older and less educated than his counterparts elsewhere. It helps explain why many ordinary Egyptians are unwilling to take the risk of building an enterprise from the ground up: coming up with an idea, implementing a business plan, hiring and training workers, and competing with hundreds or maybe thousands of other people around the world who are trying to do the same thing.

"Look, people can make easy money in Egypt," Hani Kassis, who runs a family-owned stationery and plastic products business, told me. "Licensing is easy money, real estate is easy money, imports are easy money." So why would you want to do anything so hard?

FOLLOWING THE INDUSTRY exhibition, Riham received an order to produce forty-five hundred pieces of a Thomas & Friends gray T-shirt, her factory's largest contract to date. She bought more fabric for clothes and also found a better supplier for bedsheets. She hired two former Kabo employees who impressed her as hardworking and used to operating under a strict system like hers. The young woman named Rahma was proving a capable successor to Sara, who continued to sew on the assembly line in her final months before getting married. Two young men operated the knitting machines downstairs, and they helped out on the sewing floor when they weren't busy.

A couple of weeks after the exhibition, an employee named Naglaa told Riham that she was pregnant and had to quit her job.

Riham reminded her of another employee who had continued working until close to her due date. "She was tough and she was good, you saw her."

"No, no, my husband refuses. My father had a quarrel with my husband, and we're having problems."

"Okay. Fine."

Then came Rahma, who was doing so well as Riham's number two. "I want to sit at home," she said. "I don't want to work." She explained that she was having a disagreement with her father over her employment.

"Give me your father's phone number, so I can call him," Riham said.

"No. I have to sit at home tomorrow."

"Why? Not tomorrow! This is the twenty-fifth of the month. Complete your month, and then . . ."

"No, I have to sit at home tomorrow!"

One by one the other workers came, and each one had a different pretext for leaving. Rehab's father didn't want her crossing the Cairo Desert Road to get to work every day—it was too dangerous. Adel, who worked on the Singer machine, said he had gotten an offer to work somewhere else with a 25 percent raise. He asked for a day off and Riham agreed, but she later found out that he had taken the personal belongings he usually kept at work, including his shoes and his radio, and left for good. Mona quit, and Amal, and all the rest, including the two young men she had so recently hired.

The last person to approach Riham was Sara. "I didn't want to tell you because I didn't want to upset you," she said. "But I'm going to get married next month, so I have to sit at home."

"Okay, go!"

It had happened to her before, exactly like this. When Riham first started out in the garment business, she had hired an entire production line of workers, then lost them all when they jumped to a rival factory;

their ties to one another outweighed any loyalty they felt toward her. Since then, Riham had taken care never to hire a group of friends into her factory together, but she guessed that this time her employees had gotten offers from another firm and moved over as one. Because they left without giving two weeks' notice, Riham wasn't required to pay their last month's salary, but she calculated what she owed and tried to get the money to them anyway. There was still a chance they might return.

Around this time, Riham went into one of her factory's storerooms to pick up some items to fulfill an order. As she looked around the space, she had an uneasy feeling. "No, this isn't the right quantity," she said to herself. Riham ordered an inventory of her stock, and the results shocked her: Half of the bundles she had stored in that room were gone.

Her system had always been to put the items her factory made in a large storage room that was equipped with a surveillance camera. Everything there was intact. The missing goods, which included the diaper covers and bedsheets from China, had been put in a temporary space because the other area was full. The items were still in their original packaging and highly portable, Riham realized now. That space had no security camera.

AFTERWARD, SHE AND Mustafa remembered isolated incidents that had struck them as odd at the time. One evening a former employee named Sayyid, who monitored the knitting machines on the night shift, had been spotted on the security footage carrying a large bundle out of the main storeroom. On a different night, Mustafa saw Sayyid taking the elevator to the roof for no apparent reason, and once he had let into the factory a former co-worker who had no business being there. "So lots of things happened, but we didn't think anything of it," Riham told me.

The theft of brand-new imported articles worth more than $3,300 had most likely originated inside her own factory. These were the items that Mustafa had bought almost two years earlier, that had made their way across the ocean on a container ship, that had waited patiently at the port of Alexandria while Riham navigated red tape and paid fines, that had been on proud display and admired like rare jewels through two rounds of the Nelly Kids Fashion Fair. They were the goods that customers, finally, wanted to buy.

Mustafa got in touch with a former classmate who worked in the district police department to ask for help. The man's response was that of bureaucrats and security guards who don't feel like getting out of their chairs: *Go find your stolen goods,* he said, *and we'll arrest the person who has them.* Mustafa's classmate explained the institution's priorities: "We don't move from the police station unless someone is killed, or if there's something that has to do with national security or politics."

Riham called up a longtime employee named Suzanne, who had quit along with everyone else. "Tell all the workers that if anyone took anything, I don't want to know who it is," Riham said to her. "I want them just to bring the things back. I'm not going to tell anything to the police; I'm not going to make any scenes or problems or say anything about them in the place where they're working." But no one called.

She suspected that the young man on the night shift had stolen the goods—the evidence on the tapes suggested that—but Riham thought her other employees must have been involved. Why else had they all left in that mysterious, and yet coordinated, fashion? And why hadn't a single worker called her since the robbery to express sympathy and to ask how she was?

More and more, she found herself wondering about Sara. Sara, who had the run of the factory when Riham wasn't around, who had frequently borrowed the key to the storeroom, whom Riham trusted implicitly. She recalled that Sara had mentioned someone messing with one of the sewing machines, and Riham had examined a few hours of video footage but found nothing. Now she wondered if Sara had been testing the factory's surveillance system to see how it worked.

In her last months on the job, Sara had been demoted and become increasingly negative about everything. I noticed this the last time I spoke with her, but then a sense of discontent had threaded through all the conversations we'd had together.

I'm annoyed, but I don't know what to do about it, she had told me.

I don't know how I'm going to get used to being alone at home all day.

We let them do it.

She had found pleasure and accomplishment through work but had been forced to give it all up in order to get married. It was possible to blame her father for this, or her future husband, or the society she lived in. But maybe Sara had taken her dissatisfaction and pinned it all on Riham, who had shown her another path through life but one that wasn't available to her after all. A person in this situation, many Egyptians believed, might cast the *ayn al-hasoud,* the "evil eye," on someone whose fortune was better than her own.

"I think she started to look at me with envy," Riham told me. "There are so many things she wants, and now she knows she's not going to get them." She continued, "People watch things on television, and they think: This is their life now. But this is not our life. We're not drinking wine all the time, or sitting in our huge apartments, or driving fancy cars. Maybe they think that because I'm the factory owner, I have so much money."

"Sara changed, at the end," Riham said. "Her eyes changed."

WHATEVER HARDSHIPS AN entrepreneur in Egypt faces are compounded if she's a woman. Women have fewer assets at their disposal to start a business or to pledge as collateral for a loan. They have weaker professional networks and less mobility, and their lower education levels may trap them in marginal activities that don't have much of a payoff. And for every woman who starts a business, there are many others who are put off by societal or family pressure to stay home.

Only 5 percent of Egyptian women are early-stage entrepreneurs, and 1 percent run established businesses; these are among the lowest rates in the world. Their ventures are smaller than those run by men—often just a single person—and have nothing in common with the businessmen at the far end of the socioeconomic scale (being a parasitic entrepreneur, like so many things in Egypt, is a privilege reserved for males). Women-owned firms are less likely to export the goods they make or to use advanced technology; fewer than one in five, according to one study, use the internet to promote their products or find customers. They're less likely to be legally registered, and more commonly found in rural areas doing small-scale trade that's tied to agriculture: a woman peddling eggs or baked goods in the market, Rania raising chickens or selling sugarcane to her neighbors.

But the women who do build successful businesses present a surprisingly different profile. Among legally registered enterprises, those owned by women are as large, well established, and productive as companies with male owners. They're *more* technologically sophisticated, *more* likely to export, and *more* adept at using email and websites to communicate with clients.

"Women are always being challenged to prove themselves," Sahar Nasr, who was formerly the World Bank's lead economist for the Middle East, told me. (She later served four years as a government minister.) "So they always want to advance their business, to prove that they can do it and do it better."

That description fitted Riham to a T, and it also applied to other female business proprietors I met all over the country. In the Upper Egyptian village of Tayyiba, I had talked to a middle-aged mother of six children named Hamdia Abdel Halim who designed and sewed *abaya*s for the women in her neighborhood, even though "my son is embarrassed that people are coming to the house and asking me to do things for them." A woman named Sawsan ran a children's clothing shop in Minya on her own, serving customers and stocking shelves and attending trade fairs and visiting factories and mopping the floors and staying

open until two o'clock every morning ("When I first started the business, I thought my husband would do the marketing and find the traders, but I realized that I had to do it myself"). In the same industrial
zone as Riham, I met a friend of hers named Samah El-Sayyid, who had
started at age eighteen as a factory assistant and worked her way into
management while also learning Italian and studying nights for her college diploma. She now ran a clothing factory that employed thirty-five
people, in partnership with a Bangladeshi man. "It was very important
for me not to work with an Egyptian man," she explained, "because they
never respect women."

Women could hold their own in the business world, but it wasn't a
mystery why so few of them tried. Almost every female entrepreneur I
met, whether she was single, married, divorced, or widowed, had pushed
back against opposition from her family when she started out. Every
woman told me she knew of others who admired her success but were
afraid to try the same thing for themselves. A poll of female business
owners in Alexandria found that of all the factors that might determine
success—choice of industry, access to financing, institutional support—
the most important is whether the entrepreneur's family agrees to her
doing it at all.

On a summer evening in 2017, I visited Riham at home for the first
time. She gave me the requisite tour of the apartment she and Ahmed
had moved into after they married, peppered with commentary about
all the furniture she wished she didn't own.

The front door opened on a living room that was so long that it contained two living rooms, each with its matched set of Louis Quatorze
gilded chairs. "I didn't want this. I wish the room stopped here," Riham
said, as she stood in the middle of the space and bisected it with one
arm. "In the old days, people entertained large numbers of guests, but

now they just eat out and don't need this much seating." She grabbed a handful of heavy floor-length curtains—"I'm washing these by hand, which is a lot of work"—then showed me a kitchen, a bedroom, and a cozy sitting room with a loveseat ("This is where people actually want to sit"). I had imagined that Riham had won her home renovation battles with her father—there was no *niche,* no chiffonier. But now I realized it had probably been a draw.

We sat down in one of her twin living rooms, and I told Riham I was sorry to hear about the theft in her factory.

She blamed the broader societal breakdown that followed the 2011 revolution. "People are losing control," Riham told me. "They destroyed education, they destroyed role models, they destroyed everything since Mubarak's day, and it's getting worse." She continued, "Last night my sister was telling me this revolution brought out the worst in people. I told her, 'No, in the very early days it brought out the best in everyone.'" As time went on, Riham felt, her countrymen became disappointed because all the turbulence had brought nothing good into their lives—only more poverty and more stress.

She and her brother had tracked down Sayyid's family and shared their suspicions about the crime. Sayyid's father visited the factory soon afterward and begged them not to go to the police. His two daughters were engaged, and the scandal could ruin them. Under pressure from his family, Sayyid confessed to the crime and agreed to compensate Riham for half the value of the stolen goods. The rest was to be paid by his former co-worker on the night shift, a young man named Mustafa, who had also been involved. But a different family situation—no sisters, less fear of disgrace—gave Mustafa maximum deniability. "His mother has three boys and he's the youngest, so she spoiled him," Riham told me. "If someone tells her 'All your kids are thieves,' it's not a problem for her." Riham still planned to go to the police if the young men didn't start repaying her soon.

Sara, she heard, had found work at a factory in another industrial zone, even though she had said she was leaving to get married. She was telling people that Riham had stolen money that belonged to her and the other workers and that she planned to file a lawsuit against her. This seemed to be a garbled reference to the factory's pension plan, to which both employer and employee contributed every month—but Riham told me she had already paid her share, which went not to the workers themselves but to the government.

At the beginning of Ramadan, Riham received a text message from her former protégée:

> The day after I left you, I went to work and I was paid 1,600 pounds, and I took all the other girls to work with me. I told everyone that actually you and your family are the thieves. You're the ones who stole from each other and now you're accusing us. Your brother pretends to be religious and goes to pray in the mosque, and he is actually a thief.

"I was so shocked that I threw up," Riham told me. "And that night I couldn't sleep."

Just then, her phone rang. Customers were still clamoring to buy the bamboo-lined Chinese diaper covers. "I have only seventeen pieces left," Riham said into the phone, "so I can't accept a big order."

She hung up, sighed, then laughed. She had sold only eighty of the diapers last year, because they were new to the market and people considered them expensive. So far this year, she already had orders for five hundred sixty pieces. But now she had nothing to sell.

We sat in silence for a while. "Ugh, it's terrible," I said at last.

Riham laughed her high, pealing laugh. "Yes, this is true."

She was trying to salvage whatever orders from the exhibition that she could. Desperate for employees, she had signed an agreement with a contractor who brought her however many people she needed on a daily basis. "It was a real mess: Every day when I came to the factory, I found new faces," Riham said. Against her better judgment, she hired a supervisor to oversee production, even though she considered supervisors "very bad people" who might poach her workers. This one, whose name was Ahmed, promptly rearranged the layout on the factory floor and changed the settings on all of her machines.

Riham asked only one thing of him. "The first time I hired a supervisor, I found out he was taking my employees and going to another factory," she told Ahmed on his first day. "If I find out you did something like this, it won't be good."

Ahmed assured her he would never do that.

Just yesterday, Riham told me, he had approached her when she got to work in the morning. It was very hot in the factory, he informed her, and the workers couldn't bear it anymore. They were all leaving together.

"What about the fifteen days' notice?" Riham demanded.

"I'm not leaving you with any unfinished work."

"*How?* There are eight sizes of pants. You finished six—and the rest?"

It did no good. "Today he left with five workers, all the good workers he met inside my factory," Riham said, breaking into peals of laughter again.

I realized suddenly why we were meeting in her apartment. Riham was keeping her distance from her employees, and she didn't want me to have contact with them either. It was crushing—from the first time I met her, she had been trying to run a business profitably but also to shape a younger generation of women, to teach them how to work hard and take pride in what they did and to stand up for what they deserved. *I want them to leave with a dream,* she had told me the first day the interns came to the factory. *I'm making a system in their heads. I'm doing this for the next generation.*

Now the company she had built over the past eleven years, Textile Leaders—*The name has a dream within it*—no longer felt like home. It was as anonymous as a bus station, populated by strangers who might pass through one day and leave the next to be replaced by others whose names and faces she didn't know. *People are losing control,* she had said about her fellow Egyptians, and that included herself.

SARA DECLINED TO speak with me. "I no longer work there. I got married," she said abruptly, when my translator called to see if we could meet.

"I have nothing to say about anything."

"I'm busy and I need to ask my husband."

Finally, many days and unanswered phone calls later: "I'm not comfortable having this conversation, and my husband said no. So we're not going to have this meeting at all." Sara turned off her phone, and we never talked again.

In the time I knew Riham, her business had weathered so many assaults that originated in distant places: A crackdown on imports, a currency devaluation, Mister Sisi, the Chinese. The attack that finally laid her low, though, came from deep within her own organization and from the people closest to her. The young men who robbed her lived in the neighborhood where she had operated for more than a decade; the young women who lied to her, left her, and turned on her were the same ones she had guided and taught and worried over as if they were her own daughters. Like Rehab, who had starved herself to escape an unwanted marriage. And Mona, who dreamed of saving money to start a factory of her own. And Sara, the quickest and most talented of them all, who had seemed likely to follow in Riham's path.

In the Delta factory it had also been the most promising worker, Rania, whose story had the saddest ending. Maybe the women who were most capable were destined to suffer the worst disappointment, just as the country's failures appear more devastating because of its blessings. The finest cotton and richest farmland in the world couldn't save Egypt from poverty and dysfunction, just as the best workers on earth can't free themselves from their circumstances. And the Nile is just a river.

I LEFT EGYPT in 2016 after five years of living there, feeling so much bleaker about the country's prospects than when I came. In all my time reporting in factories and shops and villages, I almost never came into contact with a government institution or official (other than my occasional brushes with the police). The state wasn't essential to the workings of daily life, and that fact more than anything else spoke to the country's failure. Mubarak's Egypt hadn't been a model of governance by any means, but the absence of functioning institutions also dooms a nation to slow decay, like the handsome villas all over Cairo that are being hollowed out from the inside by neglect. A government needs to make investments and implement policies to grow the economy, to handle global competition, to build a school system, to loosen the strictures of religious belief, and to empower women. The last person who attempted all these things had been Nasser. He had put forth a coherent vision of the modern and industrialized nation Egypt could become. The effort failed, but the long shadow Nasser cast shows how much one leader could accomplish, and also how little his successors have done in the half century since.

I met many individuals who were trying to tackle the country's social and economic problems. They included Riham and the executives at Delta, other factory owners and entrepreneurs, the activists who were rewriting the country's marriage and divorce laws, and the reporters at *Mada*. They had some success, but each one operated in a void—unable to find and link up with other like-minded organizations and bring about change on a larger scale. And all of them in some way ran up against a conservative family system that reached deep into the workings of daily life. Its power couldn't be undone by words on a page, by charts or targets or reducing the number of seconds it took a person to sew a seam or stretch out a waistband.

The ordinary women I got to know impressed me with their strength of personality. They were far more charismatic than their Chinese counterparts whom I had met in earlier years, who tend to shrink into the safety of the group rather than risk standing out. Egyptian women brandish their opinions like battle flags, in a way that surprises outsiders into making inaccurate conclusions. ("It's the women who really run things in Egypt" is a claim I've heard more than once, often spoken by men and in no way corresponding to reality.) Over time, these women showed me the intricate social structure that underlies daily life but remains invisible to the eye, like the warp on a loom into which the fabric is woven.

The trajectory of Egypt is determined by the dramas inside families, between fathers and daughters, women and fiancés, husbands and wives. Sara, for all her strength of character, had been unable to overcome her husband's insistence that she stay home, and Rania had suffered such emotional damage that she treated others with the same cruelty. So often a woman's talent and her eventual punishment seemed bound together. Mona in Bayyadiyya, who had devoted her life to educating herself and hundreds of others, ended up marrying a man who could neither read nor write. Doaa in the Delta factory, who had studied law and aspired to be a social worker, was hated by her own daughters because of an unjust legal system that forces divorcing mothers to give up their children. And Riham, who poured her heart into teaching her young charges to take pride in their work and to be honest about their failings, had been devastated by an act of theft by pupils who hadn't learned their lessons after all.

"You should change these things from the top, but we're trying to change them from the bottom" was one of the last things Riham said to me. The wonder was that so many people were still trying.

Egypt draws you in despite its failings, and everything you thought you hated about the place—the summer heat pressing down like a lid over the city, the smell of sweat and rotting vegetation and car exhaust, the fantastic messiness of human interactions—are what you remember most when you're away. *Umm al-Dunya*: Egypt is a place that confounds you, that will attract you with its promise and disappoint you with all the ways it can fail. And then it will draw you back with an optimism that this time things will work, and get better, which is the true faith held in the heart of every Egyptian.

A YEAR AFTER I moved to Egypt with my family, we made our first road trip with our daughters, who were two and a half. We went to Siwa, an oasis town near the Libyan border four hundred fifty miles from Cairo. One morning I took Ariel and Natasha for a ride around town in a donkey-drawn cart. Our driver, an old man with fierce dark eyes set off by a white turban, took us to his home and, since we were all female, invited us inside to meet his wife, four grown daughters and four daughters-in-law, and a gaggle of children, including a twelve-year-old girl named Fatima. She was bright and talkative—"I know how to swim, I swim in the big pool"—and wore a frilly yellow party dress. She seemed completely at ease talking to a foreign woman like me.

When I tried to take Fatima's picture, though, the old man stopped me. "She's already engaged. No pictures."

A couple of days after we returned home, I asked Ariel what she remembered about our trip. We had driven up and down steep sand dunes in a Jeep 4x4 and swum in an oasis on the edge of the Great Sand Sea. We had seen dogs, horses, a donkey, a cow, pigs, sheep, and chickens.

She said, right away, "Girl."

"What color was her dress?"

"Yellow."

It's impossible not to see the life and spark in Egypt's little girls, who twirl around in their dresses as if going to a secret party that the adults around them don't know about. When she turns fifteen or sixteen, it will be like a light switching off—she'll adopt modest clothing and demure behavior, leave school or quit her job and fashion herself into a muted version so that a man can love and accept her. And everyone around her will celebrate her happiness, and she'll join a cycle that repeats endlessly, which tells women to marry and to have babies and to snuff out the brightness in girls that's so obvious a two-year-old can see it.

TODAY RIHAM RUNS a clothing factory with fourteen employees in the Merghem Industrial Zone. It's the same facility, same location as before, but it feels different as soon as you walk inside. Most of the women are married and have experience working in the industrial zones outside Alexandria. Gone are the teenage girls Riham once trained to be loyal for the long term, and there are no interns anymore. Every new hire must present a copy of the *fiche*, a document issued by the police confirming that she doesn't have a criminal record.

Riham pays a lot more than she used to—£E2,000 a month, or about $112—but she has zero tolerance for mistakes. If an employee turns out to be unqualified for her position or works too slowly, Riham will fire her as soon as the current order is finished. She recently let three people go: one after a month and a half of work, another after two weeks, and the last one after eight days. There are no second chances anymore.

The prospect of firing someone used to keep her up at night, but now it comes more easily. "I was trying to create an environment where my employees felt safe and settled and secure about their salaries," Riham told me. "But I found out it's better to let them feel they're having a test every day."

Sometimes while she's inspecting finished pieces on the assembly line she'll chat with a worker for a while, but she's careful not to get too involved in their lives. She no longer knows whether a woman's family supports her employment, or what her fiancé or husband does for a living, if he does anything at all. She's not in touch with anyone's mother. If an employee starts talking about her personal problems, Riham politely explains that she's operating a business, not a charity. In the span of a few years, the culture of her workplace has evolved from that of a household-based enterprise in the preindustrial era to the anonymity of the modern factory floor.

"Nowadays, these are not my people. And of course, I'm not myself," she said. "I don't like myself much when I'm treating my workers like this. But this is the stage—you have to control things and get them back in line again."

A breeze came off the Mediterranean, which was visible through the windows. It was winter, two and a half years since the first time I visited Riham's factory. If the quality control person she just hired turned out well, Riham would start working in the export market again, but she was no longer interested in landing a big client. "It's too high-risk," she said. "I don't need to produce a million pieces in a month. I don't want a large number of workers. I think fifteen would be okay." That was two less than the number of employees she had when I first met her.

Downstairs, the knitting machines were idle. Various other plans that Riham had toyed with—selling higher-priced clothing items of her own design, or exporting her line of cotton bedding—were also on hold. With no expansive future to look forward to, she found herself thinking more about the past, when human connections in the workplace mattered. The things that had bothered her about the family business, with its friendships and feuds and the complete absence of an efficient system, appear to her in a different light, just as the crumbling old city, in the golden hour of late afternoon, becomes beautiful again.

Riham remembers when the Egyptian garment industry was something to be proud of. Workers felt a sense of loyalty to the place where they worked. Employers provided a good salary and generous benefits, along with small things that expressed a personal tie between them. During the Eid al-Adha holiday, Riham's uncle would give each of his employees a piece of meat, as a token of his gratitude.

The workers don't want the meat anymore; nowadays, they can eat meat whenever they want. What they really prefer is cash—to help pay for a trip, to install internet in their house, or to buy the newest mobile phone on the market, one that's much nicer than the device Riham herself owns. Whichever place offers a worker the most money, that's where she'll go; there's nothing else that motivates or binds a worker to anything.

What was gained, and what was lost, when the country joined the modern world? But maybe that's the wrong question. Egypt today is trapped in between. It's not developed enough to benefit from globalization, yet it's still damaged by its disruptions into wishing for a past that no longer exists, outside of memory.

Riham remembers when workers stayed at one place for a lifetime. In those days, the relations between owner and employee went deeper than money, and the factory was like your own family. Riham remembers.

ACKNOWLEDGMENTS

Anyone who moves to Egypt in a year of revolution with eight weeks of Arabic study and two toddlers will have to rely on the generosity and guidance of others. I am grateful for the support I received from so many people in the course of researching and writing this book.

My thanks go, first of all, to the women I knew in Egyptian factories who shared their personal stories so openly. In Minya, Rania Saeed Mohamed taught me about the dynamics of the factory world and the challenges that women face at work and at home; I thank her for her generous hospitality through many meals and overnight stays in her village. Doaa Mohsen showed me the grit and determination it takes to rise in the workplace and the education system. I also benefited from conversations with Hind Ali, Yasmin Ashraf Abu El-Magd, and the industrial engineers Sahar Ragab and Shaimaa Mohamed.

Ian Ross at the Delta Textile Factory illuminated the workings of the garment industry and gave me unfettered access to the company's plants in Minya and Cairo, for which I am grateful. Kevin Meyer explained the details of manufacturing and training and allowed me to sit in on the company's work-study classes; Mohamed Hanafy Ali let me observe recruiting sessions in the villages. Nader Adly showed faith early on that I would tell the stories of the women inside Delta with fairness and sympathy. I thank all of them for the trust and generosity they have shown me.

Riham Mohamed Galal Seif El-Din welcomed me into her factory and gave me an up-close education in manufacturing and entrepreneurship, with unfailing patience and good humor. Galal Seif El-Din shared the history of the Seif El-Din Company, and Mustafa Galal Seif El-Din explained changes in government policy. I am grateful to many of the women in Riham's factory who spoke with me about work, schooling, courtship, and marriage, including Sara Adel, Eman Abdel Hamid Mohamed, Mona, Noura, Dina, Rehab, Rahma, Amal, and the summer interns Samar Mahmoud Saad and Nourhan Mahmoud Ibrahim. I benefited from conversations about the textile industry with Mohamed Kassem, who also provided introductions to executives in the field. Thanks to Amr El-Sharnoubi and Hani Kassis, who helped me understand the challenges and rewards of running a factory in Egypt.

In Bayyadiyya, Mona Hafez Abdel-Maseeh was a resourceful guide who introduced me to shop owners and her students while also sharing her own remarkable story. Seham Salah welcomed me into her shop and home and showed me what it took to make an independent life. Tharwat Wahba at the Evangelical Theological Seminary of Cairo provided background on religious institutions in Bayyadiyya and shared contacts to people in the village. I am grateful to Rizkallah Nouh, Ayyad Habeeb Abdel-Quddous, and Sister Cecilia Vanzon for helping me understand the socioeconomic and educational circumstances of Bayyadiyya.

In Cairo, Lina Attalah helped me make sense of the political landscape and provided advice about staying safe while reporting. I am grateful to her and the talented team of editors and reporters at *Mada Masr* for allowing me to observe developments at their organization over a year and a half.

I was blessed to work with a talented group of researchers and translators during my years in Egypt. Amira El-Raghy helped me find and interview my first research subjects on trips to Alexandria, Minya, and Bayyadiyya; I benefited greatly from her energy and savvy handling of the security apparatus. Magda Magdy was a resourceful companion on multiple visits to the Delta factory, to Bayyadiyya, and on overnight stays in rural Minya; Mariam Boctor and "Mai" provided expert assistance on subsequent trips. In Alexandria, "Farah" helped me understand the lives of factory workers over many months of visits; she also coordinated reporting in other factories around the city and provided crucial fact-checking assistance during the editing process. I benefited early on from the gifted interpreting skills of Hassan El-Naggar. In their diligence and dedication, all of these people represent to me the best of Egypt.

Throughout this project, I have relied on a rich body of academic research about Egyptian society, economy, and history that helped me make sense of what I saw. A big thank you to Ragui Assaad at the University of Minnesota, whose boundless knowledge and patient explanations led me to a deeper understanding of the issues that affect working women in Egypt. Ghada Barsoum at the American University in Cairo illuminated the connections between economic development, employment, and female empowerment. Omaima Abou-Bakr at Cairo University introduced me to the ideas of Islamic feminism. Diane Singerman and Azza Soliman and her team at the Center for Egyptian Women's Legal Assistance conveyed the complexities of family law. Yasmine Moataz Ahmed was a wonderful resource and friend who guided me to scholarly works in my areas of interest.

I am indebted to Doug Hunt, whose perceptive suggestions helped bring focus and coherence to the book, especially in the early chapters. Elisabeth Kennedy took on the monumental task of imposing order and consistency on my use of Arabic words and names, and she provided invaluable context on the comparative history of religion. I am grateful to her and her husband, Darren, for their support and hospitality during our time in Egypt and for many years of friendship. Angela Hessler, my sister-in-law, applied her perceptive eye and elegant hand to create the beautiful map at the front of the book.

I am particularly grateful to have Molly Turpin of Random House as my editor; her sympathetic and subtle readings helped me develop

clearer arguments and tie many of the book's threads together. And a
big thank you to Chris Calhoun, my agent, for always championing my
work and finding the best home for it.

A fellowship from the Alicia Patterson Foundation allowed me to
make multiple trips back to Egypt to complete my reporting; at an earlier stage, the Kathryn Davis Fellowships for Peace supported my studies in the Intensive Arabic Summer Program at Middlebury College.
Dr. Mahmoud Abdalla, the director of the Arabic program, showed
kindness and flexibility in allowing Peter and me to take part in the
course while living together as a family and raising infant twins (still the
hardest thing I have ever done). I thank Matthew Olexa and Sara Dja-
maa for being such dedicated and supportive instructors.

In Cairo, we were fortunate to study at the Kalimat Language and
Cultural Centre, where Sherif El-Habibi, Sami Farag, Raafat Amin,
and Rifaat Amin were astute teachers and guides to a country in transition. I think often of Rifaat—I wish that he could be here to read my
book and set me straight about Gamal Abdel Nasser.

My daughters, Ariel and Natasha, grew up during the years that I
worked on this book, from riding in their twin stroller through the
streets of Zamalek to becoming opinionated humans who could discuss
the ideas in my book and think up a perfect title for it. I thank them for
their love and encouragement and for enduring my many moments of
stress and inattention to them throughout this process.

Finally, I owe a great debt to my husband, Peter Hessler, to whom
this book is dedicated. He undertook this journey into Egypt and Arabic with me and provided unwavering support and advice through the
process of reporting, writing, editing, and living the events described in
these pages. If *Egyptian Made* is a document of the extraordinary women
I knew there, it's also a testament to five wonderful years we spent together in *Umm al-Dunya*, the Mother of the World.

NOTES

Many of the scenes in these pages I witnessed firsthand; others were recounted to me by the people involved. I have listed the sources for facts and statistics that appear in the book.

In Minya, I met with Rania and Doaa regularly between April and June 2016, when I moved out of Cairo, and then on several return trips in 2016 and 2017. I also followed developments inside the Delta Textile Factory over this period through visits and conversations with executives and regular workers.

In Alexandria, I met with Riham from early 2015 to mid-2016 and again on return trips in 2016 and 2017.

I met with Mona and Seham Salah in the village of Bayyadiyya between late 2015 and late 2017.

From mid-2013 to late 2014, I attended staff meetings of the *Mada Masr* news website and conducted interviews with Lina Attalah, the editor-in-chief, and other editors, reporters, and individuals affiliated with the organization.

I have not altered the sequence of events, and I have used real names with a few exceptions. I have changed the names of two translators with whom I worked, "Farah" and "Mai," at their request. I also changed the names of two individuals in Riham's factory, "Dina" and "Noura," in order to protect their privacy as they revealed personal details about family members.

CHAPTER 1: THE BEST WORKERS ON EARTH

5   **For every Egyptian woman who works:** 21 percent of adult women in
    Egypt are in the labor force, defined as those between the ages of 15
    and 64 who are either engaged in economic activity for pay or unem-
    ployed but seeking such work. The figure, from 2018, is the same as the
    figure from 1998. Caroline Krafft, Ragui Assaad, and Caitlyn Keo,
    "The Evolution of Labor Supply in Egypt, 1988–2018: A Gendered
    Analysis," in *The Egyptian Labor Market: A Focus on Gender and Eco-
    nomic Vulnerability,* ed. Caroline Krafft and Ragui Assaad (Oxford:
    Oxford University Press, 2022), 30–31.

5   **percentage of women in the labor force:** The World Economic Forum
    ranks Egypt 143rd out of 146 countries surveyed, in terms of women's
    participation in the labor force. World Economic Forum, *Global Gen-
    der Gap Report 2022* (Geneva: World Economic Forum, 2022), https://
    www3.weforum.org/docs/WEF_GGGR_2022.pdf.

5   **some groups, such as college graduates:** The percentage of university-
    educated women in the labor force fell from 73 percent in 1998 to
    51 percent in 2018. Krafft, Assaad, and Keo, "The Evolution of Labor
    Supply," 32.

5   **These facts contradict the common belief:** Ragui Assaad, "Why Did
    Economic Liberalization Lead to Feminization of the Labor Force in
    Morocco and De-Feminization in Egypt?" in *Gender Impact of
    Trade Liberalization in the MENA Region, 2006* (Tunis: Center
    of Arab Women for Training and Research, 2006), https://www
    .cawtarclearinghouse.org/en/Publications/gender-impact-of-trade
    -liberalization-in-the-mena-region-2006.

6   **less likely to enter the workforce:** Egypt's female labor force participa-
    tion rate reached a high of 27 percent in 2006, then declined to 23 per-
    cent in 2012 and 21 percent in 2018. Krafft, Assaad, and Keo, "The
    Evolution of Labor Supply," 30–31.

6   **more focused on making a good marriage:** On how economic change
    has reinforced traditional ideas about the importance of marriage, see
    Sajeda Amin and Nagah H. Al-Bassusi, "Education, Wage Work, and

Marriage: Perspectives of Egyptian Working Women," *Journal of Marriage and Family* 66 (November 2004): 1287–1299, doi:10.1111/j.0022-2445.2004.00093.x.

6   **Girls and boys now attend school:** Elementary school enrollment for both boys and girls stands at 97.6 percent, and girls graduate at higher rates than boys. Ray Langsten and Tahra Hassan, "Primary Education Completion in Egypt: Trends and Determinants," *International Journal of Educational Development* 59 (March 2018): 136–145, doi: 10.1016/j.ijedudev.2017.10.013. Government surveys confirm high participation in schooling through age fourteen with virtually no difference between boys and girls. Ministry of Health and Population (Egypt), El-Zanaty and Associates, and ICF International, *Egypt Demographic and Health Survey 2014* (Cairo, Egypt and Rockville, Maryland: Ministry of Health and Population and ICF International, 2015), https://dhsprogram.com/pubs/pdf/SR223/SR223.pdf.

6   **Egyptian universities enroll more female:** According to the UNESCO Institute for Statistics, the gender parity index at the university level, which measures the ratio of women to men enrolled in public and private universities, was 1.04 in Egypt in 2018. "School Enrollment, Tertiary (gross), Gender Parity Index, Egypt, Arab Rep.," accessed June 4, 2023, https://data.worldbank.org/indicator/SE.ENR.TERT.FM.ZS?locations=EG.

6   **Women are living longer:** Female life expectancy was 73 years in 2020, compared to 66 in 1990. "Life Expectancy at Birth, Female," World Bank, accessed May 4, 2023, https://data.worldbank.org/indicator/SP.DYN.LE00.FE.IN?locations=EG.

6   **marrying later:** The median age at first marriage among women aged 25 to 49 years was 20.8 years in 2014, compared to 19.3 years in 1995. Ministry of Health and Population et al., *Egypt Demographic and Health Survey 2014;* Fatma El-Zanaty et al., *Egypt Demographic and Health Survey 1995* (Cairo, Egypt and Calverton, Maryland: National Population Council and Macro International Inc., 1996), https://www.dhsprogram.com/pubs/pdf/FR71/FR71.pdf.

6   **having fewer children:** Egypt's total fertility rate, defined as the num-

ber of children that a woman would have in her lifetime at current rates, declined from 4.4 in 1988 to 3.1 in 2018. Krafft, Assaad, and Keo, "The Evolution of Labor Supply," 20.

6 **"the gender equality paradox":** Ragui Assaad, "Making Sense of Arab Labor Markets: The Enduring Legacy of Dualism," *IZA Journal of Labor and Development* 3.1 (2014): 6, http://www.izajold.com/content /3/1/6.

6 **A World Bank study estimated:** Nadereh Chamlou and Mustapha Nabli, *Gender and Development in the Middle East and North Africa: Women in the Public Sphere* (Washington, D.C.: The World Bank Group, 2004), doi:10.1596/0-8213-5676-3.

6 **a hundred fifty years to catch up:** Ragui Assaad, "Labor Markets in the Arab World," in *The New Palgrave Dictionary of Economics*, ed. Steven N. Durlauf and Lawrence E. Blume (London: Palgrave Macmillan, 2016), 1–11, doi:10.1057/978-1-349-95121-5_2897-1.

6 **wifely submission is written into:** According to a 1985 amendment to Egyptian law, a husband need not provide for his wife if she "voluntarily declines to submit herself to her husband" or "if she goes out without the permission of her husband." Lynn Welchman, *Women and Muslim Family Laws in Arab States: A Comparative Overview of Textual Development and Advocacy* (Amsterdam: Amsterdam University Press, 2007), 171.

7 **Most women are reluctant to travel:** Ragui Assaad, *Women's Participation in Paid Employment Is a Matter of Policy not Simply Ideology,* Policy Brief 022 (Cairo: Egypt Network for Integrated Development, 2015), https://elnidaa.org/app/uploads/2019/07/PB22_women_employment _assaad.pdf. See also Ghada Barsoum, "When There is 'No Respect' at Work: Job Quality Issues for Women in Egypt's Private Sector," *OIDA International Journal of Sustainable Development* 1.1 (2010): 66–80, doi:10.31899/pgy15.1044.

7 **Unemployment in Egypt is four times higher:** Krafft, Assaad, and Keo, "The Evolution of Labor Supply," 41.

7 **"It's not about the wage":** Ragui Assaad, discussion with author, November 27, 2017.

7　**the public sector is shrinking:** The number of employees in the Egyptian government and government-owned enterprises was 5.6 million in 2020, down from 5.9 million in 2000. The figures, from the government's Central Agency for Public Mobilization and Statistics (CAPMAS), were supplied to me by Ragui Assaad.

7　**More than 40 percent:** Among employed Egyptian women, 43 percent worked in the public sector in 2018. Ragui Assaad, Abdelaziz Alsharawy, and Colette Salemi, "Is the Egyptian Economy Creating Good Jobs? Job Creation and Economic Vulnerability, 1998–2018," in *The Egyptian Labor Market: A Focus on Gender*, ed. Krafft and Assaad, 57.

7　**Between 2006 and 2012:** The number of women in the labor force dropped from 6.2 million in 2006 to 5.6 million in 2012; between 2012 and 2018, it continued to shrink at the rate of 0.1 percent per year, despite an increase in the working-age population. Krafft, Assaad, and Keo, "The Evolution of Labor Supply," 27–29.

7　**Serving as a maid or a nanny:** On the social acceptability of certain occupations over others, see Homa Hoodfar, *Between Marriage and the Market: Intimate Politics and Survival in Cairo* (Berkeley: University of California Press, 1997), 136–137.

8　**Factory work is roughly on par:** On the relatively low status of factory work for women, see Hoodfar, *Between Marriage and the Market*, 121–122; Diane Singerman, *Avenues of Participation: Family, Politics, and Networks in Urban Quarters of Cairo* (Princeton: Princeton University Press, 1995), 63, 123.

8　**"I'll go into the house":** Heba Mohamed Fathy, discussion with author, April 12, 2016.

9　**£E700, or the equivalent of $80:** This was the starting base salary for Delta factory workers in Minya in April 2016, when I first visited. I have used the Egyptian pound–dollar exchange rate from that time of 8.8 to 1. In a city like Cairo or Alexandria, an average worker's wage might be 30 percent to 70 percent higher.

9　**Young women often take jobs:** Women's participation in private-sector jobs peaks two years before marriage, drops slightly the year before, and is cut in half the year of marriage. Krafft, Assaad, and Keo, "The Evolution of Labor Supply," 38.

13 **Between 2004 and 2006:** Leslie T. Chang, *Factory Girls: From Village to City in a Changing China* (New York: Spiegel and Grau, 2008).

17 **one of the poorest parts of the country:** In 2018, 54.7 percent of the population in Minya lived below the poverty line, which puts Minya at 20th out of 23 governorates in Egypt. Minya ranks lowest among all the governorates in literacy rates and fourth from the bottom in life expectancy. Hanan Girgis, *Localization of Sustainable Development Goals in Egypt* (Cairo: Egyptian Center for Public Opinion Research [baseera], 2020), 12, 48, https://egypt.unfpa.org/sites/default/files/pub -pdf/part_i_localization_targets_7_nov.pdf; "Subnational HDI, Life Expectancy, Egypt," Global Data Lab, Radboud University, accessed July 4, 2023, https://globaldatalab.org/shdi/table/lifexp/EGY/.

30 **the traditional tools that women used:** The anthropologist M. Laetitia Cairoli observed similar dynamics among garment factory workers in the Moroccan city of Fez, where women used the idiom of family to describe their relationships with factory owners, supervisors, and their fellow workers. M. Laetitia Cairoli, "Factory as Home and Family: Female Workers in the Moroccan Garment Industry," *Human Organization* 57.2 (Summer 1998): 181–189, doi:10.17730/humo.57.2 .082j824l32711736.

31 **Bahia Nazim, owner of a factory:** Bahia Nazim, discussion with author, April 16, 2015.

31 **Hani Ibrahim, owner of a fruit and vegetable packing business:** Hani Ibrahim, discussion with author, October 20, 2014.

31 **Samah El-Sayyid, co-owner of a children's clothing factory:** Samah El-Sayyid, discussion with author, May 7, 2015.

32 **Wages were no longer tied:** Data show that before 1962, wages in manufacturing rose along with productivity; after that time, wages were tied to changes in the consumer price index. Bent Hansen, *The Political Economy of Poverty, Equity, and Growth: Egypt and Turkey* (Washington, D.C.: World Bank, 1991), 186.

32 **"The entire economic catastrophe":** Ahmed El-Bosaty, chairman and

managing director of Modern Nile Cotton, discussion with author, November 26, 2017.

32 **In his book** *Shop Floor Culture and Politics*: Samer S. Shehata, *Shop Floor Culture and Politics in Egypt* (Albany: State University of New York Press, 2009).

32 **"refashion[ing] old blades"**: Shehata, *Shop Floor Culture*, 23.

33 **"sabotage . . . pilfering, evasion"**: Shehata, *Shop Floor Culture*, 105.

33 **A USAID study**: As cited in American Chamber of Commerce in Egypt, *Improving Labor Productivity in Egypt's Ready-Made Garments Sector* (Cairo: American Chamber of Commerce in Egypt, April 2009), http://www.amcham-egypt.org/QiZ_REPORT_April09.pdf.

33 **a World Economic Forum survey**: Egypt was ranked 129th out of 141 countries for the quality of its vocational training and 133rd for the skills of graduates. World Economic Forum, *The Global Competitiveness Report 2019* (Geneva: World Economic Forum, 2019), 200, https://www3.weforum.org/docs/WEF_TheGlobalCompetitiveness Report2019.pdf.

33 **Hani Kassis, the chief executive officer**: Hani Kassis, discussion with author, December 2, 2017.

34 **"It was very, very successful"**: Medhat Kamal, discussion with author, August 17, 2017.

CHAPTER 2: STARTING FROM ZERO

36 **an Egyptian textile manufacturer named Louis Bishara**: Louis Bishara, interview by Abdel Aziz Ezz El-Arab, Dina Khalifa, and Wa'el Ismail, April and May 2005, Economic and Business History Research Centre Collection, American University in Cairo.

37 **"Cotton enabled upwardly mobile"**: Mona Abaza, *The Cotton Plantation Remembered* (Cairo: American University in Cairo Press, 2013), 66–67.

37 **"You would wake up one morning"**: Ali, journalist from a village near Minya, discussion with author, October 25, 2014.

37 **the oldest cotton futures market**: The Alexandria Cotton Futures Ex-

change was established in 1861, though cotton futures contracts had been traded on an informal basis since 1849. John Baffes and Ioannis Kaltsas, "Cotton Futures Exchanges: Their Past, Their Present, and Their Future," *Quarterly Journal of International Agriculture* 43.2 (January 2004): 153–176, https://www.researchgate.net/publication /288621163_Cotton_futures_exchanges_Their_past_their_present _and_their_future.

37 **Riham's grandfather set up a factory:** I have based my account of the history of the Seif El-Din Company on conversations with Riham and with her father, Galal Seif El-Din.

42 **largest manufacturing industry in the world:** On the history and spread of cotton around the world, see Sven Beckert, *Empire of Cotton: A Global History* (New York: Alfred A. Knopf, 2014; New York: Vintage Books, 2015), xiii.

42 **technology of spinning and weaving:** Beckert, *Empire of Cotton*, 5–6.

42 **Cotton cloth was sent as tribute:** Beckert, *Empire of Cotton*, 4.

42 **a form of tax payment:** Beckert, *Empire of Cotton*, 11.

42 **functioned as currency:** Beckert, *Empire of Cotton*, 17.

42 **fascinated by the exotic fiber:** Beckert, *Empire of Cotton*, 22.

42 **The signal event:** Beckert, *Empire of Cotton*, 22.

42 **Teachers in the religious schools:** Beckert, *Empire of Cotton*, 10.

43 **"So tight was the association":** Beckert, *Empire of Cotton*, 22.

43 **demand for Indian calico and chintz:** Sarah Fee, "The Global Craze for Cotton and Colour," *Royal Ontario Museum Magazine*, March 13, 2020, https://www.rom.on.ca/en/collections-research/magazine/the -global-craze-for-cotton-and-colour.

43 **"Cotton and colonial expansion":** Beckert, *Empire of Cotton*, 348.

43 **inextricably bound to the slave trade:** Beckert, *Empire of Cotton*, 35–38.

43 **the most fertile land in the world:** Habib Ayeb, "The Marginalization of the Small Peasantry: Egypt and Tunisia," in *Marginality and Exclusion in Egypt*, ed. Ray Bush and Habib Ayeb (London: Zed Books, 2012), 73.

43 **cotton growing was an important part:** Beckert, *Empire of Cotton*, 166.

43 **a French textile engineer:** On the history of cotton production in

Egypt, see E.R.J. Owen, *Cotton and the Egyptian Economy 1820–1914: A Study in Trade and Development* (Oxford: Clarendon Press, 1969).

44 **tried to turn Egypt into an industrialized nation:** On Mohamed Ali's industrialization program, see Robert Mabro and Samir Radwan, *The Industrialization of Egypt, 1939–1973: Policy and Performance* (New York: Oxford University Press, 1976), 10–16; Judith Tucker, *Women in Nineteenth-Century Egypt* (Cambridge: Cambridge University Press, 1985), 71–77.

44 **thirty spinning and weaving factories:** Beckert, *Empire of Cotton*, 166.

44 **thirty thousand workers:** Beckert, *Empire of Cotton*, 499n.

44 **cotton spindles per capita:** Beckert, *Empire of Cotton*, 167.

44 **"It is industry," he wrote:** Beckert, *Empire of Cotton*, 168.

44 **textile machines began to break down:** On the collapse of Mohamed Ali's industrialization effort, see Mabro and Radwan, *Industrialization of Egypt*, 16–18; Owen, *Cotton and the Egyptian Economy*, 82–83.

45 **half of the raw material:** Owen, *Cotton and the Egyptian Economy*, 46.

45 **Unlike in Great Britain and the United States:** Beckert, *Empire of Cotton*, 169.

45 **two and a half to four times:** Owen, *Cotton and the Egyptian Economy*, 29.

45 **"This twist is of superior quality":** Beckert, *Empire of Cotton*, 168.

45 **production in Egypt quintupled:** Beckert, *Empire of Cotton*, 293.

45 **40 percent of the land:** Beckert, *Empire of Cotton*, 294.

45 **integrated into the world economy:** Mabro and Radwan, *Industrialization of Egypt*, 19; Tucker, *Women in Nineteenth-Century Egypt*, 67.

46 **In *Cotton and the Egyptian Economy*:** Owen, *Cotton and the Egyptian Economy*, 356–364.

46 **the country doubled down:** On Egypt's focus on agricultural production and failure to industrialize, see Owen, *Cotton and the Egyptian Economy*, 355.

46 **Rich Egyptians invested:** Owen, *Cotton and the Egyptian Economy*, 282–283, 291–293; Mabro and Radwan, *Industrialization of Egypt*, 24–25.

46 **tens of thousands of Europeans:** According to government figures, the number of foreign residents in the country had reached nearly

80,000 by 1872 and 91,000 ten years later. Owen, *Cotton and the Egyptian Economy*, 157.

46 **illiteracy rates stayed high:** According to the 1907 census, 85 percent of the male population over 5 could neither read nor write. Owen, *Cotton and the Egyptian Economy*, 255n.

46 **"In the circumstances, it might seem":** Owen, *Cotton and the Egyptian Economy*, 304.

46 **construction of the Suez Canal:** On the building of the canal and its impact on Egypt, see Zachary Karabell, *Parting the Desert: The Creation of the Suez Canal* (New York: Alfred A. Knopf, 2003).

47 **implemented a free trade policy:** Tucker, *Women in Nineteenth-Century Egypt*, 79.

47 **"Egypt is the gift of the Nile":** Herodotus, *The Histories* 2.5.1.

50 **children as young as twelve:** The Child Law stipulates that children between twelve and fourteen can undertake seasonal work, and thirteen-year-olds can participate in training and apprenticeships. Salma Adel and Marina Safwat, *Child Labour in Egypt* (Cairo: Forum for Development and Human Rights Dialogue, June 2022), 7, https://www.fdhrd.org/wp-content/uploads/2022/06/Child-Labour-in-Egypt.pdf.

50 **attended class for three hours a day:** In 2012, close to a third of students from the ages of six to seventeen had attended primary schools that operated in shifts. Asmaa Elbadawy, "Education in Egypt: Improvements in Attainment, Problems with Quality and Inequality," in *The Egyptian Labor Market in an Era of Revolution*, ed. Ragui Assaad and Caroline Krafft (Oxford: Oxford University Press, 2015), 135.

51 **an industrialist named Talat Harb:** On the history of the Misr Spinning and Weaving Company, see Robert L. Tignor, *Egyptian Textiles and British Capital: 1930–1956* (Cairo: American University in Cairo Press, 1989), 14–17.

52 **al-Mahalla al-Kubra, a traditional center:** Tignor, *Egyptian Textiles*, 9.

52 **official communication was in Arabic:** Tignor, *Egyptian Textiles*, 15.

52 **75 percent of the domestic market:** Tignor, *Egyptian Textiles*, 45.

52 the top-down control of the industry: On the disadvantages of government involvement in the textile industry, see Tignor, *Egyptian Textiles*, 33–47.

52 a confidential report: Cited in Tignor, *Egyptian Textiles*, 34–35.

53 came and went on no fixed schedule: Roger Owen and Şevket Pamuk, *A History of Middle East Economies in the Twentieth Century* (London: I. B. Tauris, 1998), 44.

53 long-staple cotton was spun at high counts: Owen, *Cotton and the Egyptian Economy*, 199.

53 economists at the time: Tignor, *Egyptian Textiles*, 63–64.

53 a 1936 report: Mabro and Radwan, *Industrialization of Egypt*, 63.

53 The textile industry expanded: On the industry's wartime expansion, see Tignor, *Egyptian Textiles*, 48–52.

53 A 1947 study: Cited in Charles Issawi, "The Economic Development of Egypt, 1800–1960," in *The Economic History of the Middle East, 1800–1914*, ed. Charles Issawi (Chicago: University of Chicago Press, 1966), 359–374.

53 no improvement in their standard of living: Owen and Pamuk, *A History of Middle East Economies*, 35.

54 "The life of the rank and file": Robert L. Tignor, *State, Private Enterprise, and Economic Change in Egypt, 1918–1952* (Princeton: Princeton University Press, 1984), 251.

54 took over ownership of the country's banks: On state management of the economy under Nasser, see Mabro and Radwan, *Industrialization of Egypt*, 39–40, 64–75, 90–114; Owen and Pamuk, *A History of Middle East Economies*, 130–133.

54 promoted higher education: Alan Richards, *Higher Education in Egypt*, Policy Research Working Paper No. WPS862 (Washington, D.C.: World Bank, 1992), ii, https://documents1.worldbank.org/curated/en/163341468770080097/pdf/multi-page.pdf.

54 "Woman must be regarded as equal": Hoodfar, *Between Marriage and the Market*, 106.

54 Female enrollment in schools jumped: Between 1961 and 1974, the percentage of females in the student body of universities increased

from 16.3 percent to 30.4 percent. Ghada Barsoum, "Educated Young Women's Employment Decisions in Egypt: A Qualitative Account," *SAHWA Scientific Paper* 13 (March 2017): 1–26, doi:10.24241/swsp .2017.13.1.

55 **"a dumping ground"**: Owen and Pamuk, *A History of Middle East Economies,* 141.

55 **"The most important thing was to export"**: Bishara, interview.

55 **"a ruinous blow"**: The report, published by the Ministry of Agriculture and Land Reclamation, is cited in Sanna Negus, "Spinning Industry Unravels," *Business Monthly* (Cairo), November 2001, https://www .amcham.org.eg/publications/business-monthly/issues/11/November -2001/1782/spinning-industry-unravels.

55 **In 1982, the average wait**: Richards, *Higher Education,* 16.

56 **three in four young people**: Ghada Barsoum, "Young People's Job Aspirations in Egypt and the Continued Preference for a Government Job," in *Egyptian Labor Market in an Era,* ed. Assaad and Krafft, 108–126.

56 **Ghada Barsoum, an associate professor**: Ghada Barsoum, "The Public Sector as the Employer of Choice among Youth in Egypt: The Relevance of Public Service Motivation Theory," *International Journal of Public Administration* 39 (October 2015): 9, doi:10.1080/01900692 .2015.1004082.

56 **a college student named Rania**: Rania, volunteer at Country's News Foundation, discussion with author, April 19, 2016.

57 **one study about female employment**: Arlene Elowe MacLeod, "Transforming Women's Identity: The Intersection of Household and Workplace in Cairo," in *Development, Change, and Gender in Cairo: A View from the Household,* ed. Diane Singerman and Homa Hoodfar (Bloomington: Indiana University Press, 1996), 27–50.

61 **On the day I visited their factory**: I met Riham's father, Galal Seif El-Din, and toured his family's factory on February 27, 2017.

66 **still the country's most famous brand**: Egyptian cotton continues to be considered "the highest quality-graded cotton in the world." Rawiah Abdallah et al., *The Textile Cluster in Egypt* (Boston: Institute

for Strategy and Competitiveness, 2012), 5, https://www.isc.hbs.edu/
Documents/resources/courses/moc-course-at-harvard/pdf/student
-projects/Egypt_Textiles_Cluster.pdf.

66 **all of the crop that's planted:** Amirah El-Haddad, discussion with author, February 15, 2017; Abdallah, *The Textile Cluster in Egypt*, 18, 25.

66 **import almost all their cotton and polyester:** Riham Mohamed Galal Seif El-Din, discussion with author; Mohamed Kassem, discussion with author, August 6, 2017. See also Amirah El-Haddad, "Effects of the Global Crisis on the Egyptian Textiles and Clothing Sector: A Blessing in Disguise?" *International Scholarly Research Network* (October 2012): doi:10.5402/2012/941695.

66 **Egypt's free trade agreements:** Markus Loewe, *Industrial Policy in Egypt 2004–2011*, Discussion Paper No. 13 (Bonn: German Development Institute, 2013), 46, 52, doi:10.2139/ssrn.2294507; El-Haddad, "Effects of the Global Crisis."

66 **Egypt exports about $4.5 billion:** "Textiles, Exporters and Importers 2021," Observatory of Economic Complexity, accessed May 21, 2023, https://oec.world/en/profile/hs/textiles.

67 **dwarfed by exports from China:** "Textiles, Exporters and Importers 2021," Observatory of Economic Complexity, accessed May 21, 2023, https://oec.world/en/profile/hs/textiles.

67 **"As a cotton producer":** El-Haddad, "Effects of the Global Crisis," 16.

67 **manufacturing is critical:** On the importance of manufacturing to economic development and Egypt's disappointing performance, see Hansen, *The Political Economy of Poverty*, 33–109; Galal A. Amin, *Egypt's Economic Predicament: A Study in the Interaction of External Pressure, Political Folly, and Social Tension in Egypt, 1960–1990* (Leiden, the Netherlands: E.J. Brill, 1995), 85–95; Hélène Djoufelkit-Cottenet, *Egyptian Industry Since the Early 1970s: A History of Thwarted Development*, Working Paper No. 61 (Paris: Agence Française de Développement, 2008), https://www.afd.fr/en/ressources/egyptian-industry-early-1970s-history-thwarted-development.

67 **the sector makes up 15 percent:** Manufacturing accounted for 15 percent of Egypt's gross domestic product in 2021. "Manufacturing,

Value Added, % of GDP," World Bank, accessed May 21, 2023, https://data.worldbank.org/indicator/NV.IND.MANF.ZS?locations=EG. In 1955, industry and mining together made up around 16.6 percent of GDP. Owen and Pamuk, *A History of Middle East Economies,* 255.

67 **garment industry in Bangladesh:** Rachel Heath and A. Mushfiq Mobarak, "Manufacturing Growth and the Lives of Bangladeshi Women," *Journal of Development Economics* 115 (July 2015): 1–15, doi:10.1016/j.jdeveco.2015.01.006.

68 **labor-intensive manufacturing in Morocco:** Assaad, "Why Did Economic Liberalization," 14–15.

68 **Egypt has developed in a different direction:** Assaad, "Why Did Economic Liberalization," 14–15.

68 **migrated by the millions:** On international migration from Egypt, see Jackline Wahba, "Through the Keyhole: International Migration in Egypt," in *The Egyptian Labor Market in an Era,* ed. Assaad and Krafft, 198–217.

CHAPTER 3: PATTERNS IN THE CLOTH

70 **The Greek historian Herodotus:** Herodotus, *The Histories* 2.35.2–4.

70 **possessed the same legal rights:** On pharaonic-era women's legal status and rights compared to the rest of the classical world, see Joyce Tyldesley, *Daughters of Isis: Women of Ancient Egypt* (London: Penguin Books, 1995), 36–44; Janet H. Johnson, "The Legal Status of Women in Ancient Egypt," in *Mistress of the House, Mistress of Heaven: Women in Ancient Egypt,* ed. Anne K. Capel and Glenn E. Markoe (New York: Hudson Hills Press, 1996), 175–186; Gay Robins, *Women in Ancient Egypt* (London: British Museum Press, 1993), 127–141.

71 **a "wisdom" text that dates to 2400 B.C.:** Johnson, "Legal Status of Women," 175.

71 **Marriage was a private agreement:** Tyldesley, *Daughters of Isis,* 52.

71 **A contract between two workers:** Leila Ahmed, *Women and Gender in Islam* (New Haven: Yale University Press, 1992), 31.

71 **A woman could initiate divorce:** Tyldesley, *Daughters of Isis,* 56–60.

71 Women in Mesopotamia, Greece, and Rome: Tyldesley, *Daughters of Isis*, 37–39.

71 Sexual relations between unattached adults: Tyldesley, *Daughters of Isis*, 36, 54.

71 *My heart is not yet done*: Michael V. Fox, "Rereading 'The Song of Songs and the Ancient Egyptian Love Songs' Thirty Years Later," *Die Welt Des Orients* 46.1 (August 2016): 8–21, doi:10.13109/wdor.2016 .46.1.8.

72 *Beware of the woman who is a stranger*: Tyldesley, *Daughters of Isis*, 179.

72 played an active part in economic life: On women's work in pharaonic times, see Tyldesley, *Daughters of Isis*, 122–138; Catharine H. Roehrig, "Women's Work: Some Occupations of Nonroyal Women as Depicted in Ancient Egyptian Art," in *Mistress of the House*, ed. Capel and Markoe, 13–24; Robins, *Women in Ancient Egypt*, 103–126; Joshua J. Mark, "Women in Ancient Egypt," *World History Encyclopedia*, accessed June 9, 2023, https://www.worldhistory.org/article/623/women -in-ancient-egypt/.

72 Records from a workers' community: Robins, *Women in Ancient Egypt*, 129.

72 10 percent of property owners: Johnson, "Legal Status of Women," 178.

72 Hatshepsut personally led Egypt: On the prosperity and artistic innovation that marked Hatshepsut's rule, see Catharine H. Roehrig, ed., *Hatshepsut: From Queen to Pharaoh* (New York: Metropolitan Museum of Art; New Haven: Yale University Press, 2005).

72 she ruled alone as pharaoh: Nicholas Reeves, "The Gold Mask of Ankhkheperure Neferneferuaten," *Journal of Ancient Egyptian Interconnections* 7.4 (December 2015): 77–79, doi:10.2458/azu_jaei_v07i4 _reeves.

72 Four or maybe five female leaders: Scholars generally agree that ancient Egypt's female rulers included Sobeknefru, who assumed the throne as the last ruler of the Twelfth Dynasty; Hatshepsut; Tausret, who ruled after Hatshepsut at the end of the Nineteenth Dynasty; Cleopatra VII, the last queen of the Ptolemaic Dynasty; and possibly

Nefertiti. Betsy M. Bryan, "In Women Good and Bad Fortune Are on Earth: Status and Roles of Women in Egyptian Culture," in *Mistress of the House,* ed. Capel and Markoe, 29–36; Ann Macy Roth, "Models of Authority: Hatshepsut's Predecessors in Power," in Roehrig, ed., *Hatshepsut: From Queen to Pharaoh,* 12.

72 **England has had just six female rulers:** Tyldesley makes this argument in Tyldesley, *Daughters of Isis,* 212.

72 **labor that was central to women's lives:** On the involvement of ancient Egyptian women in cloth production, see Roehrig, "Women's Work," 19–24; Tyldesley, *Daughters of Isis,* 130–132.

72 **made linen cloth into garments:** On the production and importance of linen cloth in ancient Egypt, see Elizabeth Wayland Barber, *Women's Work: The First 20,000 Years* (New York: W. W. Norton, 1994), 189–200.

73 **they stole valuable linens:** Nicholas Reeves, *The Complete Tutankhamun: The King, the Tomb, the Royal Treasure* (Cairo: American University in Cairo Press, 1990), 96.

73 **hieroglyph for "weaver":** Tyldesley, *Daughters of Isis,* 131.

73 **making cloth and clothing:** For a global history of women's involvement in textile production, see Barber, *Women's Work.*

73 **"Men till the soil":** Beckert, *Empire of Cotton,* 15.

73 *Who can find a virtuous wife?:* Proverbs 31: 10–25 (New King James Version).

73 **an expression of female ingenuity:** Barber, *Women's Work,* 243.

74 *She set up a great loom:* Homer, *The Odyssey* 2.113–115.

74 **"In creating cloth":** Barber, *Women's Work,* 160–161.

74 **That changed around 1500 B.C.:** Barber, *Women's Work,* 257–272, 284–285.

74 **Greek conquest of Egypt:** For a comparison of women's status in ancient Greek and Egyptian societies, see Jane Rowlandson, ed., *Women and Society in Greek and Roman Egypt: A Sourcebook* (Cambridge: Cambridge University Press, 1998), 156, 162–164.

74 **considered the female a "deformed male":** Ahmed, *Women and Gender,* 29.

74 the same status as a child: Ahmed, *Women and Gender,* 28–29.

75 required to have a *kyrios:* On women's loss of freedoms and rights under Greek and then Roman rule, see Tyldesley, *Daughters of Isis,* 44; Ada Nifosi, *Becoming a Woman and Mother in Greco-Roman Egypt: Women's Bodies, Society, and Domestic Space* (New York: Routledge, 2019), 8–9.

75 The writings of Pisentius: Cited in T. G. Wilfong, *Women of Jeme: Lives in a Coptic Town in Late Antique Egypt* (Ann Arbor: University of Michigan Press, 2002), 26.

75 Documents from the era of Greek rule: Rowlandson, *Women and Society,* 163–164, 167–170.

75 The years of Roman administration: On women's economic activities during the Roman era, see Rowlandson, *Women and Society,* 218–279; Nifosi, *Becoming a Woman and Mother,* 36–38, 235.

75 a study of a predominantly Christian town: On the economic activities of women in the town of Jeme, see Wilfong, *Women of Jeme,* 141–149.

76 a third of the transactions: Wilfong, *Women of Jeme,* 130.

76 "In the centuries that followed": Wilfong, *Women of Jeme,* 155.

76 The earliest woven garment: Barber, *Women's Work,* 134–136.

77 the faith rejected aristocracy: On the egalitarian conception of gender in the Quran, see Ahmed, *Women and Gender,* 64–78; Barbara Freyer Stowasser, "Women and Citizenship in the Quran," in *Women, the Family, and Divorce Laws in Islamic History,* ed. Amira El-Azhary Sonbol (Syracuse: Syracuse University Press, 1996), 23–38; Asma Lamrabet, "An Egalitarian Reading of the Concepts of *Khilafah, Wilayah* and *Qiwamah,*" in *Men In Charge? Rethinking Authority in Muslim Legal Tradition,* ed. Ziba Mir-Hosseini, Mulki Al-Sharmani, and Jana Rumminger (London: Oneworld Publications, 2015), 65–87.

77 *For Muslim men and women*: Quran 33:35.

77 *I suffer not the good deeds of any*: Quran 3:195.

77 "created you from a single soul": Quran 4:1.

77 Quranic law recognized women's rights: On the legal rights women were granted under Quranic law, see Barbara Freyer Stowasser, "The

Status of Women in Early Islam," in *Muslim Women*, ed. Freda Hussain (Oxford: Routledge, 2015), 11–43.

78 **Khadija, Muhammad's first wife:** Ahmed, *Women and Gender*, 42. Ahmed argues that Khadija's conduct and economic independence were shaped by pre-Islamic society; Fatima Mernissi, *Beyond the Veil: Male-Female Dynamics in Modern Muslim Society*, revised edition (Bloomington: Indiana University Press, 1987), 51.

78 **Ordinary women sometimes joined:** On women's participation and agency in early Muslim society, see Ahmed, *Women and Gender*, 69–75; Stowasser, "The Status of Women," 34–36.

78 **"Men are the protectors and maintainers":** Quran 4:34.

78 **Men can marry outside the faith:** On men's greater legal privileges under Islam, see Stowasser, "The Status of Women," 18–20.

79 **"there are two quite different Islams":** Leila Ahmed, *A Border Passage: From Cairo to America—A Woman's Journey* (New York: Penguin Books, 2012), 123.

79 **an "Islamic feminism" movement:** On the emergence of this movement and debates about its impact, see Ziba Mir-Hosseini, "Muslim Legal Tradition and the Challenge of Gender Equality," in *Men In Charge*, ed. Mir-Hosseini, Al-Sharmani, and Rumminger, 28–29; Valentine M. Moghadam, "Islamic Feminism and Its Discontents: Toward a Resolution of the Debate," *Signs: Journal of Women in Culture and Society* 27.4 (Summer 2002): 1135–1171, doi:10.1086/339639.

79 **"The Muslim woman has only to read":** Amina Wadud, *Quran and Woman: Rereading the Sacred Text from a Woman's Perspective* (Oxford: Oxford University Press, 1999), xxii.

80 **The verse *Men are a degree above women:*** Stowasser, "Women and Citizenship," 33; Wadud, *Quran and Woman*, 68–69.

80 **Many of the rules in the Quran:** On the distinction between the Quran's principles and its recognition of social reality, see Mir-Hosseini, "Muslim Legal Tradition," 20–21.

80 *He created for you mates:* Quran 30:21.

80 **As Islam spread beyond the Arabian Peninsula:** Ahmed, *Women and Gender*, 80–85.

80   Particularly influential were the Sasanians: On the mores of the Sasanians and their impact on Muslim beliefs, see Ahmed, *Women and Gender,* 19–20.

80   Practices such as female veiling and seclusion: Ahmed, *Women and Gender,* 55–56.

80   Muhammad's wives are told: Quran 33:33, 53.

80   "draw their veils": Quran 24:31.

80   custom among the Sasanian nobility: Ahmed, *Women and Gender,* 83.

80   "the genius of Islam": Mernissi, *Beyond the Veil,* 80.

81   Pre-Islamic Arabian society had recognized: On the variety of marriage practices in pre-Islamic Arabia, including some that granted women more rights and freedoms, see Mernissi, *Beyond the Veil,* 64–85; Ahmed, *Women and Gender,* 43–45.

81   Aisha, another of his wives: Ahmed, *Women and Gender,* 43.

81   By the time of the Abbasid caliphate: Ahmed, *Women and Gender,* 79–87.

81   Omaima Abou-Bakr, a professor: Omaima Abou-Bakr, "The Interpretive Legacy of *Qiwamah* as an Exegetical Construct," in *Men In Charge,* ed. Mir-Hosseini, Al-Sharmani, and Rumminger, 44–64.

81   Abu Jafar Mohamed El-Tabari: Abou-Bakr, "Interpretive Legacy," 46.

81   Abu El-Qasim Mahmoud ibn Umar El-Zamakhshari: Abou-Bakr, "Interpretive Legacy," 48–49.

81   Ismail Ibn Kathir of Syria: Abou-Bakr, "Interpretive Legacy," 51–52.

82   "It is said that men have the privilege": Abou-Bakr, "Interpretive Legacy," 51.

82   "system of innate disposition": Abou-Bakr, "Interpretive Legacy," 54.

82   Domesticity as an evolutionary trait: Hoda Elsadda, "Gendered Citizenship: Discourses on Domesticity in the Second Half of the Nineteenth Century," *Hawwa* 4.1 (January 2006): 1–28, doi:10 .1163/156920806777504562.

82   Sayyid Qutb, one of the main theorists: Abou-Bakr, "Interpretive Legacy," 55.

82   the Grand Mufti: Stowasser, "The Status of Women," 37.

82   Doctors in Victorian England: Claire Jones, "Who Now Believes that

University Risks Giving Women a Moustache?" *The Guardian*, September 15, 2010, https://www.theguardian.com/commentisfree/2010/sep/15/women-equal-access-traditionally-male-roles.

82 **Augustine, the most influential thinker:** As cited in Ahmed, *Women and Gender*, 36.

82 **A Church father named Tertullian:** As cited in Ahmed, *Women and Gender*, 36.

83 **Judaism was also deeply patriarchal:** Ahmed, *Women and Gender*, 34.

83 **debated how to apply Islamic law:** Lama Abu-Odeh, "Modernizing Muslim Family Law: The Case of Egypt," *Vanderbilt Journal of Transnational Law* 37 (2021): 1051–1053, https://scholarship.law.vanderbilt.edu/vjtl/vol37/iss4/4/.

83 **recognized four schools of jurisprudence:** On the process of formulating legal doctrine, see Ahmed, *Women and Gender*, 89–90.

84 **"Islamic modernism" movement:** On the history and impact of Islamic modernism, see Mansoor Moaddel, *Islamic Modernism, Nationalism, and Fundamentalism: Episode and Discourse* (Chicago: University of Chicago Press, 2005).

84 **Egypt follows the Hanafi school:** Amira El-Azhary Sonbol, "Adults and Minors in Ottoman *Sharia* Courts and Modern Law," in *Women, the Family, and Divorce Laws*, ed. Sonbol, 238.

84 **Ordinary women went shopping:** On women's social activities during the medieval era, see Ahmed, *Women and Gender*, 118–120; Shirley Guthrie, *Arab Women in the Middle Ages: Private Lives and Public Roles* (London: Saqi Books, 2001), 16–22.

84 **pressed their claims in court:** On Muslim women's use of courts in premodern times, see Amira Sonbol, "Women in Shari'ah Courts: A Historical and Methodological Discussion," *Fordham International Law Journal* 27.1 (2003): 225–253, https://ir.lawnet.fordham.edu/cgi/viewcontent.cgi?article=1918&context=ilj.

84 **"Cairo is a very large town":** As cited in Guthrie, *Arab Women in the Middle Ages*, 178.

85 **the caliph El-Hakim bi-Amr Allah:** Guthrie, *Arab Women in the Middle Ages*, 135.

85 **The Sultan Barsbay:** Yossef Rapoport, *Marriage, Money, and Divorce*

in Medieval Islamic Society (Cambridge: Cambridge University Press, 2005), 36.

85 **"Some of the pious elders":** As cited in Guthrie, *Arab Women in the Middle Ages*, 17; Huda Lutfi, "Manners and Customs of Fourteenth-Century Cairene Women: Female Anarchy versus Male Sharia Order in Muslim Prescriptive Treatises," in *Women in Middle Eastern History: Shifting Boundaries in Sex and Gender,* ed. Nikki R. Keddie and Beth Baron (New Haven: Yale University Press, 1991), 99–121.

85 **a long list of female deeds:** Guthrie, *Arab Women in the Middle Ages*, 20–21; Lutfi, "Manners and Customs," 103–104.

86 **"Look how these norms":** Lutfi, "Manners and Customs," 103.

86 **worked as doctors, midwives, wet nurses:** On women's economic activity in the medieval Muslim world, see Ahmed, *Women and Gender,* 112, 115; Amira El-Azhary Sonbol, "How the *Sharia* Sees Women's Work," in *Society and Economy in Egypt and the Eastern Mediterranean, 1600–1900: Essays in Honor of André Raymond,* ed. Nelly Hanna and Raouf Abbas (Cairo: American University in Cairo Press, 2005), 157–176; Guthrie, *Arab Women in the Middle Ages,* 178–186.

86 **"The only women who did not work":** Omaima Abou-Bakr, discussion with author, May 9, 2016.

86 **women bought and sold land:** On women's property ownership, see Ahmed, *Women and Gender,* 110–112.

86 **European women would not enjoy:** Juan Cole, *Napoleon's Egypt: Invading the Middle East* (New York: Palgrave Macmillan, 2007), 79.

86 **set up and managed *waqf*s:** Guthrie, *Arab Women in the Middle Ages,* 175; Tucker, *Women in Nineteenth-Century Egypt,* 95–96.

86 **between 35 and 40 percent of transactions:** Afaf Lutfi al-Sayyid Marsot, *Women and Men in Late Eighteenth-Century Egypt* (Austin: University of Texas Press, 1995), 55.

86 **indispensable to the manufacturing of textiles:** On the economic independence of female wage-earners in the textile industry, see Rapoport, *Marriage, Money, and Divorce,* 31–50.

87 **"From an economic perspective, we need to reconsider":** Rapoport, *Marriage, Money, and Divorce,* 6.

87 **a woman's right to choose her own husband:** Judith Tucker, *In the*

House of the Law: Gender and Islamic Law in Ottoman Syria and Palestine (Berkeley: University of California Press, 1998), 46–52.

87 **a woman could initiate a divorce:** Tucker, *In the House of the Law,* 95–100.

87 **"Contrary to the ideas commonly prevailing":** Cited in Tucker, *Women in Nineteenth-Century Egypt,* 110.

90 **A nonprofit group called Harassmap:** https://harassmap.org/en/.

90 **a well-publicized United Nations study:** The organization's poll of 2,332 women, aged 10 to 35, across 7 governorates found that 99.3 percent of them reported having been subject to sexual harassment. United Nations Entity for Gender Equality and the Empowerment of Women (UN Women), *Study on Ways and Methods to Eliminate Sexual Harassment in Egypt: Results/Outcomes and Recommendations Summary* (New York: UN Women, 2013), https://s3-eu-west-1 .amazonaws.com/harassmap/media/uploaded-files/287_Summaryreport_eng_low-1.pdf.

92 **"Sexual segregation":** Mernissi, *Beyond the Veil,* 140.

93 **three-quarters of married women:** 73.7 percent of married women reported that their husbands were jealous or angry if they talked to other men. Ministry of Health and Population et al., *Demographic and Health Survey 2014,* 232.

93 **"Women in male spaces":** Mernissi, *Beyond the Veil,* 143–144.

94 **decimated the cottage trades:** On how women were marginalized by industrialization and the transition to wage labor, see Tucker, *Women in Nineteenth-Century Egypt,* 87–91, 100; Afaf Lutfi al-Sayyid Marsot, "Women and Modernization: A Reevaluation," in *Women, the Family, and Divorce Laws,* ed. Sonbol, 39–51; Marsot, *Women and Men in Late Eighteenth-Century Egypt,* 134–154.

94 **could neither buy stocks nor open:** Marsot, "Women and Modernization," 45–46.

95 **practice of female seclusion spreads:** Marsot, *Women and Men in Late Eighteenth-Century Egypt,* 117.

95 **lose the power to include conditions:** Marsot, *Women and Men in Late Eighteenth-Century Egypt,* 88.

95 **rarely register property:** Marsot, *Women and Men in Late Eighteenth-Century Egypt*, 138.

95 **Nile Delta town of Hamaqa:** Sonbol, "Adults and Minors," 250.

95 **"a reactionary desire":** Abou-Bakr, interview.

95 **Only in the realm of family law:** On the codification of Egyptian family law in the modern era and how it impacted women, see Amira El-Azhary Sonbol, "Shari'ah and State Formation: Historical Perspective," *Chicago Journal of International Law* 8.1 (2007): 59–83, https://chicagounbound.uchicago.edu/cjil/vol8/iss1/6/; Amira El-Azhary Sonbol, "The Genesis of Family Law: How *Shari'ah*, Custom, and Colonial Laws Influenced the Development of Personal Status Codes," in *Wanted: Equality and Justice in the Muslim Family*, ed. Zainah Anwar (Malaysia: Musawah, 2009), 179–207.

96 **Egypt's Christian adherents:** Non-Muslims in Egypt continue to maintain their own religious legislation in matters of marriage and divorce. Nathalie Bernard-Maugiron, *Personal Status Laws in Egypt: FAQ* (Eschborn: German Agency for Technical Cooperation, 2010), 25–29, https://horizon.documentation.ird.fr/exl-doc/pleins_textes/divers17-07/010048687.pdf.

96 **Modern Muslim states, writes a Georgetown University historian:** Sonbol, ed., *Women, the Family, and Divorce Laws*, 11.

96 **In the twentieth century, an Egyptian woman:** On women's loss of these specific rights, see Sonbol, "Adults and Minors," 251–252; Sonbol, "Law and Gender Violence in Ottoman and Modern Egypt," in *Women, the Family, and Divorce Laws*, ed. Sonbol, 281–285; Sonbol, "A History of Marriage Contracts in Egypt," in *The Islamic Marriage Contract: Case Studies in Islamic Family Law*, ed. Asifa Quraishi and Frank E. Vogel (Cambridge: Harvard University Press, 2008), 87–122.

96 **The courts could even force a wife:** Sonbol, "Shari'ah and State Formation," 81.

96 **schools to teach girls needlework:** On the restrictive nature of women's education, see Tucker, *Women in Nineteenth-Century Egypt*, 126–130.

97   **Women's magazines appeared:** Elsadda, "Gendered Citizenship."

97   **"It is the wife's duty":** As cited in Ahmed, *Women and Gender,* 159.

97   **a small but vocal women's movement:** On the emergence of feminism in Egypt in the early twentieth century, see Ahmed, *Women and Gender,* 169–188.

97   **One Egyptian woman out of every three:** Among Egyptian females aged fifteen and above, 32.6 percent are illiterate. "Literacy Rate, Adult Female, 2021," World Bank Gender Data Portal, accessed May 3, 2023, https://genderdata.worldbank.org/indicators/se-adt/.

98   **form of Islam called Wahhabism:** Human Rights Watch, *Boxed In: Women and Saudi Arabia's Male Guardianship System* (New York: Human Rights Watch, 2016), https://www.hrw.org/report/2016/07/17/boxed/women-and-saudi-arabias-male-guardianship-system.

98   **aided by the mass migration:** Many scholars have commented on the conservative pressures wrought by migration, including Amin and Al-Bassusi, "Education, Wage Work, and Marriage," 1290.

98   **resurgence of the veil:** On the rise of veiling on college campuses in Egypt, see Ahmed, *Women and Gender,* 220–222; Fadwa El Guindi, "Veiling Infitah with Muslim Ethic: Egypt's Contemporary Islamic Movement," *Social Problems* 28.4 (April 1981): 465–485, doi: 10.2307/800058.

98   **A 1982 study on Cairo University's campus:** Ahmed, *Women and Gender,* 222, 226–227.

98   **fewer than one-quarter of people:** The survey, by the Egyptian Center for Public Opinion Research "Baseera," found that only 23 percent of respondents saw married women's work as having a positive impact on families. Additionally, 83 percent of men and 72 percent of women felt that men should be given priority when employment opportunities are limited. "Egyptians' Perception Regarding Women's Social and Economic Role," Egypt National Observatory for Women, accessed May 12, 2023, https://en.enow.gov.eg/Report/World%20bank%2030%20numbers%20(NOD)20-2%20En.pdf.

99   **labor laws in most Muslim countries:** Welchman, *Women and Muslim Family Laws,* 89–90.

99   only in the past few decades: Sonbol, "How the *Sharia* Sees Women's Work," 168.

99   *To men is allotted a share of what they earned*: Quran 4:32.

99   "Some of its verses are definite": Quran 3:7.

99   People's Assembly opened debate: For background on the *khul* law and its passage, see Diane Singerman, "Rewriting Divorce in Egypt: Reclaiming Islam, Legal Activism, and Coalition Politics," in *Remaking Muslim Politics: Pluralism, Contestation, Democratization*, ed. Robert W. Hefner (Princeton: Princeton University Press, 2005), 161–188; Center for Egyptian Women's Legal Assistance, *The Harvest: Two Years After* Khol (Cairo: Center for Egyptian Women's Legal Assistance, 2003).

100 A man could divorce his wife: On Egypt's discriminatory divorce laws, see Farida Deif, *Divorced from Justice: Women's Unequal Access to Divorce in Egypt* (New York: Human Rights Watch, 2004).

101 "give something up to her husband:" Quran 2:229.

101 In a related *hadith:* Mulki Al-Sharmani, "Marriage in Islamic Interpretive Tradition: Revisiting the Legal and the Ethical," *Journal of Islamic Ethics* 2 (2018): 76–96, doi:10.1163/24685542-12340017.

101 Muslim jurisprudence thus recognizes: On Egyptian women's historical access to divorce and their loss of that right under modern law, see Sonbol, "A History of Marriage Contracts," 114–117.

101 the sum of money that her husband gave her: In Egyptian marriages, the groom pays the dower to the bride's family, who typically use it to buy furniture for the new couple's home. Singerman, "Rewriting Divorce," 110–111.

101 the country's first female judges: A 2007 presidential decree appointed thirty women to be judges, and another resolution the following year appointed twelve more. National Council for Women, *National Report on Beijing +20* (Cairo: National Council for Women, 2015), https://sustainabledevelopment.un.org/content/documents/13058Egypt_review_en_Beijing20.pdf.

101 members of the ruling National Democratic Party: Singerman, "Rewriting Divorce," 176.

101 **Representatives from the Wafd Party:** Singerman, "Rewriting Divorce," 177.

101 **A statement from Ali Nasr:** Singerman, "Rewriting Divorce," 178.

101 **"a very dirty dialogue":** Azza Soliman, discussion with author, November 12, 2016.

102 **"Most parliamentarians agreed":** For detailed coverage of the parliamentary debate, see Huda Zakareya, "*Khol*': A Socio-Legal Study," in Center for Egyptian Women's Legal Assistance, *The Harvest*, 41–66.

102 **"Husny Behalou expressed his fear":** Zakareya, "*Khol*': A Socio-Legal Study," 55.

102 **"Fayez Al Tenikhy shouted":** Zakareya, "*Khol*': A Socio-Legal Study," 53.

103 **"[Some] parliamentarians claimed":** Zakareya, "*Khol*': A Socio-Legal Study," 51–52.

103 **the need to preserve the family:** Mariz Tadrous, "The Law of *Khol*' in the Egyptian Press," in Center for Egyptian Women's Legal Assistance, *The Harvest*, 77–78.

104 *Al-Wafd* **claimed the law:** Tadrous, "The Law of *Khol*,'" 77.

104 **a Western and Zionist conspiracy:** Tadrous, "The Law of *Khol*,'" 79.

104 **Political cartoons mocked:** Nadia Sonneveld, "If Only There Was *Khul*'..." *Isim Review* 17 (Spring 2006): 50–51, https://repository.ubn.ru.nl/bitstream/handle/2066/151774/151774.pdf?sequence=1; Nadia Sonneveld, "Divorce Reform in Egypt and Morocco: Men and Women Navigating Rights and Duties," *Islamic Law and Society* 26 (January 2019): 149–178, doi:10.1163/15685195-00260A01.

104 **more than fifty thousand Egyptian women:** The total number of *khul* divorces registered in Egypt from 2010 to 2011 and from 2014 to 2020 was 52,999, though that may include a small number of other types of divorces. The data from 2012, 2013, and many of the years from 2000 to 2009 are too unclear to be useful. "Annual Bulletin of Marriage and Divorce Statistics," CAPMAS, accessed August 10, 2023, https://www.capmas.gov.eg/Pages/Publications.aspx?page_id=5104&Year=23632.

104 **countries like Jordan and Morocco:** Sonneveld, "Divorce Reform in Egypt and Morocco," 151.

104 **"It is at best a partial solution"**: Zakareya, *"Khol"*: A Socio-Legal Study," 69.

105 **"There shall be no sin"**: Quran 2:229.

CHAPTER 4: WORK STUDY

106 **the unfinished Aten Museum:** Construction began in 2002 and has dragged on for more than two decades. In early 2023, the Ministry of Tourism and Antiquities announced that the museum was expected to open soon. "New Aten Museum in Minya to Be Open for the Public," *Egyptian Streets* (Cairo), January 14, 2023, https://egyptianstreets .com/2023/01/14/new-aten-museum-in-minya-to-be-open-for-the -public/.

108 **one woman out of every five:** In rural Upper Egypt, 22 percent of women have never attended school. UN Women, *Profile of Women in Rural Egypt* (Cairo: UN Women, March 2018), https://egypt .unwomen.org/sites/default/files/Field%20Office%20Egypt/Attach ments/Publications/2018/05/Profile%20of%20rural%20women%20 %20final%20version.pdf.

108 **one out of four is married to her first cousin:** According to a government survey, 23 percent of married women in Upper Egypt between the ages of 15 and 49 report that their current, or in the case of widowed or divorced women, their most recent husband, was a first cousin. In rural Upper Egypt, the figure rises to 25.3 percent. Ministry of Health and Population et al., *Demographic and Health Survey 2014*, 92.

108 **"Egyptian Woman Reveals":** Jared Malsin, "Egyptian Woman Reveals 42-Year Secret of Survival," *The New York Times*, March 25, 2015, https://www.nytimes.com/2015/03/26/world/middleeast/egyptian -woman-reveals-42-year-secret-of-survival-pretending-to-be-a-man .html.

108 **"In that community, women don't work":** Ommeya El-Bahrawy, discussion with author, April 27, 2015.

108 **"not a single ready-made-garment factory":** Heba Handoussa, man-

aging director of the Egypt Network for Integrated Development, discussion with author, April 10, 2014.

108 **"A man always believes his eyes"**: Herodotus, *The Histories* 1.8.2.

108 **the Great Sphinx, which for many centuries lay submerged**: Built around 2500 B.C., the monument was buried for much of its life under desert sands. Brian Haughton, "The Mystery of the Great Sphinx," in *World History Encyclopedia*, June 1, 2011, https://www.worldhistory.org /article/236/the-mystery-of-the-great-sphinx/.

109 **the rock-cut tombs of Beni Hassan**: For a detailed description of the paintings, see Roehrig, "Women's Work," 21.

109 **When I came here**: I visited the Beni Hassan tombs on December 1, 2017.

114 **I met Sahar Nasr**: Sahar Nasr, discussion with author, April 26, 2015.

114 **Nasr was named**: Nasr served as Minister of International Cooperation from 2015 to 2017, and as Minister of Investment and International Cooperation from 2017 to 2019. "HE Minister, Prof. Dr. Sahar Nasr," Al-Yamamah University, accessed July 1, 2023, https://yu.edu.sa /faculty/sahar-nasr-phd/.

114 **three-fourths are unoccupied**: Mona Amer and Marian Attalah, "The School to Work Transition and Youth Economic Vulnerability in Egypt," in *The Egyptian Labor Market: A Focus on Gender*, ed. Krafft and Assaad, 125.

115 **The impetus was usually an engagement**: A study of young women in Egypt found that the central event that pushes them out of the labor force is marriage, not childbirth. Michael Gebel and Stefanie Heyne, *Transitions to Adulthood in the Middle East and North Africa: Young Women's Rising?* (London: Palgrave Macmillan, 2014), 120.

115 **I had ridden a shuttle bus**: I met Seham Forkash and her fellow villagers on May 22, 2016.

118 **The practice of measuring**: On the history and details of work study, I relied on the explanations of Kevin Meyer at Delta. See also George Kanawaty, ed., *Introduction to Work Study* (Geneva: International Labour Office, 1957).

124 **a woman's chief purpose in life**: On the centrality of marriage in

Egyptian society, see Singerman, *Avenues of Participation*, 74–131; Hoodfar, *Between Marriage and the Market*, 51–79.

124 **As she enters her teens:** Singerman, *Avenues of Participation*, 82–83, 87–88.

124 **median age of marriage:** In 2014, the median age at first marriage among women aged 25 to 49 years was 20.8 years; in rural Upper Egypt, it was 19.1 years. Ministry of Health and Population et al., *Demographic and Health Survey 2014*, 93.

125 **divorced women lose custody:** Deif, *Divorced from Justice*, 34; Bernard-Maugiron, *Personal Status Laws in Egypt*, 24.

128 **"It's considered a luxury":** Rania Salem, discussion with author, May 11, 2016.

128 **studies in rural Minya:** Rania Salem, Yuk Fai Cheong, and Kathryn M. Yount, "Is Women's Work a Pathway to Their Agency in Rural Minya, Egypt?" *Social Indicators Research: An International and Interdisciplinary Journal for Quality-of-Life Measurement* 136 (2018): 807–831, doi:10.1007/s11205-017-1573-9; Rania Salem, *Women's Economic Resources and Bargaining in Marriage: Does Egyptian Women's Status Depend on Earnings or Marriage Payments?* Gender and Work in the MENA Region Working Paper No. 18 (Cairo: Population Council, 2011), doi:10.31899/pgy2.1078.

129 **young women in nineteenth-century France:** Judith Tucker, "Egyptian Women in the Work Force: An Historical Survey," *Middle East Research and Information Project Reports* 50 (August 1976): 3–9, doi:10.2307/3010883.

129 **Places as disparate as India, Mexico, and Bangladesh:** Female employment in these countries is associated with declining fertility, delayed marriage, greater household autonomy for women, and more education for girls. "Decent Work Opportunities," Bill and Melinda Gates Foundation, accessed July 2, 2023, https://www.gatesfoundation.org/equal-is-greater/element/decent-work-opportunities/.

129 **In a village called Abu Hinnis:** I visited the Raway factory on February 10, 2016.

130 **one out of every three employed women:** 22.9 percent of employed women reported that they earned roughly the same wage as their husbands, and 9.1 percent said they earned more. Ministry of Health and Population et al., *Demographic and Health Survey 2014,* 216–217.

131 **women have pragmatic reasons:** On women's reinforcement of traditional roles, see Hoodfar, *Between Marriage and the Market,* 132–138, 166–171.

131 **"Far from questioning the basis":** Hoodfar, *Between Marriage and the Market,* 170.

131 **hid their jobs as maids or handywomen:** Hoodfar, *Between Marriage and the Market,* 112.

131 **"To prevent this,"Hoodfar wrote:** Hoodfar, *Between Marriage and the Market,* 158.

132 **a law to increase female representation:** Amany A. Khodair and Salwa A. Farrag, "Women Representation in the Egyptian Parliament: Representation or Misrepresentation?" *Developing Country Studies* 6.8 (2016): 152.

132 **a new standard for expensive trousseaux:** On the increase in marriage costs due to Sadat's Open Door policies, see Singerman, *Avenues of Participation,* 109–126; Ikran Eum, "Consumerism and Negotiations for Marriage Among the Middle- and Upper-Class Muslims in Cairo," *International Area Studies Review* 7.2 (September 2004): 171–186, doi:10.1177/223386590400700209.

132 **The videotaped plea of an activist:** "Asmaa Mahfouz and the YouTube Video that Helped Spark the Egyptian Uprising," *Democracy Now,* February 8, 2011, https://www.democracynow.org/2011/2/8/asmaa_mahfouz_the_youtube_video_that.

132 **a quarter of the million protesters:** Sharon Otterman, "Women Fight to Maintain Their Role in the Building of a New Egypt," *The New York Times,* March 5, 2011, https://www.nytimes.com/2011/03/06/world/middleeast/06cairo.html.

132 **female unemployment jumped:** The unemployment figures are from 2012, the year after the Arab Spring protests. Alia El-Mahdi, "Women's Economic Empowerment and Participation in the Labor Market

in Egypt: Constraints and Opportunities," presented at the Agence Française de Développement Conference on Women's Economic Empowerment in the Middle East and North Africa, April 15, 2015.

133   **Arab spring further eroded:** Rana Hendy, "Women's Participation in the Egyptian Labor Market: 1998–2012," in *The Egyptian Labor Market in an Era,* ed. Assaad and Krafft, 147–161.

133   **a third of the workers at Delta:** Mohamed Hanafy Ali, Delta's personnel manager, discussion with author, August 8, 2017.

134   **Egyptian mothers get custody:** According to Egyptian law, children are under the legal custody of their mother until they reach the age of fifteen. At that time, the children can decide which parent they wish to live with, unless the judge determines that it's in their interest to stay with the mother. Bernard-Maugiron, *Personal Status Laws,* 21, 24.

134   **fathers are required to pay:** Bernard-Maugiron, *Personal Status Laws,* 21–22.

134   **Unless she ceded custody:** Many divorced women find themselves in a similar situation to Doaa—forced to relinquish their custody rights because they can't provide for their children. Deif, *Divorced from Justice,* 39.

CHAPTER 5: MAIDEN VOYAGE

139   **Sara was sitting at a table:** I met Sara Adel on April 16, 2015, and spoke with her regularly over the next two years on my visits to the factory.

142   **a 1981 study of female employees:** Barbara Lethem Ibrahim, "Family Strategies: A Perspective on Women's Entry to the Labor Force in Egypt," *International Journal of Sociology of the Family* 11.2 (July–Dec. 1981): 235–249, http://www.jstor.org/stable/23027914.

143   **men who married in the 1970s:** Hoodfar, *Between Marriage and the Market,* 115.

143   **All the college-educated women:** Hoodfar, *Between Marriage and the Market,* 138.

147   **I asked Radwa about my impression:** Radwa El-Sheikh, discussion with author, June 7, 2015.

147 **Egypt has built thousands of schools:** Langsten and Hassan, "Primary Education Completion," 137.

148 **Ninety-one percent of Egyptian children:** Langsten and Hassan, "Primary Education Completion," 139.

148 **girls graduate in higher numbers:** In 2014, the elementary school completion rate for girls was 92.4 percent, compared to 90.5 percent for boys. Langsten and Hassan, "Primary Education Completion," 140.

148 **One out of four school buildings:** According to the Ministry of Education, 23.8 percent of all school buildings have been deemed unfit. Mohamed A. Zaki Ewiss, "The Availability and Quality of School Buildings in Egypt," *Journal of Research in Humanities and Social Science* 9.5 (2021): 56–72, https://www.questjournals.org/jrhss/papers/vol9 -issue5/Ser-2/H09055672.pdf. In a national survey of young people, roughly a third of students said that their schools had broken chairs and windows, and a fourth reported crowding of seats, inadequate lighting, and illegible blackboards. Rania Roushdy and Maia Sieverding, *Panel Survey of Young People in Egypt (SYPE) 2014: Generating Evidence for Policy, Programs, and Research* (Cairo: Population Council, 2015), 44, doi:10.31899/pgy9.1070.

148 **one-third of middle schools:** Only 36.3 percent of middle schools use a full-day system. Ewiss, "Availability and Quality," 65.

148 **recently ranked 130th out of 137 nations:** World Economic Forum, *The Global Competitiveness Report 2017–2018* (Geneva: World Economic Forum, 2017), 111, https://www3.weforum.org/docs/GCR2017 -2018/05FullReport/TheGlobalCompetitivenessReport2017–2018 .pdf.

148 **Egyptian families spend more:** According to a survey by the Egyptian National Institute of Planning, poor households spend 20 percent of their annual income on schooling, and a UNESCO report estimated that middle-class households spend one-third of their income on tutoring. As cited in Hania Sobhy, "The De-Facto Privatization of Secondary Education in Egypt: A Study of Private Tutoring in Technical and General Schools," *Compare: A Journal of Comparative and Interna-*

tional Education 42.1 (January 2012): 47–67, doi:10.1080/03057925.2011
.629042.

148 **teachers double as private tutors:** On the abuses inherent in the tutoring system, see Sobhy, "De-Facto Privatization," 51–62.

149 **not a single child:** Hania Sholkamy, "Constructing the Feminine . . .
and the Masculine: Child Rearing and Identity," in *Upper Egypt: Identity and Change,* ed. Nicholas Hopkins and Reem Saad (Cairo: American University in Cairo Press, 2004), 191–211. The national youth
survey also shows how education is not a path to social mobility.
Among those whose fathers were illiterate, only 8 percent attended
university, while 81 percent of the children of college-educated fathers
went on to higher education themselves. Roushdy and Sieverding,
Panel Survey, 35.

149 **a national network of technical high schools:** On the history and evolution of the vocational-school system in Egypt, see Moushira Elgeziri, "Marginalization and Self-marginalization: Commercial
Education and its Graduates," in *Marginality and Exclusion,* ed. Bush
and Ayeb, 191–218.

149 **The bureaucracy became overstaffed:** Richards, *Higher Education,* ii.

149 **confers no economic advantage:** Caroline Krafft, *Is School the Best
Route to Skills? Returns to Vocational School and Vocational Skills in
Egypt,* Working Paper No. 2013-09 (Minneapolis: Minnesota Popula-
tion Center, August 2013), doi:10.18128/MPC2013-09.

150 **"they're a trapped workforce":** A study of commuting rates shows that
women face greater constraints on mobility than men, which shuts
them out of many jobs. Ragui Assaad, "Informalization and Defemi-
nization: Explaining the Unusual Pattern in Egypt," in *Rethinking Informalization: Poverty, Precarious Jobs, and Social Protection,* ed. Neema
Kudva and Lourdes Beneria (Ithaca, New York: Internet-First University Press, 2005), http://hdl.handle.net/1813/3716.

150 **"Technical education is offered":** Elgeziri, "Marginalization and Self-
Marginalization," 213.

150 **Parents send their sons:** The idea that boys need education to get
jobs, while girls' schooling helps them become better wives and

mothers, is widespread. See Maia Sieverding and Rasha Hassan, *'Her Future is Marriage': Young People's Attitudes towards Gender Roles and the Gender Gap in Egypt* (Cairo: Population Council, 2016), doi:10.31899/pgy9.1014; Amin and Al-Bassusi, "Education, Wage Work, and Marriage," 1289.

151 **Yasmin was a troubling but typical case:** On "diploma disease" in Egypt, see Ghada Barsoum, "The Allure of 'Easy': Reflections on the Learning Experience in Private Higher Education Institutes in Egypt," *Compare: A Journal of Comparative and International Education* 47.1 (2016): doi:10.1080/03057925.2016.1153409.

153 **I met a woman whose husband:** Hamdia Abdel Halim, discussion with author, December 23, 2015.

155 **Mustafa loved the factory world:** Mustafa Galal Seif El-Din, discussion with author, November 16, 2015.

158 **£E5,000, or around $640:** In December 2015, the Egyptian pound–dollar exchange rate was 7.8 to 1.

160 **the government had imposed tariffs:** In a January 26, 2016, decree, the government announced import tariffs of between 20 and 40 percent on hundreds of products, ranging from food and clothing to toiletries and electronic devices. "Egypt Increases Tariffs on Range of Imports," Reuters, January 31, 2016, https://www.reuters.com /article/ozabs-uk-egypt-import-tariff-idAFKCN0V90CO; Bassem Abo Alabass, "Egypt's Sisi Raises Tariffs on Hundreds of Imported Goods to 40 Percent," *Ahram Online*, January 31, 2016, https://english .ahram.org.eg/NewsContentP/3/186371/Business/Egypts-Sisi-raises -tariffs-on-hundreds-of-imported.aspx.

160 **anyone who wanted to bring products:** Tamer Hafez, "Import Restrictions Draw Mixed Reviews," *Business Monthly* (Cairo), February 2016, https://www.amcham.org.eg/publications/business-monthly /issues/242/February-2016/3404/import-restrictions-draw-mixed -reviews.

161 **a woman who wove palm leaves:** Roda Abdullah Zaki Gabriel, discussion with author, February 10, 2016.

162 **Sons followed their fathers into trades:** Tyldesley, *Daughters of Isis*, 14.

Chapter 6: Downtown

165 **twenty thousand people:** According to census results and official estimates, the population of Bayyadiyya in 2021 was 23,550. "Egypt, Cities and Towns, Al-Bayadiyah," City Population, accessed August 3, 2023, https://www.citypopulation.de/en/egypt/cities/.

166 **A priest named Sameh Farouk:** Sameh Farouk, discussion with author, November 19, 2015.

168 **If the returnees invested:** Nationally, only a small proportion of migrant remittances are used to establish small businesses, improve agricultural practices, or undertake other forms of productive investment. A survey of two hundred families receiving remittances across four Egyptian governorates found that only 5.6 percent had invested the money in either small- or medium-size business ventures. International Organization for Migration, *A Study on Remittances and Investment Opportunities for Egyptian Migrants* (Cairo: International Organization for Migration, 2010), https://www.mfw4a.org/publication/study-remittances-and-investment-opportunities-egyptian-migrants.

168 **largest source of migrant labor:** Anda David, Nelly Elmallakh, and Jackline Wahba, "Internal versus International Migration in Egypt: Together or Far Apart," in *The Egyptian Labor Market: A Focus on Gender*, ed. Krafft and Assaad, 197–224.

168 **eight million men:** The figure is an estimate from CAPMAS. Roushdy and Sieverding, *Panel Survey*, 70.

168 **a *negative* impact on growth:** Rasha Qutb, "Migrants' Remittances and Economic Growth in Egypt: An Empirical Analysis from 1980 to 2017," *Review of Economics and Political Science* 7.3 (March 2021): 154–176, doi:10.1108/REPS-10-2018-0011.

169 **They can't travel overseas for work:** Egyptian migration is male dominated; almost 98 percent of migrants were men in 2018. David, Elmallakh, and Wahba, "Internal versus International Migration," 210.

169 **"We have a problem":** Rizkallah Nouh, pastor of the Evangelical Church of Bayyadiyya, discussion with author, April 13, 2016.

169   **four years of an average rural family's income:** The average annual income of a rural family in the 2019–2020 fiscal year was £E59,700.
Nehal Samir, "Egypt Poverty Rate Decreases for First Time in Twenty
Years: CAPMAS," *Daily News Egypt*, December 4, 2020, https://www
.dailynewsegypt.com/2020/12/03/egypt-poverty-rate-decreases-for
-1st-time-in-20-years-capmas/.

170   **One study of Egyptian households:** A survey of 394 Egyptian couples
in which the husband had migrated to an Arab country found that
return migration increases the predicted total number of children by
1.37. Simone Bertoli and Francesca Marchetta, "Bringing It All Back
Home: Return Migration and Fertility Choices," *World Development*
65 (January 2015): 27–40, doi:10.1016/j.worlddev.2013.08.006.

170   **In Jordan, a similar survey:** Michele Tuccio and Jackline Wahba, *Can
I Have Permission to Leave the House? Return Migration and the Transfer of Gender Norms,* IZA Discussion Paper No. 9216 (Bonn: Institute
for the Study of Labor, July 2015), doi:10.2139/ssrn.2655237.

170   **He may set up a private bank account:** In her fieldwork in several low-
income Cairo neighborhoods, Homa Hoodfar found that the wives of
migrants often had less control over, and access to, a husband's earnings after he migrated. Homa Hoodfar, "Egyptian Male Migration
and Urban Families Left Behind: 'Feminization of the Egyptian Family' or a Reaffirmation of Traditional Gender Roles?" in *Development,
Change, and Gender*, ed. Singerman and Hoodfar, 51–79.

171   **a wife is more likely to drop out:** Christine Binzel and Ragui Assaad,
*Egyptian Men Working Abroad: Labor Supply Responses by the Women
Left Behind,* IZA Discussion Paper No. 5589 (Bonn: Institute for the
Study of Labor, March 2011), doi:10.2139/ssrn.1796584.

173   **thousands of mom-and-pop shops:** Small groceries dominate the
country's fragmented retail sector, and goods often pass through six or
seven layers of intermediaries; the modern trade accounts for only 10
percent of total sales. Tielman Nieuwoudt, "Egypt's MaxAB: Transforming the Small Grocery Trade," The Supply Chain Lab (blog), accessed July 8, 2023, https://thesupplychainlab.blog/2019/11/22/egypts
-maxab-transforming-the-small-grocery-trade/.

176 **"We face south"**: Heba Afify, "Sectarian Borders," *Mada Masr* (Cairo), January 2, 2018, https://www.madamasr.com/en/2018/01/02/feature /politics/sectarian-borders/.

176 **home to large numbers of Christians**: The greatest concentration of Christians in Upper Egypt is found in the governorate of Asyut, where they make up about 20–25 percent of the population, followed by Minya and Sohag (about 15–20 percent each), and Qena (about 8–10 percent). Nicholas Hopkins and Reem Saad, "The Region of Upper Egypt: Identity and Change," in *Upper Egypt: Identity and Change*, ed. Hopkins and Saad, 8.

176 **In 2011, in another part of Minya**: "Two Dead, Eight Injured in Minya Sectarian Clashes," *Daily News Egypt*, April 20, 2011, https://www .dailynewsegypt.com/2011/04/20/two-dead-eight-injured-in-minya -sectarian-clashes/.

176 **More than a dozen churches**: "Egypt: Mass Attacks on Churches," Human Rights Watch, August 21, 2013, https://www.hrw.org /news/2013/08/21/egypt-mass-attacks-churches.

176 **American Presbyterian missionaries**: Tharwat Wahba, chairman of the missions department at the Evangelical Theological Seminary of Cairo, and a native of a village near Bayyadiyya, shared with me the history of Christian organizations in the area.

177 **a Jesuit priest**: The priest, Henry Ayrout, established the Catholic Association for Schools in Egypt in 1940, which eventually became the Association of Upper Egypt for Education and Development. Michel Labib Salib, executive director of the Association of Upper Egypt for Education and Development, discussion with author, December 2, 2015.

177 **Bayyadiyya has five Coptic Orthodox churches**: Wahba, interview.

177 **A public elementary and middle school**: Ayyad Habeeb Abdel-Quddous, principal of New Bayyadiyya Preparatory School, discussion with author, November 2, 2016.

177 **When Malaka Refai, a project officer**: Malaka Refai, discussion with author, February 3, 2016.

178 **Christian women have greater mobility**: Salem, Cheong, and Yount, "Is Women's Work a Pathway?"

178 **the importance of female virtue:** Febe Armanios, "The 'Virtuous Woman': Images of Gender in Modern Coptic Society," *Middle Eastern Studies* 38.1 (January 2002): 110–130, doi:10.1080/714004436.

178 **"The stronger the Islamic brand":** Mohamed Afifi, "Reflections on the Personal Laws of Egyptian Copts," in *Women, the Family, and Divorce Laws*, ed. Sonbol, 202–215.

178 **took me to see a priest:** I met Timouthaous on February 10, 2016.

180 **During the era of Ottoman rule, Coptic officials:** Afifi, "Reflections on the Personal Laws," 205–207.

180 **went so far as to recognize polygamy:** On the struggles over polygamy within the Coptic Church, see Afifi, "Reflections on the Personal Laws," 207–208.

180 **On the question of inheritance:** Sonbol, "Shari'ah and State Formation," 73.

180 **One afternoon I visited the pastor:** I met with the pastor, Rizkallah Nouh, the school principal, Ayyad Habeeb Abdel-Quddous, and Sister Cecilia Vanzon on November 2, 2016.

181 **"A student may be in sixth grade":** The national survey of youth found that among young people who had attended school for five years, half of them can't read or write and 40 percent can't do basic addition or subtraction. Roushdy and Sieverding, *Panel Survey*, 38.

181 **young women are prone to forgetting:** A study of illiterate and semi-literate women in Cairo found that many women who had gone to school later lost their literacy skills through lack of use. K. R. Kamphoefner, "What's the Use? The Household, Low-Income Women, and Literacy," in *Development, Change, and Gender*, ed. Singerman and Hoodfar, 80–109; Hoodfar, *Between Marriage and the Market*, 36–37.

182 **twenty women had assembled:** I met Mona's students on November 5, 2016.

186 **women who live on the margins:** In a study of an Upper Egyptian village, the anthropologist Reem Saad found that the female members of a low-status tribe enjoyed more freedom to work, move around, and set up businesses. Reem Saad, "Margins and Frontiers," in *Marginality and Exclusion*, ed. Bush and Ayeb, 97–111. A study of female Bedouin

animal herders in southern Egypt found that only the community's poorest women and widows were interested in pursuing new methods to cultivate feed for their livestock. Joanna Sharp et al., "Doing Gender and Development: Understanding Empowerment and Local Gender Relations," *Transactions of the Institute of British Geographers* 28.3 (September 2003): 281–291, doi:10.1111/1475-5661.00093.

CHAPTER 7: EXCESS MOTIONS

190 **a young woman named Walaa:** Walaa, discussion with author, October 30, 2014.

194 **an Italian Ph.D. student:** For accounts of Regeni's killing, see Alexander Stille, "Who Murdered Giulio Regeni?" *The Guardian,* October 4, 2016, https://www.theguardian.com/world/2016/oct/04/egypt-murder -giulio-regeni; Margherita Stancati, "An Italian Student Was Murdered in Egypt. Italy Says It Has Solved the Mystery," *The Wall Street Journal,* December 14, 2020, https://www.wsj.com/articles/an-italian -student-was-murdered-in-egypt-italy-says-it-has-solved-the -mystery-11607951422.

196 **the Personal Profile Analysis:** "Personal Profile Analysis (PPA)," British Psychological Society, accessed July 1, 2023, doi:10.53841/bpstest .2003.ppa.

198 **the work of an American psychologist:** On Marston's work, see "William M. Marston," Disc Insights, accessed July 1, 2023, https:// discinsights.com/william-marston; "History of DiSC," Disc Profile, accessed July 1, 2023, https://www.discprofile.com/what-is-disc /history-of-disc.

205 **The operator of a single-needle lockstitch:** Meyer, interview.

205 **"Use of the human body":** Kanawaty, *Introduction to Work Study,* 140–141.

207 **according to one study, the gap between official policy:** This finding, which comes from the Arab Reform Initiative's Democracy Index, is cited in Robert Springborg, "Egypt's Economic Transition: Challenges and Prospects," *International Development Policy* 7 (2017): 3, doi:10.4000/poldev.2277.

220 **In the winter of 2005:** I visited Chen Meirong and her family from February 1–13, 2005.

229 **"Five interviews out of nine":** Hoodfar, *Between Marriage and the Market*, 33.

230 **Married couples, Hoodfar observed:** On marital disputes over a husband's financial contribution to the household, see Hoodfar, *Between Marriage and the Market*, 142–154.

230 **"by nature men have sticky fingers":** Hoodfar, *Between Marriage and the Market*, 129.

231 **"On closer observation":** Hoodfar, *Between Marriage and the Market*, 149, 161.

231 **When the parents of a young woman:** On the detailed and sometimes adversarial nature of marriage negotiations, see Hoodfar, *Between Marriage and the Market*, 66–74.

232 **requirement that a man support his sisters:** Hoodfar, *Between Marriage and the Market*, 233.

232 **"The close link between mother and son":** Mernissi, *Beyond the Veil*, 121.

232 **"In a traditional setting":** Mernissi, *Beyond the Veil*, 132–135.

232 **writes about household disputes:** Singerman, *Avenues of Participation*, 57–61.

233 **a marriage engagement that collapsed:** Singerman, *Avenues of Participation*, 89–90.

233 **The economist Amartya Sen:** Homa Hoodfar explores this idea in Hoodfar, *Between Marriage and the Market*, 12.

233 **Egypt's divorce rate is rising:** The year 2021 saw 255,000 new divorces and 880,000 new marriages. In 2011, there were 152,000 divorces and 898,000 marriages. The figures, from CAPMAS, were supplied to me by Ragui Assaad.

233 **less than 2 percent:** Assaad, interview.

236 **more than 9 percent every year:** Since 1978, gross domestic product growth in China has averaged more than 9 percent a year. "The World Bank in China," World Bank, accessed July 9, 2023, https://www.worldbank.org/en/country/china/overview.

236 **seven hundred million people:** "How Well-Off Is China's Middle Class?" China Power Project, Center for Strategic and International Studies, April 26, 2017, https://chinapower.csis.org/china-middle -class/.

236 **economy has grown at less than half:** Since the 1990s, Egypt's GDP has grown on average 4.3 percent annually. Organization for Economic Co-operation and Development (OECD) et al., "Egypt's Path to Prosperity," in *Production Transformation Policy Review of Egypt: Embracing Change, Achieving Prosperity* (Paris: OECD Publishing, 2021), https://doi.org/10.1787/302fec4b-en.

237 **human habitation is confined:** Because most of the country is desert, only 7.7 percent of Egypt's area is inhabited. "Egypt, Country Background," United Nations Children's Fund, accessed July 9, 2023, https://www.unicef.org/egypt/country-background.

237 **"I was the first girl in the village":** Samia Farah Youssef, discussion with author, October 22, 2015.

237 **"When countries seek to industrialize":** Marsot, "Women and Modernization," 50.

Chapter 8: The Weight of a Dream

245 **Sara explained to me:** For a more detailed example of a typical trousseau, see Singerman, *Avenues of Participation*, 115–116.

247 **informal savings associations:** On the workings of the *gamiyya*, see Singerman, *Avenues of Participation*, 124–130, 154–157; Hoodfar, *Between Marriage and the Market*, 219–222.

249 **wedding of an Emir's daughter:** Rapoport, *Marriage, Money, and Divorce*, 12–13.

249 **three wooden *dikka* chests:** Rapoport, *Marriage, Money, and Divorce*, 15.

249 **trousseaux for twelve hundred brides:** Rapoport, *Marriage, Money, and Divorce*, 16.

250 **two rooms of furniture:** Singerman, *Avenues of Participation*, 120.

250 **average cost of marriage:** Although the groom and his family typically

cover two-thirds of the total cost of marriage, this figure provides a useful metric. Ragui Assaad and Caroline Krafft, *The Economics of Marriage in North Africa*, WIDER Working Paper 2014/067 (Helsinki: United Nations University-World Institute for Development Economics Research, 2014), doi:10.35188/UNU-WIDER/2014/788-2.

250 **"Young men generally expect"**: Singerman, *Avenues of Participation*, 122.

250 **"She began opening box after box"**: Singerman, *Avenues of Participation*, 114.

251 **Young people are delaying marriage**: Amin and Al-Bassusi, "Education, Wage Work, and Marriage."

251 **Some scholars see this accumulation**: Hoodfar, *Between Marriage and the Market*, 204–208.

252 **The father of one of them**: Mahmoud Ibrahim Ahmed, discussion with author, October 8, 2015.

255 **Romance follows this frantic timetable**: Singerman also observes that the choice of a mate is often made hastily. Singerman, *Avenues of Participation*, 79–80.

255 **Arranged marriages aren't common**: Amin and Al-Bassusi also make this point. Amin and Al-Bassusi, "Education, Wage Work, and Marriage," 1295.

255 **a husband's "secret life"**: Jaime E. Mendoza, Maram Tolba, and Yasmine Saleh, "Strengthening Marriages in Egypt: Impact of Divorce on Women," *Behavioral Sciences* 10.1 (December 2019): 1–8, doi:10.3390/bs10010014.

256 **young women and their families could attach conditions**: On the prevalence and content of marriage contracts before the modern era, see Abdal-Rehim Abdal-Rahman Abdal-Rehim, "The Family and Gender Laws in Egypt During the Ottoman Period," in *Women, the Family, and Divorce Laws*, ed. Sonbol, 96–111; Nelly Hanna, "Marriage Among Merchant Families in Seventeenth-Century Cairo," in *Women, the Family, and Divorce Laws*, ed. Sonbol, 143–154; Rapoport, *Marriage, Money, and Divorce*, 74–76; Sonbol, "A History of Marriage Contracts," 87–122.

256 **would-be brides are allowed**: On women's reluctance to add terms to their marriage contracts, see Deif, *Divorced from Justice*, 18–19.

256 **In the 1980s, a group of activists:** On the effort to draft a new marriage contract, see Singerman, "Rewriting Divorce," 171–174; Mulki Al-Sharmani, *Recent Reforms in Personal Status Laws and Women's Empowerment: Family Courts in Egypt* (Cairo: American University in Cairo Social Research Center, 2007), https://www.scribd.com/document /128195665/Recent-Reforms-in-Personal-Status-Laws-and-Women -s-Empowerment-Family-Courts-in-Egypt.

256 **Today, it's often the man:** Hoodfar, *Between Marriage and the Market*, 72–73.

257 **a young woman named Yasmin:** Yasmin Ashraf Abu El-Magd, discussion with author, August 8, 2017.

258 **devalued the Egyptian pound:** On November 3, 2016, the central bank devalued the pound to 13 against the dollar, from the earlier rate of 8.8. Nour Youssef and Diaa Hadid, "Egypt Floats Currency, Appeasing I.M.F. at Risk of Enraging Poor," *The New York Times,* November 3, 2016, https://www.nytimes.com/2016/11/04/world/middleeast/egypt -currency-pound-float-imf.html.

259 **£E1,000 a month, about $65:** The value of the Egyptian pound continued to fall. I have used the Egyptian pound–dollar exchange rate from this time of 16 to 1.

263 **A member of a government committee:** Mohamed El-Dabash, member of the Committee of 50, discussion with author, November 17, 2013.

266 **prefer to wed older men:** Hoodfar, *Between Marriage and the Market*, 58–59.

266 **Azza Soliman, the lawyer:** Soliman, interview.

CHAPTER 9: FREEDOM

271 **the University of Minya's continuing education division:** A number of public universities in Egypt run such programs, which allow high school graduates to take evening and weekend classes toward a university degree. Barsoum, "The Allure of 'Easy,'" 11n.

275 **"This is a trend in Egypt":** Alia El-Mahdi, discussion with author, November 26, 2014.

276 **"The men see beautiful women on TV"**: Ali, journalist from a village near Minya, discussion with author, October 25, 2014.

276 **Until the law was changed in 1985**: Nathalie Bernard-Maugiron and Baudouin Dupret, "Breaking Up the Family: Divorce in Egyptian Law and Practice," *Hawwa* 6.1 (April 2008): 52–74, doi :10.1163/156920808X298921.

276 **several months of compulsory mediation**: Deif, *Divorced from Justice*, 26–27.

276 **Many family court arbitrators**: Deif, *Divorced from Justice*, 26–28.

276 **A senior member of the National Center**: Deif, *Divorced from Justice*, 19.

277 **doesn't recognize joint marital assets**: Deif, *Divorced from Justice*, 36.

277 **husbands are required to return**: Deif, *Divorced from Justice*, 20.

277 **the courts' inability to enforce**: Deif, *Divorced from Justice*, 32–34.

277 **Eighty-eight percent of women**: Salem, *Women's Economic Resources*, 32.

277 **women who pursue *khul* give up that right**: Deif, *Divorced from Justice*, 39.

277 **remain in unhappy marriages**: This includes wives who have suffered domestic abuse but lack the means to get divorced. Deif, *Divorced from Justice*, 42–46.

277 **divorce was freely practiced**: Rapoport, *Marriage, Money, and Divorce*, 5–7, 69–88.

277 **one-third of marriages**: Rapoport, *Marriage, Money, and Divorce*, 5, 82–84.

277 **Women initiated the splits**: Rapoport, *Marriage, Money, and Divorce*, 88.

277 **"The majority of divorces"**: Rapoport, *Marriage, Money, and Divorce*, 69–70.

278 **Women usually gained custody**: Abdal-Rehim, "Family and Gender Laws," 108.

278 **according to the Maliki school**: Sonbol, "Women in Shari'ah Courts," 234.

278 **Women used this inconsistency**: Sonbol, "Shari'ah and State Formation," 78.

278 **In September 2017, a member of parliament:** Gawaher El-Taher, director of the Access to Justice program at the Center for Egyptian Women's Legal Assistance, discussion with author, December 4, 2017.

278 **women and men would have equal access:** El-Taher, interview.

279 **The bill's supporters are continuing to meet:** Nada Nashat, Center for Egyptian Women's Legal Assistance, email message to author, July 22, 2023.

282 **a woman named Eman Abdel Hamid Mohamed:** Eman Abdel Hamid Mohamed, discussion with author, November 9, 2016.

282 **common for brothers to marry sisters:** Kara Cooney, *The Woman Who Would Be King: Hatshepsut's Rise to Power in Ancient Egypt* (New York: Crown, 2014), 20–22.

282 **three generations of brother-sister unions:** Toby Wilkinson, *The Rise and Fall of Ancient Egypt* (London: Bloomsbury Publishing, 2010), 222.

282 **Marriage between first cousins:** Quran 33:50.

282 **One in every three marriages:** 31.5 percent of married women between the ages of 15 and 49 report that their current or most recent husband was a blood relative. In rural Upper Egypt, the rate is 47.9 percent. Ministry of Health and Population et al., *Demographic and Health Survey 2014*, 91–92.

282 **a figure that has held steady:** Diane Singerman, *The Economic Imperatives of Marriage: Emerging Practices and Identities Among Youth in the Middle East*, Middle East Youth Initiative Working Paper No. 6 (Washington, D.C.: Wolfensohn Center for Development, September 2007), 23, doi:10.2139/ssrn.1087433.

282 **The practice is most common:** On the prevalence of kin marriage in Cairo, see Singerman, *Avenues of Participation*, 78–79; Hoodfar, *Between Marriage and the Market*, 55–56.

282 **A union between paternal first cousins:** Rania Salem, "Changes in the Institution of Marriage in Egypt from 1998 to 2012," in *The Egyptian Labor Market in an Era*, ed. Assaad and Krafft, 173.

283 **a study of married women in Egypt:** A national survey of 7,196 married women found no association between wedding a relative and ownership of land or other assets, calling into question the belief that kin marriage is an economic strategy to consolidate family wealth.

Rania Salem and Sarah Shah, *Correlates of Kin Marriage in Egypt, Jordan, and Tunisia,* Working Paper No. 1067 (Cairo: Economic Research Forum, 2016), 14, https://erf.org.eg/publications/correlates-of -kin-marriage-in-egypt-jordan-and-tunisia/.

283   **marrying a relative is cheaper:** Singerman found that marrying a relative reduced costs by 25 percent. Singerman, *Economic Imperatives,* 23.

283   **almost all of them had been introduced:** Among married Egyptians aged 35 and under, 96 percent met their spouse through relatives, friends, and neighbors, rather than in institutional settings such as work or school. Roushdy and Sieverding, *Panel Survey,* 88.

283   **one out of five young women:** Gebel and Heyne, *Transitions to Adulthood,* 172.

283   **"Far more flirting":** Singerman, *Avenues of Participation,* 96.

285   **a study by two sociologists:** Salem and Shah, *Correlates of Kin Marriage,* 15.

CHAPTER 10: EGYPTIAN MADE

289   **1 to 2 percent of the population:** I have used two different measures as a proxy for membership in the upper class. Among women between the ages of 20 and 64, fewer than 1 percent attended a private foreign-language school at the elementary level. And 2.3 percent of women in this age group come from families in which both parents have a college degree. The figures, from the 2018 Egypt Labor Market Panel Survey, were supplied to me by Ragui Assaad.

289   **92 percent of men *and women:*** The figure, from the World Values Survey, is cited in Gebel and Heyne, *Transitions to Adulthood,* 32.

290   **Men no longer object:** Rania, interview.

290   **A woman named Marie Louis Bishara:** Maria Louis Bishara, discussion with author, August 6, 2017.

290   **"You can't isolate the problems":** Hanan Abdalla, discussion with author, November 21, 2013.

291   **the Year of the Woman:** "This is the second day of the Egypt Women Can conference," *al-Youm al-Sabi',* July 3, 2017.

291 "This conference should change": "Maya Morsi, the head of the National Council for Women," *al-Youm al-Sabi'*, July 7, 2017.

291 "a big problem with NGOs": Fatima Metwally, discussion with author, April 19, 2016.

292 styled themselves as benevolent fathers: For an exploration of this idea, see Mihaila Yordanova, "Father Figures," *Journal of Arabic and Islamic Studies* 17 (2018): 492–498, doi:10.5617/jais.6139.

292 an Egyptian news website: https://www.madamasr.com/en.

294 "I want to delete": Mohamad Adam, email message to author, September 27, 2014.

294 By the time my article ran: Leslie T. Chang, "The News Website That's Keeping Press Freedom Alive in Egypt," *The Guardian*, January 27, 2015, https://www.theguardian.com/news/2015/jan/27/-sp-online-news paper-keeping-press-freedom-alive-egypt.

295 "The article is rude": Omar Said, email message to author, January 28, 2015.

295 "this quote will certainly destroy": Maha ElNabawi, email message to author, January 27, 2015.

301 "Debase a woman": Mernissi, *Beyond the Veil*, 48.

301 The first community of Muslims: Ahmed, *Women and Gender*, 52; Mernissi, *Beyond the Veil*, 80.

302 "If you fear that you shall not": Quran 4:3.

302 "You are never able to be fair": Quran 4:129.

302 never meant to be practiced widely: Wadud, *Quran and Woman*, 82–83.

302 in his lifetime had thirteen wives: Mernissi, *Beyond the Veil*, 51.

302 Islamic conquests transformed the region: On the gradual diminishment of women's status from the time of the Islamic conquests into the Abbasid era, see Ahmed, *Women and Gender*, 79–87.

302 "concubines and other objects": Ahmed, *Women and Gender*, 67, 83.

302 Muhammad himself was said: Mernissi, *Beyond the Veil*, 70.

303 letter that dates to the Abbasid period: Ahmed, *Women and Gender*, 85.

303 Polygamy was a frequent cause: Abdal-Rehim, "Family and Gender Laws," 107.

303 **"Pain figures in the lives":** Ahmed, *Women and Gender*, 183.

303 **Sharawi and other activists:** On early efforts to limit polygamy, see Zakareya, *"Khol'*: A Socio-Legal Study," 44–45.

304 **The Nasser government twice prepared:** Fauzi M. Najjar, "Egypt's Laws of Personal Status," *Arab Studies Quarterly* 10.3 (Summer 1988): 319–344, https://www.jstor.org/stable/41854165.

304 **Sadat, in 1979, tried:** Najjar, "Egypt's Laws of Personal Status," 323–331.

304 **A 2004 draft:** Welchman, *Women and Muslim Family Laws*, 86.

304 **"the holiest of our holies":** Najjar, "Egypt's Laws of Personal Status," 329.

304 **Fewer than 3 percent:** Specifically, 2.7 percent of currently married women between the ages of 15 and 49 have co-wives; in rural Upper Egypt, the figure is 3.1 percent. Ministry of Health and Population et al., *Demographic and Health Survey 2014*, 90–91.

304 **10 percent of marriages:** Kirsten H. Bach, "Changing Family and Marriage Patterns in an Aswan Village," in *Upper Egypt: Identity and Change*, ed. Hopkins and Saad, 179.

304 **men invariably said a husband:** Hoodfar, *Between Marriage and the Market*, 75.

305 **young wives, she wrote, worried constantly:** Hoodfar, *Between Marriage and the Market*, 248–250.

305 **Almost all of the women:** Hoodfar, *Between Marriage and the Market*, 75–76.

305 **"men make themselves valuable":** Mernissi, *Beyond the Veil*, 115.

305 **"I just did it to spite her":** I spoke with Yasser on September 14, 2018.

307 *Every unhappy family:* Leo Tolstoy, *Anna Karenina* (Hertfordshire: Wordsworth Editions, 1995), 1.

309 **a template for other investors:** Ian Ross, discussion with author, August 14, 2018.

309 **"They're doing very well":** Kassem, interview.

310 **Some months later:** Ross, interview.

CHAPTER 11: HARD MONEY

315 **An outside visitor:** I visited the Kabo factory and interviewed Amr El-Sharnoubi on August 14, 2017.

315 **Established in 1940, Kabo was merged:** El-Sharnoubi, interview. See also "El-Nasr Clothing & Textiles Co.," EMIS, accessed July 11, 2023, https://www.emis.com/php/company-profile/EG/El-Nasr_Clothing ___Textiles_Co_SAE__النصر_للملابس_و_المنسوجات_-_ كابو__en_1437065.html#:~:text=El%2DNasr%20Clothing%20 and%20Textiles,the%20middle%20east%20and%20worldwide.

316 **Nasser-era labor laws:** Kassem, interview.

318 **On the far northwestern edge:** Fadel Marzouk, discussion with author, August 7, 2017.

319 **a diplomat named Mohamed Kassem:** Kassem, interview.

320 **A study of entrepreneurial activity:** 6.6 percent of Egyptian adults are early stage entrepreneurs, defined as running a business that is less than 3.5 years old, which places Egypt 41st out of 49 countries. Only 2.6 percent of adults own an established business more than 3.5 years old, which places Egypt 46th out of 49 countries. Global Entrepreneurship Monitor, *Global Entrepreneurship Monitor 2022/2023 Global Report: Adapting to a "New Normal"* (London: GEM, 2023), https://www.gemconsortium.org/reports/latest-global-report.

321 **dominated by foreigners:** Robert Tignor, "The Economic Activities of Foreigners in Egypt, 1920–1950: From Millet to Haute Bourgeoisie," *Comparative Studies in Society and History* 22.3 (July 1980): 416–449, doi:10.1017/S0010417500009427.

321 **"Boot-mending, as well as boot-making":** As cited in Issawi, "The Economic Development of Egypt, 1800–1960," 365.

321 **to double the value:** Owen, *Cotton and the Egyptian Economy*, 283.

321 **relied on certain businessmen:** On Nasser's policies toward private businessmen, see Safinaz El Tarouty, *Businessmen, Clientelism, and Authoritarianism in Egypt* (New York: Palgrave Macmillan, 2015), 37–53, doi:10.1057/9781137493385.

321 **"parasitic entrepreneurs":** On the rise of these entrepreneurs under

Sadat, see Loewe, *Industrial Policy in Egypt,* 22; El Tarouty, *Business-men, Clientelism.*

321 **Mubarak maintained this policy:** El Tarouty, *Businessmen, Clientelism.*

322 **a survey by Cairo University:** Mohamed El Dahshan, Ahmed H. Tolba, and Tamer Badreldin, "Enabling Entrepreneurship in Egypt: Toward a Sustainable Dynamic Model," *Innovations: Technology, Governance, Globalization* 7.2 (2012): 83–106, doi:10.1162/INOV_a_00130.

322 **the Egyptian man of *bisnis:*** On the characteristics of Egyptian entrepreneurs, see Loewe, *Industrial Policy in Egypt,* 17.

326 **Women have fewer assets:** On the challenges that female entrepreneurs face, see International Labour Organization, *Women's Entrepreneurship Development Assessment—Egypt* (Cairo: ILO Publications, 2016), https://www.ilo.org/wcmsp5/groups/public/---ed_emp/---emp_ent/---ifp_seed/documents/publication/wcms_551168.pdf; Reham Rizk and Ali Rashed, "Trends and Patterns of Women's Entrepreneurship in Egypt," in *The Egyptian Labor Market: A Focus on Gender,* ed. Krafft and Assaad, 174–196.

327 **5 percent of Egyptian women:** 5.7 percent of Egyptian women are early stage entrepreneurs, defined as running a business that is less than 3.5 years old; the country ranks 38th out of 47 nations surveyed. One percent of women in the country own an established business more than 3.5 years old, making Egypt the lowest among all the countries surveyed. Global Entrepreneurship Monitor, *Global Entrepreneurship Monitor 2021/22 Women's Entrepreneurship Report: From Crisis to Opportunity* (London: GEM, 2022), https://www.gemconsortium.org/reports/womens-entrepreneurship.

327 **Their ventures are smaller:** On the characteristics of female-owned enterprises, see International Labour Organization, *Women's Entrepreneurship Development;* Rizk and Rashed, "Trends and Patterns of Women's Entrepreneurship."

327 **Among legally registered enterprises:** The findings are from a World Bank study of close to a thousand firms in the manufacturing and service sectors in Egypt. Nadereh Chamlou, Leora Klapper, and Silvia Muzi, *The Environment for Women's Entrepreneurship in the Middle*

East and North Africa Region (Washington, D.C.: The World Bank Group, 2008), doi:10.1596/978-0-8213-7495-5.

327 **"Women are always being challenged":** Nasr, interview.

327 **a middle-aged mother of six:** Halim, interview.

327 **A woman named Sawsan:** Sawsan, discussion with author, October 21, 2015.

328 **a friend of hers named Samah El-Sayyid:** El-Sayyid, interview.

328 **poll of female business owners:** Sahar Mounir, consultant with the International Labor Organization and head of the Women in Business unit at the Federation of Egyptian Industries, shared the survey results with me on April 27, 2015.

INDEX

ABOUT THE AUTHOR

LESLIE T. CHANG has written about women in the developing world for two decades. Her book *Factory Girls: From Village to City in a Changing China* was named a *New York Times* Notable Book and has been translated into ten languages. Chang is a recipient of the PEN USA Literary Award, the Asian American Literary Award, the Tiziano Terzani International Literary Prize, the Quality Paperback Book Club New Visions Award, and the Alicia Patterson Foundation Fellowship. From 2011 to 2016, Chang lived in Cairo, Egypt. Before that, Chang lived in China for a decade as a correspondent for *The Wall Street Journal*. She has also written for *The New Yorker*, *The New York Review of Books*, and *National Geographic*. She and her husband, the writer Peter Hessler, live in southwestern Colorado with their twin daughters.

ABOUT THE TYPE

This book was set in Caslon, a typeface first designed in 1722 by William Caslon (1692–1766). Its widespread use by most English printers in the early eighteenth century soon supplanted the Dutch typefaces that had formerly prevailed. The roman is considered a "workhorse" typeface due to its pleasant, open appearance, while the italic is exceedingly decorative.